DATE DUE

FEB 2 3 2006	
JUN 1 2 2006	
SEP 1 0 2006	
FEB 1 0 2008	
MAY 0 8 2010	
MAY 0 8 2010	
MAR 1 8 2013	

THE MAKING OF A TERRORIST

THE MAKING OF A TERRORIST

RECRUITMENT, TRAINING, AND ROOT CAUSES

Volume III: Root Causes

Edited by James J. F. Forest

PRAEGER SECURITY INTERNATIONAL
Westport, Connecticut · London

Library of Congress Cataloging-in-Publication Data

The making of a terrorist : recruitment, training, and root causes / edited by
James J. F. Forest.
     p. cm.
  Includes bibliographical references and index.
  ISBN 0–275–98543–1 ((set) : alk. paper)—ISBN 0–275–98544–X ((vol. i) :
alk. paper)—ISBN 0–275–98545–8 ((vol. ii) : alk. paper)—ISBN 0–275–98546–6
((vol. iii) : alk. paper) 1. Terrorism. 2. Terrorists. I. Forest, James J. F.
  HV6431.M353 2006
  303.6'25—dc22   2005016849

British Library Cataloguing in Publication Data is available.

Library of Congress Catalog Card Number: 2005016849
ISBN: 0-275-98543-1 (set)
     0-275-98544-X (vol. I)
     0-275-98545-8 (vol. II)
     0-275-98546-6 (vol. III)

First published in 2006

Praeger Security International, 88 Post Road West, Westport, CT 06881
An imprint of Greenwood Publishing Group, Inc.
www.praeger.com

Printed in the United States of America

The paper used in this book complies with the
Permanent Paper Standard issued by the National
Information Standards Organization (Z39.48-1984).

10 9 8 7 6 5 4 3 2 1

Contents

Part II Religious and Socioeconomic Dimensions

Part III Alternative Views on Root Causes of Terrorism

Preface

A wide variety of topics can be explored within the general category of "root causes of terrorism." Further, there is also a considerable diversity of opinion about what this term means. The themes chosen for this volume are meant to represent this diversity, rather than encompass the entire spectrum of possible topics. The chapters are organized into three general areas: those dealing in the realm of politics, those addressing socioeconomic or religious dimensions, and those which either transcend all these simultaneously or address topics outside them.

Part I: Political Dimensions

In the first chapter of this section, Erica Chenoweth (a terrorism researcher at the University of Colorado, Boulder) examines the assertion that terrorist groups take haven in weak, failed, and collapsed states—and particularly those without a strong tradition of democracy. She contends that this assumed relationship between nondemocracy, state weakness, and terrorism is deficient. Levels of democracy do not necessarily diminish the likelihood of terrorist development. Instead, the political stability of the existing regime is the most significant factor affecting the origins of terrorism. Her analysis indicates that politically unstable regimes—regardless of regime type—are more likely than stable regimes to provide hospitable environments for terrorist organizations to develop. The essential argument here is that the "permissive conditions" of politically unstable regimes inhibit domestic institutional mechanisms that could potentially prevent terrorist organizations from taking root in particular countries. Therefore, the international community should seek to provide multilateral, legitimate support to transitioning states in order to provide the institutional framework by which a transitioning state can develop.[1]

In the next chapter, Paul Pillar—a twenty-eight-year veteran of the U.S. intelligence community and former deputy chief of the Counterterrorist Center at the Central Intelligence Agency—describes how a superpower's foreign policies can engender resentment on the part of certain aggrieved populations and explores the ingredients that are most likely to be found among policies resented by members of the Muslim world. U.S. policies that Muslims perceive as being on the wrong side of a conflict between Muslims and non-Muslims are resented both for the policy itself and for the U.S. motives that they are deemed to demonstrate. A second attribute that makes certain U.S. policies more likely than others to evoke resentment is that they play to other negative stereotypes or preconceptions about the United States. A third ingredient of a policy particularly suited for incurring resentment is in its potential for vivid events that by their very nature may carry emotional impact—especially people dying and suffering as a result of military action. From his analysis, it is clear that public diplomacy has an important role to play in shaping perceptions abroad of the United States and its policies.

Hassan Abbas, a former government official from Pakistan, delves deeper into this topic of public diplomacy in the next chapter. Clearly, he argues, the war of ideas and the battle for the "hearts and minds" of Muslims is by no means over. He draws on analyses of U.S. public diplomacy in Pakistan and Iran to illuminate lessons learned for consideration—for example, he notes, "closing the channels of communication and dialogue has never proved to be a productive measure." His recommendations for U.S. policymakers include acknowledging past mistakes, understanding the limitations of public diplomacy, employing efficient feedback mechanisms to assess the impact of specific policies, establishing and encouraging forums for people-to-people interaction, framing important issues in more constructive ways than "you are either with us or against us," and supporting reform of the education sector in Muslim countries, especially where madrasa networks are entrenched.

West Point Professor Ruth Margolies Beitler continues the discussion of U.S. foreign policies and public diplomacy in the next chapter. She notes that American policy toward Israel remains a potent source of discontent and reverberates throughout the Arab and Muslim world. Indeed, it is commonplace in the Middle East to hear comments espousing the view that if only the United States would modify or cease its support for Israel, hatred against the United States would end. Her analysis reveals that while the United States has supported Israel's existence, it has not always supported its policies, and yet the overwhelming assessment in the Muslim and Arab world is that the United States retains little objectivity when dealing with the Israeli-Palestinian issue. In reality, whether or not the United States is evenhanded when it comes to the Arab world and Israel is almost insignificant, she argues; the key factor fostering resentment in the Middle East is *the perception* that the United States maintains a double standard. Thus, given the prominent role this issue has come to play in public statements of Osama bin Laden and others calling for a global jihad, it is imperative for the United States to lessen al Qaeda's appeal to discontented populations in the Middle East by ensuring a greater balance—or *perception of balance*—with regard to its policies toward the Arab World.

Professor Mohammed Hafez of the University of Missouri–Kansas City also addresses discontented populations in the Middle East with his chapter on how Islamic opposition movements have adopted a variety of strategies to affect social and political change. His discussion addresses two important questions: Why do some Islamic movements turn to rebellion and why do previously nonviolent militants turn to violence? Islamic rebellion, he argues, is a product of institutional exclusion and indiscriminate state repression, particularly following an extended period of Islamic mobilization. Drawing on the political histories of Algeria and Egypt, he concludes that the choice between moderation and violence in Islamic movements during a democratization process is shaped by state policies, especially by the degree of system accessibility and the nature of state repression. If the democratic process grants Islamists substantive access to state institutions, the opposition will be channeled toward conventional political participation and will shun violence. If, on the other hand, the state denies Islamists access and applies repression indiscriminately—punishing both moderate and radical proponents of political opposition—Islamists will tend to resort to militancy.

The tendency to resort to militancy is also the topic of the final chapter of this section, by Professor Eugenia Guilmartin of the United States Military Academy, which examines how ideology, personality, and rejection of commonly respected government institutions play an important role in the making of a right-wing extremist in America. Her discussion examines the ideology of the extreme right-wing in America—an ideology of limited government and maximum property rights, opposition to taxes, support for the right to bear arms, and opposition to world government. This is followed by an analysis of personal characteristics, in particular a heightened focus on certain grievances and the rejection of political institutions, that seem most common among right-wing extremists and domestic terrorists. Her research indicates that while various types of right-wing groups—including militias, common law courts, sovereign citizens, tax protesters, and survivalists—differ in which aspect of the government they fail to recognize, they all reject some commonly respected government institution.

Part II: Religious and Socioeconomic Dimensions

The first chapter of this section, by researcher Susanna Pearce at Trinity College in Dublin, Ireland, examines the relationship between religion and violence. Rather than viewing religion as a sole cause of violence, her analysis illuminates how religion contributes to violence in specific cases. The discussion focuses on three qualities of religion as an explanation of why religion intensifies a conflict. In her model, religious doctrine supplies the motivation, a religious organization grafts on its hierarchal structure, and a religious diaspora provides resources to sustain a movement through a prolonged violent struggle. In each of these unique characteristics, religion has the capacity to escalate and sustain violence in a confrontation between individuals or groups. Overall, her chapter offers a unique analysis through which the relationship between religion and violence can be better understood.

Religious doctrine of a different nature is the topic of the next chapter, in which Professor Michael Barkun of Syracuse University explores the relationship between terrorism and apocalyptic ideologies. For religious believers, particularly many Christians, Doomsday has a fairly exact meaning, represented in two complementary scenarios: In one, time will cease with God's Last Judgment and the world will be destroyed and replaced by "a new heaven and a new earth"; in the other, this event will be preceded by a sequence of stages, during which escalating conflict between good and evil forces will result in the final, titanic battle of Armageddon. In addition to Christianity, apocalyptic strains may also be found in Islam, in association with the appearance of a salvationist Mahdi; in the Buddhist vision of a "Buddha of the future"; and in Native American beliefs about the ancestors' return. Here, as in Christianity, the destruction of the old and corrupt implies the appearance of something new and pure. Given that religious terrorists are widely thought to be the most likely source of a WMD attack in the foreseeable future, this review of apocalyptic ideologies is particularly salient in understanding contemporary terrorism.

The next several chapters of the volume address issues of a more economic orientation, beginning with a discussion on the relationship between terrorism in the Middle East and the oil extraction efforts of the West. Massachusetts Professor Michael Klare[2] examines three key aspects of this relationship: the intersection of European colonialism and the onset of oil production in the Middle East; the nature of U.S. ties with leaders of the oil-producing nations; and the strategic role of oil infrastructure in the war between the terrorists and their opponents. From the extremists' perspective, he notes, the pursuit of Middle Eastern oil is but the latest chapter in a long drive by Western nations to overpower Islamic societies, occupy their lands, and extract their precious resources. Further, these communities are largely devoted to an ancient religious tradition that is thought to be under attack by the West, and it does not help matters that the pursuers of oil are mostly adherents to a different religious tradition that is closely associated with centuries of invasion and conquest. Under these circumstances, he argues, it will probably take the demise of petroleum as the world's leading source of energy to sever the ties between oil and violence altogether.

In the next chapter, Stanford University Professor Paul Ehrlich and Michigan State Professor Jianguo (Jack) Liu address the persistent demographic and socioeconomic factors that can facilitate 9/11-type terrorism and make it easier to recruit terrorists. In particular, their analysis highlights the important and complex relationship between demographic variables and political instability in the developing world. For example, increased birthrates and the age composition of populations in these countries affects resource consumption, prices, government revenues and expenditures, demand for jobs, and labor wages. Differences between developing countries and the developed world are striking—for example, the total fertility rate of Jews born in Israel is under three, approaching replacement level, while that of Palestinians in the Gaza Strip is over seven, the highest of any national-level entity. The implications for these trends on terrorism and terrorist recruitment suggest that without dramatic action, the demographic and socioeconomic conditions in Islamic nations in the Middle East, South Central and Southeast Asia could continue to support terrorism and terrorists for many decades to come.

The following chapter, by MIT researcher Vanda Felbab-Brown, explores the intersection of terrorism and the global drug trade. Her analysis of the Taliban, the Peruvian insurgent group Sendero Luminoso, and the Colombian insurgent group FARC (Revolutionary Armed Forces of Colombia) reveals how drug cartels have used terror to protect their profits while the demand for (and cultivation of) drugs supports terrorism. Specifically, terrorist groups derive three sets of gains from their involvement with the illicit economy: increased *physical capabilities* (money and weapons); increased *freedom of action* (the ability to optimize tactics and strategies); and increased *political capital* (legitimacy, relationship with the local population, the willingness of the local population to withhold intelligence on the terrorist organization from the government, and the willingness to provide intelligence about government units to the terrorist organization). In essence, as long as a global drug trade—in which there is high consumer demand and lucrative rewards for production and trafficking—exists, terrorist groups will continue to profit from this trade, and can be expected to commit violent acts in order to protect these profits.

The final chapter of this section also deals with the global economy, but from a much different perspective. Professor Michael Mousseau, of Koç University in Istanbul, Turkey, draws on research by economic historians to show how two distinct norms of economic integration—contracting and reciprocity—give rise to two distinct political cultures that legitimate, re-

spectively, liberal democracy and collective authoritarianism. In liberal democracies, economic transactions are based on contracting, which requires
a recognition of the equal rights of strangers as well as religious and cultural tolerance. In contrast, economic environments where reciprocity is the
norm—as is the case for many developing nations—trust and cooperation
is based more on in-group beliefs and values, loyalty to in-group leaders,
and distrust of outsiders. From this perspective, one begins to see how globalization has contributed to exacerbating conflict between the developed
and developing worlds, particularly when free trade between the developed
and developing world hurts the local economy and worsens the conditions
of the urban jobless, increasing the dependency of millions who blame the
foreigners for their conditions.

Part III: Alternative Views on Root Causes of Terrorism

The final section of this volume begins with internationally renowned political theorist Benjamin Barber's chapter on the relationship between terrorism and interdependence. He argues that the contemporary struggle
against terrorism can be seen as the collision between two forces: one an
integrative modernization and aggressive economic and cultural globalization, which can be called McWorld; and the other a fragmentary tribalism
and reactionary fundamentalism, which can be called Jihad. As globalization has led to increasing interdependence, he argues, we must learn to contain and regulate the anarchy that foments both the destructiveness of
terrorists and the injustices of global capital. Only the globalization of civic
and democratic institutions is likely to offer a way out of the ongoing war
between Jihad and McWorld, and this requires a new understanding of
global democratic interdependence.

A globally interdependent perspective is also the subject of the next chapter, authored by two officers of the U.S. Army: Dr. Cindy Jebb, a Colonel
and Professor at the United States Military Academy, and Madelfia Abb, a
Lieutenant Colonel and Instructor at the U.S. Army Command and General Staff College. Their chapter explores the intellectual framework of
human security and draws from living-systems theory to illuminate definitions and concepts that are then applied to the human, political, and terrorist systems. Their analysis reveals how failed states impact security at
the individual level and particularly, how the process of globalization and
failed states create, sever, and influence the interconnectedness of the three
living systems. In essence, they argue, framing the challenge of terrorism
through the living-systems theory may help policymakers better understand
the significance of human security in the fight against terrorism.

From a similar perspective, regarding individual human security, Bryn
Mawr College Professor Clark McCauley's chapter argues that the rise of

the modern nation-state that began with the French Revolution has been accompanied by a slow but steady erosion of the distinction between soldiers and civilians. This has been exacerbated by countless instances of state-sponsored violence against its own citizens. In war against internal enemies, he notes, the modern state has cited the threat to its own power to justify killing disaffected ethnic and political categories among its own civilians. Such attacks have killed 130 million in the twentieth century. In comparison, guerrillas and terrorists have killed approximately half a million civilians in the twentieth century. Thus, he argues, our understanding of terrorism must include a recognition that a state's killing of its own civilians is not irrelevant and may have some influence on how terrorists view the morality of killing noncombatants in pursuit of their political or religious objectives.

The next chapter provides a unique discussion on how dimensions of environment and geography—specifically, the physical landscape in which terrorists live—can be seen as root influences for terrorism. Coauthored by Professor Peter Liotta, Executive Director of the Pell Center for International Relations and Public Policy, and Professor James Miskel, Vice President for Policy Studies at Alidade, Inc., this chapter argues that environment and geography provide both context and opportunity for the making of a terrorist, particularly in numerous locations across the Lagos-Cairo-Karachi-Jakarta arc of megacities where jobs and educational opportunities are increasingly unavailable, resulting in discontent, crime, and urban instability. Other locations of concern within this arc include the slums to which tens of millions of refugees have come from other (primarily rural) parts of the developing world. To combat the potential for these locations to serve as breeding grounds for terrorism, they argue, more focus must fall on internal public sector reform and public security improvements in states where governance is currently failing or where urban population growth is likely to induce failure at the municipal level.

Finally, Karin von Hippel, a Senior Research Fellow at the Center for Defense Studies at King's College, London, provides a concise summary of themes covered in many of the chapters in this volume and examines developments in six main areas that have emerged in the public debate as causal and facilitating factors for international terrorism. These six areas— poverty, weak and collapsed states, wars hijacked by Islamic extremists, fundamentalist charities, radicalization in Europe and North America, and the "democracy deficit"—need deeper analysis to understand how they may facilitate terrorist recruitment and support. Further, she argues, while some energy has been dedicated to understanding and tackling these factors in the three years since the attacks in America, the response has not been adequate. The rhetoric on both sides of the Atlantic has not yet been satisfactorily matched by realistic and robust reforms. In essence, the threat posed by transnational terrorism can only be defeated through a dedicated and coordinated transnational response, one that not only focuses on the symptoms, but also on the causes.

Conclusion

The final volume of the *Making of a Terrorist* series is perhaps the most ambitious, as it seeks to fill a significant gap in the field of terrorism studies by entering the contested terrain of "root causes." As these chapters demonstrate, the diversity of topics scattered around this terrain indicates there is still much to explore and learn. With so many roots, facilitators and trigger causes, and so much disagreement about the relative importance of any of them, surely there is ample opportunity for new generations of bright, creative thinkers to engage this field of inquiry.

Acknowledgments

The views expressed herein are those of the author and do not purport to reflect the position of the United States Military Academy, the Department of the Army, or the Department of Defense.

Acknowledgments

A massive endeavor such as this requires a great deal of support from one's colleagues, family and friends, as well as generous amounts of caffeine and hubris. Thankfully, I have not suffered for lack of any of these. For their continued support, I extend my sincere gratitude foremost to the faculty and staff of the Combating Terrorism Center (CTC) at West Point (Jarret, Kip, Bill, Brian, Lianne, Daniella, Thalia, Jeff, Janice, Jude, and Reid), from whom I continue to learn much every day. Two men in particular—General (R) Wayne Downing, Chair of the CTC, and Brigadier General (R) Russell Howard, former Head of the Department of Social Sciences at West Point and founding Director of the CTC—have inspired countless others with their leadership, counterterrorism expertise, and commitment to improving our nation's security, and I am grateful for the opportunity to learn from them. Guidance and suggestions from USMA Academy Professor (and Colonel) Cindy Jebb and Dr. Rohan Gunaratna (Senior Fellow at the CTC) were also very helpful in identifying themes and authors for this project. And my faculty colleagues throughout West Point—and particularly the Department of Social Sciences—have been a continual source of support and assistance.

Over the last few years, I have been intrigued and inspired by colleagues and friends who study terrorism and counterterrorism—many of whose words are represented in the pages of these volumes. Each of the chapters in these volumes is the product of thoughtful research and analysis, and I offer my heartfelt thanks to the authors for their hard work and commitment to excellence. It is my sincere hope that all the collective effort put into this project will inspire a new generation to pursue further research in the field of terrorism and counterterrorism studies.

Finally, and of course most importantly, I owe a great debt of gratitude to my wife Alicia, who provided an incredible amount of patience and understanding through long nights and weekends while I disappeared into the solitary world of editing. Her support during this process was particularly phenomenal given that while I was working to produce the final manuscript of these volumes, she was working on the final term of a demanding pregnancy. Book and baby are now being introduced to the world at roughly the same time; thus, with the appropriately optimistic and hopeful energy that newborns bring, I dedicate this book to my new daughter, Chloe Lynn. I pray that she and all those of her generation will grow up in a world where the scourge of terrorism is better understood, prevented, and defeated.

CHAPTER 1

Exploring Root Causes of Terrorism: An Introduction

JAMES J. F. FOREST

Of the three themes addressed in the volumes of this publication—recruitment, training, and root causes—the latter term is perhaps the least well-known or understood. Clearly, terrorism has complex historical, political, social, and economic roots, and thus evades any simplistic sort of cause-effect analysis. And yet, the term "root causes" has often been used in prominent policy statements and speeches, calling on us all to "address the root causes of terrorism" without really explaining what this term means.

On 22 September 2003, UN Secretary-General Kofi Annan convened a one-day conference, "Fighting Terrorism for Humanity," in New York City. In his opening address, Annan declared,

> Terrorism will only be defeated if we act to solve the political disputes or long-standing conflicts that generate support for it. . . . If we do not, we should find ourselves acting as recruiting sergeants for the very terrorists we seek to suppress. . . . To fight terrorism, we must not only fight terrorists. We have to win hearts and minds.[1]

Among this gathering of terrorism experts and national leaders were eighteen heads of state, including French President Jacques Chirac, Italian Prime Minister Silvio Berlusconi, Pakistani President Pervez Musharraf, and Afghan President Hamid Karzai. If one might find an official definition of root causes, this should be the place.

Participants at this conference discussed the report of an international panel of terrorism experts, convened in Oslo, Norway, in June 2003, which sought to debunk certain myths about terrorism.[2] The experts agreed that there was only a weak and indirect relationship between poverty and terrorism and that state sponsorship is not a "root cause" of terrorism. However, as Tore Bjørgo of the Norwegian Institute of International Affairs (the convener of the Oslo meeting) acknowledged in his introductory remarks to the report, there are complex definitional problems inherent in using the term "root causes" to describe factors that lead to terrorism.

> One problem is that the more deep-rooted a cause is (for example, "poverty" or "modernization"), the more general it becomes, and the less directly is it related to terrorism. On the opposite extreme are "trigger causes"—those immediate circumstances and events that provoke people to take recourse to terrorist action. A "root cause" perspective should also be supplemented by an actor-oriented approach to understand the dynamics of the terrorist process.[3]

This multidimensional perspective of terrorism is an important one: As described later in this chapter, the synthesis of environment and actors—in framing both deep-rooted and trigger causes—is a key focus of this third volume of *The Making of a Terrorist*.

The Oslo report proceeds to cite a lack of democracy, civil liberties, and rule of law as a precondition for many forms of domestic terrorism, along with extremist secular or religious ideologies, and the presence of charismatic, ideological leaders.[4] "Increased repression and coercion are likely to feed terrorism, rather than reducing it," the report notes, adding that "extremist ideologies that promote hatred and terrorism should be confronted on ideological grounds by investing more effort into challenging them politically, and not only by the use of coercive force."[5]

The ideas and suggestions contained in the Oslo report provide a useful starting point for exploring the so-called "root causes" of terrorism more fully. Thus far in this publication we have examined the lure of terror groups, including how and where recruitment takes place, as well as various developmental processes and places that help transform the new recruit into a competent terrorist. This third and final volume of the *Making of a Terrorist* series explores some of the underlying causes that lead to the formation of terror groups in the first place. The volume naturally cannot address all known or potential causes, nor can this brief introductory essay. Rather, the intention here is to reflect upon and illuminate the diversity of perspectives that inform our understanding of the wellsprings from which terrorism flows. This introductory chapter of Volume III: *Root Causes* describes in general terms what the existing research literature suggests about some of the root causes of terrorism, providing some conceptual background for the remaining chapters of this volume.

A Simplistic View of Root Causes

When explaining the phenomenon of global terrorism to my students at West Point, I typically draw on some version of the following formula: 1) Terrorism is a tactic, chosen and used by an individual or group; and 2) it is chosen because they seek some type of objective—often of a political, social, criminal, economic, and/or religious nature—and believe terrorism to be the most effective means by which they can achieve that objective. This admittedly simplistic view of terrorism implies a much broader and more important basic issue: The choice to engage in terrorism is driven by a belief that the present is inadequate, and something must be done in order to ensure a better future. Thus, from political revolutionaries to religious militants, the results are similar in terms of their adoption of politically violent tactics as a means to achieve their objectives. Dissatisfaction with the status quo has led to terrorist group formation in Ireland, Italy, Egypt, Germany, Sri Lanka, Japan, Indonesia, the Philippines, the United States, and many other nations. Moreover, terrorism has proven effective in bringing about change, from the perspective of some observers. For example, terrorism drove the powerful United States (and later Israel) out of Lebanon and convinced the French to pull out of Algeria.

In many cases, acts of terrorism are carried out by individuals consumed by hatred towards others, along with a willingness and ability to kill without remorse or regard for those who may die from their terrorist act. A good deal of this animosity—particularly in the developing world—may stem from a perception that they have been victimized by corrupt governments, backed by powerful nations and multinational corporations that have little concern for their lives, needs, or suffering. This results in what psychologist John Mack describes as "a reservoir of misery, hurt, helplessness, and rage from which the foot soldiers of terrorism can be recruited."[6] However, it can also be said that hatred in the soul of the terrorist is a symptom of something deeper, a central dissatisfaction with one's place in this world vis-à-vis others, and it is this dynamic aspect to human relations that leads to the following suggestion: A central element found within many root causes of terrorism is the pursuit of power.

Terrorism and the Pursuit of Power

The ongoing discussion about root causes of terrorism has many flavors, but a common theme, if there is one, appears to be related to the unequal distribution of power on local, national, or global levels. The unequal distribution of power feeds a perception of "us versus them," a perception found in all ideologies associated with politically violent groups and movements. From Bill Gale's rabid white-supremacy radio shows in the United

States to the firebrand imams in the mosques of Riyadh or Finsbury Park, London, the hardships and challenges "we" face can be framed in terms of what "they" are or (more likely) what "they" have done to us. As noted scholar Bernard Lewis recently observed, " 'Who did this to us?' is of course a common human response when things are going badly, and many in the Middle East, past and present, have asked this question."[7] In this light, "we" desire a redistribution of power in order to have more control over our destiny, and one could argue that many terrorist groups use violence as the way to bring this about.

A cursory look at the stated objectives of some of the world's more notorious terrorist groups exemplifies this view. Ethnic separatist groups like the Liberation Tigers of Tamil Eelam (LTTE, in Sri Lanka), the Abu Sayyaf Group (ASG, in the Philippines), and the *Euskadi Ta Askatasuna, Batasuna* (Basque Homeland and Freedom, or ETA, in Spain) all want the power to form their own recognized, sovereign entity, carved out of an existing nation-state. Groups engaged in the Middle East *intifada*— like the al-Aqsa Martyrs Brigade, Hamas, the Palestinian Islamic Jihad, and the Palestine Liberation Front—want the power to establish an Islamic Palestinian state. Other groups want the power to establish an Islamic state in their own region, including Ansar al-Islam (in Iraq), the Armed Islamic Group (in Algeria), al-Gama'at al-Islamiyya (in Egypt), the Islamic Movement of Uzbekistan (in Central Asia), Jemaah Islamiyah (in Southeast Asia), and al Qaeda. In all cases, these groups seek power to change the status quo, to forge a future that they do not believe will come about naturally, and are thus determined to use terrorism to achieve their objectives.

Political repression is clearly an important reflection of this unequal distribution of power. When a government exhibits outright hostility and commits open violence against members of its citizenry, this represents a form of the powerful subjugating the relatively powerless. States that engage in such behavior range from rogue states like Iraq to allies of the democratic West, like Egypt. In the case of the former, Saddam Hussein's use of chemical weapons to subdue the Kurdish populations in the north of Iraq is a well-known extreme example of state terrorism. Meanwhile, as researcher Jack Beatty recently noted,

> A glance at the Human Rights Watch report on Egypt for last year reveals a political tourniquet: suspects arrested and held without being charged, dissidents tried by military courts, parties outlawed, opposition candidates from Islamic parties jailed on security charges just before elections and thus kept from winning office, torture used to extract confessions, and political prisoners dying while in custody. The United States gives Egypt $1.2 billion in military aid every year, and doubtless Egypt uses a considerable amount of that to keep the tourniquet tight.[8]

This Egyptian representation of the unequal distribution of power is particularly salient given the *fatwas* issued by Osama bin Laden and his colleagues (like Ayyman al-Zawahiri, a former leader of the Egyptian Islamic Jihad) as well as other ideological statements supporting the global jihad movement.[9]

Another dimension to viewing terrorism as the pursuit of power comes in the form of opposition to political corruption. When a government fails to adhere to the conventional social contract between governor and the governed, its citizens become disenfranchised and seek the power to force change, launching a variety of revolutionary movements throughout history.[10] Corrupt governments seek to maintain and increase their power over others (and over resources) by any means necessary, while the powerless see the corruption and look for ways to combat it—even through violent acts of terrorism, as that may be perceived as their only form of recourse. By extension, U.S. foreign policies that are seen to prop up corrupt regimes, or constrain the potential for achieving a group's objectives, lead the members of that group to focus on the United States as a target of terrorist activity in the hopes of compelling a change in those policies.

Power (and the desire for it) is also seen in the relationship between weak or failed states and terrorist activity. In weak states, the absence of rule of law or peaceful ways to resolve conflict can lead those seeking power to use violent means to achieve their objectives. In these kinds of impoverished states, where security can be readily purchased by the highest bidder, the powerful do what they want, while the powerless are made to do their bidding. Further, a full-fledged failed state can be seen as both a facilitator for terrorism *and* a root cause, in that the power vacuum inherent in a failed state leads groups (either from within or from outside its borders) to adopt violence as a means to seek power and control over the future direction of that state, while the absence of a functioning state government allows the country to serve as a safe haven for terrorist organizations and activities.

From this perspective, recent events in Nepal are particularly worrisome. For nine years, the people of this country have suffered through a civil war that has raged between government forces and Maoist guerillas seeking to impose a communist state.[11] Around 11,000 have been killed, and the government has abandoned much of the country to the guerrillas since the uprising began. According to one account, "As Nepal descends towards becoming a failed state, its conflict threatens to spill over into neighboring countries, spreading unrest and perhaps even terror across parts of South Asia."[12] Meanwhile, on 1 February 2005, Nepal's King Gyanendra announced that he was declaring a state of emergency, sacking the government and assuming direct rule for three years. Political leaders, including the former prime minister, were placed under house arrest, local news media were censored (with soldiers posted in newsrooms in the capital,

Katmandu, to enforce a ban on criticizing the king's move), and across the country local and international phone lines, mobile networks, and internet services were suspended.[13] Here, a seemingly repressive governmental reaction to an ongoing insurgency (itself a sign of dissatisfaction with the status quo, particularly given that the guerrillas are calling for an elected assembly to draft a new constitution), while much of the country remains in chaos, represents a fairly robust collection of potential root causes for terrorist activity.

A similar case is found on the African continent, where the oil-rich country of Sudan has seen four decades of civil war between the Arab Muslims of the North and the African-Animist-Christian South.[14] The roots of this conflict lie in the government-led Arabization and Islamization of the North (where the country's capital, Khartoum, is located) and the resistance to those forces in the South. The imposition of Islamic law by the country's leaders triggered the formation of the Sudan People's Liberation Movement (SPLM) and its military wing, the SPL Army, whose declared objective is the creation of a new, secular, democratic, pluralistic Sudan. According to historian Frances Deng, an "acute crisis of national identity is at the core of this conflict, which is exacerbated by conflict-related famine, a collapsing economy, and insecurity brought on by a disintegrating political situation."[15] As this country increasingly raises the specter of a potentially failing state—particularly given events in the Darfur region over the last few years—its recent history as a safe haven for Osama bin Laden and his al Qaeda cronies is cause for increasing concern for U.S. counterterrorism professionals.

Another possible root cause of terrorism, related to the pursuit of power, is seen in the form of relatively powerless groups or individuals seeking the ability to extract revenge for injustices (real or perceived) against a far more powerful adversary. As discussed by psychologist Raymond Hamden in Volume 1 of this publication, any group of people who have been victimized by another feel justified in striking back by any means necessary. In the case of Iraq, for example, Hussein's use of chemical weapons against the Iranians during the 1980s and the Kurds during the 1990s engendered a natural desire among both populations to "get back" at Hussein, explaining somewhat their delight at his recent removal from power by the United States and its allies.

However, closer scrutiny reveals stark differences between these two examples of WMD usage and the desire for revenge they produced. In the first case, Iraq used WMD against Iranian forces in the context of a war, and it is widely known that atrocities are all too common in most any kind of war. However, in the second case, the government of Iraq slaughtered unarmed Kurdish men, women and children, wiping out entire villages not as part of a war but rather in an attempt to terrorize other Kurdish villages and keep them from causing more trouble for the regime. Thus, Iranians may feel justified in seeking revenge for wartime atrocities, and can do so within the context of interstate relations, while in contrast, the Kurds seek retribution for murderous injustices, but they have no state mechanisms with which to seek justice. From this perspective, one might expect the Kurds to feel that terrorist attacks and assassination attempts are their only recourse.

In another dimension of root causes, the finite limits of the world's resources create a condition of relative scarcity for various groups of people, leading to conflict and potential violence between individuals and groups who seek to control the use of those resources. In seeking the power to decide what to do with a country's natural endowment, such as land, oil, diamonds, and water, some have resorted to terrorism as a tactic for compelling others into reluctant agreement with their preferred agenda. This dimension of unequal power distribution is likely to become worse in the decades ahead, for many reasons. Droughts have increased in frequency and intensity in parts of Africa and Asia over the past four decades, and degraded soils have lowered global agricultural yields by 13 percent since 1945 while the world's population is growing at a rate of 77 million per year. Energy resources like oil and natural gas are in high demand around the world, but their supplies are limited in quantity and quality; as demand increases, we may expect to see increasing conflict over the power to control the use of these resources.

Land is a particularly important finite resource and source of conflict; indeed, a relatively tiny strip of land plays a key role in the deadly Middle East conflict. Both Palestinians and Jews focus on the "occupation" of "our land" by the other. Zionists wail about the "evil forces who have become stronger in our Holy Land,"[16] while Palestinians focus on a history of Israeli forces entering villages and driving entire populations out into what became the refugee settlements in Gaza, West Bank, Lebanon, and elsewhere. Israeli Prime Minister Yitzhak Rabin was assassinated by Yigal Amir, an Orthodox student, because of his plan to evacuate a small settler enclave in Hebron as part of the Oslo Accords he signed with Yassir Arafat in 1993.[17] Throughout its history, terrorism has been used (by both Muslims and Jewish extremists) to disrupt the Middle East peace process. Those conducting the terrorist acts are not the decision makers in this process, but instead are the relatively powerless, seeking ways to shape the course of future events that concern them, especially when these events concern a bit of highly coveted land.

Further, the crisis in the Middle East can also be seen as a struggle over the power of the Palestinian people to govern themselves within territorial boundaries defined by them, and the power of the Israelis to enjoy security and prosperity within territorial borders they define for themselves. Curiously, as scholar Michael Oren recently observed, much of the land acquired by the Israelis was actually accidental:

Israel's original plan during the 1967 war was to destroy Egypt's air force and knock out the Egyptian army's first line of defense. But the IDF moved so quickly and encountered such weak resistance that the goal kept changing. . . . The territorial conquests were not planned—the Sinai Peninsula, the West Bank, the Golan Heights, Jerusalem's old city. . . . It was these unplanned conquests, which tripled Israel's size and left 1.2 million Palestinian homeless and under Israel's control, that created the conditions for the stand-off in today's Middle East.[18]

The intersection between terrorism and the pursuit of power can also be found among criminal organizations and drug cartels. From Afghanistan and Burma to Colombia and Peru, violence has been used around the world to terrorize local populations into acquiescing to—even facilitating—the drug trade and other criminal activities. Powerful gangs and drug lords in Los Angeles and New York City regularly use terror to expand their territory, protect their profitable activities from potential rivals, and convince the citizens of their neighborhood not to cooperate with the authorities.

In sum, terrorism can be seen from one point of view as a tactic used in the pursuit of power to achieve some form of political, social, criminal, economic, religious, or other objective. At a most basic level, those with a comparatively greater position of power over others and over their own futures typically have relatively little incentive to use terrorism to achieve their goals. When one has power, one's goals can be achieved through other means. But the relatively powerless, engaged in a struggle with the powerful over resources and the shape of their future, may resort to terrorism as a primary way by which to influence the evolution of history. From this perspective, it is intuitive to suggest that only through the global spread of democracy—in which all groups, large and small, have equal opportunity to influence the course of future events—will we ever find a way to bring about the decline of terrorism. However, democracies require compromise, and it is here that the argument hits a stumbling block: In true democracies, small groups, particularly those with relatively unpopular social, political, or religious agendas, are often unable to achieve their objectives, and a willingness to compromise may not be among their core values in the first place. This is a particularly worrisome factor in today's era of sacred terror, where terrorism is being used as a tactic for achieving an ideologically absolutist agenda without regard for the niceties of diplomatic negotiation or democratic compromise.

The Pursuit of Power in the Age of Sacred Terror

In most cases, religious-oriented terrorism seeks to bring about changes that are aligned with the values and doctrines of a particular religion—or, as in the case of Aum Shinrikyō, a religious cult. Because these changes are not seen as attainable through nonviolent means, groups like al Qaeda, Jemaah Islamiyah, and the Moro Islamic Front have adopted terrorist activity in pursuit of the power to achieve their ideological goals. Religious ideologies can be a powerful motivator for human action because religion, as psychologist John Mack and others have noted,

> deals with spiritual or ultimate human concerns, such as life or death, our highest values and selves, the roots of evil, the existence of God, the nature of divinity and goodness, whether there is some sort of life after the body has died, the idea of the infinite and the eternal, defining the boundaries of reality itself, and the possibility of a human community governed by universal love. Religious assumptions shape our minds from childhood, and for this reason religious systems and institutions have had, and continue to have, extraordinary power to affect the course of human history.[19]

As catalyst for change (or attempts to bring about change), few belief systems can match the power of religious ideologies. As British researcher J. P. Larsson has observed, there are several unique aspects to religion which help explain how and why violence may be condoned and necessary to achieve ideologically-related goals. First, these ideologies are often *theologically supremacist*,[20] meaning that all believers assume superiority over nonbelievers, who are not privy to the truth of the religion. Second, most are *exclusivist*—believers are a chosen people, or their territory is a holy land. Third, many are *absolutist*—it is not possible to be a half-hearted believer, and you are either totally within the system or totally without it. Further, only the true believers are guaranteed salvation and victory, whereas the enemies and the unbelievers—as well as those who have taken no stance whatsoever—are condemned to some sort of eternal punishment or damnation, as well as death. Overall, religious ideologies help foster *polarizing values* in terms of right and wrong, good and evil, light and dark— values which can be co-opted by terrorist organizations to convert a devout believer into a lethal killer.

The most worrisome representation of these polarizing values is seen among today's religious extremists. From the Muslim Brotherhood (founded in Egypt in 1928 and responsible for numerous terror attacks and assassinations) to American anti-abortion extremist Paul Hill (convicted of terrorizing and killing members of the medical profession), religious ideals have led to violent acts that are perpetrated by individuals who believe their actions are sanctioned by a higher power. Indeed, most extremist movements and groups have an additionally powerful element in their belief systems—the conviction that God *requires* them to commit violent acts for the sake of all humankind. Thus, with the righteousness that comes from believing that God on your side, what need or incentive is there for negotiation or compromise?

In one of the most eloquent descriptions to date of religious terrorism,

Harvard researcher Jessica Stern describes how her interviews with extremist Christians, Jews, and Muslims revealed a sort of "spiritual intoxication," a spiritual high or addiction derived from the fulfillment of God's will (or the individual's interpretation thereof).[21] For these individuals, religion has helped them simplify an otherwise complex life, and becoming part of a radical movement has given them support, a sense of purpose, an outlet in which to express their grievances (sometimes related to personal or social humiliation), and "new identities as martyrs on behalf of a purported spiritual cause."[22] In a unique form of transcendental experience, the religious extremist seems to

> enter into a kind of trance, where the world is divided neatly between good and evil, victim and oppressor. Uncertainty and ambiguity, always painful to experience, are banished. There is no room for the other person's point of view. Because they believe their cause is just, and because the population they hope to protect is purportedly so deprived, abused and helpless, they persuade themselves that any action—even a heinous crime—is justified. They believe that God is on their side.[23]

Radical militant Islam warrants particular attention because of the intersection of modern-day geopolitical concerns and ideological goals, the achievement of which, the extremists argue, requires violence, even suicidal violence, through which an individual can earn his or her way into paradise while in the service of restoring the Caliphate. As religion expert Olivier Roy notes, today's radical Islamic movements are

> very conservative . . . [members are] struggling for the total implementation of shari'ah, and do not care for social and economic issues as did the Islamists. They are closer to Saudi Wahhabism than to the left-influenced revolutionary Islam of Khomeini. . . . Their only strategic agenda is to wage jihad in order to reconstitute the "Muslim community" (*ummah*) beyond the national and ethnic divides. Hence, their support for various jihads at the periphery of the Muslim world: Kashmir, the Philippines, Chechnya, Uzbekistan, Bosnia, and so forth. In this sense, they are truly global. . . . [Further], they recruit among uprooted cosmopolitans, de-territorialized militants, themselves a sociological product of globalization; many migrated in order to find employment or education opportunities; they easily travel and change their citizenship; in their use of English, computers, satellite phones, and other technology, they are the authentic product of the modern, globalized world. Their battlefield is the whole world, from New Jersey to the Philippines.[24]

Today, many nations of the once-mighty Islamic world are struggling economically, socially, and politically. Indeed, members of the global Islamic jihad often see themselves as oppressed and threatened defenders of

Islam, more than seeking the spread of Islam.[25] The relationship between modern-day geopolitical realities of the Islamic world and religious ideological goals is an important component of al Qaeda's view of the world, as reflected in the 12 October 1996 *fatwa* issued by Osama bin Laden: "The people of Islam have suffered from aggression, iniquity and injustice imposed by the Zionist-crusader alliance and their collaborators. . . ."[26] Following a litany of grievances and perceived injustices, this document calls upon all Muslims "to express our anger and hate . . . [as] a very important moral gesture" and requests support for the mujahideen "by supplying them with the necessary information, materials and arms. Security men are especially asked to cover up for the mujahideen and to assist them as much as possible against the occupying enemy; and to spread rumors, fear and discouragement among the members of the enemy forces."[27] Finally, bin Laden notes how Muslim "youths believe in what has been told by Allah and His messenger . . . about the greatness of the reward for the mujahideen and Martyrs. . . . He will guide them and improve their condition and cause them to enter the garden—paradise—which He has made known to them."[28]

The intersection of Muslim ideology and the strategic goals of al Qaeda (and its affiliated groups) has spawned what terrorism researcher Marc Sageman calls the Global Salafi Jihad. Salafists, he notes, "advocate a strict interpretation of the Quran" and believe that because the leaders of modern-day Muslim societies "refuse to impose Sharia, the strict Quranic law and true Islamic way of life . . . [they] are accused of being apostates, deserving death."[29] Members of the Global Salafi Jihad believe that to overthrow these corrupt regimes and "reinstate the fallen Caliphate and regain its lost glory," they must first recognize that "the United States would never allow this to happen, [thus] the global jihad must defeat this country . . . [and needs to] inflict the maximum casualties against this opponent."[30]

What makes the Global Salafi Jihad so important is that ideology coupled with what some have called the "strategic logic" of suicide bombing[31] creates a force that seeks an absolute, uncompromising vision of the future, and is willing to use smart weapons (human bombs) as a means to change policy and behavior. As Sageman notes, members of this radical movement are encouraged to "concentrate on the method of martyrdom operations as the most efficient in terms of damages and least costly to the jihad."[32] Further, in the process of conducting suicide attacks, these individuals are demonstrating their view of what devout Muslims should be willing to do in the service of God. In sum, terrorist attacks from New York to Bali to Madrid to Casablanca can all be seen as representations of devout faith combined with the use of lethal tactics in the pursuit of power to secure a future aligned with that faith. When the power to achieve their goals has been attained, this logic argues, the Global Salafi Jihad will cease its terror attacks and begin the task of governing the Islamic state and organizing a new world order more to their liking. Thus, in the realm of religious extremism, death (both martyrdom and the murder of others) is seen as but a means to an end, and the uncompromising nature of terrorist groups who embrace this view accounts for some of the most deadly forms of terrorism in the world today.

Conclusion

To sum up, dissatisfaction with the conditions of the present, combined with an inability (or perceived inability) to shape a future more to their liking, contributes to the formation of groups who seek violence as a means for gaining the power necessary to achieve their objectives. When these groups are infused with a sense of religious purpose, the results can be all the more uncompromising and lethal. While the basic texts of every major monotheistic faith emphasize peaceful tolerance and good works, religious ideologies can be (and all too often have been) used to justify the worst instances of terrorist violence. Also, it is important to note that in the global war on terror, perceptions matter. Perceptions of political, social, economic, or religious oppression are often as powerful a motivator for terrorist activity as the real existence of such oppression.

Of course, in a comparatively few cases, individuals may use terrorism for completely unfathomable reasons, like perhaps some warped sense of satisfaction or morbid joy at the suffering of others. During the thirteenth century, as terrorism expert David Rapoport has noted, a group known as the Thugs intended for

> their victims to experience terror and to express it visibly for the pleasure of Kali, the Hindu Goddess of terror and destruction. . . . Murder was the Thugs' main objective, [and] they believed that death actually benefited the victim, who would surely enter paradise, whereas Thugs who failed to comply with Kali's commands would become impotent, and their families would become either extinct or experience many misfortunes.[33]

Here, while terrorism was conducted without any overarching political goals, the perpetrators of these violent acts felt the need to do so because they believed that such actions were required in order to secure a particular vision of the future for themselves and their victims.

In more modern times in the United States, a similarly warped sense of satisfaction was sought by such individuals as the Tylenol killer, who laced capsules with arsenic in the fall of 1982 (terrorizing the American public and drug industry in the process) but was never apprehended,[34] and Ted Kaczynski (a.k.a., the Unabomber), whose infamy stems from his deadly campaign of mailing homemade bombs that killed three people and wounded twenty-three others in sixteen separate incidents from 1978 to 1995. In cases such as these, the terrorist may be reflecting what psychologist Jerrold Post describes as a consequence of psychological forces in which a polarizing and absolutist "us versus them" rhetoric reflects an underlying view of "the establishment" as the source of all evil, and provides a psychologically satisfying explanation for what has gone wrong in their lives. The fixed logical conclusion of the terrorist—that the establishment must be destroyed—is driven by the terrorist's search for identity, Post argues, and as he strikes out against the establishment he is attempting to destroy the enemy within. This, one could argue, is the pursuit of power in a different form and yet is closely related to the terrorist group motivations discussed earlier in this chapter in the sense that here, too, the individual is seeking the power to achieve a certain vision of his or her future, based on an inherent dissatisfaction with their present.

It must be reemphasized here that the pursuit of power is not *the* root cause of terrorism—indeed, there is no one discrete root cause—but it is one important dimension of many root causes and thus worth consideration. As most experts agree, a complex, multilayered stack of root causes has contributed to the rise of terrorism worldwide. Poverty and social disadvantage alone will not typically lead to violence, nor will religious indoctrination or the absence of a strong state. But it is the combination of root causes to which we must focus our attention.

Returning to the United Nations conference and the Oslo report described at the beginning of this chapter, one theme stands out through much of the debate over what to do about root causes of terrorism: Political and economic reforms are needed. Jitka Malecková (of Charles University, Prague), one of the experts cited in the report, noted that "terrorists are more likely to come from countries that lack civil liberties, suggesting that freedom of expression may provide an alternative to terrorism."[35] This sentiment is echoed by the U.S. government's *9/11 Commission Report*, which notes that there is clearly a need for economic and political reform throughout much of the Middle East and Central Asia:

> Economic openness is essential. Terrorism is not caused by poverty. Indeed, many terrorists come from relatively well-off families. Yet when people lose hope, when societies break down, when countries fragment, the breeding grounds for terrorism are created. Backward economic policies and repressive political regimes slip into societies that are without hope, where ambitions and passions have no constructive outlet.[36]

Finding, fixing, and preventing these "breeding grounds for terrorists" is surely the most daunting task of the global war on terrorism. Clearly, no single nation can meet the challenges represented in this volume on its own. Failure to ensure a globally coordinated, integrated, and long-term response to the root causes of terrorism could very well ensure that our children and grandchildren live in a world under constant threat of terror attacks close to home. Let us try hard not to endow them with such a future. It is to this objective that the chapters of this volume now contribute.

Acknowledgments

The views expressed herein are those of the author and do not purport to reflect the position of the United States Military Academy, the Department of the Army, or the Department of Defense.

PART I

POLITICAL DIMENSIONS

CHAPTER 2

Instability and Opportunity: The Origins of Terrorism in Weak and Failed States

ERICA CHENOWETH

The U.S. National Security Strategy, released in September 2002, codified a rigorous new foreign policy initiative. Under this initiative, security policy focuses on certain "rogue" states that pursue weapons of mass destruction programs, as well as "weak" states that support or harbor terrorists. As this document observes, "the events of September 11, 2001, taught us that weak states, like Afghanistan, can pose as great a danger to our nation as strong states . . . poverty, weak institutions, and corruption can make weak states vulnerable to terrorist networks and drug cartels within their borders."[1] The underlying logic of this statement is that terrorist groups take haven in weak, failed, and collapsed states. This concept of state strength is often associated with freedom and democracy. However, throughout the world one can observe democratic states that are "weak" and autocratic states that are "strong." These contradictions suggest a more complex relationship between democracy and state strength than the simple dichotomies commonly used to describe them.

The National Security Strategy further indicates an implicit assumption that weak, failed, or collapsed states are more likely to harbor terrorists, thus calling for foreign aid to developing nations in order to diminish the likelihood of terrorist organizations in these regions. For instance, in order to combat global terrorism, the George W. Bush administration claims that it will contain or democratize weak states, thus strengthening them and, in effect, making them less hospitable to terrorist organizations.

This chapter contends that this assumed relationship between non-democracy, state weakness, and terrorism is deficient. Levels of democracy do not necessarily diminish the likelihood of terrorist development. Instead, the political stability of the existing regime is the most significant factor affecting the origins of terrorism. This analysis indicates that politically unstable regimes—regardless of regime type—are more likely than stable regimes to provide hospitable environments for terrorist organizations to develop. The essential argument is that the "permissive conditions" of politically unstable regimes inhibit domestic institutional mechanisms that could potentially prevent terrorist organizations from taking root in particular countries.

This argument is significant for several reasons. First, it contributes to existing literatures on both state strength and the origins of terrorism. Moreover, it contradicts conventional wisdom concerning the nature of terrorism and its relationship to democratic forms of government. Finally, it introduces some important considerations that could inform analysts and decision makers regarding security policy, such as focusing on relative political stability rather than democracy and development, increasing efforts at multilateral cooperation with local intelligence agencies, and recognizing new forms of transnational terrorist organization.[2]

Defining State Strength

The concept of "state strength" became prominent in the 1970s and has been useful for development scholars in distinguishing different degrees of governance. It is especially popular among policymakers, who find the classification of states as "weak" or "strong" useful in prescribing foreign policy. State strength is difficult to categorize because many scholars use ill-defined, ambiguous terms and indicators, and they use these terms quite loosely. However, several new volumes by Robert I. Rotberg[3] provide valuable criteria by which we can better evaluate state strength. The general consensus is that states can fall into four different categories: strong, weak, failed, and collapsed. Rotberg contends that states exist to provide mechanisms by which to deliver public or political goods to people living within a designated territory. The state assembles and channels crucial interests among the citizenry, providing for the common welfare and defense. While all states fail and succeed to varying degrees across these dimensions, "it is according to their performance—according to the levels of their effective delivery of the most crucial political goods—that strong states may be distinguished from weak ones, and weak states from failed or collapsed states."[4] Furthermore, states can move back and forth among the differing categories of the continuum.

What are "political goods"? They are often intangible and difficult to quantify, encompassing expectations that exist between the ruler and the ruled. Rotberg contends that political goods exist in a hierarchy, and the most vital good is the supply of human security. The state is responsible for preventing cross-border threats and domestic crime, as well as providing mechanisms through which citizens can resolve their disputes without resort to violent means.[5] With strong institutions, the rule of law can be established and enforced with varying degrees of equity—property rights and laws, a judicial system, and a system that supports norms of fair play. Another political good enables citizens to "participate freely, openly, and fully in politics and the political process" through fundamental civil and human rights, the right to compete for office, and respect and support for national and regional political institutions.[6] Other vital goods may include medical and health care, educational systems, physical infrastructure, communications infrastructure, a money and banking system, promotion of civil society, and methods of regulating the sharing of environmental commons.[7]

State strength exists on a continuum, combining many of the factors enumerated above. Strong states perform well across each of these categories, and they tend to provide many of the goods in the hierarchy. They demonstrate clear control over their territories and deliver a wide range of political goods to their citizens.

Weak states contain a mixed profile, satisfying expectations in some areas while performing poorly in others. Although the "weak" classification refers to a broad continuum of states, it is a distinct category. Some states may be inherently weak because of geographical, physical, or fundamental economic constraints, or they may be fundamentally strong with a situational or temporary weakness due to internal crisis or conflict. Weak states may also experience a combination of these circumstances.

In Rotberg's view, weak states are typically characterized by unresolved ethnic or religious tensions, high urban crime rates, and diminished ability to deliver other public goods, including physical infrastructure and educational systems. There is often a decline in relative GDP per capita and other economic indicators, while levels of corruption increase.[8]

Failed states are "tense, deeply conflicted, dangerous, and contested bitterly by warring factions."[9] Internal or external violence can be intense and unending. Failed states are unable to control their borders, and state regimes may prey on their own constituents. Criminal violence increases, while the government provides virtually no political goods. Infrastructures are deteriorating, and other institutions are flawed. Often the only functional institution in such states is the executive. Rarely do viable domestic currencies circulate, so other international currencies replace them. Other characteristics of failed or failing states include poor health care and school systems, food shortages and widespread hunger, and diminishing levels of annual per capita GDP. The executive branch may still be "strong," because a dictator may have a strong hold over his population. However, the executive is unable to deliver political goods to the population. One example of this is the Sudan, where the citizens have suffered a consistent loss of political goods while the executive has maintained a large degree of power over its population.

A collapsed state is an extreme type of failed state—one in which there is a literal authority vacuum. Political goods are obtained through private or ad hoc means.[10] The citizens become "inhabitants," and the rulers become strongmen who provide the only semblance of security. Many states move between failure and collapse. The failed states of the 1990s, according to Rotberg, are Afghanistan, Angola, Burundi, Congo, Liberia, Sierra Leone, and the Sudan, whereas Somalia is a collapsed state.[11]

Rotberg's synthesis is valuable because it provides indicators that can be both quantitatively and qualitatively measured. This chapter highlights the importance of political stability as a key indicator of state strength.[12] This indicator measures whether a population perceives its government to clearly control its lands and people. Conversely, a government is unstable if its population does not perceive it to control the nation's territory and constituents. Political stability, which reflects that the government exerts clear control—and therefore provides the public good of human security—describes at least one vital aspect of state strength. A dataset of political stability indicators is available at the World Bank, so this measure is both useful and accessible for analyzing state strength.

State Weakness and Origins of Terrorism: A Connection?

The George W. Bush administration favors the approach that nondemocracies are more likely than democracies to sponsor or host terrorist groups, either directly or indirectly. And yet there have been numerous studies evaluating the relationship between terrorism and democracy, which have found that terrorist organizations are more likely to thrive in democracies than in nondemocracies.[13] Despite such studies, however, policy makers and scholars have continued to argue vehemently that democracy will defeat terrorism. In fact, members of the Bush administration have strongly asserted that spreading freedom and liberty around the world will help to alleviate or eliminate the terrorist problem.

In contrast to such assertions, this chapter argues that political instability, or the inability of a government to demonstrate clear control over its population, is the most salient factor in terrorist development. Unstable regimes can occur in democratic or nondemocratic political systems. Because terrorist groups will gravitate toward or originate within political vacuums, a government's inability or unwillingness to prevent terrorism provides opportunities for terrorist organizations to take root.

What are these so-called "opportunities"? The reasons that terrorists would prefer to develop in politically unstable environments rather than stable ones seem clear.[14] First, in unstable systems, a lack of enforcement, accountability, and monitoring capacity exists. The implication, therefore, is that in the absence of strong security institutions, terrorist organizations can flourish with or without state consent.

The second reason that terrorists are so attracted by political instability is because they are themselves political actors who are reacting to some established order. In fact, terrorism expert Bruce Hoffman goes so far as to assert that "terrorism is designed to create power where there is none, or to consolidate power where there is very little."[15] Not only are the means placed at the terrorists' disposal by the permissive environment in which they operate, but they also thrive on the absence of political power by occupying a legitimate political space which has been left open by instability. In essence, *terrorism develops wherever it can.* A politically unstable state, therefore, provides the "permissive conditions" that allow such groups to prosper. Under such conditions, terrorist groups can engage in illicit activities undetected. Military, police, and intelligence units are ill-equipped or undersupported in their counterterrorist initiatives. Moreover, terrorist groups can solicit assistance from local sympathizers, who provide shelter and other supports to such groups. The population may have little confidence in its government's ability to protect it, so populations may be more hospitable to terrorist groups recruiting or hiding in local areas without fear of government intervention. In some cases, terrorist groups may establish their own rules of legality and morality, while also providing security to supporters (thus compensating for the lack of security provided by the state).

Therefore, the development or infiltration of terrorist groups occurs on two levels. One level is the terrorist group itself, which perceives an opening or a vacuum. The other level is the government, where an unstable system is unable or unwilling to combat terrorist development.

Very simply, it makes sense that terrorist groups should be attracted to states with no institutions to inhibit them; further, populations that perceive their governments as unstable may therefore be more "terrorist-friendly" than other populations may be. Such conditions may exist in both democratic and nondemocratic systems.[16]

One significant implication of this argument is that we can expect to observe terrorist activity in transitioning states. There are several kinds of relevant transitions, including the transition from autocracy to democracy and from interim government to democracy. Many studies have determined a strong correlation between transitions to democracy and political instability.[17] Moreover, the transition from an interim government imposed by an occupying force to a democratic government may be susceptible to increased instability (as witnessed most recently in Iraq). Therefore, the transition of interim or authoritarian governments to democratic ones may lead to infiltration or development of terrorist organizations during the time of transition. In the short term, therefore, democracy cannot prevent terrorist emergence. On the contrary, political stability is the most salient variable. This assertion challenges the claims of policy makers concerning the importance of spreading democracy in order to win the global war on terror, suggesting a more nuanced relationship between weak or undemocratic states and the presence of terrorist groups.

Case Studies—Indonesia, Afghanistan, and the Philippines

Developments in Indonesia, Afghanistan, and the Philippines illustrate the nature of the relationship between political instability and origins of terrorism. In fact, all three cases reinforce the argument that political instability makes a terrorist presence more likely, especially during times of transition.

Indonesia

Indonesia has been designated a "weak state" by many observers.[18] The average life expectancy is 66.2 years, and there is very little public expenditure on education or health. Indonesia is burdened with a large deficit and high rates of illiteracy, especially in rural areas. Other indicators of weakness include Indonesia's poor infrastructure, a large discrepancy between male and female earning capacity, high levels of corruption, low quality of regulation and government effectiveness, poor enforcement of the rule of law, and a high degree of political instability. In other words, Indonesia is weak in terms of its government's perceived ability to exercise clear control over its population.

During the Sukarno and Suharto regimes, Indonesia experienced de facto authoritarian rule. Despite accusations of human rights violations and oppression, the state itself was somewhat "stable" politically: There was no dispute regarding who controlled the state. Terrorist activity was virtually nonexistent, although during the 1960s and 1970s revolutionary nationalist terrorist groups began to form. For instance, members of a South Moluccan group sought independence from Indonesia and used terrorist methods to draw attention to themselves and their objectives.[19]

However, these terrorist groups were quickly dismembered due to the state's strong hand. Moreover, during Suharto's rule, extremist Islamic movements were expelled from Indonesia. In fact, "the tightly regulated political and security environment in Indonesia under Suharto forced Indonesian Islamists who supported the anti-Soviet Afghan campaign to relocate to Malaysia in 1985."[20] Indonesia experienced virtually no foreign terrorist development during Suharto's rule because of the relative stability of this regime and the lack of tolerance for such movements, which diminished the opportunity for terrorist groups to form.

In general, this stability remained unchallenged until the Asian Financial Crisis provided the exogenous shock and subsequent circumstances that threatened Suharto's authority. Virtually overnight, Suharto lost legitimacy and authority in his country, and the nation underwent a regime change and a transition to free democratic elections. Another consequence of this political instability was the infiltration of terrorist groups who were waiting in the wings for just such an occasion. For instance, intelligence agencies in both the Philippines and Spain independently reported the existence of terrorist training camps in Indonesia beginning in the late 1990s.[21] While some Indonesians had fled to the Philippines to receive training from the Moro Islamic Liberation Front (MILF), they were able to return to their country and establish bases there. Members of the MILF referred to these Indonesians as the "Indonesian Islamic Liberation Front" (IILF), a name based on its Philippines counterpart. Currently three known terrorist organizations of significant size reside in Indonesia: Jemaah Islamiyah ("Islamic Community," or JI), al Qaeda, and the IILF. Two of these groups, as well as others associated with al Qaeda, originated from Indonesia itself but only gained significant attention after the fall of Suharto. The current al Qaeda groups began as small cells that later became affiliated with this global network, as have so many local groups worldwide with similar ideological persuasions. However, extremist Islam is not necessarily a popular ideology in Indonesia, whose leaders tend to be quite moderate and progressive in their interpretations of Islam.[22]

Unfortunately, Indonesian intelligence has had considerable difficulty detecting or diminishing terrorist activities within its borders. The establishment of local training camps, the movement of these groups throughout the islands of Indonesia, and illicit fundraising perpetrated by these groups has gone relatively unpunished. In Indonesia, then, political instability has caused the government to be less effective against the proliferation of terrorist organizations. Because of the transition from Suharto's regime to an open democracy, the elites in the government have been unable to create a sound and unified antiterrorist policy. Government inaction is creating a greater public space in which terrorism can flourish, while the Indonesian elite are divided on how to respond. The presence of terrorist organizations are sustained not because of lack of democracy in Indonesia; they thrive because of the inability of the government to demonstrate political stability and clear control.

Afghanistan

Afghanistan has been described alternately as a formerly "failed" state that has improved to "weak" status, or a "collapsed" state that has improved to "failed." One major problem is that quality data in Afghanistan on a national level is unavailable, largely due to its weakness and recent collapse or failure. The very absence of this data speaks to the poor conditions in Afghanistan. What data does exist suggests that life expectancy is around 42.8 years, around two-thirds of the adult population is illiterate, 87 percent of the population has no sustainable access to an improved water source, and there are only nineteen physicians per 100,000 people. Afghanistan plays host to millions of displaced peoples from other countries, and there are extremely low levels of government effectiveness, accountability, control over political corruption, and ability to enforce the rule of law. The country is characterized by large levels of gender inequality, particularly in education, political participation, and civil rights. Finally, Afghanistan has experienced significant political instability over the last several decades.

Not surprisingly, then, Afghanistan contains many terrorist organizations—14, according to the U.S. Department of State.[23] The origins of Afghanistan's involvement in terrorism lie in several decades of foreign occupation. During periods of British, Soviet, and American occupation, the interim governments in Afghanistan have been characterized as having limited clear control over their country. Especially following the British occupation, Afghanistan struggled to define itself as a sovereign state. With the Cold War and Soviet involvement in Afghanistan, the existence of a clear, independent government was disputed. Instead, tribes, clans, and warlords dominated the country's political landscape.

Indeed, the only unified body within the Afghan nation over the past two decades has been the mass of mujahideen fighters. At the end of the Soviet occupation in 1989, the Najibullah regime attempted to exercise control and authority over Afghanistan. However, this regime began to collapse because of mujahideen pressure soon after Soviet withdrawal. By the early 1990s, the mujahideen had taken over the government, but they were incapable of ruling with any sense of unity. Persistent infighting crippled potential responses and undermined perceptions of the state's ability to govern.

Amid the famine, disease, and enduring ethnic struggles of the mid-1990s, Afghanistan continued to suffer politically and socially. Simultaneously, terrorist organizations began to take root. In the wake of these seemingly hopeless conditions, the Taliban came into power (with support from neighboring Pakistan). A group of religious students armed with extremist Islamic ideology and anti-Soviet weaponry, the Taliban successfully overthrew the government and declared political authority over the entire country. By 1997, "the general consensus was that the Taliban had won the war and were, in effect, the masters of the whole of Afghanistan."[24]

However, this initial conclusion was mistaken. While the Taliban were ruthless in their attempts to enforce Islamic law among the people of Afghanistan, they were unable to maintain control over many aspects of the loose society. Although the Taliban used forceful measures to control Afghanistan, large portions of the country remained disunited, unmonitored, and overrun by drug lords and warlords. By April 1998, for instance, the Taliban controlled only two-thirds of the country, while the remainder was controlled by the Northern Alliance.[25] Obviously, a government which has no authority over one-third of its territory does not have clear control. An example of this lack of control, even in its more subdued regions, was the Taliban's inability to monitor or regulate the narcotics trade. Further, while the Taliban initially attempted to ban the drug trade, before long they began to profit immensely from the narcotics industry.[26] As a matter of fact, the Taliban were able to raise some money from tolls of transport as well as narcotics trafficking, but they were unable to raise enough money to reconcile debts from bribes or provide for provisions, fuel, or other supplies required for sustained welfare.[27] Although such activity certainly occurred out of material interest, these failures demonstrate the inability of the Taliban to govern effectively within the political realm.

The withdrawal of narcotics bans reflected an attitude of "if you can't beat 'em, join 'em," an approach to governance which also provided ample opportunity for terrorist groups to take advantage of the Taliban's tenuous rule over Afghanistan. Despite human rights violations and extreme oppression over parts of the population, the government was unable to deter terrorist groups from organizing and establishing themselves within the borders. In fact, the Taliban were found to be quite tolerant—even supportive—of Muslim terrorist groups. This support, implicit or explicit, can be attributed to the Taliban's inability to secure political stability. While the Taliban shared ideologies with terrorist networks such as al Qaeda, it is probable that al Qaeda chose to establish itself in Afghanistan because of its perception of the Taliban's relative weakness in governance. For instance, Osama bin Laden was well aware of the Taliban's inability to exile him: "While they would ensure that [bin Laden] would not carry out political or military activity from Afghan soil, they would not expel him and still less would they hand him over for trial."[28] The Taliban's lack of response to terrorist programs and operations were more related to their inability to react than their unwillingness to react.

Today, Afghanistan continues to suffer tremendous levels of famine, poverty, and disease. The country's ethnic and cultural diversity, coupled with its political and ethnic conflicts, resulting in refugee displacements virtually everywhere, has made re-creating national unity virtually impossible. With the inability of transitional ruling bodies to demonstrate clear control, it is unlikely that Afghanistan will eradicate terrorist organizations anytime soon, whether or not it evolves into a successful democracy. Further, one can easily argue that without the intervention of the United States and other members of the international community since 2001, the situation in Afghanistan would be far worse.

The Philippines

A final example of these critical issues is seen in the case of the Philippines. While this state is one of the more "successful" democracies in Southeast

Asia—and is the "strongest" state included in this discussion—it still experiences a moderate degree of state weakness. Granted, the life expectancy in the Philippines is a respectable 69.5 years, and there have been recent improvements concerning levels of public spending on education and health. However, the Philippines has extremely high levels of debt: Public spending on debt is four times higher than on education and public health combined. Females in the Philippines can expect to earn half as much as their male counterparts, and there are significant amounts of the general population without access to sanitary conditions or clean water. Government effectiveness—particularly the state's ability to enforce the rule of law and control corruption—is low relative to comparable states. Most important, however, is the fact that the Philippines has experienced high degrees of political instability.

There are five known terrorist organizations in the Philippines. One of the most prominent groups is the MILF, a separatist movement that operated in Mindanao from 1971–96. At this point in the history of the Philippines, the central government had no counterterrorist mechanisms to prevent the development of these organizations, particularly in the loosely governed south.[29] When President Ferdinand Marcos left power in the mid-1980s, the Philippines experienced a transition to de facto democracy. Not surprisingly, terrorist organizations proliferated in conjunction with this transition. Jemaah Islamiyah took root in the Philippines during this time, and the MILF became more powerful. Al Qaeda has had an established presence in the Philippines since the late 1990s. In fact, al Qaeda operatives have used various locations within the Philippines to train terrorists who have subsequently become active in Indonesia and elsewhere.

Development projects have had little or no effect on the existence of terrorist organizations in the Philippines; further, these reforms have been poorly implemented, with much of the needed funds passing through corrupt channels.[30] Instead, political instability, marked in part by confusing and indeterminate elections in recent years, allowed terrorist groups to flourish in the Philippines. Moreover, during the course of reforms, the elite were in conflict with each other regarding the best course of action. This case reinforces the familiar pattern of a state's inability to exercise authority over its population and territory, creating permissive conditions for terrorist activity in the meantime.

Recently, however, political stability in the Philippines has improved. With support from the international community, elected officials have demonstrated clearer control over the country. Moreover, the government has taken some effective measures against terrorist organizations within its borders. Elite disunity has been mitigated by the presence of U.S. military forces, which have helped improve Filipino military tactics and intelligence in the war against terrorism.

Because of contributions from the international community and troop

support, places like Mindanao and Manila have made considerable achievements in counterterrorism, and Indonesia has strengthened intelligence
forces in all areas of the country.[31] Since 1996, for instance, the newly developed Filipino intelligence forces have gathered information on terrorist
activity in the Philippines and in other Southeast Asian countries. In November 2001, in response to 9/11, the Philippines intelligence community
launched a successful operation to disrupt the al Qaeda network in the
country.[32]

While such measures have developed political stability, they have only
begun to address the well-developed terrorist presence in existence for over
fifteen years. However, allowing for foreign military assistance in developing and reinforcing perceptions of political stability has strengthened Filipino political institutions and provided a united front against terrorism.
The Philippines thus provides an instructive test case for successful improvement in the war on terrorism, mostly due to the supplemental support of the international community in strengthening the stability of the
political system, thus eliminating space within which terrorist groups can
operate.

In sum, political instability within each of these countries has provided
a significantly hospitable atmosphere for terrorism to develop, regardless
of regime type. Critics may argue that the examples used to support this
argument are suspect because each contains a large Muslim population.
Can Islamist ideology just as easily explain the origins of terrorism in these
states? A reasonable answer is no; further, using Islamist ideology as an indicator of terrorist development is not only misinformed, but also dangerous. First, not all regions with large Muslim populations produce a high
number of terrorist groups. An example would be the large Muslim populations within European countries, China, and other Asian states. Moreover, many terrorist groups emanate out of non-Muslim, Western,
industrialized democracies, such as Ireland, Germany, and the United
States. Finally, associating terrorism exclusively with Muslim populations
results in misdirected policies as well as oversimplifications of the enemy,
which can only exacerbate tensions between Islamic and Western states. In
other words, Muslim terrorists are not the only terrorists in the world, nor
are states with high Muslim populations the only states that produce terrorists. Indeed, democratic systems that have undergone a transition, or
some degree of uncertainty in the political system, are also susceptible to
terrorist growth. An example of a "strong" state that underwent a political transition, thus creating an opening for terrorist development, is Spain.
During General Francisco Franco's military authoritarian rule, virtually no
terrorist groups existed. However, following the *coup d'état* that devastated
Franco's regime, Euskadi Ta Askatasuna (or "Basque Fatherland and Liberty," commonly known as the ETA) developed in Spain almost immediately. An ethnic separatist group, the ETA has employed terrorist tactics to

convey its political message. Indeed, while the ETA has ideological origins in the era preceding Franco's fall, the group became truly active following the fall of Franco and during the 1980s and 1990s recruited more followers and advanced its method and scope of attacks. Therefore, political instability, often provoked by a political transition, is the most likely condition in which terrorist groups flourish.

Conclusion

This analysis leads to the following conclusion: A critical relationship exists between the relative political instability of a state and the origins of terrorism. Contrary to most conventional assumptions, however, the weakness that permits terrorist exploitation is not related to nondemocracy. Instead, the relationship is influenced by the relative political instability of a state and its institutions. The cases of Indonesia, Afghanistan, and the Philippines demonstrate this relationship. In each of these states, during key points of political transition, terrorist organizations began to take root. Political instability in turn creates the power vacuum or permissive conditions that permit the infiltration and establishment of terrorist organizations, whereas states with strong, stable systems are able to expel terrorist influence or stop them from forming in the first place.

The results of this analysis indicate that political stability is more desirable than democracy in some states—especially those that wish to contain and dispel terrorist threats. However, while these results seem to argue that governments should crack down on terrorism and revoke civil liberties in order to maintain stability, this is not necessarily a desirable outcome. On the contrary, it is important to remember that "stability, no less than revolution, may have its own kind of terror."[33] Overall, it is important to acknowledge the complexities in relationships between freedom, state failure, and terrorism. Instead of reducing the relationship to simple dichotomies such as terrorism and the absence of terrorism, freedom and repression, or strong and weak, policy makers, scholars, and citizens should be aware of the trade-offs of democratization. Of course, democracy itself may be the most desirable political system for many people in many countries, but democracy may come with a decrease in stability,[34] and a decrease in stability will provide the opportunity for terrorist groups to develop. The presence of terrorist groups may then affect the quality of democracy, either by physical harm imposed by terrorists upon the population or by democratic governments revoking civil liberties in favor of extreme security measures. Under either circumstance, countries may suffer from social unrest, economic disruption, mistrust, and fear.

An irony in recent history is that the United States launched wars in Afghanistan and Iraq in order to extinguish the terrorist threats residing in or supported by each state. With an agenda to liberate and democratize each nation, the United States has effectively toppled each regime with the expectation that the terrorist problem would be eliminated. According to this analysis, however, the levels of democracy that develop in either country are—at least in the short term—unrelated to the terrorist threat. What has occurred instead is the creation of a power vacuum where no one is in clear control—an example of political instability. Thus, we can expect to see an increase of terrorist activity and organization in these regions rather than a decrease. Further, the less stable and organized a state becomes, the more stable and organized a terrorist presence can become. In effect, instead of eradicating the threat, U.S. security policy has (at least temporarily) exacerbated it. We can also expect to see increased terrorist activity originating from other weak states, such as many of those on the African continent or in South America.

Policy makers cannot always fight "evil" (terrorism) with "good" (democracy). Instead, the nature of terrorism and political instability necessitates a trade-off in values between democracy and political stability. First, policy makers should not make broad, sweeping generalizations about "rogue," Islamic, or authoritarian states. Moreover, governments would be well advised to monitor terrorist development in states in which a political transition is occurring. Counterterrorist analysts should also focus on the causes behind political instability and state weakness in order to mitigate possible threats, shifting the focus away from undemocratic regimes. Once these threats are identified, analysts should use context-based policy alternatives and recommendations based upon local conditions and trends. For instance, in the Philippines case, a strong intelligence community has benefited from foreign support and improved antiterrorist conditions. Strong intelligence may not exist in some of the other cases, like Indonesia. The international community should therefore focus on increased support, cooperation, and communication with foreign intelligence forces while distinguishing politically unstable states from the terrorist organizations residing within its borders.

What, then, should the international community do about dictators and authoritarian regimes? There are several possible options. One suggestion is to avoid deposing dictators, instead providing incentives to democratize and gradually shaping institutions that will eventually support democracy in those states.[35] For instance, some argue that the best way to promote democracy is to build institutions that support democracy, such as the rule of law, and encourage voter participation and elections only after such institutions have coagulated.[36] The second option follows from the first, suggesting that institutionalization must come prior to democratization in order for successful transitions to occur. Therefore, the international community should seek to provide multilateral, legitimate support to transitioning states in order to provide the institutional framework by which a transitioning state can develop.[37]

Finally, the international community should embrace the changing nature of terrorism as a global force with international networking capabilities. Small sects of larger organizations like al Qaeda can take root in many countries. Thus, we can expect to find small cells of this organization (or others like it) existing in countries with low levels of political stability.

Addressing the primacy of political instability may not complete the puzzle of state weakness and terrorist development but at a minimum should inform academic inquiry and policy decisions regarding the problem of terrorism.

Acknowledgments

The author would like to thank Jessica Teets, Orion Lewis, James Smith, James Forest, Colin Dueck, Susan Clarke, and Steve Chan for comments on previous drafts of this chapter.

CHAPTER 3

Superpower Foreign Policies: A Source for Global Resentment

PAUL R. PILLAR

The public words and actions of some terrorists provide the most obvious clues that perceptions of, and animosity toward, U.S. foreign policies can be roots of terrorism. The United States or its overseas interests had increasingly become, even prior to the attacks of September 2001, prime targets of international terrorist attacks. The leaders of terrorist groups regularly denounce U.S. policies ranging from military operations to diplomatic postures. And it has become a more frequently discussed issue in public debate within the United States whether America's own actions may anger those who might resort to terrorism, motivate those who do resort to it, and thereby increase the number of Americans who will become victims of future terrorist attacks.

The policy relevance of this issue is clear; less clear are the specific policy implications. The issue underlies many questions, which this chapter explores but does not necessarily answer. Just how important, for example, are responses to superpower policies compared with other roots of terrorism? The rhetoric of terrorist leaders may be an indicator of what issues they believe resonate with the wider audiences they are addressing, but it is not necessarily an accurate gauge of terrorists' motivations, including their own.

Another question concerns the linkage between policies made in Washington and the pain and resentment felt by would-be terrorists in foreign lands. Even for most Americans, foreign policy is not a major concern. It has not figured highly in most recent presidential elections (2004 being an exception). Should foreigners be expected to focus so intently on it that some of them are driven to the extreme of committing terrorist acts? Perhaps the answer requires distinguishing between what causes individuals to become terrorists in the first place and other—also important—issues concerning terrorism, such as what increases the sympathy that larger populations have for terrorist groups and what affects the decisions of those groups about which countries or targets to attack.

Yet another question is whether that which most angers and motivates terrorists are specific U.S. policies or inherent attributes of being a superpower. In other words, is the problem more what the United States *does* or what it *is*? The answer affects where responsibility does and does not lie and, more importantly, what can and cannot be changed. And finally, to the extent that the motivators for terrorists are policies rather than attributes, which policies are they, and which particular aspects of those policies?

Even if reasonably clear answers could be given to those questions—and they are mostly complex questions without clear and simple answers—this would not resolve the related policy debates. The resentment that a policy may cause is only one of the counterterrorist considerations in weighing that policy, however important that resentment may be in generating terrorists and stimulating terrorist acts. Even at the level of the individual would-be terrorist, the same policies that engender resentment may also evoke other emotions, such as fear or awe, that conceivably could have beneficial effects from a counterterrorist point of view. This raises the old question of whether it is better to be feared or liked (or admired, or respected).

Looking beyond the possibly conflicting emotions at the individual level, policies that cause resentment may serve other potentially useful counterterrorist purposes. A military operation, for example, may anger a population that experiences or witnesses its collateral damage, while also eliminating a terrorist leader, camp, or haven. What is the net effect on the terrorist threat? It is a question that Israeli military actions against Palestinians raise almost every week.

Taking an even broader perspective, one must remember that counterterrorism is not the sole interest at stake in formulating foreign policy, no matter how preeminent an interest it has become in the United States since the 9/11 attacks. Superpowers, like other powers, pursue multiple interests through their foreign policies. Some things they do may have a negative effect on counterterrorism—possibly because of the ire they cause among foreigners—but still may be worth doing for other reasons.

None of the foregoing is intended to downplay the significance that resentment over U.S. policies has on the severity and persistence of international terrorism. But as with almost everything else in counterterrorism, analysis of the problems is complicated, and enactment of the solutions involves significant costs and trade-offs.

Importance to the Individual

A superpower's foreign policy matters to the would-be terrorist insofar as he (or she) sees it as affecting either his immediate daily life and welfare or a larger community—usually one defined in terms of religion or ethnicity—from which he derives his identity.

The policies of the sole superpower, the United States, affect the welfare of foreigners in multiple ways, but most of the effects are indirect. Tariffs or quotas that the United States imposes on goods it imports (be they catfish or textiles), for example, affect the livelihoods of foreigners working in the industries in question and have second-order effects on the standards of living of their countrymen. Few people outside of trade ministries and leaders in the private sector understand what is going on, however, and issues of access to markets is not the stuff of which terrorists tend to be made.

Effects on daily lives are more likely to become a root of terrorism when people feel the immediate, harsh, highly visible hand of either an occupying power or a repressive regime. And the United States will be a target of popular wrath if it is seen as supporting that hand. The leading example is the anger of Palestinians who feel every day the yoke of Israel, and who express their anger both at Israel and at the United States, which is widely, even though incorrectly, assumed to have a role in almost everything Israel does.

The Palestinian situation is a particularly acute instance of a phenomenon seen in a different form elsewhere in the Middle East. Many Arabs feel stifled and oppressed not by an occupier such as Israel but by their own governments, which preside over unreformed economies and unresponsive political systems. Other chapters in this volume explore how these economic and political conditions can foster terrorism. The U.S. angle is that once again Washington is seen as—and resented for—providing support to prop up the local oppressor. How much this adds to the level of terrorist recruitment that would occur anyway (because of local conditions) is a matter of conjecture. Possibly, it affects the choice of targets of terrorists at least as much as their recruitment. But the image of the United States as the big devil supporting local devils figures prominently in, for example, the view of Saudi Arabia that Osama bin Laden propagates.

A malign image of the United States potentially has even greater motivating power when it involves perceived attacks not just on individuals' daily lives and material circumstances but on their very sources of identity, or on a community defined by that identity. The motivating power is greater in that it can reach not just those who are directly and materially affected but all those who share the identity and consider themselves part of the same community. Thus, many Arabs feel the pain of Palestinian Arabs even if they have no other connection with Palestine besides a shared identity as Arabs. Indonesian Muslim clerics and their followers may feel the pain of Palestinians solely based on religious affinity. In both instances, these people may resent the United States insofar as they believe Washington is responsible for the Palestinians' plight. A major root of Islamist terrorism is the pain that Muslims feel over what they perceive as U.S. depredations against fellow Muslims.

The Historical and Religious Context

Centuries of confrontation between the Muslim world and the largely Judeo-Christian West influence contemporary radical Islamists' attitudes toward the United States. The rhetoric of bin Laden and other terrorist leaders harkens back to the Crusades of the eleventh through thirteenth centuries, the reconquest of Iberia in the fifteenth century, and other past collisions between the Islamic and Christian worlds. The perspective of the Islamist terrorists is very long-term and very broad. They regard their campaign in the same terms as have some Western scholars: as a clash between two entire civilizations, rooted in differences of culture and particularly of religion.[1]

Of course, the United States had nothing to do with the endeavors of Richard the Lion-hearted, Ferdinand and Isabella, or any of the other leaders from the West who did battle with Muslims before the United States even existed. Nor was it responsible for the European colonialism that also has provided some of the background for the radical Islamists' view of an aggrieved Muslim world having long suffered injustices inflicted by the West. As the leader of today's West, however, the United States has inherited this historical baggage.

When the United States was not the only superpower, it had company as a target of hostility among the Islamists. It was not even the chief target during the 1980s (the final decade of existence of the other previous superpower, the Soviet Union). The Soviet occupation of Afghanistan from 1979 to 1989 was, throughout that period, the main front line of conflict along the borders of the Islamic world. For the Islamists, Afghanistan had the right combination of ingredients to make it the leading battleground of its time for jihad, or holy war: resistance to a foreign, mostly non-Muslim, power that had invaded an overwhelmingly Muslim country in time to keep its client regime from being overthrown. Since the break-up of the Soviet Union, the remnants of Moscow's confrontation with the Islamic world have continued in the Caucasus, particularly represented by the terrorism and other bloodshed revolving around Chechnya. Chechnya does have some salience for the Islamists. Mohammed Atta and several of his 9/11 co-conspirators, for example, were planning to go to Chechnya to fight there before being diverted to the attack on the United States.[2] But Chechnya is inside the Russian federation, and today's Russia clearly is not a superpower with the will and capability to project power in ways that would make it as major a combatant against the Islamic world as it was in Afghanistan.

The United States provided assistance to the Islamists in the Afghan war against the Soviets. Any implied alliance, however, was purely one of convenience rather than sentiment. America's posture during that war has not spared it from assuming the USSR's role as the leading target of jihad. The impact of warfare in Afghanistan on subsequent international terrorism included not only the development of terrorist-related skills among those who fought there and the forging of ties between jihadists of different nationalities. The defeat of the Soviets (marked by the withdrawal of Soviet troops from Afghanistan in 1989 and the toppling of Moscow's client Najibullah in 1992) was also an inspiration to the jihadists—a demonstration that their version of holy war could beat even a superpower. If this could be done against one superpower (in the case of the USSR, contributing to its dissolution), it can be done as well, believe the jihadists, to the other one. Moscow's misadventure in Afghanistan was its parting shot as a superpower, one that continues to plague the victor of the Cold War today.

Everything the United States does within—or that affects—the Muslim world today is viewed through lenses colored by centuries of confrontation between that world and the West. Here arises the question of how much the resentment against the United States that can undergird terrorism is a product of what it is and how much is a response to what it does. Insofar as the United States suffers from being the beneficiary of a history of past clashes between two civilizations, it clearly is the former. Simply being the big guy—on a block, or on the globe—probably also contributes to resentment mixed with envy or with suspicion of how the big guy will use his strength among some of the less powerful. In addition, some of what may be resented is intrinsic to the very concept of a superpower—the ability to project power and influence all over the world. In the case of the United States, much of that influence consists of a propagation of culture that is a result not so much of U.S. foreign policy but rather of globalization and U.S. economic strength. MTV and Big Macs have spread throughout the world—including the Muslim world, to the chagrin of the Islamists—not because of decisions made in Washington but because America is large, rich, and creative, and as such has a disproportionate influence on what flows over the world's airwaves and trade routes.

The Salience of Policies

All of these factors that are not linked to specific U.S. policies contribute to what is probably an irreducible minimum of animosity from the Islamists, no matter what Washington decides to do on the global stage. Beyond that minimum, however, there is still ample room for resentment towards the United States to be higher or lower depending on what the United States does; in essence, policies do matter. Terrorist statements and other manifestations of anger that mention specific U.S. policies are one indication of that. Another indication is the variation in the level of anger. Polls that track attitudes of foreign publics toward the United States have shown two marked patterns in recent years: The standing of the United States in the Muslim world is significantly lower than elsewhere, and opinion of the United States, particularly among Muslims, has been getting increasingly unfavorable.[3] Wherever changes are seen, one must look for causal factors that may explain that change. In this instance, changing attitudes toward the United States may be attributed to changing U.S. policies rather than the more permanent aspects of being a superpower.

The declining favorability of the United States in such polls may reflect not only changes in certain U.S. policies but also an increase in the extent to which foreign policies in general, as distinct from history and the unchanging attributes of states, tend to shape attitudes overseas. Foreign publics are more likely to react to the current policies of the United States or other foreign powers than they would have been even a decade ago because they are more exposed to news of those policies. The information revolution and expansion of mass media permit the transmission of that news more quickly and to more people, and if it is the sort of news that makes people angry, blood can boil at broadband speed. A citizen of Saudi Arabia would have had difficulty following the events involving Iraq in 1990–91, for example, being largely dependent on government-controlled news organizations that reported even important news (such as Iraq's invasion of Kuwait) late and declined to report some things altogether. A decade later, Saudis could receive news from Iraq on a near-real-time basis from news organizations battling for scoops, especially Arab satellite television stations such as al Arabiya and al Jazeera.

Ingredients of Resented Policies

The grounding of Muslim resentment in a centuries-old history of confrontation between the Islamic world and the West leads to the first and probably most important characteristic of U.S. policies that are prone to incite still more resentment: being seen on the "wrong side" of any conflict that pits Muslims against non-Muslims. Religion has become the lens through which many Muslims view any U.S. posture or policy, and which influences their interpretations of the rightness or wrongness of the American position. What matters most to them is whether the United States is for or against the interests of the *ummah*, the community of fellow believers.

This manner of interpreting and evaluating U.S. policies has the appeal of simplicity and the emotive power of being grounded in individual faith. It obviates the analytical labor required to examine the specific issues and circumstances that any individual conflict entails or the rationales that a government may have for a particular policy. It has the attraction and imperviousness of a "you're either for us or against us" perspective. Holders of such a perspective are not easily moved by arguments that point to the justice or necessity of the U.S. policy in question or the fair-mindedness that underlies the policy. All that matters to them is whose side the United States is on.

Being seen as taking sides does not require the United States to actually be a direct party to a conflict, although the perception of side-taking is clearest when that is the case. The resented U.S. posture may entail support to an ally that is in conflict with Muslims. It may involve a diplomatic position such as a vote or veto at the United Nations. It may even be a matter of U.S. inaction when others think action is necessary—for example, a perceived tardiness in coming to the support of persecuted Muslims during the Bosnian civil war.

U.S. policies that Muslims perceive as being on the wrong side of a conflict between Muslims and non-Muslims are resented both for the policy itself and for the U.S. motives that they are deemed to demonstrate. Many critics believe the United States pursues policies that hurt the interests of Muslims not just because this is an unfortunate by-product of foreign policies formulated for other reasons, but because the United States *wants* to hurt Muslims. Some even believed that Washington kept aloof from the Bosnian war as long as it did because it was happy to see Serbs kill off Muslims. A negative cycle of perceptions thus sustains a jaundiced view of the United States. The very suspicions that lead to a critical scrutiny of U.S. policy, without giving Washington any benefit of doubt, leads to an imputing of hostile motives that darkens even further the negative image of the United States in the Muslim world. Given such malign interpretations, recent U.S. policies are added to an ever-expanding lore of supposedly unfriendly American acts through the years.

A second attribute that makes certain U.S. policies more likely than others to evoke resentment is that they play to other negative stereotypes or preconceptions about the United States (beyond the perception that it is anti-Muslim). Some of those preconceptions are associated with being the most powerful nation on earth—for example, critics may argue that power itself is an overriding objective, that Washington will ride roughshod over other interests to expand its power, and that it is quick to use the form of power in which it enjoys the greatest advantage, which is military power. Other preconceptions are related to stereotypes of American culture and values—for example, that U.S. motivations are centered on materialism and greed, if not rapaciousness.

A third ingredient of a policy particularly suited for incurring resentment is in its potential for vivid events that by their very nature may carry emotional impact, especially people dying and suffering as a result of military action. The emotive force comes from the visuals. Televised pictures of death and destruction can stir whole populations into anger—including anger against whatever outside power is deemed even partly responsible—more quickly than any words about the policies themselves.

None of these ingredients are essential for resentment. Not all U.S. foreign policies that have incurred animosity abroad have exhibited them all. The more an issue embodies these attributes in combination, however, the greater the risk of generating ill will that contributes to anti-U.S. terrorism.

The issue that has been at the center of the broadest and most persistent negative sentiments toward U.S. foreign policy is the conflict between Israelis and Arabs, particularly the dimension that pits Israel against the Palestinians. The conflict has long been the most salient and frequently voiced grievance against the United States in the Middle East. Ethnicity explains part of the prominence of the issue, in that it involves Arabs sympathizing with fellow Arabs (as well as sharing the pain and humiliation of Arab armies having been soundly defeated by Israel in past wars). The conflict has increasingly acquired a religious flavor, however, which was less apparent during its early years. This transformation is reflected in the changes in leadership of the Palestinian resistance. For instance, one of the most prominent groups in that resistance during the 1960s and 1970s was the Popular Front for the Liberation of Palestine, led by a Christian (and Marxist), George Habash. Today, the most effective Palestinian group resisting Israel is Hamas, an offshoot of the Muslim Brotherhood whose acronymic name stands for the Islamic Resistance Movement.

Most of the issues in dispute between Israel and the Palestinians (and other Arab neighbors) are straightforward contests over land and resources, with the religious aspect simply being that most of the contestants on one side are Muslim, and most on the other side are Jewish. But what is probably the most intractable issue—the status of Jerusalem—has an inherently religious dimension. The question of who is to control a city with holy places revered by three religions has defined the conflict for many who care deeply about it because of their religious identity but otherwise do not have a direct stake in Palestine. For example, the leadership of Saudi Arabia has stated that all Muslims have a direct interest in the status of Jerusalem and that it is not a matter for only Palestinians to decide, even though on other issues in dispute with Israel, the Saudis would accept whatever the Palestinians were willing to accept. Because of the religious dimension, many Muslims perceive the Israeli-Palestinian conflict as one more chapter in the historic confrontation between the Muslim world and the Judeo-Christian West. In this view, Israel is a kind of Western excrescence—a beachhead created by the West on the shores of the world of Islam, similar to the kingdoms and castles the Crusaders erected during the Middle Ages. The context of centuries-old religiously based strife is what gives the Arab-Israeli conflict tremendous resonance throughout the Muslim world.

The United States plays a very prominent role in all this as the prime backer and ally of Israel. The material and diplomatic support that Washington gives Israel, from arms sales to vetoes at the United Nations Security Council, complements a perception of the United States as leader of the Judeo-Christian West, using Israel as a means for pursuing confrontation with the Muslim world. The details of U.S. policy and the many instances in which U.S. and Israeli policies diverge are noticed by Muslim elites but make little difference to broader Muslim populations, for whom the overall pattern is what matters. It would be very difficult for the United States to stop receiving a generous share of the animosity directed against Israel, until and unless the conflict over Palestine is resolved.

The Arab-Israeli conflict therefore displays a key ingredient of modern conflicts that fit neatly into a historical image of religiously based confrontation between the Muslim world and the West. To a lesser extent, it also evokes other stereotypes and common perceptions of the United States. The principal perception involved has been that U.S. policy is in thrall to the "Jewish lobby" and that strong U.S. support to Israel reflects strong Israeli influence over Washington. Interestingly, one of the recent political patterns in the United States that helps to break down that perception has its own religious dimension and tends to sustain the larger image of religiously based confrontation with Islam. That pattern is the very strong support for Israel that comes from fundamentalist elements of Protestant Christianity, some of the strongest from any quarter in the United States. That support, and the explicitly religious basis for it, may be noticed even more by some Muslims overseas than it tends to be inside the United States. It strengthens in their eyes the hyphen in the adjective "Judeo-Christian" that describes their Western adversary.

The other ingredient of an issue that tends to generate resentment—the visual impact of death and destruction—has certainly been part of the Israeli-Palestinian conflict as well. The Palestinian children wounded in Israeli air strikes, and the piles of rubble left after Israeli bulldozers level Palestinian houses, are prime material for the likes of al Jazeera (or the Hizballah television station al-Manar) to broadcast to audiences throughout the Middle East. Perhaps part of the purpose for some terrorist attacks against Israel is to provoke Israeli retaliation that will generate more of these sorts of images. And again, the United States, even if it had nothing to do with the fresh events, is also a target of anger because of its close association with Israel and the belief that it is largely up to the United States to somehow solve the Palestinian problem.

Since the 1967 Middle East war, the Arab-Israeli conflict has been far ahead of any other issue among grievances that Middle Easterners (and to a lesser extent Muslims worldwide) voice against the United States. Beginning in March 2003, a second big grievance has emerged to rival the Arab-Israeli conflict in its impact: the invasion and occupation of Iraq displays in abundance the attributes of an initiative especially likely to incur wide-spread resentment against the United States, which indeed it has. The initiation of a war (not, as in the driving of the Iraqis out of Kuwait in 1991, the reversal of someone else's aggression) against one of the largest and most prominent Muslim states plays directly into the misperception of a United States bent on using its power to bludgeon Muslims—notwithstanding how despised Iraqi dictator Saddam Hussein was throughout much of the region. The capacity for generating ill-will that is focused narrowly on the United States may be even greater than with the Palestinian issue because the actions in question are those of the United States itself, not merely those of its ally Israel.

The war plays into other negative stereotypes of the United States, including the perception of a superpower bent on using its military might to expand its presence overseas and thereby facilitate further use of that power. Iraq's oil wealth also fosters the belief that control of an economic resource rather than liberation of an oppressed people was the principal driver of U.S. policy or (in an even harsher view) that plundering the resources of Muslims was a principal goal of the operation.

The deaths, injuries, and physical damage that are the concomitant consequences of warfare obviously have been another key ingredient in the impact of the operation in Iraq, amplified by broadcasts far beyond Iraq of visual images of the casualties and destruction. This is the main respect in which resentment from a military campaign—a shooting war—goes beyond whatever resentment results from a quieter overseas military presence. The latter can indeed be a source of resentment, as reflected in Osama bin Laden's propagandistic exploitation of the U.S. military presence that remained in Saudi Arabia after the war in Kuwait in 1991. But people actually dying as a consequence of U.S. guns being fired or bombs being dropped will always present a more powerful image.

The impact on terrorism of the resentment stemming from the Iraq operation was apparent from the first months of the occupation. Iraq quickly became, in President George W. Bush's words, a "central front in the war on terror" in the form of an escalating insurgency that included true terrorism against civilian targets as well as attacks against coalition military forces. The perpetrators have included a variety of Iraqi elements, both secular and religious. They have also included non-Iraqi Islamists who have been drawn into the fight against what they would describe as the infidel invader. Iraq has become the latest and biggest jihad or holy war, filling a role that had been played earlier by conflicts in Afghanistan and, to a lesser extent, Bosnia and Chechnya. Iraq is now the place to be for jihadists seeking their route to an afterlife in paradise, and the United States is the enemy they want to fight to get there.

There will be other U.S. policies that will incur varying degrees of hostility in the Muslim world and still others that will be sources of resentment for non-Muslim populations. Some of those resentments will be intense enough among some individuals to motivate them to turn to terrorism. But the conflicts over Palestine and Iraq will continue to be, until one or both are settled, the leading issues capable of driving angry people to that extreme.

Exploitation by Terrorist Leaders

Resentment toward the policies of the United States or another major power can affect not only the decisions of individuals to become terrorists but also the decisions of groups regarding the tempo and targets of their terrorist operations, or whether to conduct terrorist operations at all. Such operational decisions by groups tend to be responses to specific U.S. policies, in contrast to the behavior of individuals, who tend to be swayed more by general images of the United States.

The activities of Lebanese Hizballah during the 1980s are an example of a group responding with terrorism to a specific U.S. foreign policy initiative—in this case, military intervention in Lebanon. Hizballah wanted the United States out of Lebanon, to help clear the playing field for an expansion of its own influence. The bombing of the U.S. Embassy and Marine Barracks in Beirut in 1983 and other terrorist attacks at the time were intended to accomplish that goal. The goal was achieved when the United States withdrew its forces from Lebanon in 1984. Hizballah conducted other attacks against U.S. interests over the next decade, and it still voices hostility toward a variety of U.S. policies. The absence of any anti-U.S. terrorist attacks involving Hizballah since the Khobar Towers bombing in Saudi Arabia in 1996, however, shows that sustained, general anger against Washington is insufficient to drive the group into more terrorist attacks—particularly in light of all that Hizballah has achieved through nonterrorist means in expanding its power and prestige in Lebanon. If Hizballah were to use its still-potent terrorist capabilities to attack U.S. interests once again, it probably would be in response to new U.S. initiatives that specifically threatened Hizballah's interests, such as military operations within Lebanon or against Hizballah's patron Iran.

The responses of group leaders to U.S. policies can affect the extent to which resentment drives individuals to become terrorists. Groups can play upon existing anti-U.S. sentiment to enhance their own recruitment, whether or not they are engaged in anti-U.S. attacks themselves. And ones who do attempt anti-U.S. attacks play up anti-U.S. themes even more, to justify their operations as well as to recruit new members. Much of the anti-U.S. proselytization takes place at a one-to-one level, behind closed doors in apartments and in mosques. But as Osama bin Laden has demonstrated, it also can take the form of propaganda with a worldwide reach.

Bin Laden has played a unique role in this regard, and not just because of the reach of his propaganda or the way he has combined the roles of propagandist and operational group leader. The doctrine bin Laden has espoused derives in most respects from earlier Islamist writers and preachers, dating back centuries.[4] His principal goals involve the overthrow of the established order in much of the Muslim world, especially his former homeland of Saudi Arabia. In this regard, the war he has tried to wage is primarily a civil war within the Islamic world.[5] Against the backdrop of setbacks in trying to get such a civil war going, bin Laden's stroke of evil genius—his one original contribution to ideology, and the one aspect of his doctrine that has most clearly driven his operational strategy—was to direct his main fire at the United States. The ultimate goal remained the sweeping away of regimes in the Muslim (especially Arab) world and the establishment of a new Caliphate. But the primary near-term target of both the propaganda and the terrorist attacks was Washington.

Bin Laden's anti-U.S. focus could advance his ultimate goal in two ways. One was to drive a wedge between the United States and its Muslim allies, perhaps weakening the latter. The increased strains in the relationship between the United States and Saudi Arabia—the home of most of the 9/11 hijackers—since the 9/11 attacks could be seen as a partial success for bin Laden in this regard. The other advantage of playing directly and loudly on anti-U.S. themes was that they were much more popular and resonant than almost any other themes bin Laden could sound. Standing up to the United States has won bin Laden admiration among millions, even among those who do not condone his terrorist attacks and who would never think of participating in such attacks themselves. This broader sympathy has helped al Qaeda in numerous ways, including maintaining financial support and weakening some counterterrorist efforts against it, despite the significant blows that these efforts have inflicted on the organization since 9/11. Within a smaller audience, the anti-U.S. themes have been an energizing force and a valuable recruitment tool for Islamist groups. In the hands of a master propagandist like bin Laden, the impact of the themes has been all the greater.

Bin Laden, and those who echo his rhetoric, have exploited all the potentially effective anti-U.S. angles, even ones in which they have little or no direct stake. The Palestinian issue is one of those angles; bin Laden has milked it rhetorically, just as many others have, even though al Qaeda and groups affiliated with it have had almost no role in that conflict. Iraq has become another theme—again, for bin Laden just as for many others—although in Iraq, bin Laden has taken a back seat to other terrorists, particularly those led by Abu Musab al-Zarqawi.

Since 9/11, bin Laden's exploitation of opposition to the United States, and the operational strategy he derived from that exploitation, have shaped the way many people (and especially most Americans) think about terrorism. But bin Laden's approach is certainly not the only way a terrorist group, even an Islamic one (and even one with specific grievances against Washington) may regard the United States. Hamas has not conducted attacks against U.S. interests (notwithstanding some U.S. citizens becoming incidental victims in attacks against Israel) and has repeatedly identified its sole adversary as Israel and its sole interest as the future of Palestine. However much resentment there may be among Hamas's constituents in the Palestinian territories, for the group to come after the United States would not serve its objective of gaining power as the recognized leader of the Palestinians. Similar calculations enter into the strategy of non-Islamic groups seeking power over their own territories, such as the Liberation Tigers of Tamil Eelam in Sri Lanka.

For now, however, the principal way in which the United States and its foreign policies figure into the thinking of terrorists and would-be terrorists—certainly the way most damaging to the United States—is the way put forth in bin Laden's doctrine: as the prime object of animosity and the prime target for attack. Bin Laden the operational terrorist leader has suffered severe setbacks in recent years; bin Laden the ideologist can take satisfaction in how much impact he has had. His poisonous manipulation of anti-U.S. sentiment has spread far beyond al Qaeda and seems likely to outlive both al Qaeda and himself. It will probably continue to support the recruitment of terrorists for years to come.

Reducing the Resentment

Given the significant part resentment toward the United States plays in the likelihood of people turning themselves into terrorists, it is important to consider how much that resentment can be reduced and how to reduce it. It can indeed be reduced, but with some significant limits. One of those limits is set by the simple fact that the U.S. is a superpower. The portion of the ill-will toward the United States that is a response to its very size, power, and influence cannot be reduced. In addition, insofar as some resented policies are an almost inherent aspect of being a superpower—such as policies having to do with the peaceful projection of power around the globe—these are also not easily changeable, at least not without significant damage to fulfilling the responsibilities, and enjoying the benefits, of being a superpower.

A different set of complications involves statements and behavior in the United States that are not part of official policy, but that nonetheless contribute to perceptions that put U.S. policies in an unfavorable light. Some of these statements and actions are more controllable than others. Emanations from popular American culture (for example, Hollywood movies and television shows that contribute to an image of America as materialist or violent) cannot be prevented, at least not without an unacceptable degree of censorship. But statements by U.S. officials in nonofficial settings that portray U.S. actions in religious terms, adding to perceptions of a Christian-versus-Muslim struggle, can be controlled through reassignments or tighter discipline. Far less controllable are statements by prominent American evangelists that are openly hostile to Islam, but the damage might be limited if such utterances were quickly condemned officially as contrary to U.S. policy and to American values.

Public diplomacy has an important role to play in shaping perceptions abroad of the United States and its policies. As a recent officially commissioned report argued, much more can be done with the instrument of public diplomacy to explain U.S. policies and to counter negative perceptions of the United States among foreigners.[6] The same report acknowledged, however, that those perceptions are shaped first of all by the content of the policies themselves, no matter how deft the public diplomacy may be. Whether selling toothpaste or foreign policy, the quality of the product affects sales.

So it comes in the end to U.S. foreign policy itself. That means there will always be trade-offs and competing priorities to consider, since policies that are effective in avoiding the sorts of resentment capable of breeding additional terrorists are not necessarily the most effective ones for achieving other objectives. Given the many difficulties and limitations in using other instruments for combating terrorism, however, much attention needs to be given—as a high priority in all deliberations on U.S. foreign policy—to the effects that U.S. actions may have on anger abroad and on the possibility of that anger generating still more terrorism.

CHAPTER 4

A Failure to Communicate: American Public Diplomacy in the Islamic World

HASSAN ABBAS

As we consider public diplomacy in the twenty-first century, we are mindful that our voice competes amidst the cacophony of voices shaping global opinion. Today, with the Internet, satellite radio and TV networks providing instantaneous and often unfiltered information, public diplomacy is more important and more difficult than ever before. No matter how powerful our military, we will not be able to achieve all our foreign policy objectives if we lose the war of ideas. In public diplomacy, we must use our most powerful tools: Truth, credibility, and openness.

—*Senator Joseph R. Biden Jr.*[1]

To put it bluntly, it is a hard fact that America's image in the Islamic world has nose-dived in recent years. Moreover, this trend signifying unfavorable opinion of the West in general and the United States in particular is not merely confined to the Muslim states—Muslim communities in Europe and North America by and large also show similar tendencies, though the changes in ratings have been less sharp. Numerous polls and surveys conducted by various credible organizations and independent professionals strongly indicate the widespread prevalence of such perceptions.[2] Arguably, al Qaeda and its like-minded affiliates in the post 9/11 tragedy scenario have been quite effective in their pubic relations campaign. The extent of the "collateral damage" during the U.S.-led Afghan campaign (2001–02), the insurgency crisis in Iraq in response to preemptive U.S. military action (2003), and the lingering Israeli-Palestinian conflict have only added fuel to the fire of Muslims' discontent and grievances. However, the war of ideas and the battle for the "hearts and minds" of Muslims is by no means over. To understand the intricacies of the situation, we need to look at terrorism and religious extremism in terms of an ideology based on bigotry, narrow-mindedness, and violence-friendly dogma which in essence is reflective of a bad idea at work. The most efficient and potent way to counter such ideas is by challenging and discrediting these with superior ideas and ideals. Daisy-cutter bombs and cruise missiles can only eliminate physical targets, not the mindset that produces hate and hostility. And when it comes to ideas, the United States has no deficiency in terms of creativity and capability to come up with constructive solutions. The success of the Marshall Plan in Europe in the aftermath of the World War II is a convincing testimony to this fact.

There is no dearth of voices of reason within the Islamic world as well who believe in pluralism, freedom, and peaceful coexistence. Such forces should be co-opted, since without Muslim partners the U.S. public diplomacy endeavors will have no legs to stand upon. However, such collaborations cannot be fruitful unless these are an outcome of consistent policies that are transparent and serve the interests of all sides involved. Diplomacy is not a tool to advance and express political objectives in a sugar-coated monologue—rather, it involves listening to the other side, making adjustments, and demonstrating a capacity to engage in a meaningful dialogue.

This chapter makes an attempt to understand how communication failure between the United States and the Muslim world has transformed the "Islam and the West" discourse into an "Islam versus the United States" debate in the minds of many. It is worth probing why the "clash of civilizations"[3] theory remains a more popular discussion theme rather than proposals like "dialogue among civilizations"[4] and "enlightened moderation."[5] There are counterarguments to the view that the rise of negative perceptions about the United States among Muslims is a consequence merely of a failure to communicate and nothing more—an argument which will be examined in this chapter. To study these issues in some detail, U.S. public diplomacy *vis-à-vis* Pakistan and Iran will serve as the primary focus of the chapter. However, the policy recommendations and conclusions drawn from these analyses have much broader implications.

The Case of Pakistan

Pakistan, a nuclear-armed country of 150 million Muslims, with well-entrenched religious political parties—having strong representation in provincial and national assemblies—and around half a dozen active religious militant groups operating in the state (despite being officially banned), is also one of the most important U.S. allies in the war on terror. The country is unique in the sense that it has enjoyed the best of relations with the United States during different phases of its history, but it is also considered by analysts as a potential worst foreign policy nightmare for the United States in times to come.[6]

Recent data gathered by Pew Research Center[7] provide interesting insights into the recent shifts in Pakistani public opinion about the United States. Comparisons can also be drawn with Turkey and Jordan, in order to place opinions of Pakistanis *vis-à-vis* a secular and an Arab state. As indicated in Table 4.1, a majority of those surveyed in all three of these countries hold an unfavorable opinion toward the United States, and this has held constant (with some variation) for several years. In addition to the trends shown in Table 1, the March 2004 survey conducted by the Pew Center also revealed that:

- 60 percent of Pakistanis oppose the American war on terrorism whereas 56 percent of Turks and 78 percent of Jordanians think likewise;

- Osama bin Laden is viewed favorably by 65 percent of Pakistanis, 11 percent of Turks, and 55 percent of Jordanians;

Table 4.1

Perceptions toward the United States

	Favorable	Somewhat Unfavorable	Very Unfavorable
		PAKISTAN	
March 2004	21%	11%	50%
May 2003	13%	10%	71%
Summer 2002	10%	11%	58%
		TURKEY	
March 2004	30%	18%	45%
May 2003	15%	15%	68%
Summer 2002	30%	13%	42%
		JORDAN	
March 2004	5%	26%	67%
May 2003	1%	16%	83%
Summer 2002	25%	18%	57%

Source: "A Year After Iraq War: Mistrust of America in Europe Ever Higher, Muslim Anger Persists." *Pew Research Center for the People and the Press*, 16 March 2004.

- among those who doubt American sincerity in the war on terrorism, 51 percent of Pakistanis, 47 percent of Turks, and 53 percent of Jordanians believe that the war is meant to target those Muslim countries that are known for having unfavorable view of the United States; and

- 51 percent of Pakistanis, 47 percent of Turks, and 56 percent of Jordanians say that as a result of the Iraq war they are less confident that the United States really wants to promote democracy globally.

It is interesting to note that Pakistani public opinion trends are generally similar to those of Turkey and Jordon, except for one striking and alarming indicator: huge support for Osama bin Laden. However, Pew surveys and a few other studies—including one conducted by the U.S. State Department—also show that a clear majority of Pakistanis support General Pervez Musharraf.[8] Musharraf had taken a courageous U-turn after the 9/11 attacks when he halted Pakistan's support to the Taliban and initiated a clampdown on Pakistani religious militant groups operating in Indian-controlled Kashmir, as well as moving against Wahhabi-sponsored groups involved in sectarian killings inside Pakistan. It is a common belief in Pakistan that he is strongly pursuing pro-American policies and that the U.S. administration values his support and contribution in the war on terror. The arrests of leading al Qaeda operators from Pakistan, along with Pakistani-U.S. military collaboration in the Waziristan tribal belt in the hunt for al Qaeda, are examples reflecting a warming-up of relations between the two states. It has not been smooth sailing for Musharraf, however. He was lucky to survive two major assassination attempts on his life by religious fanatics in late 2003. The exposure of Dr. Abdul Qadeer Khan's nuclear proliferation activities in late 2003/early 2004 by the U.S. intelligence community was another big test for Musharraf; apparently Khan's shop was closed as a consequence, and the U.S. administration is satisfied with the progress on the issue so far. Dr. A. Q. Khan publicly confessed that he committed the crimes, and Musharraf pardoned him given Khan's status as the founder of Pakistan's nuclear bomb. The way the United States handled the issue helped Musharraf in the domestic Pakistani context. Still, most Pakistanis harbor an ingrained distrust of American policies and there is a history to it. No effective diplomacy model can work for the United States in Pakistan without first understanding that background. A brief analysis of U.S.-Pakistani relations since 1947 is pertinent here in this context.

A Brief History of U.S.-Pakistani Relations from a Pakistani Perspective

As soon as British India was partitioned into a Hindu-majority India and Muslim-majority Pakistan on 14 August 1947, the region witnessed another divide in the foreign policy orientation of the two newborn countries. The Cold War had set in and the socialist leaning of the Indian leadership helped it gravitate towards the Soviet Union, while the Western orientation of Pakistan's leadership (coupled with its security needs) ensured its alignment with the United States. As early as 9 September 1947 Mohammad Ali Jinnah (the founder of Pakistan) stated in a cabinet meeting: "Our interests lie with the two great democratic countries, namely U.K. and U.S.A., rather than with Russia."[9] On the American side, a National Security Council "Top Secret" report prepared in early 1951 maintained that "in Pakistan, the communists have acquired considerable influence in press circles, among intellectuals and in certain labor unions" and argued that domination of "Pakistan by unfriendly powers, either directly or through subservient indigenous regimes would constitute a serious threat to the national security of the U.S."[10] Similar assessments led to increased American interest in the country and the United States signed a Mutual Aid Assistance Agreement with Pakistan in May 1954. A few months later, Pakistan joined the South East Asia Treaty Organization (SEATO), and in February 1955 it entered the Baghdad Pact (later called CENTO), bringing the two states closer to each other and making Pakistan a frontline state against the expansion of communism. Pakistan's army was desperate to get military hardware and weapons from the United States as the perceived threat from India—especially in reference to the Kashmir conflict—was rising with every passing year. In pursuit of this goal, General Ayub Khan, the then commander-in-chief of the Pakistan army, even went to the extent in 1953 (while talking to the U.S. Assistant Secretary of State Henry Byroade) of saying, "Our army can be your army if you want us."[11]

The relationship continued to get cozier; in 1958–59, Pakistan agreed to the establishment of an American base in Peshawar—a secret intelligence facility—and would allow the United States to operate U-2 spy planes from this base. This was considered an excellent place from which to monitor signals from Soviet missile test sites and to intercept other sensitive communications. However, this landed Pakistan in trouble when, in May 1960, a U-2 plane was shot down over Soviet territory. Nikita Khrushchev, the Soviet leader, gave a stern warning to Pakistan for supporting this U.S. project and conveyed to Pakistan that Peshawar had been marked in red on their maps.

With the arrival of John F. Kennedy in the U.S. presidency in 1960, the U.S. focus began shifting towards India, and some members of the new administration even suggested that military aid to Pakistan was a blunder and that it should be reduced. Pakistan's leadership was greatly distressed by this turn of events. Still, when war erupted between China and India in October 1962, and the United States asked the Pakistan government to "make a positive gesture of sympathy and restraint" towards India,[12] Pakistan complied. However, to the dismay of Pakistan, when the India-Pakistan war broke out in 1965, the United States took a neutral position, and Pakistan felt that they had been let down by its senior ally just when its help was most needed. This was the first time that unfavorable opinion about the United States was felt across the board in Pakistan.

Interstate relations returned to normal during the President Nixon era when Pakistan helped open a secret U.S.-Chinese diplomatic channel (1969–71). A secret visit of the U.S. Secretary of State Henry Kissinger to China was arranged by Pakistan in July 1971, which ultimately led to President Nixon's unprecedented visit to China and the formalization of the Sino-American rapprochement, to the chagrin of the Soviet Union. The Nixon administration returned the favor when hostilities broke out between India and Pakistan in 1971 in the East Pakistan sector. Nixon directly warned the Soviet Union, which was supporting India, by saying, "If the Indians continued their military operations (against West Pakistan), we must inevitably look towards a confrontation between the USSR and the U.S. The Soviet Union has a treaty with India; we have one with Pakistan."[13] Pakistan lost East Pakistan (Bangladesh), but the western wing (present-day Pakistan) was saved largely through the U.S. political and diplomatic support. However, Pakistanis perhaps were expecting more *vis-à-vis* the eastern wing, without realizing that the autocratic and oppressive policies of Pakistan's military leadership were primarily responsible for the massive anti-Pakistan movement in its eastern wing.

The next crucial episode in this context unraveled in the late 1970s, when the United States decided to cut off economic aid to Pakistan as a form of punishment for pursuing nuclear ambitions. What really cut deep and really wounded Pakistan was that India, which had been the first to embark on the nuclear path, continued to receive U.S. attention and aid. It was difficult for Pakistanis to understand how the United States could dump an ally of long standing and embrace the ally of its most rabid adversary. The situation changed dramatically when Soviet forces marched into Afghanistan in 1979 and the United States assessed that it direly needed its old ally in the region.

General Zia-ul-Haq, the Pakistani head of state at the time, decided to fully support the Afghan resistance movement to halt the Soviet ambitions in the region. He led the diplomatic offensive against the USSR; gave shelter to the fleeing Afghan refugees, and provided clandestine military assistance to the Afghan resistance (the mujahideen). After the Shah of Iran had fled Iran in 1979, Zia-ul-Haq had already allowed the U.S. Central Intelligence Agency to set up an electronic eavesdropping facility in Pakistan,[14] and by July 1979 a limited amount of nonmilitary U.S. aid had started to be funneled to the Afghan resistance through Pakistan. In this effort, General Zia saw a coincidence of interest between Pakistan and the United States. In response, the United States decided to look the other way as far as Pakistan's nuclear program was concerned, while also ignoring the fact that General Zia had imposed military rule in the country in 1977, dislodging a democratic set-up. In the early 1980s, the Reagan administration quickly pushed through a $3.2 billion aid package for Pakistan and also sanctioned the sale of F-16s, making Pakistan the closest regional ally of the United States all over again.

In the process, the United States also convinced Saudi Arabia to match its own contribution to the Afghan war effort on a "dollar for dollar" basis. General Zia used some of this financing to support the religious seminaries and military training camps in the border areas between Pakistan and Afghanistan where most of the Afghan refugees were based—to train and prepare the young Afghans to go back to Afghanistan and fight the Soviets. As a result, madrasas (religious seminaries) mushroomed, and their output increased exponentially, as did the radicalization of Islam in the region. Donated by their parents at a tender age, these soldiers of God were crafted for one function alone—to kill the infidel communists or die trying, and to view either outcome as the ultimate victory. It is hard enough to produce such men, and 10 times harder to decommission them. But that was something their sponsors would learn in the future, and it was only the present that counted. In that time, they were the ill-clad, lean, hungry, and weather-beaten heroes who started bleeding a superpower to a standstill.

Pakistan was paying a heavy price for being a part of this endeavor. By 1987, of 777 terrorist incidents recorded worldwide, 90 percent had taken place in Pakistan,[15] mostly orchestrated by the KGB and leftist Afghan supporters of the Soviet campaign. But with steady U.S. financial and military support to the Afghan mujahideen, Soviets were increasingly on the receiving end of the violence. Faced with military humiliation and increasing financial burden of the occupation, Soviet leader Mikhail Gorbachev announced in 1987 that his forces would withdraw from Afghanistan within a year. At this point, a divergence of Pakistani-U.S. interests manifested itself, reflecting different expectations of both the countries. The United States just wanted to see the Soviet Union out of Afghanistan and did not much care what happened to the country after that, as evident from the statement of U.S. State Department's Michael Armacost: "Our main interest was getting the Russians out. Afghanistan, as such, was remote from U.S. concerns. The United States was not much interested in the internal Afghan setup and did not have much capacity to understand this."[16] As soon as the Soviets left Afghanistan in 1989, the Americans left Pakistan. Pakistan had helped America to sow the winds of change in Afghanistan, but when it came time to reap the whirlwind, it had to do it alone. The abandonment of Pakistan by America left Pakistan more than 3 million Afghan refugees to care for; thousands of madrasas funded by Saudi money, militarizing the youth; a Kalashnikov culture, such that one could rent an automatic gun in Karachi at less than two dollars an hour; and last but not least, a flourishing drug trade. This turn of fortunes was to lay the groundwork for a tragedy, the full ramifications of which cannot be fully measured yet.

When all these monumental developments were taking place, General Zia—along with twenty other senior Pakistani army officials; Arnold Lewis Raphel, the U.S. Ambassador to Pakistan; and Brig. Gen. Herbert Wasson, the U.S. defense representative—died in a mysterious air crash in August 1988. To this day, the U.S. official position is that the crash was an accident, whereas an overwhelming view among Pakistanis (corroborated by various investigations) is that it was an assassination. Also, one of the most popular conspiracy theories in the country is that the United States was involved in it.[17] These divergent perceptions speak volumes about how most Pakistanis view the United States.

In the aftermath of this crisis, the United States rightly supported the revival of democracy in Pakistan. However, the new government led by Prime Minister Benazir Bhutto (1989–90)—the first elected woman leader of any Muslim state—had to face a new challenge when, on 1 October 1990, President George H. W. Bush refused to provide the requisite certification to Congress in reference to Pakistan's efforts to acquire nuclear weapons. The U.S. aid to Pakistan was abruptly cut off. The way the people of Pakistan saw it was that when their country had fulfilled its part of the contract in supporting the Afghan jihad and the United States had no further need of Pakistan, it simply struck camp and left. The U.S. position was that since the last certification, its intelligence reports indicated that Pakistan had produced more weapons-grade uranium and had machined it to form uranium cores for weapons manufacturing. Consequently, the delivery of F-16 fighter aircraft that Pakistan had already paid for was also halted.

All this was happening while the Kashmir insurgency in India was heating up. Demobilized Afghan veterans, mostly of Arab origin, and Pakistanis who had received their battle inoculation in Afghanistan had found another arena for the employment of their talents, and started to drift into Kashmir. The Pakistani intelligence was only too happy to facilitate this shift. Meanwhile, different Afghan groups were busy destroying what was left of Afghanistan. The madrasa network had produced a new breed of fanatics, calling themselves the Taliban, who took over Afghanistan in 1994 with the help of Pakistani intelligence services. The 1990s also witnessed the rise of religious militant groups in Pakistan. The unemployed youth of Pakistan had found an occupation, an ideology, and a new family in which they found bonding and brotherhood. As to the political orientation of religious militant groups, a statement of Hafiz Saeed, the leader of Lashkar-e-Taiba (army of the pure) truly reflects the extremists' worldview: "We believe in the Huntington's clash of civilizations, and our jihad will continue until Islam becomes the dominant religion."[18] In retrospect, many Pakistanis believe that things could have been different if the United States had remained constructively involved in the region.

Pakistan faced increasing isolation internationally due to its support of the Kashmir insurgency and its pro-Taliban stance. A U.S. State Department report, *Patterns of Global Terrorism—1999*,[19] appropriately pinpointed South Asia for the first time as a major center of international terrorism. The report asserted that Pakistan "has tolerated terrorists living and moving freely within its territory," besides supporting "groups that engage in violence in Kashmir." In addition, the report urged Islamabad to close certain madrasas "that actually serve as conduits for terrorism," but the United States had very little leverage to ensure that Pakistan was even listening at this point.

In 2000, U.S. President William Clinton, while on a brief visit to Pakistan, highlighted a new understanding of U.S.-Pakistani relations in a televised address to the people of Pakistan:

> I ask Pakistan also to be a leader in non-proliferation . . . in your own self-interest and to help us prevent dangerous technologies from spreading. . . . I understand your concerns about Kashmir. I share your conviction that human rights of all its people must be respected. But a stark truth must also be faced—there is no military solution to Kashmir. . . . I hope you will be able to meet the difficult challenges. . . . If you do not, there is a danger that Pakistan may grow even more isolated. . . . But if you do meet these challenges, our full economic and political partnership can be restored for the benefit of the people of Pakistan.[20]

Many Pakistanis completely agreed with President Clinton's viewpoint.[21] *Dawn*, the leading English daily of Pakistan aptly said in its editorial the next day, "His [Clinton's] speech leaves little scope for mounting the high horse of injured Pakistani patriotism, because he was guilty of neither of these solecisms and, if anything, came across as a deeply concerned well-wisher of Pakistan."[22] Despite the goodwill on both sides, there was little headway, as skepticism on both sides was stronger than the hopes, and the track record of keeping commitments was not something that engendered trust.

Post-9/11 Scenario

The 9/11 tragedy changed this scenario significantly. Within twenty-four hours of the tragedy, General Musharraf received his first call from Wendy Chamberlain (the U.S. Ambassador to Pakistan), who expressed the hope that Pakistan would come on board and extend all its cooperation to the United States in bringing the perpetrators of the terrorist act to justice. Musharraf gave her the assurances she sought but could not restrain himself from enumerating Pakistan's past experiences of cooperation with America and the list of broken promises which represented the compensation Pakistan often received from such alliances. Ambassador Chamberlain assured him that this time it would be different.

Then, in an important policy speech addressing the nation on 12 January 2002, Musharraf banned Jaish-i-Mohammad, Lashkar-i-Taiba, Sipah-i-Sahaba, Tehrik-i-Jaferia, and Tanzim Nifaz-i-Shariat-i-Mohammadi.[23] His remarks made on the occasion were also courageous and bold:

> The day of reckoning has come. Do we want Pakistan to become a theocratic state? Do we believe that religious education alone is enough for governance or do we want Pakistan to emerge as a progressive and dynamic Islamic welfare state? . . . Look at what this extremist minority is doing . . . Mosques are being misused for propagating and inciting hatred against each other's sect and beliefs. . . . The extremist minority must realize that Pakistan is not responsible of waging armed jihad in the world.[24]

Consequently, Pakistan fully supported the U.S.-led military campaign in Afghanistan beginning in November 2001, and later Musharraf also halted the support of Pakistani-sponsored militant groups in Kashmir. But in response Pakistan also expected that the U.S. administration would help it resolve the lingering Kashmir conflict. U.S. efforts have indeed played a crucial role in de-escalating the military tensions between India and Pakistan in 2002–03, and a bilateral peace process was launched in early 2004, but a resolution of the conflict is still elusive.

Musharraf's credibility within Pakistan, however, started tumbling with the passage of time. The rise in popularity of religious political parties, as evident from the October 2002 national and provincial elections, was just one indicator of that. The anti-American feeling in the wake of Taliban's fall translated into an increased vote bank for these parties. An example of the political ideals of the Muttahida Majlis-i-Amal (MMA)—a coalition of six Islamist pro-Sharia, pro-Taliban, anti-West parties that hold the balance of power in Pakistan—comes from one of its major leaders, Qazi Hussain Ahmed, who declared in a public meeting in March 2003 that "I salute the Iraqi soldier who killed five U.S. marines in a suicide attack" and added that jihad was "the only option to halt the U.S. aggression in Iraq."[25] Musharraf is also blamed by some Pakistanis for sidelining the mainstream liberal political parties in elections and for introducing undemocratic amendments to the constitution entrenching his personal position but damaging democratic institutions.

Another major reason behind Musharraf's declining support is the widely held belief among Pakistanis that despite his strong support to the U.S war on terror, there have been very few benefits for Pakistan. According to the U.S. Central Command (CENTCOM), Pakistan's economy suffered a loss of over U.S.$10 billion from October 2001 to October 2002, particularly due to declines in tourism and investments, losses caused to civil aviation, and increases in the rates of insurance. This information and assessment by CENTCOM was immediately taken off its official website as soon it was reported in the Pakistani press in May 2003.[26] The report did not help Musharraf, to say the least. He was accused of selling Pakistan short. Besides loan waivers, President Bush in June 2003 pledged a $3 billion aid package to Pakistan, to be disbursed over five years (tied to annual reviews of Pakistan's cooperation in the war on terrorism), but it surprised many Pakistanis that half of it was earmarked for armed forces and defense procurements. Ordinary Pakistanis interpreted it as a revival of the Pakistan Army–Pentagon relationship. It is questionable whether this is a prudent policy for the United States to pursue from a long-term perspective.

The Case of Iran

In the words of Thomas Friedman, renowned *New York Times* columnist, there is an enormous longing in Iran, especially among young Iranians, for a resumption of relations with the U.S.[27] He also points out that the Iranian street, in comparison to that of other Muslim states, is more pro-American. To political observers, this change of heart was clearly evident in the aftermath of 9/11. In his first interview with an American publication, Iranian President Khatami told the *New York Times* in November 2001 that "the horrific terrorist attacks of September 11, 2001 in the United States were perpetrated by [a] cult of fanatics who had self-mutilated their ears and tongues, and could only communicate with perceived opponents through carnage and devastation."[28] A few months later, in response to an offer made by Senator Joseph Biden, the then-chairman of the Senate Foreign Relations Committee, to meet Iranian parliamentarians, Iran's official spokesman said that Iran would not oppose direct talks with American legislators.

Iran even quietly offered support for the U.S. campaign in Afghanistan; this was understandable, as Iran had supported the Afghan Northern Alliance against the Taliban all along. In the backdrop of these developments, when Secretary of State Colin Powell shook hands with the Iranian foreign minister, Kamal Kharrazi, at the UN headquarters in New York City in November 2001, it was rightly deemed as "the most tantalizing hint of rapprochement between the U.S. and Iran since the Islamic revolution and the hostage crisis in 1979."[29] The hopes generated by this episode were dashed, however, when President George W. Bush branded Iran as a part of the "axis of evil" during his State of the Union address in January 2002. Despite this setback of sorts, Iran was certainly relieved to see Saddam Hussein removed from power, as Iranians bitterly remember the Iran-Iraq war of the 1980s, in which Saddam had used chemical weapons against them. The Iraq crisis complicated the possibilities of a revival of U.S.-Iran diplomatic channels, but the emergence of a Shiite-led government in Iraq after the 2005 elections is naturally satisfying for Iran, providing another opportunity to open up lines of communication. On the other hand, Iran's pursuit of nuclear weapons and support for Hizballah are crucial factors that are relevant from an American perspective. This is a radically different scenario from the times when Iran was among the most favorite allies of the United States—the days when the Shah of Iran was at the helm of affairs. How and why it all changed is an interesting an intriguing episode of history which is vital to understanding the subject under discussion.

A Brief History of Iran-U.S. Relations

During the first half of the twentieth century, the United States enjoyed cordial relations with Iran, which was also an ally of the British. The first jolt to the relations came in 1953, when the U.S. Central Intelligence Agency, initially instigated by the British, orchestrated the downfall of the popular Iranian prime minister, Mohammed Mossadegh.[30] Previous to this, Mossadegh had bravely refused to be manipulated by British control of Iran's oil industry, and had nationalized the Anglo-Iranian Oil Company. Iranians have not forgotten the CIA episode, which is widely viewed as the first betrayal by their ally. The Shah of Iran was re-installed (by the West) as King in the aftermath of the 1953 "coup," and though he introduced many progressive economic and administrative reforms in the country, his repressive policies tarnished his image and profile in the eyes of Iranians. Political turmoil was in the making in Iran, but ironically, successive American administrations failed to decipher the signs. While the religious establishment led by Ayatollah Khomeini—along with Iran's intelligentsia—continued to criticize the government, the United States ignored the red flags and maintained a steady level of military and political support to the Shah. Between 1972 and 1976, the U.S. military sales to Iran amounted to $16.2 billion alone.[31]

The Shah continued to use torture and repressive measures to tackle his opponents and critics, which eventually led to a massive public uprising. Religious centers were at the forefront of this movement, which raised the credentials of the religious leadership and eventually helped them take control of the country in a bloody revolution in 1979. The contours of this rebellion were also anti-American; Iranians saw the United States as the major supporter of the Shah and his regime. As the United States had failed to gauge what was so clearly written on the wall, it found itself out of touch with reality and without any contacts with the new leadership. Fearful of a repeat of the 1953 affair, the revolutionary regime cut all its ties with the United States. A zealous group of supporters of the new enterprise, in an unexpected move, took American diplomats as hostages at the U.S. Embassy in Tehran, leading to a bitter crisis and closing the doors of any possible reconciliation at the time. Since then, U.S.-Iranian relations have continued to go downhill, entrenching mutual distrust, animosity, and confrontation.

These trends have slowly pushed the two countries along a perpetual diplomatic collision course. Both states question each others' motives and actions, and without an attempt by both sides to answer other side's concerns, no reconciliation is in sight. For their part, Iranians questions such as:

- Why did the United States oppose the Iranian Revolution?
- Why did the United States support Saddam Hussein's invasion of Iran in 1980?
- What was the real purpose of the July 1987 attack on an Iranian civilian airliner, killing all 260 on board?
- Why is the United States enforcing an economic embargo that produces great hardship and suffering to all the Iranian people?
- Why is the United States constantly trying to exclude Iran from an appropriate regional role, while militarily supporting Kuwait, the United Arab Emirates, and other Gulf states?
- Why is the United States creating hurdles in Iranian efforts to develop oil pipeline links with Central Asia?

While the United States response to these questions has been less than adequate, Americans have their own questions, including:

- Why does Iran seek to build weapons of mass destruction?
- How does Iran justify taking American diplomats as hostages in the aftermath of the revolution, in clear violation of international law?
- How does Iran justify its worsening human rights record?
- Why does Iran support Hizballah and terrorism in Middle East?
- Why is Iran holding al Qaeda operatives and not handing them over to the United States?
- Why is Iran supporting radical Shiite groups in Iraq and complicating U.S. efforts in Iraq?

The Prevailing Political Scenario in Iran

Though most Iranians are proud of the 1979 revolution, their expectations of positive change remains unfulfilled. They were looking for social justice and spiritual fulfillment, but soon after the success, Ayatollah Khomeini—the leader of the revolution—admonished the people by saying that the purpose of the revolution was not "to have less expensive melons" but to lead a more elevated life.[32] Also unexpectedly, Khomeini saddled Iran with something not all his supporters bargained for: the doctrine of *velayat-i-faqih*, or the rule of the jurist. This doctrine effectively delivered autocratic executive powers to Iran's clerics, even though the new constitution provided for a democratically elected legislature and president to govern the state under the guidance of religious authorities.

As a result of the religious leadership's failure to make a real difference in the life of the people, disillusionment and discontent gradually took root, and opposition to state policies became popular. Iran has a history of intellectual ferment and its vibrant society is known for strongly reacting to repression and dogmatic tendencies of the state. Scholars like Abdol Karim Soroush, Mohsin Kadivar, and 2003 Nobel Peace Prize winner Shirin Ebadi are a few examples of courageous Iranians who raised their voices against the excesses of the postrevolution religious leadership. Though they deserve support from the West—and especially the United States—they needed no instigation or provocation to embark on this path and this differentiation must be kept in mind by those who want change in terms of engaging Iran constructively.

For instance, Soroush's open criticism of the Iranian clergy and its ways of handling the state had a discernible impact on the intellectual climate of the country. This discourse gained increasing popularity during the 1990s, especially among the urban middle class, and proved to be much more than merely a philosophical debate; it had a significant impact on the formulation of public policy in Iran, on the larger Iranian polity, and even on Iran's relations with the outside world.[33] Arguably, the rise of reformist Mohammad Khatami to the Presidency of Iran in 1997 was an outcome of this trend. Moreover, in recent years these debates have attained mass currency and have moved into the domain of popular journals, newspapers, book shops, and the street. There has been a strong reaction by the religious establishment to this trend, through autocratic measures against media as well as election manipulation, but this has led to further lack of support for the clergy among the people.

The story of Iran today is one of economic decline: Its per-capita income is a third of what it was before the revolution, oil production is two-thirds of the 1979 level, and the middle class is being squeezed by chronically high inflation and widespread unemployment, while (most importantly) two-thirds of Iran's population is under thirty.[34] The 1979 revolution faces a profound challenge from this new and disenchanted generation, widely known in Iran as "the third force."[35] At this juncture, any outside pressure or activity in terms of a choreographed "regime change" can discredit the brave and courageous Iranians who are challenging the status quo from within Iran.

Iran desperately needs economic progress to satisfy its burgeoning population of young people. About 1 million Iranians enter the workforce each year, while only 300,000 new jobs are created.[36] The situation will surely worsen as long as Iran remains isolated globally. In this context, Graham E. Fuller of the Rand Corporation argued in 1998 that Washington should consider partial lifting of restrictions on trade with Iran as a key gesture of good faith, as U.S.-sponsored economic sanctions have largely benefited the hard-liners in Iran who prefer confrontation as a way of legitimizing their policies.[37] This recommendation is still valid, as the beneficiary of such a development will be the people of Iran, and there is no better way to earn their goodwill and prove to them that the U.S. believes in empowering people. In addition, people-to-people contact and dialogue is an effective way to overcome several decades of suspicion.

Conclusions and Recommendations[38]

Lately, there has been a concerted endeavor on the part of the U.S. administration to rethink and reevaluate its public diplomacy efforts in the Islamic world. Various congressional hearings and official reports have focused on the issue, and numerous new programs are underway, ranging from the creation of media outlets for the Arab audience—in order to counter the al Jazeera effect—to reaching out to different Muslim countries and explaining the American perspective. The unfortunate Abu Ghraib prison affair was a setback to these U.S. efforts, having a negative impact on Muslim public opinion. Also, many Muslims continue to believe that the U.S. war on terror in reality is a war against Muslims. This false assertion needs to be challenged more strongly. The litmus test in the eyes of Muslims, however, is the Israeli-Palestinian issue. It is pertinent to point out here that majority of Muslims—despite their skepticisms about American polices—still look towards the United States for a just resolution of the lingering Middle East conflict, indicating that Muslims trust that effective American involvement will lead to a fair conclusion of the dispute.

With reference to the U.S. public diplomacy front in Pakistan and Iran, as well as in the Islamic world more generally, the following measures are worth considering:

1. Acknowledging past mistakes—or providing a truthful explanation of controversial events like that of the 1953 overthrow of Iranian Prime Minister Mossadegh and walking out of Afghanistan and Pakistan after the Soviet withdrawal from Afghanistan in 1989—can go a long way in raising U.S. prestige in the region and in encouraging Iranians and Pakistanis to accept what went wrong on their part.

2. Understanding the limitations of public diplomacy is crucial, as it cannot be a substitute for policies that are self-evident in terms of their rationale and good reason.

3. Effective diplomacy needs an efficient feedback mechanism to assess the impact of specific policies.

4. Most Muslim countries are being governed by rulers who are autocratic and lack democratic credentials. The United States at times unnecessarily gets blamed for the oppressive policies of such rulers, because they are perceived as U.S. partners. For instance, it is almost an element of faith in Pakistan that all military dictators have had the support of the United States, and people question why the United States has not been as supportive of democratic institutions and popular political movements.

5. Forums for people-to-people contact deserve more attention as a way of promoting a better understanding of American political system, values, and freedoms.

6. Regardless of the nature of political differences, closing the channels of communication and dialogue has never proved to be a productive measure. The shutting down of diplomatic relations with Iran since 1979 has proved to be counterproductive, though of course Iran's postrevolution policies played a significant part in forcing the United States to take that path.

7. Muslim-Americans and those living in other Western countries can act as bridges between the West and Muslims. The message is as important as the messenger in the avenues of public diplomacy.

8. To frame the issues in terms of "you are either with us or against us" is often interpreted as an arrogant way to approach one's allies and potential partners. Such proposals might be effective in the short term, given the overwhelming U.S. military superiority, but are not expected to deliver in the long term.

9. Many political analysts make the case that Muslim moderates should be engaged and supported by the United States. On the contrary, scholars like Tariq Ramadan and Yusuf Islam (Cat Stevens), who are widely perceived by Muslims as progressive and anti religious extremists, were refused entry in the United States, creating a wrong impression. More so, no explanations were given by the Department of Homeland Security as to the charges against them. Such public diplomacy blunders can be avoided by a more careful preparation of the lists of individuals who belong to such categories as "person of interest."

10. U.S. aid for reform of the education sector in Muslim countries, especially where madrasa networks are entrenched, can gain the respect of those who want better education for their children but are forced by financial pressures to send their kids to madrasas that provide free boarding and food.

11. Many times, misgivings and misperceptions are an outcome of a lack of access to basic information. Many conspiracy theories, which are a favorite pastime in many parts of the Muslim world, will die their own death if accurate and easily accessible information is available. For instance, partnerships with popular websites and media outlets in the Muslim world can be fruitful. Coupled with this, support for the free press in the Muslim world will help anti-extremist voices to freely disseminate their opinions.

12. Finally, and importantly, a better understanding of cultural and religious sensitivities, language skills and the history of the U.S. relations with countries of interest will be an asset for successful public diplomacy.

CHAPTER 5

The Complex Relationship between Global Terrorism and U.S. Support for Israel

RUTH MARGOLIES BEITLER

In the quest to determine the underlying causes of terrorism, it is commonplace in the Middle East to hear comments espousing the view that if only the United States would modify or cease its support for Israel, hatred against the United States would end. Producer Saul Landau, who released a film on Iraq entitled *Iraq Voices from the Street*, summed up his opinion of the Arab world's justification for its resentment of the United States with the following pithy remark: "It's the occupation, stupid."[1] Following the September 11 terrorist attacks on the United States, many Arab countries expressed sympathy for the victims of the violence, yet quickly blamed U.S. policies in the Middle East for the terrorists' discontent, especially U.S. support for Israel. One only needs to examine the religious edicts of Islamic militants—including Osama bin Laden and Ayman al-Zawahiri, the highest ranking members of al Qaeda—to reveal the explicit connection that is often made between U.S. support of Israel and terrorist actions.

American policy toward Israel remains a potent source of discontent and reverberates throughout the Arab and Muslim world. As one of the most intractable global problems, the Palestinian-Israeli conflict affects U.S. strategic interests in the Middle East. Persistent turmoil between Israelis and Palestinians hampers U.S. objectives *vis-à-vis* the global war on terrorism, as well as its goals of rebuilding a democratic Iraq and fostering greater political liberalization in a region where democracy has yet to take hold. As such, it is crucial to understand the perceived or actual interconnection that many people contend exists between global terrorism and American policies supporting Israel.

This chapter examines the complex relationship between U.S. policy regarding Israel and the impact that relationship has on the roots of global terrorism. The overwhelming assessment in the Muslim and Arab world is that the United States retains little objectivity when dealing with the Israeli-Palestinian issue. It is this perception that fosters antipathy for the United States and justifies, in the minds of the terrorists, their actions. Although on the surface these interconnections between U.S. support for Israel and violent action appear as unambiguous motivators for terrorist actions, they mask a crucial issue. Both the Muslim and Arab world use the Palestinian issue to deflect discontent for the lack of democratic reform within their societies. Highlighting U.S. support for Israel and the perceived indifference to the predicaments of the Arab world provides fodder for the terrorist groups, while simultaneously turning public opinion away from the deficiencies of their own regimes.

In reality, whether or not the United States is even-handed when it comes to the Arab world and Israel is almost insignificant. The key factor fostering resentment in the Middle East is *the perception* that the United States maintains a double standard. The United States is not viewed as an unbiased player or honest broker in the region. From the Palestinian and Arab standpoint, U.S. policy in the Middle East often reflects hypocrisy, requiring Arabs to do one thing while sanctioning opposite activities by the Israelis. The Arab press is rife with examples of Arab leaders denouncing U.S. policy in the region as one of "double standards."

Therefore, to understand this multifaceted relationship between U.S. support of Israel and global terrorism, the first section of this chapter presents a short historical overview of U.S. policy to elucidate that while the United States has supported Israel's existence, it has not always supported its policies. The second section assesses Arab reaction to American policy and explores the development of the negative perception of U.S. policy with regards to Israel. The third section provides a survey of statements made by Arab leaders and Islamic militants, revealing their assessment of the linkages between U.S. support for Israel and the perceived American indifference to the plight of the Arab and Muslim world. Historically, U.S. policy towards Israel has varied between staunch support and indifference, although it has rarely been appraised as even-handed.

U.S. Policy Toward Israel: A Historical Overview

U.S. relations and attitudes toward Israel have always been complicated matters. When Israel was created in 1948, members of the U.S. government clashed over whether or not recognizing the nascent Jewish state was a liability given the United States' relationship with the Arab world, more specifically, the Persian Gulf. Additionally, as Moscow became more involved in the Middle East, Washington believed that it was imperative to cultivate friendly relations with stable Arab regimes in the region in order to stave off communist influence. During the period prior to Israel's declaration as a state, a debate between the U.S. Department of State and the White House ensued, with the former contending that support for the Zionist State would jeopardize relations with the Arab world.[2] Yet President Harry Truman was swayed by Zionist arguments and supported the creation of the State of Israel, much to the dismay of the State Department.

President Dwight Eisenhower took a different approach toward Israel than did President Truman. Concerned with Soviet expansion in the Middle East, Eisenhower—along with his Secretary of State, John Foster Dulles—saw Israel as a strategic liability.[3] In 1953, when Israel diverted the headwaters of the Jordan River, Eisenhower sent his envoy, Eric Johnston, to mediate between the parties and secure a plan to resolve the dispute. The United States exerted economic pressure on Israel by threatening to withhold $50 million in aid. Furthermore, when Israel, France, and Britain colluded and precipitated the Suez Crisis in 1956, an infuriated Eisenhower forced Israel's withdrawal of troops from the Sinai Peninsula. Eisenhower's reaction earned him respect from Arab leaders, who later agreed to support the Eisenhower Doctrine.

However, although many scholars have suggested that the gradual shift in U.S. policy toward closer relations with Israel began with the Kennedy and Johnson administrations, Douglas Little[4] contends that it was Eisenhower who planted the seed for closer ties with Israel: With the Soviet inroads in the region and the potential for anti-American sentiment from revolutionary Arab nationalism, Eisenhower recognized Israel's potential as an important ally. Kennedy was the first president to sell military equipment to Israel and in a meeting with Israeli Foreign Minister Golda Meir spoke for the first time of the "special relationship between Israel and the United States."[5] Johnson solidified the closer relations between the United States and Israel by supporting the Jewish state with weapons, despite a continued "Arabist" perspective in the State Department.

Under President Richard Nixon, the pendulum moved firmly towards a strong military connection with Israel, although initially, President Nixon's administration was preoccupied with the Vietnam War. In fact, when Henry Kissinger became Secretary of State, he convinced Anwar Sadat, the President of Egypt, that an alliance with Washington would be more beneficial than one with the Soviets and hence tried to balance America's contradictory interests in the region. Maintaining a secure Israel and unfettered access to oil remained an intricate balancing act for all American administrations. President Sadat launched a surprise attack against Israel in October 1973, jeopardizing the existence of the small state. As such, this war pushed the United States into a closer military relationship with Israel to deter the Jewish state's total collapse and to curb expanded Soviet influence in the region. President Nixon authorized a full-scale airlift to Israel after being informed of a Soviet airlift to Syria.[6]

President Jimmy Carter's administration postulated that holding out for a comprehensive peace treaty with all of the Arab States was in America's strategic interest. Because of this, coupled with his emphasis on human rights, Carter was accepted by the Arab world as more engaged in their issues. President Sadat and Israeli Prime Minister Menachem Begin signed a historic peace treaty between their two countries, but ignored a comprehensive settlement involving all Arab states. Specifically, the agreement dropped linkage with the Palestinian issue. Following the peace treaty, the United States pledged billions of dollars in aid to Egypt while maintaining strong assurances for the security of Israel.

During President Ronald Reagan's administration, Israel was seen as an important strategic ally in the Cold War, and Reagan tacitly and explicitly supported some of Israel's most controversial policies—such as its destruction of Iraq's Osirak nuclear reactor in 1981 and the invasion of Lebanon in 1982 to curb Katusha rocket attacks into Northern Israel. In actuality, the United States opposed Israel's 1982 "Peace for Galilee" operation when the mission broadened to advance on Beirut. Further, although President Reagan condemned the Osirak attack in a United Nations Security Council vote and suspended delivery of F-16 fighter jets that had been sold to Israel, the Arab world was outraged at what they perceived as a mild American response to an egregious attack on a nation's sovereignty. The Arab world contrasted this with the American reaction to Turkey's invasion of Cyprus in 1974, when the United States implemented a complete military supplies embargo on that country.[7]

President George H. W. Bush attempted to distance himself from the right-wing Likud government of Israeli Prime Minister Yitzhak Shamir and to push the Arab states and Israel into negotiations following the first Gulf War in 1991. President Bush's aid to Kuwait after the invasion by Iraq in 1990–91 earned him some credibility in the Arab world as a more even-handed player in that tense regional arena. Consequently, he convinced the Arab states to join the Madrid conference and undertake bilateral and multilateral negotiations with the Israelis. President Bush opened talks with the Palestinians and also withheld financial aid to Israel in order to pressure Prime Minister Shamir to cease construction in the West Bank and Gaza Strip.

Diverting from his predecessor's acrimonious relationship with Israel's leadership, President William Clinton fostered warm relations with Prime Minister Yitzhak Rabin and was optimistic—following the signing of the Oslo Accords between the Israelis and Palestinians in 1993—that the region was on the road to a sustained peace. However, the Camp David summit, sponsored by the United States in July 2000 between Israeli Prime Minister Ehud Barak and Palestinian Chairman Yassir Arafat, failed to resolve final status issues for the creation of a Palestinian state. President Clinton outwardly blamed Chairman Arafat for the demise of the talks and the instigation of the al-Aqsa *intifada*. The Arab world rejected the suggestion that Prime Minister Barak had offered the Palestinians the best deal that they would ever receive. The termination of the summit solidified the perception in the Arab world that the United States did not have a balanced approach to the conflict.

When President George W. Bush became president, he initially neglected the Israeli-Palestinian peace process, but was pushed firmly into the Israeli camp following the attacks on September 11. For the Bush administration, Israel's war against suicide bombings and the American-led global war on terror nurtured a profound camaraderie between the two nations. This connection, coupled with President Bush's strong ties with the religious right, which vociferously supports Israel, has left no doubt regarding the Bush administration's affection for Israel. The March 2003 American invasion of Iraq to topple Saddam Hussein's regime has further exacerbated tensions between President Bush and the Arab and Muslim world.

Reaction to U.S. Policy

U.S. policy toward Israel in the early years of Israel's existence evolved during a complex and precarious period of Arab independence following decades of colonial influence. This historical backdrop shaped Arab leaders' reaction to anything that was perceived as an encroachment on the independence of countries in the region. Although global terrorism was not a concern during the early years of Israel's existence, Arab reaction to what was perceived as a pro-Israel policy was explosive. Israel was viewed as a neocolonialist entity in the midst of a region vying for its true independence.

After the United States rescinded on a commitment to fund the Aswan Dam project in 1956, Nasser (the President of Egypt) nationalized the Suez Canal and moved Egypt toward closer relations with the Soviets. Significantly, he also adopted a more rejectionist stance regarding both Israel and the West. Furthermore, Egypt and Syria formed the United Arab Republic (UAR) in 1958, hoping to mobilize the Arab nations to oppose continued Western encroachment in the region. In Jordan, during that same year, supporters of Nasser's vision were caught preparing to execute a coup against the pro-Western monarch, King Hussein, who was not perceived as sufficiently anti-Israel.[8] Although the Eisenhower administration conceded the utility of support for Israel, it also recognized that policy's potential for "Arab radicalization and gravitation towards the Soviets."[9] In 1963, significant protests erupted in Jordan, demanding that King Hussein join Nasser's "union for the liberation of Palestine."[10]

In 1970, members of the Palestinian Front for the Liberation of Palestine (PFLP) blew up British, Swiss, and American airplanes on an unused airstrip in the Jordanian desert. Although the motivation for the hijackings of the British and Swiss planes was to demand the release of Palestinian prisoners held in their countries, the seizure of a TWA plane was meant to convince the United States to exert pressure on Israel to meet Palestinian stipulations. Clearly, the issue of Palestine has continually mobilized the Arab world. As such, it is logical that U.S. support for Israeli actions that negatively impact the Palestinians will provoke a reaction in the Arab world. Additionally, despite numerous examples in history where the opposite held true, many in the Middle East assert that the United States retains the ability to pressure Israel to comply with its demands.

Some scholars contend that the main ideologue behind al Qaeda's organization is not Osama bin Laden but Ayman al-Zawahiri, who had been the leader of the militant Egyptian Islamic Jihad movement. There is an interesting link between the Nasserist rejectionist trend that emerged in the 1960s and al Qaeda's current ideology. Al-Zawahiri, a product of Nasser's Egypt, tries to court Muslims to join his militant camp by using the issue of Palestine as an ideological hook. Yet Nasser and al-Zawahiri diverge significantly in the ideological roots for their actions. Some strands of the early theological roots of al Qaeda can be linked to a twelfth-century Muslim scholar, Taqi al Din Ibn Tamiyya, who stressed jihad's militant nature (rather than stressing a personal struggle to follow the Koran and live a virtuous life). Ibn Tamiyya also legitimized the use of rebellion against Muslim rulers who did not obey or enforce Islamic law.[11] For al-Zawahiri, the rejection of Israel and an attempt to actively transform the policy of states which accept Israel's existence undoubtedly reflect an interpretation of Ibn Tamiyya's teachings. Al-Zawahiri contends that Arab and Muslim states have "sold out by the mere fact that they accepted the authority of the United Nations and the very idea that any Jew might remain in any part of Palestine."[12]

Ibn Tamiyya's teachings were extraordinarily influential due to the way in which he interpreted the concept of jihad. In Islam, jihad has several distinct meanings. First, it refers to a personal struggle to follow the Koran and live by the teachings of the prophet Muhammed. Second, jihad can be interpreted as a Muslim's obligation for nonviolent struggle if Islam is being threatened from within the community. A third meaning calls for a more militant jihad to defend the religion against nonbelievers. As mentioned previously, Ibn Tamiyya emphasized the obligation of Muslims to revolt against unjust Muslim rulers. Although many in the West believe that a goal of militant Islamic groups is to create a nation based on *sharia* or Islamic law, al-Zawahiri stresses the issue of Palestine. Therefore, a country such as Saudi Arabia—whose government is based on *sharia* law, but is allied with the United States—is considered by al-Zawahiri as an unjust Muslim state denying true Islamic law.[13]

In many cases, U.S. support of Israel evokes a cynicism in the Arab and

Muslim world. For example, when President George W. Bush referred to Israeli Prime Minister Ariel Sharon as a "man of peace," reaction in the Arab press was biting and sarcastic. Additionally, conspiracy theories circulating in the Arab world—including a well-publicized conjecture that the United States, in collusion with the Mossad, was responsible for the September 11 attacks—reflect the growing antipathy toward the American relationship with the Jewish State.

Terrorist Groups and U.S. Policy

A survey of statements made by Arab world leaders and militant terrorist groups reveals their perception of an interconnection between global terrorism and U.S. policy supporting Israel. Many militant Islamic groups refer to America's relationship with Israel when justifying their violent attacks. Arab leaders, even those with good relations with the United States, have urged government officials to modify U.S. policy and pursue a more balanced approach in the Middle East. When President George W. Bush telephoned Yemen's president, Ali Abdallah Salih, to thank him for his cooperation in pursuing the group responsible for carrying out the attack on a Navy ship (the USS *Cole*) during the summer of 2000, President Salih encouraged President Bush to persuade the Israelis to halt their operations against the Palestinians.[14]

U.S. sponsorship of Israel becomes an issue almost every time Israel implements a controversial policy. Following Israel's assassination of two leaders of Hamas—the Islamic Resistance Group—in the Gaza Strip, President Hosni Mubarak of Egypt declared that "there is hatred of Americans like never before in the region."[15] His anger stemmed from U.S. statements positing that Israel has the right to defend itself from terror, instead of condemning Israeli action. Although the United States counts Egypt among its closest allies in the Middle East and labels it as a moderate Arab state, a broad segment of the population resents what people perceive as indifference to the Palestinian plight. Prior to the U.S. invasion of Iraq in March 2003, an Egyptian woman was asked whether Saddam Hussein posed a threat in the Middle East with chemical weapons, and specifically to Israel. She responded that "Israel has chemical weapons as well, and the United States does not attack Israel for that."[16] Clearly, acrimony towards U.S. policy in the Middle East is increasing and "the more they resent the United States, the more they sympathize with Bin Laden."[17]

For many in the Muslim world, the distinction between Israeli action and U.S. policy is nonexistent. The perception remains that Israel acts with either overt or tacit U.S. approval. For example, in 1996, Israel attacked Hizballah bases in Lebanon and killed (according to some reports) more than 150 civilians. This action reverberated throughout the Middle East, eliciting harsh reaction in several Arab nations. According to Eric Watkins, the Saudis were livid that the United States did not condemn the Israeli attack.[18] As a result of growing internal unrest in the Kingdom, the Saudi royal family distanced itself from U.S. views. Likewise, a commentary from Egypt's progovernment newspaper, *Al-Ahram*, following the U.S. invasion of Iraq vividly illuminates the fact that many in the Arab world do not distinguish between U.S. and Israeli policy: "The simultaneous use of excessive force against civilians in Palestine and Iraq by the occupation forces will only lead to more anger, wrath, suicide bombings and booby-trapped cars."[19]

In a commentary from the Iranian newspaper, *Jomhuri-ye Eslami*, the author contends that the UN inspection team in Iraq for ten years was actually a puppet of the American and Israeli government. He continues by saying that "Richard Butler, one of the leaders of the special team responsible for disarming Iraq known as UNSCOM, acted like an Israeli agent."[20] Likewise, the Secretary-General of Hizballah, Sayyed Hassan Nasrallah, proclaimed that Israel and the United States are aligned against the Palestinians: "Nowadays, we must comprehend that the battle and enemy are one; that we are facing one camp, which is the American-'Israeli', a collection of Zionism in America and within the 'Israeli' entity."[21]

As early as 1988, Abdullah Azzam—the founder of the al-Kifah Refugee Services, a movement connected to the Pakistan-based Office of Services that would later become al Qaeda—preached global jihad to his followers: "Every Muslim on earth should unsheathe his sword and fight to liberate Palestine."[22] Azzam raised money in the United States while advocating the importance of global jihad. It was during this period that one of the first Islamic terror cells was organized in the United States. Terrorists involved in the 1993 World Trade Center bombings have been connected to Abdullah Azzam.

Militant leaders have justified their terrorist actions by citing U.S. support for Israel as a provocation. When explaining the bombings at the Khobar towers in Saudi Arabia in 1996, which killed nineteen American service members, bin Laden clearly connected U.S. policy towards Israel as validation for the action: "We feel for our brothers in Palestine and Lebanon. The explosion at Khobar towers did not come as a direct result of American occupation but as a result of American behavior against Muslims. When sixty Jews are killed inside Palestine, all the world gathers within seven days to criticize this action, while the deaths of 600,000 Iraqi children did not receive the same reaction."[23]

In March 1997, bin Laden claimed in comments during a CNN interview that "we declared jihad against the U.S. government, because the U.S. government is unjust, criminal and tyrannical. It has committed acts that are extremely unjust, hideous and criminal whether directly or through its support of the Israeli occupation."[24] Several statements alluding to the close association of the United States with Israel also emerged in Osama bin Laden's 1998 "Declaration of the World Islamic Front for Jihad Against the Jews and the Crusaders." According to the declaration, the murder of Americans, whether civilian or military, is an obligation for every Muslim "until the Aqsa Mosque and the Haram Mosque are freed from their grip and until their armies, shattered and broken-winged, depart from all the lands of Islam, incapable of threatening any Muslim."[25] In one recording obtained by the television network al Jazeera, bin Laden urged his followers to continue the jihad against "crusaders in Baghdad" and "the situation in Jerusalem under the deceptions of the road map and the Geneva initiative."[26]

Likewise, al-Zawahiri asserts that the issue of Palestine features prominently as a catalyst for his militant activities. Al-Zawahiri subsequently became bin Laden's second-in-command after he adopted the view that Islamic groups needed to act beyond the boundaries of their states. Al-Zawahiri details his thinking regarding the Palestine issue in a document he wrote entitled "The Cure for Believers' Hearts."[27] In the document, he posits that any nation that supports Israel is characterized as an enemy, making it a legitimate target for attack.

In a tape recording made by al-Zawahiri, his statements concerning the United States and Israel offer a glimpse of the injustice with which he views U.S. support, not only of Israel's policies, but also backing of the Jewish state's creation: "It was the Americans who decided over sixty years ago to create Israel. And they haven't stopped supporting it from then until today. They won't allow anyone to hinder it or its aims."[28] As a consequence of his view of history, his suggestion for Muslim youth is to resist the "crusaders."

Prior to the U.S. invasion of Iraq in March 2003, al Jazeera aired a videotape allegedly made by bin Laden. During the broadcast, bin Laden unambiguously blamed U.S. support for Israel and its intention to invade Iraq for Muslim disaffection:

> We are following with utmost concern the Crusaders' preparations to occupy the former capital of Islam (Baghdad), loot the fortunes of the Muslims and install a puppet regime on you that follows its masters in Washington and Tel Aviv like the rest of the treacherous puppet Arab governments, as a prelude to the formation of Greater Israel.[29]

Many militants profess that Jews control the American government, and it is not uncommon to find copies of a virulently anti-Semitic book, *The Protocols of the Elders of Zion*, circulating in Arab states.

In an interview with a Western journalist, bin Laden excoriated the Saudi regime for inviting U.S. troops onto its soil during the Gulf War in 1991. He held that by doing so, the Saudi regime "revealed their deception. They had given their support to nations that were fighting against Muslims. They helped Yemen Communists against the southern Yemeni Muslims and helped Arafat's regime fight Hamas."[30] Consequently, Saudi Arabia is seen as a legitimate target for the wrath of Islamic militants as part of their jihad against an unjust regime.

Historically, the United States has not given Israel unconditional support for its policies, but has always supported the country's right to exist. For militant Muslims, the very existence of the Jewish state is an affront to Islam. The reality of Jews residing in the "holy land" is unacceptable, despite Islam's allowance for a protected minority status for Jews and Christians, referred to as "people of the book." In Islam, although Jews are considered a protected minority, or *Dhimmi*, the notion of Jews controlling territory in Muslim land is antithetical. In ancient times, Jews and Christians were required to pay taxes and abide by the Muslim rulers. Thus, it is not solely American support of Israeli policies that enrages the militants, but the fundamental conviction that Israel has a right to exist.

Furthermore, for many al Qaeda and militant Muslim groups, there is little distinction between Jews and Israel, and both are portrayed with anti-Semitic overtones. During a sermon in Gaza, Ahmad Abu Halabiya, a former rector of the Islamic University of Gaza, professed,

> Have no mercy on the Jews, no matter where they are, in any country. Fight them, wherever you are. Wherever you are, kill those Jews and those Americans who are like them and those who stand by them. They are all in one trench against the Arabs and the Muslims because they established Israel here, in the beating heart of the Arab world, in Palestine.[31]

Additionally, Arab states have resurrected the concept of blood libel from medieval Christian times, portraying Jews as murderers who require human blood to make holiday food. In 2002 an educated Saudi Arabian journalist published an article (which he later recanted) in *al-Riyadh*, a government daily, entitled, "Jews Use Teenagers' Blood for Purim Pastries."

From all this, the question still remains whether global terrorism can be attributed to U.S. support for Israel, or at least whether terrorist groups employ the issue to evoke a response from Arab and Muslim populations. On closer inspection, although the Palestinian issue resonates with Arab and Muslim populations, and fuels anger at the United States, Arab governments manipulate the matter for their personal gain by deflecting discontent from their undemocratic policies and their inability to meet the economic and political demands of their populations. For example, Egypt suffers from a lack of political liberalization and severe economic crises. If the United States is viewed as continuing to support Mubarak's authoritarian rule, while simultaneously calling for regime change in other states—specifically within the Palestinian Authority—anti-American sentiment and terrorism will most likely increase. It is evident that there has been an intensification of public anti-U.S. views in the Egyptian media. Hamdy Qandil, a television personality who harshly criticizes American and Israeli policy *vis-à-vis* the Palestinians and the global war on terrorism, has gained popularity.[32] U.S. officials believe that the Egyptian regime allows the show to air in order for the population to vent frustration over U.S. action in Afghanistan and the deteriorating situation in the West Bank and Gaza Strip.[33]

Therefore, the antagonism that many feel towards the United States reflects dissent with corrupt regimes that are perceived to be "propped up" by American support. Paradoxically, states such as Saudi Arabia and Egypt are required to sanction, on some level, the anti-U.S. sentiments often expressed in mosques and through the media in order to contain internal unrest within their countries. Yet they are also required, by the nature of state and strategic interests, "to provide diplomatic or other practical support for U.S. policies that offend public sensitivities."[34] For the militants, the linkage between these two issues is clear: Any country that deals with the United States condones its policies towards Israel.

Conclusion

The roots of terrorist rage and discontent are mired in religion, politics, and millenarian ideology. Al Qaeda, under the leadership of bin Laden and al-Zawahiri, have manipulated U.S. support for Israel to intensify anti-American sentiment and increase recruitment for their organization. Undoubtedly, the Arab and Muslim world identify with the Palestinian issue on either an ethnic or religious level, and it is these aspects that are exploited by the terrorist groups to mobilize their followers. At the very least, the relationship between Israel and the United States, coupled with the militants' perception of U.S. indifference to Arab and Muslim grievances, produces a very potent motivator for the recruitment and violent activity of terrorists.

Removing the Israeli-Palestinian question from the agenda will not solve the problems endemic to that region and, moreover, the issue only resounds with a subset of all global terrorists. As such, its resolution will not extinguish the challenge of global terrorism, though it can have a positive outcome.[35] Although a core of militant Islamists will remain instigators of violence, for President George W. Bush and his new cabinet finding a solution to the Israeli-Palestinian problem may decrease tension in the region and have significant ramifications for the global war on terror. Since the Palestinian issue resonates strongly with Arab populations, creating a Palestinian state has the potential to remove a compelling recruitment tool for Osama bin Laden. One issue is unmistakable. Unless the United States is willing to allow the destruction of the Jewish state, al Qaeda and other Islamic militant groups will not be appeased. As such, it is imperative for the United States to lessen al Qaeda's appeal to discontented populations in the Middle East by ensuring a greater balance—or *perception of balance*—with regard to its policies toward the Arab World.

Acknowledgments

The views expressed herein are those of the authors and do not purport to reflect the position of the United States Military Academy, the Department of the Army, or the Department of Defense.

CHAPTER 6

Political Repression and Violent Rebellion in the Muslim World

MOHAMMED M. HAFEZ

Since the 1970s, following decades of Western secularization and modernization, the Muslim world has witnessed an Islamic revival characterized by the spread of public displays of piety, growing mosque attendance, and the spread of Islamic networks, social movements, and political parties.[1] Young men and women in the universities gravitated toward Islamic social clubs and unions, and Islamic activists reaped the benefits by expanding their representation in local student elections. Where and when allowed, Islamists organized political parties and played an active role in Islamizing their politics. Islamic fundamentalism, as it came to be known, contested the hold of secular leftists and nationalists in almost every arena of competition—student unions, professional associations, local and national elections, and in the cultural sphere. Even the state-controlled media of secular regimes had to placate the growing religious sentiment of its public by adopting more religious programming as well as censoring content deemed inappropriate or sinful. Networks of charity and nongovernmental mosques were created by entrepreneurial Islamic activists who saw an opportunity to present viable public spaces free from the "corrupting" influence of the secular state, as well as to foster legitimacy for the Islamic movement through tangible provisions to the public. The Iranian revolution in 1979, and the liberation of Afghanistan by Islamic rebels (*mujahideen*) from Soviet forces a decade later reinforced the trend toward Islamic activism.

The 1980s and 1990s witnessed Islamic rebellions and violence in many countries and almost every region of the Muslim world, including Afghanistan, Algeria, Chechnya, Egypt, Indonesia, Iraq, Kashmir, the occupied Palestinian territories, Philippines, Syria, Lebanon, Tajikistan, Uzbekistan, and Yemen. In many of these countries, Islamic insurgency garnered some (if not mass) support from the broader public and turned into protracted conflicts with "residual" attacks that have continued to this day. Some see this turn to violence as a natural progression toward radicalization in inherently intolerant and antimodern Islamic movements. Following more than a decade of organizing and recruiting members, some observers maintain, radical Islamists saw an opportunity to capitalize on their growing power and turned to rebellion in order to establish Islamic states.[2]

This chapter argues that Islamic violence since the 1980s is not a product of inherent tendencies toward radicalism and militancy. On the contrary, Islamic opposition movements have adopted a variety of strategies to affect social and political change. Some opt for militancy, violence and revolution—as the recent histories of Algeria, Egypt, and Iraq demonstrate—but many more eschew violence and seek accommodation with their secular states. Islamists in Turkey, Jordan, Morocco, Malaysia, and Indonesia, to name a few, are generally committed to legality, gradualism, and constitutionalism. Many more avoid politics altogether and seek to affect change through education and social reforms at the grassroots level; they promote the moral rejuvenation of their communities without taking up arms or participating in parliaments. In most cases, Islamic movements are not "born" violent. Instead, proponents of violence develop coteries of militants from within established, predominantly nonviolent Islamic movements. This observation raises two questions: Why do some Islamic movements turn to rebellion and why do previously nonviolent militants turn to violence?

Islamic rebellion is a product of an ill-fated combination of institutional exclusion and the indiscriminate repression that threatens the organizational resources of Islamic movements and the lives of their activists. It is often a defensive reaction to an overly repressive regime that misapplies its repression in ways that radicalizes, rather than deters, movement activists and supporters. Thus, violent Islamic militancy is not a natural outgrowth of Islamic activism, but a contingent development that arises when exclusionary and illegitimate regimes apply repression to remove social forces that pose serious challenges to their political rule.

Regime Legitimacy Crises and the Rise of Islamic Challenge

To understand the widespread phenomenon of Islamic violence in the Muslim world, we must begin with the social transformations that shaped the lives of millions of Muslims in the postcolonial era. Following independence from their former colonial rulers, many revolutionary governments promoted rapid structural, demographic, and social transformations in order to modernize their societies. These reforms entailed the expansion of secondary and university education, development of public-sector employment, implementation of land reforms and Western-style legal systems, nationalization of religious institutions, modification of personal status codes, and promotion of state-led industrialization. Secular leaders and technocratic elites with an affinity toward Western models of development usually carried out these reforms with the intent of consolidating their rule, expanding their legitimacy, and promoting genuine economic progress for their societies. They equated successful development with secularization and Westernization of society and saw institutions rooted in rural economies and religious traditions as impediments to modernization. Kamal Ataturk in Turkey, Reza Shah in Iran, Habib Bourguiba in Tunisia, Houari Boumedienne in Algeria, and Gamal Abdel Nasser in Egypt are primary examples of postcolonial modernizing reformers who embraced secular and Western models of development and relegated religion to the private sphere.

These postcolonial transformations, despite improving the lot of many people, manifested serious contradictions. Industrialization, initially a source of national pride, quickly turned into a heavy burden on society that could only be sustained through national debt. The expansion of education significantly increased literacy rates and produced many engineers, doctors, and lawyers. However, prospects for meaningful employment for this "new middle class" diminished over time; many of the new professionals could not find employment or simply withered away in state-sector jobs where their talents were underutilized. Land reforms did not improve the lot of peasants, but instead forced many of them to migrate to already overcrowded cities, where they ended up in shantytowns. Legal reforms did not ensure the rule of law or put an end to corruption; instead, they became the principle means by which to deprive civil society of independent expression.

Meanwhile, the rhetoric of "progress" that accompanied efforts at modernization produced high expectations among people. Many state regimes sought legitimacy by promoting grandiose national projects that promised to raise the living standards of ordinary people and combat poverty, inequality, and exploitation associated with preindependence years. Thus, many people came to believe that hard work and education could result in a better life for themselves and their children. This talk of progress resulted in a rapid increase in urbanization, as many peasants flocked to cities expecting to benefit from modern education and employment. As time passed, however, it became apparent that the attempt at state-led development in Muslim societies disproportionately benefited a well-positioned few while leaving many with unfulfilled expectations and broken promises.

This failure to meet the rising expectations of ordinary people and the crude emulation of Western lifestyles resulted in feelings of generalized discontent and alienation, creating an opportunity for Islamic movements to step forward as untainted critics of secularism and excessive Westernization. Islamists did not just offer a critique of existing social arrangements;

they also advanced social and charitable projects, presenting a tangible alternative to secular governments. In Egypt, for instance, Islamic groups in impoverished neighborhoods organized food distribution to families during the holidays. In Algeria, Islamists organized "free" mosques to circumvent sermons approved by secular state officials. In almost every Muslim country, Islamic activists sought to compete with leftists and nationalists over the vision and direction of their societies. Underlying this Islamic challenge was a genuine cultural shift toward greater religiosity in everyday living. Women donned their headscarves and men grew their beards. Muslims began to purchase books on Islam, Islamic history, and contemporary figures of Islamic revivalism. The spread of heightened Islamic consciousness created a cultural opportunity for politicizing religion and demanding a "return to Islam." Islamic groups began to organize around political issues and, when possible, formed parties in order to challenge the hold of secular nationalists on government. Their ultimate aim was to establish governments bound by Islamic law (*sharia*).[3]

The resurgence of Islamic movements as serious competitors in the political process has put many regimes on the defensive. Many sought to harness the political energy of Islamic activists in order to balance against internal opposition forces. However, they soon came to realize that Islamic movements have a momentum of their own that could bring them to rule over the state, either through elections—as in Algeria and Turkey—or by force, as in Iran and Afghanistan. Many state regimes have sought to discover through trial and error a formula with which to counter the "threat" posed to their rule by Islamic opposition forces. Some have chosen a strategy of unmitigated repression (for example, Tunisia since 1990, Algeria since 1992, and Syria in 1982). Others, such as Jordan, Indonesia, Malaysia and Pakistan, have opted for formal inclusion. Still others have chosen a mixed strategy of toleration and repression (for example, Turkey since the 1970s, Egypt during the 1980s, and Morocco since the 1990s). It is safe to say that none of these state strategies has produced consistent results. In Tunisia and Syria, repression effectively eliminated the Islamic opposition; in Algeria, repression intensified its resolve and led to violent rebellions. In Indonesia and Malaysia, political incorporation appears to have placated the Islamists; in the Sudan and Pakistan, inclusion gave them prominence without necessarily lessening their determination to Islamize society. In Morocco and Turkey, a strategy of partial toleration and repression appears to have succeeded in keeping Islamic groups in line; in Egypt, this mixed strategy has failed to prevent Islamic terrorism.[4]

Although the reactions of governments to Islamic politics have varied between accommodation and exclusion, or co-optation and repression, nearly all sought to maneuver in order to avoid ceding real power to Islamic opposition movements in the system. In other words, governments that were increasingly viewed by a large segment of the public as corrupt, illegitimate, and ineffectual in running state affairs did not seek to implement reforms to end the crises posed by their rule. Instead, they engaged in legal and institutional machinations to provide Islamic opposition forces with procedural access to institutional politics but simultaneously sought to deny them (and any opposition for that matter) substantive influence in the political process. This circumscribed inclusion resulted in two dynamics that ultimately contributed to mass Islamic rebellions in some of these societies.

The first dynamic was the expansion of Islamic networks and legitimacy in society, which generated material and political resources for the Islamic opposition which could be mobilized for rebellion. The policy of partial inclusion allowed Islamists to grow in strength and popularize their message, which meant that they had societal and organizational resources with which to fight state repression and political exclusion. The second dynamic was the delegitimation of moderate Islamic strategies. While Islamic forces were growing in strength, their ability to affect change through conventional channels of politics was hindered by regimes that consolidated power in few institutions that were outside of the reach of Islamists. Thus, moderates who wanted to work within the system were constantly frustrated by their inability to exert power. More dangerously, their radical critics pointed out their futility in implementing reforms through conventional political processes. As a result, radical strategies became more appealing to the broader Islamic movement. To understand the impact of these two dynamics on Islamic movement contention, the following section of this chapter will chart the links among political exclusion, state repression, and violent rebellion in Algeria and Egypt, two countries that witnessed persistent patterns of political violence during the 1990s.

Exclusion, Repression, and Rebellion: The Cases of Algeria and Egypt

The contemporary Islamic movements in Algeria and Egypt were forged during the 1970s and 1980s. Like all social movements, Islamic movements in Algeria and Egypt represented various tendencies ranging from apolitical social reformers to violent ideologues and extremists. Overall, however, Islamic movements in both countries did not emerge as radical projects bent on the revolutionary overthrow of secular states or violent destruction of secular societies. On the contrary, the prevailing tendency was oriented toward the gradual redirection of Muslims into a "more Islamic" path and competition with Marxist and nationalist thought, particularly on university campuses.[5] The relative quiescence of Islamic movements in Algeria and Egypt during the 1970s and 1980s can be observed in their pattern of relative nonmilitancy, especially when compared to the 1990s. As Figure 6.1 indicates, Islamists in Algeria and Egypt rarely engaged in extra-institutional

Figure 6.1
Islamist Activism in Algeria and Egypt, 1970–2001
(Demonstrations, Clashes, Assassinations, Bombings, and Massacres)

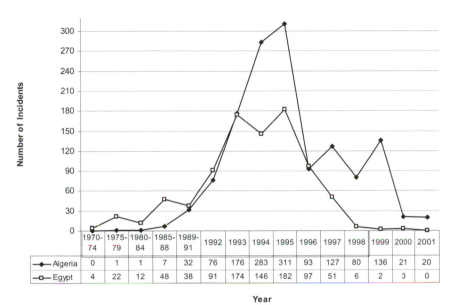

	1970-74	1975-79	1980-84	1985-88	1989-91	1992	1993	1994	1995	1996	1997	1998	1999	2000	2001
Algeria	0	1	1	7	32	76	176	283	311	93	127	80	136	21	20
Egypt	4	22	12	48	38	91	174	146	182	97	51	6	2	3	0

Year

mobilization against the state during the formative phases of their movements.

To be sure, armed Islamic groups did emerge during this time in both
countries. In Algeria, the *Mouvement Algérien Islamique Armée*, better
known as the Bouyali group, began to take organizational form in 1982
after a merger of several smaller groups under the leadership of Mustapha
Bouyali. Although this group did muster the support of approximately 600
activists (mainly south of Algiers), it never posed a serious challenge to the
Algerian state and was largely shunned by other Islamists and preachers at
the time.[6] In Egypt, the 1970s witnessed the rise of several radical groups,
including *Jama'it al-Muslimun* (The Society of Muslims) and *Shabab
Muhammad* (Muhammad's Youth). Both of these organizations adopted a
distinctively radical ideology and went as far as to engage in violent activities against the state. However, their violence was limited to a few note-
worthy incidents, and both quickly succumbed to state repression.[7]

During the 1980s and early 1990s, Islamic extra-institutional militancy
and violent activities increased in both countries, but remained well below
the level of mass rebellion. In Algeria, the relative quiescence of the Islamic
movement during the early 1980s was shattered by a series of mainly peace-

ful demonstrations and rallies that brought together thousands of Islamists from 1989 to 1991. These public mobilizations were largely intended to popularize the message of an emerging Islamic party and to illustrate the power of Islamic organizing in the context of electoral campaigns. In Egypt, violence marked the first two years of the 1980s. The most prominent incident of antistate violence, of course, is the assassination of President Anwar Sadat in October 1981. The expansion in violence coincided with the radicalization of some of the Upper Egypt Islamic students organized around *al-Jama'a al-Islamiyya* (henceforth the *Jama'a*), many of whom took up a revolutionary strategy by merging forces with an incipient radical organization called *al-Jihad*.[8] Despite the noticeable increase in Islamic militancy during the first two years of the 1980s, the Egyptian Islamic movement did not turn to sustained insurgency, as evinced by the relatively limited and sporadic violence in the years 1982–1986. Islamic militancy reemerged between 1986 and 1991. Much of the violence was carried out by the *Jama'a* and struck at "soft" targets, such as musical festivals, weddings, cinemas, and churches, as well as any individual perceived to be engaging in "sin." This was not revolutionary violence intent on toppling the state.

Patterns of violence significantly changed in 1992, the year that ushered in Islamic rebellions in both Algeria and Egypt. In Algeria, the prevailing strategy of the movement from 1992 to 1997 was armed insurgency. Initially, this armed struggle took the form of dispersed and unorganized clashes with security forces. Over the course of time, insurgents organized themselves into numerous armed groups, the two most prominent of which were the *Groupe Islamique Armé* (GIA or Armed Islamic Group) and *Armée Islamique du Salut* (AIS or Islamic Salvation Army). The latter officially gave up its insurgency in 1997 and disarmed its cadres in 1999. The former has split into numerous groups, including the Salafist Group for Preaching and Combat (GSPC). The GSPC was formed by a former GIA commander who broke with the group in 1996 after accusing it of spilling the blood of innocent people, raping women, and pilfering property. The GSPC differentiates itself from the GIA by only targeting soldiers and security forces mainly around east Algeria and by 1999 had replaced the GIA as the leading armed group with approximately 1,200 to 1,500 armed insurgents. It refused to abide by the AIS cease-fire called in 1997 or any other peace efforts that followed, resulting in continuing violence to this day.[9] The insurgency in Algeria resulted in over 100,000 deaths and injuries, while Egypt witnessed a total of 741 incidents of violence between 1992 and 1997, resulting in 1,442 deaths and 1,779 injuries. This violence was overwhelmingly the work of the *Jama'a*; the *Jihad* group played a minor role in the insurgency, while the Muslim Brotherhood (MB) shunned violence altogether.[10] The insurgency came to an end in 1997 after the *Jama'a* declared a ceasefire.

In sum, the contemporary Algerian and Egyptian Islamic movements that emerged in the 1970s and 1980s were not "naturally" radical movements bent on violent rebellion. Proponents of revolutionary violence were a small part of a broader social movement. It was only in 1992 that militancy became more prominent in Algeria's and Egypt's Islamic movements.

Exclusion, Repression, and Rebellion in Algeria

In 1989, Algeria's President Chadli Benjedid embarked on major political and institutional reforms in the aftermath of the October 1988 riots, which protested deteriorating living conditions and rampant government corruption. It was widely believed that institutional reforms were a way to absorb the anger of the public over economic mismanagement. These reforms began with the announcement that the National Liberation Front (FLN), which had ruled Algeria as the sole legitimate party since independence in 1962, would no longer directly manage the state, oversee elections, or appoint candidates. The 1989 constitution gave the right to form political parties, thus officially abandoning one-party rule.[11] These reforms, among others, signaled a significant opening in the system and appeared to have ushered in a new era in Algeria.

Islamists took advantage of nearly every aspect of institutional and political openness. In March 1989, Islamist came together to form the *Front Islamique du Salut* (FIS) as a political party. Although the FIS was a political party that sought to work within the system, it was also a populist movement that organized rallies, marches, and demonstrations to highlight its demands and exhibit its popularity to the larger public. Its rallies and demonstrations easily mobilized thousands of supporters, and at times brought out hundreds of thousands. Led by Abassi Madani and Ali Belhaj, two Islamic activists who gained notoriety during the 1980s, the FIS presented the public with two faces, one moderate and the other radical. Abassi sought to reassure the public of FIS's good intentions and intrinsically moderate message, particularly when it came to issues of democracy and individual liberties. Although Abassi declared his preference for *al-shura* (Islamic tradition of consultation) over democracy, he defined the former as a system that permits freedom of expression, encourages self-criticism and accountability, and precludes political monopoly. In contrast to those who argue that "only God legislates," Abassi maintained that "it is the people that rule, and no government should exist without the will of the people; Islamists are not enemies of democracy."[12] However, his deputy Ali Belhaj did not hesitate to give fiery speeches in which he denounced democracy, the state, and opponents in vitriolic terms. Belhaj declared that democracy is "an un-Islamic institution," and that any victory for Islamists through the polls would be "not a victory for democracy but a victory for Islam."[13]

The radical rhetoric and populist militancy of the FIS may not have been wise, but it was not a revolutionary party bent on taking state power at any cost. A closer examination of the period 1989–91 indicates the extent to which the FIS was willing to accommodate the state and limit its militancy to remain a legitimate actor in the political process. The FIS participated in local government elections as a political party, winning the majority of communal and departmental assemblies. The success of the FIS led to major electoral reforms prior to the national elections that were intended to gerrymander voting districts to give greater representation to southern regions of Algeria, where the FLN was likely to dominate. As a result, the FIS called for a peaceful general strike in May 1991 to ensure that the democratic process was not sabotaged by the ruling regime. On the first day of the strike, organizers with loudspeakers urged supporters to avoid any violence even in self-defense or in response to provocation.[14] During the strike, the FIS maintained constant contact with government mediators and negotiated an agreement with the Prime Minister to peacefully occupy the capital squares. When Ahmed Ghozali, the new Prime Minister, took over he negotiated an end to the demonstrations. An escalation in violence and rhetoric came after security forces began arresting mainstream FIS activists. This prompted Abassi and Belhaj to declare their willingness to confront the regime with force if it did not cease its arrests and provocations against the party. As a result, both Abassi and Belhaj were arrested.[15]

After the arrest of its principal leaders, the FIS took measures to ensure it remained a legitimate actor in the system. In July 1991 it held a conference to sort out its strategy. At least three tendencies emerged during the conference. One group, led by Said Gushi, a founding member of the FIS, believed that Algeria was not ripe for an Islamic state. Therefore, the FIS should not seek to rule but instead should limit itself to a secondary role of preaching. Another group led by the radicals Said Mekhloufi and Qameredin Kharban wanted to boycott the elections and exert pressure on the regime to release FIS leaders and repeal the biased electoral laws through mass mobilization. This group believed that the FIS controlled the street and, therefore, could flex its muscles in the face of the regime. The third group, led by Abdelkader Hachani, did not want the withdrawal of the FIS from the political arena or a boycott of the elections. Instead, it wanted to continue with the electoral path but was uncertain of the appropriate course of action to take. Hachani's immediate objective was to expand the membership of the FIS consultative council to counter the influence of the Gushi group and quiet the radical elements that threatened to unleash repression against the organization.

Hachani succeeded in raising the number of members from thirty-eight to fifty. Many of the new members were not part of the FIS founding committees. The FIS froze the membership of five consultative council members, including Mekhloufi and Kharban, and it issued a public communiqué announcing its decision, thus signaling to the regime that it will not tolerate those who advocate militancy and violence.[16] The new FIS provisional leader Hachani moderated the tone of the party and did not organize rallies until it was made legal to do so again. When armed Islamists outside of the FIS killed three policemen in November 1991 in an attack on a border post, the FIS was quick to distance itself from the attack and condemned it. Finally, although the FIS publicly declared its intention to boycott the national elections scheduled for December 1991, it prepared for them all along and participated in them. According to FIS leader Rabeh Kebir, Hachani wanted to stay on the electoral path all along. However, the FIS wanted to "deflect the attention of the regime to the possibility of our non-participation as we gathered our ranks and prepared for the elections and determined the nominees."[17] The FIS won 188 out of 430 national assembly seats in the first round of the elections and was poised to win an overwhelming majority of seats in the second round of voting. However, at this point the military stepped in to stop the electoral process.

The military did not just seek to deny the FIS the ability to dominate the national assembly; it sought to exclude the party from politics altogether. After the dissolution of the national assembly and cancellation of the elections, the military regime declared a state of emergency, suspended the FIS, and closed down its headquarters. In March, the FIS was formally dissolved, and this decision was confirmed by the Supreme Court the following month. In July, a military court sentenced Abassi and Belhaj to twelve years in prison. In November, the state empowered authorities to close down charitable and cultural organizations associated with the FIS, and more than 300 councils controlled by the FIS were dissolved.

The military unleashed a campaign of repression after three years of Islamic organizing and mobilization, which culminated with a near landslide victory for the Islamic party. In those three years, Islamists organized social services—medical clinics, youth clubs, and market cooperatives—that allowed activists to regularly work together. It also put them directly in touch with their communities, which facilitated the development of links with potential recruits. As one observer put it, "At its height the FIS could mobilize hundreds of thousands of people in the space of a few hours."[18] These links also meant that Islamists could draw political and material support from their communities in times of need. After extending Islamists the right to form political parties and giving them space for mass mobilization in the early 1990s, the state applied an undifferentiated policy of repression. Thus, by the time repression came in 1992, Islamists had much to lose if they did not fight back and, more importantly, they had organizational resources and popular legitimacy with which to resist repression.

Following the coup, many FIS activists began to clash with security forces all over the country. Initially these clashes were spontaneous expressions of anger, but shortly thereafter they became premeditated attacks against police stations and individual security officers. More significantly, Islamists organized militias and began to hold meetings to unify the ranks of the emerging armed movement. The armed movement initially coalesced around the radical groups that opted to stay outside of the FIS apparatus from 1989 to 1991. The newly formed GIA succeeded in significantly expanding its ranks in the aftermath of the coup.[19] The radicals appeared to have been right all along in their assessment of the electoral process and the Algerian regime. Their argument had always been that to establish an Islamic state, Islamists must prepare for jihad. However, whereas opponents of revolutionary violence within the FIS could successfully argue that the electoral option made jihad unnecessary, it could not credibly do so after the coup. As former FLN leader Abdelhamid Mehri explains, "When the [electoral] experiment was aborted, it boosted the extremist wing that claimed that democracy is a game in the hands of the regime, and the regime will cancel democracy if it is not in its interest."[20]

The military regime had a combined strategy of political repression of the FIS and dialogue with other political parties and civic associations, in an effort to establish legitimacy for the coup. In October 1993, the Commission on National Dialogue was established to organize a National Reconciliation Conference, which was intended to bring Algeria's political parties together to arrive at a consensus. In May 1994, a new quasi-parliamentary body, the National Transition Council, was created, consisting of 175 seats to be filled by state-appointed representatives of political parties, professional associations, and trade unions, but excluding the FIS. However, all these efforts failed to win the military regime the legitimacy it was seeking, principally because the major secular parties refused to recognize the authority of the new institutions. Instead, they called for the reinstatement of the electoral process and inclusion of the FIS in national dialogue.[21]

The political marginalization of the FIS—which was willing to play by the rules of electoral politics—and the indiscriminate repression of the state created fertile ground for political violence. The rebellion of Algerian Islamists in 1992 was not inevitable. While the FIS engaged in radical rhetoric prior to 1992, it was not a violently insurgent movement bent on revolution. Political exclusion of Islamists from 1992 to 1997 was the main impetus for mass revolt. The FIS justified its jihad strictly in terms of fighting for the people's right to choose their representatives. In an open letter addressed to all Algerians, Madani Mezraq, the national commander of the AIS, argued that "the youth had no choice but resisting the aggressors and fighting for the sake of regaining the rights of the oppressed."[22] Responding to charges of terrorism, Rabeh Kebir rhetorically asked,

Who is the bearer of violence that must be condemned? Is it not the military tyranny that violated the constitution and trampled on the law and pursued state terrorism? Did the Islamic Salvation Front not enter elections twice in a legitimate manner . . . and not rely on any violence?[23]

Even the undemocratic and uncompromising Ali Belhaj points to the 1992 coup as the real cause of violence. In one of the letters issued from his prison cell, he eloquently sums up the impact of institutional exclusion and repression on the Algeria Islamist movement:

> We made a promise to ourselves to proceed on the peaceful path in our political struggle to reach power as long as the regime abided by that path. Our goal is the creation of an Islamic state according to the choice of the Muslim Algerian people and through the ballot box. . . . But as soon as the [FIS] won, the tyrannical regime launched a coup against the choice of the people, stopped the electoral course, and opened concentration camps and prisons for the innocent.[24]

Exclusion, Repression, and Rebellion in Egypt

Similar to Algeria, the Islamist revolt in Egypt was partly a response to the politics of exclusion that served to delegitimize the ruling regime and the moderate Islamists who insisted on working through state institutions. After a period of institutional openness, the Egyptian ruling regime embarked on a policy of deliberalization in the early 1990s, which contributed—at least in part—to the legitimization of Islamic violence. During the mid-1980s, in an effort to shore up its legitimacy, the regime of Hosni Mubarak permitted political liberalization, which included allowing Islamists to play an indirect role in electoral politics. The most notable measure of liberalization was the expansion of opposition forces in the National Assembly. Whereas in the 1979 People's Assembly only thirty-two out of 372 seats went to the opposition (almost 9%), in 1984 the opposition won fifty-eight seats out of 448 (almost 13%), and in the 1987 elections it won 100 out of 458 seats—a little more than 22 percent.

More importantly, during those years the state allowed the participation of the Muslim Brotherhood (MB) in parliamentary and local government elections. The MB was not given the status of a party, but it was able to form alliances with legal opposition parties, including the secular *New Wafd* in 1984 and the Labor and Liberal Parties in 1987.[25] In 1984, the MB won eight seats, while in the 1987 election it took thirty-six seats, making it the leading opposition force in parliament. In exchange for this access to the political process, the MB consistently and unequivocally reaffirmed its commitment to pluralism, gradualism, and nonviolence. The MB was in the forefront of challenging the ruling party and government through parliamentary questioning of state ministers. It also insisted on the application of Islamic law, and it was relentless in demanding respect for democratic freedoms and human rights, an end to mass arrests and torture in detention centers, and electoral reforms to ensure a fair and effective democratic process.[26]

In parliament, the MB was able to push through a number of reforms such as expanding religious content in the education curriculum, increasing the hours of religious programming on radio and television, and censoring materials deemed inappropriate for television.[27] However, the MB made it a point not to question the legitimacy of President Mubarak or his ability to rule. As a matter of fact, the MB supported the renomination of Mubarak for president in 1987. Their criticism, instead, targeted the ruling party and government ministers, as well as particular policies. The MB justified its use of the parliamentary arena on the grounds that it allowed it to disseminate its message and influence the rulers of Egypt.

However, mere formal inclusion of Islamists in the political system during the 1980s did not placate the radicals, who came to view the MB as an instrument of the regime. Aboud Zumur, the leader of the Jihad Organization, chided the MB for failing to secure a political party, pointing out that "whereas France, Germany, and Italy permit the formation of a religious party, Egypt is proud of the fact it does not permit such a party."[28] The *Jama'a* rejected the path of political accommodation and opted to organize a social movement based on a loosely structured network of social organizations. It believed that the Islamic state must be created through a revolutionary Islamic mass movement, and pursued a dual strategy of social reformism and direct militant action to build such a movement. Over time, the *Jama'a* developed a network of mosques through which it established social services to aid the poor and cultivate the legitimacy of the group in towns and villages.[29] The *Jama'a* was able to establish "liberated zones" in some of the towns of Upper Egypt and Greater Cairo. It controlled hundreds of mosques and organized social welfare services out of them to help their impoverished communities. These activities included distributing meat and rice during religious holidays and providing school supplies and clothing to poor families at the beginning of each school year. They also set up "reconciliation committees" to mediate conflict in neighborhoods on the basis of Islamic laws. These activities were known to the local authorities because the *Jama'a* made it a point to publicize them, in order to increase its legitimacy among the people.[30] As a result of its efforts, the group expanded its ranks in Asyut, al-Minya, Beni Swayf, Souhaj, Qina, Aswan, Imbaba, Ain Shems, Boulaq al-Dikrour, and al-Amraniya.

The *Jama'a* believed that direct militant action was justified by the Islamic precept of "commanding the good and prohibiting the forbidden." Such actions included the disruption of musical festivals and wedding ceremonies, destroying video clubs, attacking beer deliveries and bars, and segregating men and women in the universities and the neighborhoods. These actions went largely unpunished by the local authorities or national government as long as Islamists limited their activities to Upper Egypt. Despite its antistate rhetoric, the *Jama'a* did not launch any notable attacks on the state during the 1980s. Instead, much of its violence was directed at "soft" targets. Thus, by the end of the 1980s, the Islamic movement was divided between an accommodative wing led by the MB—which was eager to play a political role through the heavily circumscribed institutional channels of the state—and a marginal radical wing led by the *Jama'a*, which was concentrated in the towns and villages of Upper Egypt and some of the suburbs of Greater Cairo.

In the early 1990s, the Egyptian regime realized that its policy of partial inclusion of Islamists was not bearing fruit. The MB had been growing in strength, especially among professional associations, while the radicals were expanding their mobilization capacity. The ruling regime thus reversed its policies by merging all Islamists into one category of "subversives." The MB faced greater restriction on its ability to play even a limited role in the political arena. The 1990s began with the state issuing electoral Law 206 of 1990—to replace Law 188, which was deemed unconstitutional by the Supreme Court—in essence redrawing (or gerrymandering) the voting districts in such a blatantly unfair way as to privilege the ruling National Democratic Party (NDP).[31] In protest, the opposition—including the MB—decided to boycott the 1990 parliamentary elections. As a result, in 1990 only seven seats (less than 2%) went to the official opposition. The 1990 parliament was thus proportionally less representative of the opposition than the 1979 one, which had allotted the opposition almost 9 percent of the seats.

The 1995 elections resulted in a comparable outcome, but for entirely different reasons. First, the opposition—including the MB—did not boycott the 1995 elections. However, prior to both rounds of the election, the state carried out a wave of arrests against hundreds of MB representatives and cadres, in order to prevent them from running an effective campaign; indeed, to block them from putting forward candidates altogether. Days before the election, the state sentenced fifty-four leading MB members to prison terms ranging from three to five years. As a result, only one of the 150 MB candidates made it to the People's Assembly, and he was removed in 1996 for being a member of an illegal organization. The 1995 parliament thus had only had sixteen representatives of the opposition, less than 3 percent. In other words, the political opposition was less represented in parliament during the 1990s than it had been during the 1980s.[32]

The exclusion of the MB was not limited to only the institutional and professional arenas. In 1993, the authorities began to impose restrictions on the MB's participation in professional syndicates, effectively closing some of them down under the pretext of reforming their election bylaws. In that year, President Mubarak called for a National Dialogue, which convened in July 1994. However, the MB and other Islamic organizations were not allowed to participate, due to their illegal status. During this period, the state began to harass midlevel MB cadres and leaders through periodic arrests and internment, on the grounds that they belonged to an unlawful organization.[33]

The stagnation of institutional politics and exclusion of the MB in the early and mid-1990s appeared to secure the revolutionary convictions of the radicals: Islamists cannot advance their cause through institutional channels. In one communiqué, the *Jama'a* rhetorically asked, "What has the Muslim Brotherhood, since its inception until now, achieved of the goals and objectives of Islam, the hopes and needs of the Muslims, and the tasks and requirements of the age?" It added, "What is astonishing is that every time the MB rushes to issue its statements of moral condemnation, denunciation, and disavowal of all that is jihad—it calls it terrorism—the more the government redoubles its constraints against it and strikes it nonstop."[34] Talat Fouad Qasim, one of the prominent leaders of the *Jama'a*, rejected MB's parliamentary strategy on the following grounds: "We view the regime's confrontation with the Islamists as one of stages: at first comes (the confrontation with) the *Jama'a al-Islamiyya*, and then comes the turn of the MB. [The regime] will not permit it to enjoy its seats in parliament and in the syndicates."[35] The Jihad Organization criticized the MB strategy on similar grounds, noting in its publication *al-Mujahideen* (The Holy Fighters) that

> all the peacefulness and gradualism upheld by the [Muslim] Brothers during their political struggles, and their work through the regime's legitimate, legal channels did not save them from being handcuffed, tried in front of military courts, and dragged to prisons. All the while, their preachers declare that they will not be provoked and will not attempt confrontation.[36]

In sum, the institutional exclusion and growing harassment of Islamists by the state, especially those who advocated working through the system, gave credence to the claims of radicals.

Political exclusion was accompanied by indiscriminate repression, resulting in a widening cycle of violence. In 1990, the state assassinated Ala Muhyi al-Din, the official spokesman of the *Jama'a*, which led the group to form an armed wing. The *Jama'a* assassinated Rifat al-Mahjoub, former speaker of parliament, in retaliation for the killing of Muhyi al-Din. This assassination led the state to carryout a massive sweep in Asyut, Cairo, and Beni Swayf, which resulted in thousands of arrests. The crackdown on Islamists, however, did not fully develop until mid- and late 1992, two years after the initial crackdown and six years since the resurgence of radical Islamic organizing in 1986. Three events appear to have initiated the nationwide crackdown: the March 1992 clash between Muslims and Christians in Manshiyat Nasir in Upper Egypt, where at least thirteen people were killed; the assassination of the prominent secular intellectual Faraj Fuda in June 1992; and the attacks on tourists that began in June 1992. In May 1992 the state deployed approximately 2,000 soldiers in the Asyut district of Dairut to impose a curfew, following a series of demonstrations and clashes between Islamists and the police. In December 1992 the state sent approximately 16,000 soldiers to "liberate" Imbaba in Greater Cairo. In January 1993, 8,000 soldiers participated in searches for Islamists in Masarah, Dairut, Sanaba, Manshiyat Nasir, and Dairut al-Sharif. In April 1993, an additional force of 5,000 soldiers was deployed in Asyut.

State repression encompassed not only the hardcore militants of the *Jama'a*; it also included their supporters, families, and anyone suspected of harboring Islamic tendencies.[37] The number of people arrested during the 1990s, especially when compared to the late 1980s, indicates that the state cast its net widely.[38] Between 1992 and 1997, more than 47,000 people were arrested, a number that is surely greater than the number of active Islamic militants throughout Egypt. In addition to mass arrests, the authorities began to engage in "hostage taking," whereby the relatives—especially the wives—of suspected militants were detained until the latter turned themselves in to the authorities.[39] Those arrested were regularly mistreated and, worse, tortured. The fact that repression was reactive meant that radical Islamists had an added incentive to defend the material and organizational resources they had accumulated during the 1980s. As the documents and statements of *Jama'a* activists indicate, its branches began their struggle against the state not as an attempt to topple the regime, but as a way to stop mass arrests, torture, and the takeover of private mosques.[40] The lack of credible legal and institutional avenues for political contestation meant that Islamists had two options: succumb to repression or fight back to preserve the gains of their movement. They opted to rebel.

Implications for Counterterrorism in the Muslim World

The attacks of September 11, 2001, on the United States, and the subsequent wars on terrorism and Iraq, have brought to the forefront the perennial debate about the desirability and feasibility of democracy in the Muslim world. The official policy of Western governments is that democracy is urgently needed in the Muslim world and offers a potential solution to the protracted conflicts and terrorism stemming from that part of the globe. The questions are, what type of democracy should this be, and is there a place for Islamic movements in it? The Western camp is divided between the accommodationists, who want to include Islamists in the political process, and the confrontationalists, who see Islamists as a threat to democratization.[41] To the accommodationists, the inclusion of Islamists—based on a political pact that delineates the parameters of proper political conduct—could lead to moderation, pragmatism and, ultimately, a genuine democratic process.[42] To the confrontationalists, the inclusion of Islamists—who are inherently antidemocratic and deeply anti-Western—could lead to theocracy, regional instability, and international terrorism.

This chapter has argued that the choice between moderation and violence in Islamic movements during a democratization process is shaped by state policies, especially the degree of system accessibility and the nature of state repression. If the democratic process grants Islamists substantive access to state institutions, the opposition will be channeled toward conventional political participation and shun violence. If, on the other hand, the state denies Islamists access and if the state applies repression indiscriminately—punishing both moderate and radical proponents of political opposition—Islamists will be channeled toward militancy. Further, this likelihood increases if repression is applied after an extended period of Islamic mobilization.

The cases of Algeria and Egypt demonstrate that when Muslims encounter institutional exclusion and indiscriminate repression they are likely to rebel. In Algeria, Islamists rebelled after the military cancelled elections, banned the most prominent Islamic party (the FIS) and arrested thousands of its supporters *en masse*. Thereafter, the state engaged in a brutal campaign of repression that entailed extrajudicial killings, disappearances, and torture. Repression came after two years of mobilizing and organizing supporters for electoral participation. In Egypt, insurgency broke out during a period of political deliberalization and after the state made the crucial decision to dismantle (with brute force) loosely-structured networks of radical Islamists in Upper Egypt. After allowing militants to organize on the periphery of Egyptian society during the 1980s, the authorities sought to crush the *Jama'a* during the early 1990s. Repression in the context of political exclusion gave legitimacy to violent strategies. Even the peaceful Muslim Brotherhood movement encountered greater restrictions on its conduct during the 1990s, despite its unequivocal denunciation of militant violence. Similar to the Algerian military, the Egyptian government provided few avenues for nonmilitant forms of contention; it effectively channeled the opposition toward rebellion.

Recent history from the Muslim world suggests that a number of Islamic movements and governments have internalized some of Algeria's and Egypt's lessons. During the 2002 parliamentary elections in Morocco, the Islamic-oriented Party of Justice and Development refrained from making overtly religious rhetoric, avoided threatening declarations against the established order or secular parties, and went so far as to limit the number of parliamentary candidates in order to avoid an overwhelming victory that could possibly frighten the ruling regime. In Turkey, also in 2002, the Islamic-leaning Justice and Development Party adapted its political rhetoric and programs to Turkey's constitutional constraints on overt Islamic mobilization in the political process. Thus, governments in both Morocco and Turkey have allowed Islamists to participate in institutional politics. For their part, Islamists have learned to negotiate the boundaries of their political systems. The Moroccan and Turkish models are far from perfect, but they are feasible given the precariousness of transitioning from authoritarianism to democracy in a world where democratic ideals and advocates are sparse. Institutional inclusion and a policy of selective repression facilitate political institutionalization of Islamists. The success or failure of democratization in the Muslim world will likely depend, at least in part, on astute leaders—both within the state and the Islamic opposition—who have studied and taken to heart the lessons of Algeria and Egypt.

CHAPTER 7

Rejection of Political Institutions by Right-Wing Extremists in the United States

EUGENIA K. GUILMARTIN

Anthony Russo, editor of a New York right-wing journal, was shot in late 2004 when he threatened police with a rifle following a low-speed police chase. According to the journalist who had followed Russo's rise and fall as a local right-wing militia leader, Russo's behavior was as much the result of personal and economic stresses as any extreme political belief:

> It wasn't the fear of a UN invasion, a feud with local politicians or an allergic reaction to a conspiracy that propelled Anthony Russo into the confrontation . . . what dogged him the past few months were the same worries that consume lots of people: A loan company wanted to foreclose on his house. There was a breakup with a woman. At sixty-four, blind in one eye and financially destitute, Russo was alone.[1]

What distinguished Russo from any other person down on his luck was a reputation for being a hostile neighbor, serving citizens with bogus legal papers for trespassing, proclaiming himself a common-law "sheriff," and suing local police for $45 million for violating his civil rights during a traffic stop related to unlicensed driving (a red-flag offense for the "no government identification" crowd). Even his closest neighbors feared him.

This chapter examines the volatile combination of a bullying personality and personal and economic grievances that lead some Americans like Russo to engage in confrontational right-wing activities. The discussion begins with a brief look at the ideology of the extreme right-wing in America, followed by a description of the right-wing groups most commonly found in the United States. This is followed by an examination of personal characteristics—particularly a heightened focus on certain grievances and the rejection of political institutions—which seem most common among right-wing extremists and domestic terrorists. Next, the chapter provides an example of a local extremist, engaged in low-level terrorizing activity, who illustrates the type of personality that can be called a "political bully." Finally, this analysis concludes that the combination of ideology, personality, and rejection of commonly respected government institutions plays an important role in the making of a right-wing extremist in America.

Ideology

What does the Far Right believe in? Without the benefit of a party convention or platform, the Far Right has a diverse and decentralized set of ideas about the role of government and where the current federal government goes astray. At its core, if a core exists at all, the ideology generally affirms states' rights, personal property rights, the right to bear arms, opposition to taxes, opposition to world government—a "New World Order"—and, thus, opposition to the United Nations.

These core tenets are not individually exclusive to the Far Right. Many Republicans, and more than a few Democrats, are progun, antitax or anti-United Nations. When sovereign citizen and Army Specialist Michael New took his stand and faced court-martial for not wearing a UN beret in 1995, thirty-three members of the House cosponsored the American Hero Restoration Act to condemn his court-martial and call upon the president to restore New's rank.[2] Similarly, seventy-three Republicans and 6 Democrats of the House cosponsored a bill to prohibit troops from being required to wear UN insignia.[3] However, while elected officials will often support laws favorable to the Far Right, only a few consistently uphold nearly all the tenets of this ideology. Only eight members of Congress have publicly endorsed or been associated with right-wing groups like militias since 1992, making up far less than 1 percent of all national lawmakers this past decade.[4]

These five beliefs—in states' rights, personal property rights, the right to bear arms, opposition to taxes, and opposition to the United Nations—are not individually exclusive to the Far Right, but when bundled together and coupled with a rejection of the mainstream Republican or Democratic parties, they clearly identify an adherent of the Far Right. One would be hard pressed to find a right-wing organization that is antigun (though three creative or confused souls somewhere probably lay claim to this issue). Similarly, one would have to search extensively to find a website that advocates raising the federal income tax rates or increasing U.S. support to the United Nations.

What role do third parties play in right-wing activity? At the ideological level, adherents of the Far Right most agree with either the Libertarian or

Constitution Party, depending on one's social conservatism. Both parties, however, have gone to lengths to distance themselves from more extreme members. The Libertarian Party requires candidates and members to sign an oath "against the initiation of force."[5] Still, Colorado Libertarians discovered in November 2002 that the Denver Police Department kept intelligence files on its members, labeling it a "Militia type organization, pro gun rights."[6] Party officials were outraged, claiming involvement only in ordinary political activity such as fielding candidates, lobbying, and participating in legal demonstrations. The Constitution Party has had greater image problems since the Southern Poverty Law Center (SPLC) began listing it on an annual report of "Patriot Groups." The national chairman told reporters "We don't advocate any kind of violence or militant movement. . . . We're not trying to overthrow the government. We're not a hate group. We don't subscribe to any extreme anti-government doctrine."[7] The editor of the SPLC report, Mark Potok, defends this inclusion based on the Constitution Party's beliefs in conspiracy theories, abolishing bureaucracy, and returning the country to traditional Christian values. Potok admits that 2000 presidential candidate Howard Phillips shoulders most of the responsibility for the "Patriot" tag, since Phillips has alleged associations with neo-Confederate groups.[8] The link between third parties and right-wing criminal activities is unproven. What is more likely is that the hard right, dissatisfied with Republican and Democrat platforms, sees third-party ideas advocated by the Libertarian and Constitution parties as attractive.

Right-Wing Groups

The ideology of the Far Right serves as a rallying point for a wide range of groups. Newspapers, government reports, and law enforcement documents refer to these groups as militias, common-law courts, and tax-protest groups. Their followers are called militiamen and militiawomen, patriots, Freemen, sovereign citizens, tax protesters, survivalists and, less specifically, "extremists." Often these terms are used interchangeably in news stories, leading to inaccuracies. The Oklahoma City bombing, for example, generated initial public interest in militia groups even though Timothy McVeigh, Terry Nichols, and Michael Fortier were not militia members. The inaccuracy seems to have originated with McVeigh's progun beliefs, his sales of extremist literature, and his calls to two right-wing compounds in search of postbombing safe haven. While the men attended a meeting of the Michigan Militia (and by some accounts were kicked out), court records show that Terry Nichols—the man who introduced McVeigh to antigovernmental beliefs—was instead a "sovereign citizen," or one who rejects nearly all government above the county level. In another example, the Bureau of Alcohol, Tobacco, and Firearms assault near Waco, Texas, became an important symbol (to right-wing groups) of an abusive Department of Justice, even though the Branch Davidians themselves were not a right-wing organization. Amassing an arsenal and preparing for the apocalypse is consistent with survivalist tactics, but the Davidians are more accurately described as a religious cult.

Though there is ample confusion in the popular press, enough differences exist to categorize right-wing adherents into general groups of militias, common-law courts, sovereign citizens, tax protesters, and survivalists. These groups do not differ primarily by age, education, income, or level of violence. Instead, groups differ by which political institutions they choose to reject.

Militias reject federal defense forces and are pro–Second Amendment above all, with a military chain of command conducting military training. Their mission is to create citizen defense organizations under the charter of the Second Amendment, which states, "A well regulated Militia, being necessary to the security of a free State, the right of the people to keep and bear Arms, shall not be infringed." Most militias are defensive, training and equipping to protect their communities against federal law enforcement agents, United States military, or foreign soldiers who will invade the United States under the auspices of the "New World Order."

Consistent with their pro–Second Amendment beliefs, many militiamen and women are gun collectors and sportsmen who just happen to have a greater-than-average distrust of the government. Militia of Montana's John Trochmann and Bob Fletcher told the Senate Judiciary Committee Subcommittee on Terrorism, Technology and Government Information on 15 June 1995 that militia members were merely a "giant neighborhood watch."[9] In some cases, law enforcement officials agree.[10] The FBI formally encourages law enforcers to open a dialogue with militia groups that engage only in defensive preparations and are law abiding or have only been suspected of minor property crimes or weapons violations.[11] In other cases, the militia runs afoul of the law. It is no surprise that militia members are arrested on weapons and explosives charges, for buying or selling illegal weapons, for owning destructive devices, or for conspiracy to seize weapons from armories and military installations.[12] The militia is primarily a defensive movement, and an effective defense depends on owning sufficient firepower! In some cases, however, militia members are charged with offensive plots to attack symbols of (in their view) an illegitimate government; examples include the San Joaquin, California, militia's plot to blow up propane tanks for the Millennium, and the Colorado First Light Infantry's plot to destroy federal targets in 1996.[13]

Where militias reject armies, common-law courts reject the courts, creating a parallel judiciary based loosely on British common law, Biblical texts, the *Citizens Rule Book*, and the "organic" Constitution (the original Constitution and the Bill of Rights). Adherents are pro–property rights and antijudiciary, directly challenging laws with a complicated subset of legal and political arguments that have been documented by Bernard Sussman in a legal guide for other attorneys.[14] Common-law courts are offensive rather than defensive. Groups hold their own proceedings, issuing "summonses" and warrants. The state of Minnesota, for example, was embarrassed to find that an alternate "Supreme Court" was holding its proceedings in a government building, and Ohio's Supreme Court Justice met with leaders of a parallel legal body once the common-law courts grew to cover 60 of the 88 of the counties in his state.[15] Common-law advocates are often arrested for impersonating public officials, harassment, obstruction of justice, and filing "bogus" legal documents—a crime in many states crafted specifically to counter their tactics.[16]

Sovereign citizens and "Freemen" like the Montana Freemen and Republic of Texas share the militias' focus on defensive preparations and the common-law courts' belief in active defiance of an unjust government. Unlike militias and common-law courts, sovereign citizens reject nearly all political rules and elected officials rather than establish alternate institutions like armies and courts. The charter of the sovereign citizen is the Posse Comitatus's doctrine of "power of the county," which believes in local control, rejection of legal authority, and a hidden political history.[17] Groups subscribe to the belief that each man or woman is "sovereign" or a free person and is not required to give up individual liberties by registering information like Social Security numbers, license applications, census forms, or public school enrollment. True to their names, sovereign citizens and Freemen withdraw from ordinary political life and operate in their own independent political world. They live in closed communities, resorting to common-law tactics when their members face legitimate authorities. Freemen will print their own money, either bogus checks or "comptroller warrants," claiming assets against political enemies. Consistent with their beliefs, these members of the Far Right will often be charged on multiple counts of driving without a license or registration, filing bogus liens and harassment, and resisting any authority above the level of county sheriff.

Tax protesters share many of the common-law and sovereign citizen rhetoric, since all three trace their organizational lineage to the Posse Comitatus of the 1970s. Tax protesters, however, are issue specific; they selectively reject government taxation, as embodied in the federal and state tax code. Tax protest arguments are varied and creative, but many emphasize that the Sixteenth Amendment was never properly ratified, or that wages are not income, or that only federal employees, residents of Washington, DC, and U.S. territories should be taxed.[18] Tax protesters are normally charged with tax evasion, "frivolous nonfiling," threatening tax collectors, and bogus legal arguments like the previous two groups. Tax protesters are also the most likely of all groups to ensnare ordinary citizens in their schemes.

The State of California, for example, released a public service announcement to warn taxpayers of slave reparation claims by black separatist movements and "De-Taxing" claims by Freemen.[19]

Survivalists sever all ties to political bodies and rules. They do not create alternate institutions, like militias and common-law courts, or make their own rules, like sovereign citizens and tax protesters. Survivalists instead stockpile food and supplies to survive the pending takeover—a worldview that earned them some respect during the Y2K/Millennium scare. Their lifestyle has been described as living "off the grid" without modern electricity or utilities. Survivalists value medical skills, hunting, fishing, marksmanship, food preservation, and home schooling. Survivalists sometimes organize in compounds with other families and share some of the same defensive preparations as the militia. They normally fight only when officials serve warrants or raise their suspicions, like the infamous 1992 Ruby Ridge standoff in Idaho.

Membership in these five subgroups is in no way mutually exclusive. Many people belong to more than one group. Most common-law courts include sovereign citizens, for example, and many survivalists subscribe to militia publications. In a way, the Far Right could be considered one athletic team with both general and specialized players of varying skill, commitment, and endurance. The importance of these distinctions is to understand that groups differ in rejection of political rules and institutions. These variations are summarized in Table 7.1. Militias reject federal defenses, common-law courts reject the judicial system, sovereign citizens reject the bureaucracy and any authority above county level, tax protesters reject revenue collection, and survivalists reject all formal government.

It is important to note that the use of the term "group" suggests a level of organization and size that is often absent from the most dangerous and threatening elements of the right wing. Those who are most receptive to

Table 7.1

Right-Wing Groups Classified by Rejection of Governmental Institutions

Group	Rejected Governmental body	Rejected Political rules
Militias	Defense	—
Common-Law Courts	Judicial	—
Sovereign Citizens	—	Any authority above county level; Any bureaucracy (not elected)
Tax Protesters	—	Federal income tax (sometimes state)
Survivalists	All bodies	All rules

the ultraright are often driven by ideas of "superpatriotism," a sense that the individual knows what is best for society, and a need to command respect. Simply put, these people are "chiefs" without many followers. This helps to explain why the most frightening right-wing groups often break apart, given enough time, while the largest and most stable (commonly the militia), are often benign.

A Key Decision: Rejection of Political Institutions

The first characteristic of one who is likely to engage in right-wing extremist activities is that he rejects the rules of the game. While the media classify the most violent acts against Americans as terrorism, and violence increases the likelihood of media attention, violence is neither necessary nor sufficient for terrorism. Violence without ideological motivation, such as John Hinckley's assassination attempt on President Reagan, is not terrorism, while a bloodless computer virus attack on U.S. government computer networks most surely is terrorism. As described in other chapters of this publication, terrorism is commonly viewed as a tactic used to compel certain types of behavior, including a change in government policies. In the realm of domestic terrorism, the most important force to consider is an individual's (or group's) rejection of political institutions, and what this rejectionism indicates in terms of a propensity for political violence.

However, the same force also compels individuals and groups to engage in activities which, while some may not consider them terrorism, are nonetheless damaging to others within their community and thus deserve more attention. Further, the unfortunate overemphasis (in the media and the scholarly community) on violence and abnormality creates two problems in the study of right-wing extremism. First, it gives an incorrect picture of the phenomenon, and second, it is mere conjecture resulting in persistent puzzles and missed opportunities in the study of American antigovernmental movements. The focus on violence explains why scholars keep searching for a critical mass of powerless and fearful people particularly susceptible to lashing out at perceived enemies and come up short empirically. It explains why they fail to foresee the escalation of violence in situations like the Republic of Texas standoff where previously nonviolent sovereign citizens kidnapped two neighbors and shot at lawmen. It explains why they look for abnormal psyches and stories of personal failure and find instead seemingly ordinary neighbors, family members, and community leaders in the ranks of the hard right.[20]

Adherents of the Far Right, all with antigovernmental beliefs and all dissatisfied with the status quo, differ widely in their choices of political participation. As we already know, some choose violence and some do not. But antigovernmental political action offers another set of choices: partic-

Figure 7.1

Antigovernmental Activity by Rejection of the Political System and Commitment to Violence

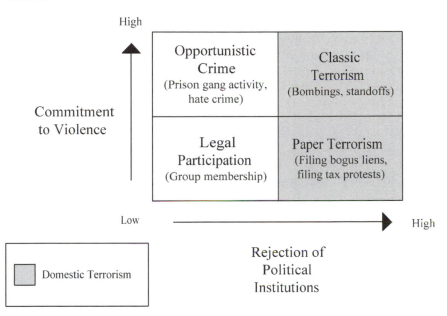

ipate according to the rules of the game or reject them outright. While most of the current research in domestic terrorism explores the violent/nonviolent dimension, it can be argued that varying commitment to political institutions better explains the puzzles surrounding American right-wing terrorist groups. Figure 7.1 thus offers a concept of domestic terrorism which emphasizes the important role played by an individual's (or group's) rejection of political institutions.

From bottom to top, one sees an increasing willingness to use violence. Those who reject violence are in the bottom half; those who are willing to use violent means are in the top half. The second dimension, from left to right, is an increasing willingness to reject political institutions. Those who accept the political system are in the left half, while those who reject the political bodies, rules, and officials are in the right half. From this analysis, it seems clear that those individuals most likely to engage in right-wing extremist activities fit comfortably in the rightmost portion of this figure— among those who reject political rules—regardless of their taste for violence.

These two dimensions create four quadrants with distinctly different patterns of activity. The top left quadrant encompasses those who hold antigovernmental beliefs but are happy to exploit others in the status quo, most notably white supremacist prison gangs.[21] It may seem counterintuitive for someone to employ violence and yet accept the political and legal system. This, however, is the nature of crime; the criminal gains most when others obey the law. An orderly environment is ideal for the predator. Gangs are not terrorists, despite their right-wing beliefs, since their desired end-state is dominance in the status quo, not the overthrow or disruption of government. The bottom left quadrant includes those who accept the rules of the game and express their antigovernmental sentiments legally through group meetings, publications, or radio programs. As offensive or far-fetched as their ideas may be, these adherents are not terrorists. And their very ability to organize, compromise, and peacefully discuss their beliefs makes them very different from the political bullies who run afoul of the law.

The top right quadrant includes those who are violent and reject the rules of the game. This group includes the most familiar cases: Eric Rudolph, McVeigh and associates, the Kehoe family of Washington—the "classic terrorists." The bottom right quadrant represents those who engage in physically nonviolent harassment, including the newer phenomenon of "paper terrorism." These right-wing supporters may not employ violence, presently or ever, but they reject the political rules and organizations that impose order on society. While one may not think of terrorism when a group of Missourians harasses a judge with a $10.8 million lien, this illegal coercion aims to threaten public servants and cripple the government in the same manner as a bomb threat.[22] Both the bomber and the paper terrorist live in the right half of this universe, among those right-wing supporters who reject political institutions—our courts, our laws, our military, and our system of law enforcement—regardless of their use of violence.

This concept of domestic terrorism is more than an exercise in sorting cases and grouping extremists. It has an implications for how one understands terrorist movements. If rejection of political rules is a determining factor in domestic terrorism, then individuals most likely to engage in domestic terrorism will be those who want to be active in their communities, but at the same time are unhappy with mainstream government and participation or are ill suited to work in groups. Likely terrorists will feel tension between wanting to be involved in a group with an important mission, but rejecting existing organizations and activities that might provide an outlet for these desires. If, instead, a predilection for violence is the defining characteristic of a likely terrorist, than at-risk individuals may be those who feel the most frustration, rage, powerlessness, sense of failure or confusion. We would expect to find people with strong emotions seeking an easy outlet.

Extremism and Domestic Terrorists

For several decades, policy makers and law-enforcement officials in the United States have sought a better understanding of personal attributes and

socioeconomic factors that may be related to participation in domestic terrorism. What factors increase the likelihood of unlawful or extreme political activities? Answers to this question have been elusive. Domestic
terrorist attacks are rare, though destructive, limiting research opportunities to only a few hundred observable cases. Domestic terrorism is not state
sponsored and therefore not easily understood in an international policy
context. Economic and social tensions in the United States have been relatively mild compared to those in Latin America, Eastern Europe, and Asia,
leaving perfectly useful theories of civil war and popular revolution with
little explanatory power in studies of American politics. Similarly, psychological theories have been frustrated by the seeming normality of Far-Right
adherents. Sociologist James Aho recalls a colleague leaving his last will
and testament before meeting with Idaho neo-Nazis. No threat material-
ized. The researcher encountered only a "smattering of gray-haired retired
folks, a grandfather-like leader living in comfortable surroundings with his
devoted wife and dogs, and an atmosphere of conviviality and openness."[23]
Elinor Burkett had a similar experience with right-wing women:

> When I went in search of militiawomen, I expected to find Bubba tramping
> through the woods, his wife in tow. Or some semiliterate wackos spouting
> off about black helicopters sent by the United Nations to impose the New
> World Order, while their girlfriends brought them cold beers. But for every
> woman I found flashing a militia membership card because she believed her
> husband . . . I found a dozen . . . terrified about what their children were
> learning in school and about the crime rate in their neighborhoods.[24]

Anecdotes of otherwise normal behavior, however, cannot overshadow the
traits that most distinguish possible terrorists from others: beliefs in bizarre
conspiracies, intolerant tactics, and, most of all, a willingness to break the
law in the name of an ideology.

How do we reconcile illegal terrorist acts with profiles of "normal"
Americans who commit them? Part of the puzzle becomes clearer when we
consider terrorism not just in terms of violence, but also in terms of an active and public rejection of government institutions. While the nature of
terrorism naturally leads social scientists to look for abnormal psychologies and significant personal and professional failure—all contributing to a
predilection for violence—terrorism is as much a function of political participation as it is an outlet for failure, powerlessness, or rage. There is a
central conflict: Terrorists are caught between a call to participate and a
rejection of those mainstream organizations that would otherwise provide
an outlet for these activities.

Biographical sketches of American right-wing leaders provide reason to
believe that violent tendencies are foundational to terrorism.[25] A Who's
Who of the right illustrates the point. Tom Metzger, leader of the White

Aryan Resistance, lost a civil suit in which he was found guilty of supporting men who murdered an Ethiopian man in Portland, Oregon, and faced criminal charges in a vigilante plot against Mexican immigrants. Louis Beam of the Ku Klux Klan was involved in a shootout with authorities in Mexico prior to his extradition to the United States for his role in attacks on Vietnamese fishermen in Galveston Bay. Mark Koernke, former leader of the Michigan Militia, is in jail for aiding fellow militiamen who murdered a disloyal associate. Before his death in 2002, William Pierce of the National Alliance spoke often and publicly of violence against Jews and Black Americans; Pierce's *The Turner Diaries*, written under the pen name Andrew Macdonald, inspired a string of violence by "The Order" during the 1980s, and was a favored reading of terrorists like Timothy McVeigh, Terry Nichols, and Michael Fortier during the 1990s. Clearly, no one would consider Metzger, Beam, Koernke, or Piece to be a model citizen or good neighbor.

The biographical sketches of right-wing leaders are consistent with currents of racism, anti-Semitism, and antipluralism that run throughout right-wing literature. Racism is thinly disguised in positions against immigration, welfare, crime, and affirmative action. Tax protesters and sovereign citizen groups distinguish "sovereign citizens" from minorities who were granted rights in the Thirteenth, Fourteenth, and Fifteenth Amendments. In other cases, racism is overt. Some right-wing adherents greet each other with "Fourteen words"—shorthand for the fourteen-word-long slogan, "We must secure the existence of our people and a future for white children."[26] Pierce's *Hunter* (the sequel to *Turner Diaries*, also published under the pen name Andrew Macdonald) tells the story of a nationwide vigilante mission to kill blacks, interracial couples and other nonwhite Americans.[27]

Anti-Semitic themes are even more prevalent. While savvy groups avoid obvious slurs in newsletters and websites, the key players in the New World Order are clearly Jewish "international bankers," "Northeastern business leaders," and "money lenders." In one of the more shocking anti-Jewish acts of the right, members of The Order killed Denver radio talk show host Alan Berg in 1984. More recently, three young men were arrested in 1999 for placing pipe bombs on the doorstep of a Santa Clara County, California, judge they mistakenly thought to be Jewish.[28]

Finally, the Far Right is known for its antipluralism. Extremists are uncompromising and unwilling to engage in political discussions. Obviously, there is good reason to consider that extremism is rooted in a confrontational predisposition.

Profiles of right-wing leaders, rhetoric, and tactics may emphasize violence and intolerance, but observations of rank-and-file members are not as clear-cut. In most cases, right-wing terrorists are not indiscriminately violent; target selection follows patterns of classic terrorism rather than group violence. An analysis of over 500 cases of crimes in the mid-1990s, for example, shows that only around 14 percent targeted minorities, gays, or Jewish Americans.[29] In all other cases, terrorists selected public officials, government buildings, or other symbolic targets. Even the Ku Klux Klan, the most salient racist organization to most Americans, has shifted missions to attack public officials rather than black Americans. Morris Dees's 1996 study of extremist elites shows that leaders subverted racist and anti-Semitic themes in favor of antigovernmental messages, in order to appeal to a more patriotic and rights-conscious recruitment base.[30] Additionally, right-wing activities involve more minorities than popularly reported. In 1997, more than 100 New York City public employees of all races employed both Moorish Nation and Montana Freemen tactics in a widespread tax protest. Militias seeking law enforcement or military expertise often welcome minority members. The United States Special Operations Citizens' Militia of Florida proclaims, "We are in no way a racist group! We are totally against racism. We do not tolerate racism at all!"[31] The High Desert Militia of Southern California agrees, "Some of us are devout Christians, Catholics or Jews, others may be merely spritual [*sic*], while still others make it a point of not informing us of such matters. . . . We are in no way associated with or promote racism or bigotry."[32] Indeed, several conspiracy theories identify racism as a sign of pending takeover. Some believe the government will incite a race war as justification for bringing foreign troops into the United States and declaring martial law. Many terrorists are hateful and intolerant, but their common enemy appears to be the government.

Contrary to studies of the Wallace-era South, modern terrorists do not appear to be distinctive and pathological. Instead, these Americans feel a heightened sense of political efficacy, doggedly researching "common law," preparing quasi-legal documents, meeting, and training. They believe a good economy has lulled the nation into inactivity and only a vigilant few will be able to fight the federal government. This drive to save the country from unseen enemies has been called "superpatriotism." The Southern Poverty Law Center's Morris Dees offers as an example McVeigh's concerns about U.S. involvement in Somalia and Iraq, FBI actions at Waco and Ruby Ridge, and rural economic strife. According to Dees, McVeigh "probably honestly believed he had to sound an alarm to wake up a sleeping people before we all became slaves to a tyrannical government. . . . He loves his country. He is, he believes, a true patriot."[33]

Paradoxically, these people who crave political action are also the ones who reject political groups. While the Constitution Party's antitax, progun, anti-UN, and pro family platform is sympathetic to fears of the hardcore Right, Constitution Party activities are limited to fielding candidates for local races, drafting anti-UN ordinances and disseminating party materials. Terrorists have little patience for such legal activities and consider party activists sell-outs. Similarly, the issue-friendly Libertarian party, with a free-market, low-tax and anti-federal government message, has disappointed many who agree with the ideology but not with the vehicle.[34] This tension between wanting to belong to a group and yet shunning mainstream group activities makes right-wing organizations particularly fragile. As the head of a regional criminal intelligence unit explained, many terrorist groups self-destruct since each member wants to be a part of something important but no one wants to compromise with other group members—an integral function of any organization.[35]

While journalists concentrate on the implausibility of right-wing conspiracies, many adherents are drawn to the movement because of real and personal setbacks at the hands of lower-level government bureaucrats. Some had bad experiences with divorce courts, tax assessors, zoning commissions, or school boards. Ben Long of the Montana Human Rights Commission has also noted a higher-than-expected rate of disabled workers and disabled veterans in Montana's right-wing groups.[36] In Santa Clara, California, journalist Rick Sine explained a tax protester's rationale for participation:

> Jesse blames government for two traumatic experiences in his life. First, he faced a huge tax bill for a home he had inherited. Then, he had to pay an $80,000 divorce settlement after a marriage of just one year. "You don't wake up one day and decide you're going to protest the system,"[he says]. "You go through a process."[37]

Terrorist tactics are surely unjustified, but they may be symptomatic of legitimate grievances. Overall, though, while there is some reason to believe that terrorism is linked to an abnormal psychology, other observations indicate that terrorists may be involved in a peculiar form of political participation involving a heightened sense of political efficacy, personal grievances, rejection of mainstream organizations, and a lack of confidence in the government.

Political Bullies: A Case Study

In 2003, U.S. Representative James Sensenbrenner Jr. (R-WI) introduced the Involuntary Bankruptcy Improvement Act in the House of Representatives, while Senators Russ Feingold (D-WI) and Herb Kohl (D-WI) were cosponsoring similar legislation in the Senate to prevent right-wing extremists from declaring their political enemies involuntarily bankrupt.[38] This legislation made its way to the U.S. Capitol in direct response to Steven Magritz, a Fredonia, Wisconsin, landowner who wreaked havoc with the personal and financial lives of thirty-six public officials in response to a property foreclosure. Ozaukee County Board Chairman Gus Wirth, a victim of Magritz' malicious "paper terrorism," said, "It's terrible that a person needs an act of Congress to clear their name while serving the public."[39]

Magritz's story begins ordinarily enough, and did not start with the harassment of public officials. Like other Americans facing financial troubles, Magritz and his wife failed to pay property taxes on their home and surrounding forty acres for more than two years. When the county began proceedings to repossess the property, Magritz sent back the notices with bogus paperwork and sovereign citizen documents. He then contacted the registrar of deeds to transfer the property to himself or his wife as "sovereign entities"—a sovereign citizen and tax protester tactic used to declare a person is not subject to the laws of the United States. When the registrar refused these filings, he attempted to pay his taxes with fake bills and foreign currency. These, too, were refused. After three years of nonpayment, the county sought to evict him from the property. Magritz refused to leave the property.[40]

Wisconsin officials had enough experience with sovereign citizens and those who subscribe to Posse Comitatus to know that Magritz would be most likely to accept the authority of the county sheriff—a "constitutional authority"—so they requested that the sheriff's office evict the couple. However, unbeknownst to the local supervisors, officers, and county counsel, Magritz begin to retaliate against the government in a two-pronged attack. He filed liens against the public officials, exploiting a Wisconsin system that allows consumers or merchants to claim money owed to them online under the state's Uniform Commercial Code. He also declared his enemies involuntarily bankrupt. The public officials were unaware of these attacks until they tried to sell property or their credit cards came back declined. Once the extent of Magritz's harassment was exposed, it took countless hours notifying banks, state agencies, and credit card companies about the frivolous liens and bankruptcies before they were able to regain their financial lives. For these attacks, Mr. Magritz was sentenced to five years in jail.

Was Magritz threatening? Most of the officials who came in contact with him feared no violence. Instead they reported a "continual low-key intimidation" which took the form of exhausting circular conversations, verbal baiting, and a failure to verbally disengage from them when it became apparent that a conversation would not result in compromise or consensus.[41] What motivated Magritz? Quite reasonably, he was upset by the loss of his homestead. His actions, however, depart from those who would seek to resolve their problems within the system or seek help of others. For example, County Corporation Counsel Dennis Kenealy, the county's civil attorney, noted that Magritz's activities were counterproductive insofar as he spent a nontrivial amount of money and time to file the frivolous documents. Nor was he financially unsophisticated, having been paid in the past to prepare other families' taxes as a financial planner. Kenealy believes that "on a personal level he bought into this philosophy and felt ignored." As observed earlier in this chapter, those two elements embody the forces that converge in one who is likely to embrace right-wing extremism: a previously held belief in right-wing ideology coupled with a bullying personality. All that it took to activate this paper terrorist was the right misfortune, in this case a foreclosure.

Conclusion

The Magritz case helps illustrate the forces that converge in a person who is vulnerable to the extreme right-wing activities in America today. The common ideology of limited government and maximum property rights, the opposition to taxes, the right to bear arms, and opposition to world government appeal to those who wish to live private lives without the influence of the government. The various types of right-wing groups—militias, common-law courts, sovereign citizens, tax protesters, and survivalists—differ in which aspect of the government they refuse to recognize, but they all reject some commonly respected government institution. When one suffers personal misfortune such as Steven Magritz did, one need only subscribe to the beliefs of the group that rejects the government agent most responsible for the personal, political, or economic grievance. In Magritz's case, both tax protest and sovereign citizen activity were a perfect fit for one who did not believe in taxes and wanted to be an "entity of one." Disaffected citizens may escalate to violence or threats, or they may remain entirely nonviolent, as did Magritz. The more important decision in the making of an extremist is the decision to reject the political rules of the game—those institutions, authorities, norms, and rules that allow reasonable people to compromise in a free and responsive political system.

From jail where he is serving a five-year sentence, Magritz wrote to the local newspaper to protest the clean up and replacing of the septic system on his lot: "How much more injury is the county going to cause? When will people wake up? Is there no honor?" For a political bully such as Magritz, being ignored in jail would be the final, and worst, injury.

PART II

RELIGIOUS AND SOCIOECONOMIC DIMENSIONS

CHAPTER 8

Religious Sources of Violence

SUSANNA PEARCE

Observing the headlines of the daily news and even the conclusions of many academic case studies, one can be forgiven for assuming without investigation that there is an inevitable relationship between religion and violence. Religion is claimed as the motivation for individual violence the world over, as well as for group violence in Sudan, Nigeria, Algeria, Northern Ireland, the former Soviet republics, Tibet, Philippines, and Indonesia, not to mention the Middle East. Most researchers would agree that there is a more complex motivation that causes a person or group to engage in violence and that religion is not a sole instigator of conflict nor a sole cause of perpetual violence. It is, however, often presumed that religion plays at least *some* role in the worldwide increase in violence because of numerous anecdotal instances. The extent to which religion is a prime cause of violence will not be investigated in this chapter; rather, the issue at hand is synthesizing previous research into a framework that allows one to then evaluate the impact of religion on the level of violence. This chapter sets out a model through which the relationship between religion and violence can be better understood. Before considering a framework of analysis, however, it is necessary to define the phenomenon being analyzed: What is religious violence?

Defining "Religious Violence"

The popular media seem to characterize any violence between groups or individuals of largely different religious identities as religious violence, regardless of the issue in dispute. Within the academic literature on religious violence, a primordial perspective supports this view and argues that religious identities (as well as other identities) will always be in tension with each other. Those tensions are temporarily subdued by the institutional structure of the state, but when the structure is removed, the tensions again surface though the issue in dispute or the spark of the conflict may not be religious. This can be referred to as an *identity-oriented* definition and measurement.

The difficulty with the identity-oriented definition is that it does not account for the relevance of religion to the dispute. Such a definition lumps together both the Bosnian wars, where religious expressions during massacres were frequent, and the Falkland Wars, where the United Kingdom and Argentina fought for territorial control of the strategic islands. Clearly, these two conflicts involve religion to different degrees. Using an identity-oriented definition also raises the issue of the blurred boundaries between religious identities and ethnic or national identities. In many cases, the three identities are so intertwined that making a differentiation between them (and analysis of only one of them) virtually impossible. Are the various Yugoslav conflicts to be viewed as between Serbs, Croats, and Bosnians or between Orthodox Christians, Catholics, and Muslims? Distinguishing between the role of religious identities and the role of ethnic and national identities on the violence in the conflicts is a daunting task, particularly if one uses an identity-oriented definition.

An alternative definition focuses on the issues in dispute between two groups, regardless of the identities of the groups. Within the academic literature, the issue-oriented definition is supported by an instrumental perspective which argues that religion is not a source of conflict (as the primordial perspective suggests), but a tool used by either side to legitimize their actions and mobilize support. As such, many instrumentalists would argue that a political conflict based on a religious disagreement is very rare; rather, religion is a secondary factor in the nature of a conflict. This can be referred to as an *issue-oriented* definition.

There are several difficulties with the issue-oriented definition. First, it is often difficult to ascertain the central issue in a complex web of disputes and propaganda that surround a conflict. The list of issues is seemingly endless, and often a specific case belongs to multiple categories of issues. The discrepancies are a result of the varying ways used to identify the central issue of a conflict. For instance, a conflict over the sovereignty of a given territory that is claimed by two competing groups would generally be categorized as secessionist because the sovereignty or authority over the area is the primary issue for both sides. It could also be categorized as nationalist if the minority group is a somewhat cohesive ethnic group (or claims to be such) and wishes to establish a homeland for their nation. Or, if the minority was a coherent economic class wishing to install a government that favors their class, the conflict may best be described as a class conflict.

An additional problem is that there are often many goals for one group, and determining which one defines a conflict can be difficult. In Northern Ireland, for instance, Sinn Fein is equally committed to removing British control of Northern Ireland *and* to creating a Marxist state.[1] It would be difficult to determine which goal comes before the other, as they are so intertwined in Sinn Fein's ideology. Thus, Sinn Fein and the Northern Ireland conflict could be categorized as either a conflict over territory or as a Marxist conflict.

Furthermore, many groups see themselves involved in a conflict of which the other party is unaware. The al Qaeda movement is an excellent example. In 1996 (long before the United States recognized a war against al Qaeda and terrorism), Osama bin Laden issued a *fatwa* (or religious declaration) that described the American actions in the Gulf War as a "clear declaration of war on God, His Messenger and Muslims."[2] Yet the American government saw their actions as defending Kuwait's sovereignty (or more likely, defending Western access to Kuwait's oil) from a more terrestrial enemy, Saddam Hussein. From bin Laden's perspective, the conflict between the United States and Iraq was religious, while from the American perspective, the conflict was territorial.

This chapter will consider religious violence in both its identity-oriented and issue-oriented varieties, in order to evaluate the full scope of the religious sources of violence. What this chapter aims to do is set out a framework for understanding the impact that religion has on violence. It does not mean to state that religion is a sole cause of violence, but lays the groundwork for analyzing how it contributes to violence in specific cases. The framework is intended to be a means by which we can evaluate the extent of the relationship between religion and violence.

The Model

The frequency and potency of religious conflicts leaves little doubt that religion has some role to play in intensifying violence. This chapter focuses on three qualities of religion as an explanation of why religion intensifies a conflict. In the model provided here (encapsulated in Figure 8.1), religious doctrine supplies the motivation, a religious organization grafts in its hierarchal structure, and a religious diaspora provides resources to sustain a movement through a prolonged violent struggle. In each of these unique characteristics, religion has the capacity to escalate and sustain violence in a confrontation between individuals or groups.

Religious Doctrine

Religious doctrine includes the violent traditions and myths, as well as the metaphysical worldview that are passed through generations of faithful ad-

Figure 8.1
Religion's Influence on the Intensity of a Conflict

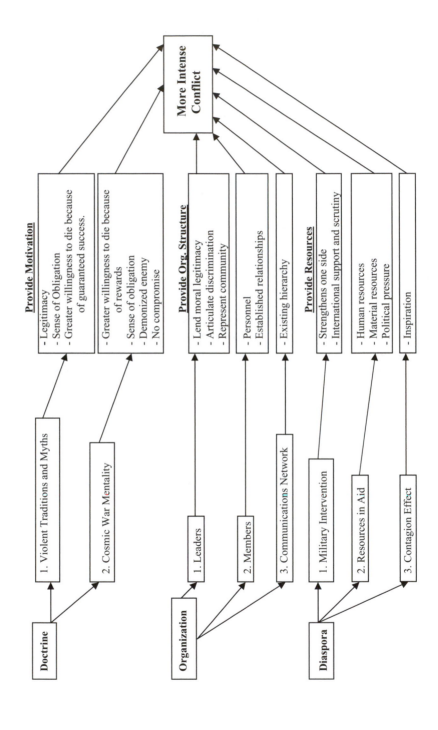

herents. This doctrine, when referenced by a group's leadership, serves to legitimize a violent strategy. In referencing the doctrine, the leadership creates a group of followers with a greater willingness and sense of obligation to die in the struggle without compromise.

Violent traditions and myths are a central component of all five of the world's major religions (Buddhism, Christianity, Hinduism, Islam, and Judaism). The concept of jihad in Islam, which obligates the Muslim to fight against corruption either in oneself or in the world, has been much discussed in recent years.[3] Muhammed himself set the precedent by which some Muslims have justified their violent strategies. The sacred historical texts of Christians and Jews also offer myths that are used to justify violence. The Jewish Torah and Christian Old Testament chronicle battle after battle in which God commanded the Israelites to enter and conquer a foreign land. In some cases, they were even commanded by God to kill the women and children and were chastised when they failed to completely obey. The most prominent sacred Hindu text, the Bhagavad Gita, also narrates a significant battle that was encouraged by Krishna. The warrior Arjuna was hesitant about going through with the battle because he was related to the tribes on both sides, but in the Bhagavad Gita account, Krishna implores Arjuna to fight and Arjuna dutifully obeys. Violent myths in the Buddhist tradition are less prominent, though the traditions established—particularly in Sri Lanka, where militaries conquered the island in the name of Buddhism—serve as sacred precedents that can legitimize contemporary violence.

The instances where these traditions are used as a legitimizer of violence are numerous and prominent. To take only one example, the Christ-killer tradition in Christianity was adapted by the Serbs to hold the Muslims responsible for the martyrdom of Christ and therefore legitimate targets of retribution. In the Christian tradition, the Sanhedrin (the Jewish political council that ruled Palestine during Jesus's lifetime) pressured Pontius Pilate to execute Jesus by crucifixion for claiming to be the King of Jews. Pilate, unwilling to be held responsible for the religious leader's death, allowed the Jewish public to decide Jesus's fate, and they ultimately decided to execute Jesus. Throughout history, Christians have periodically attacked Jews for being responsible for Christ's death. During the Crusades, those Christians who did not join the pilgrimage to Jerusalem did their part in carrying out Pope Urban's proclamation by punishing the local Jews physically for their role in Jesus's death. Again during World War II, Hitler brought the Christ-killer tradition into his notion of Aryan nationalism that legitimized attacks on European Jews. Even more recent, there are those who feared that Mel Gibson's release of a new dramatization of Jesus's death, *The Passion of the Christ*, would lead to a new wave of attacks on Jews.

The Christ-killer tradition was brought into the conflict and perpetuated the violence. The Serbian Christians were able to graft the tradition into

their own national history and thereby hold the Bosnian Muslims responsible for Christ-killing (figuratively), despite their nonexistence at the time
of Christ. The historical event in Serb-Bosnian relations that was re-
interpreted through the Christ-killer tradition occurred in the fourteenth
century. The Serb army, led by Prince Lazar, collided with the Ottoman
Turks in Kosovo. Prince Lazar was killed in the battle, and the Serbs were
subsequently overtaken by the Ottomans. As author Michael Sells observes,
Serb writers in the nineteenth century "transformed Lazar into an explicit
Christ figure, surrounded by a group of disciples, partaking of a Last Sup-
per, and betrayed by a Judas. Lazar's death represents the death of the Serb
nation, which will not be resurrected until Lazar is raised from the dead
and the descendants of Lazar's killers are purged from the Serbian people.
In this story, the Ottoman Turks play the role of the Christ killers. Vuk
Brankovic, the Serb who betrays the battle plans to the Ottoman army, becomes the Christ killer within. In the nationalist myth, Vuk Brankovic represents the Slavs who converted to Islam under the Ottomans and any Serb
who would live with them or tolerate them."[4]

Holding the Muslims responsible for "the death of the Serb nation"
(though the Serb nation exists to this day), and figuratively attacking Christ
in the form of the Serb nation, left the ordinary Serbs with little option
than to defend themselves against the vicious aggressors. Of course, this
Christ-killer interpretation of the Serb nationalist myth has existed for
nearly 200 years, and modern violence against the Muslims was not widespread until the 1990s. Much of the blame for igniting the violence can be
put on Slobodon Milosevic, who visited Kosovo in 1989 to commemorate
the six hundredth anniversary of Lazar's death and reminded the Serbs of
the attacks on their identity and the national Christ figure. As the crowd
chanted "Kosovo is Serb," Milosevic spoke of the unity of the Serb identity
and the necessity of going to battle while standing in front of a backdrop
of peonies (flowers that symbolize Lazar's blood), an Orthodox cross, and
the slogan "Only Unity Saves the Serb."[5] The event served to initiate a process of division between the Serbs and Muslims that escalated to violence
within a few years.

Not only do violent religious traditions serve to legitimize violence by
providing a historical grievance, but they also provide a pattern of behavior for a group in conflict. When the faithful read about their spiritual ancestors who had disagreements with a state or government and reacted with
violence, it sets a precedent. Likewise, when their spiritual ancestors chose
a nonviolent strategy, the group can pattern their behavior after these
prominent predecessors. Rev. Martin Luther King Jr. for example, noted
how Jesus chose to reform the Palestinian state through peaceful means and
replicated his behavior by encouraging members of the civil rights movement to use civil disobedience in the face of harsh oppression, rather than
turning to bombings, hijackings, or guerrilla tactics.

Furthermore, reading the stories about how a deity allowed their ancestors to prevail despite their military weakness gives hope to the faithful who may recognize their uphill struggle. For example, within Judaism and Christianity is the story of the Israelites and the Red Sea. As the event is described in the Bible, Pharaoh released the Israelites from their slavery in Egypt. As the Israelites began their exile, Pharaoh changed his mind and sent his army after them; the army found the Israelites at the Red Sea. With the Israelites surrounded by the army on one side and the sea on the other, it seemed inevitable that Pharaoh's army would eliminate them or take them back as slaves. But God intervened on behalf of the Israelites and saved them from what seemed to be sure destruction. The Red Sea parted and allowed the Israelites to cross on dry land.[6] As the Bible states, "If God is for us, who can be against us."[7] Such examples give even the weakest hope of success.

Religious identities are not unique in their capacity to encourage violence by referencing violent traditions and myths; thus, this alone would not lead one to expect religion to cause a conflict to be more violent. Ethnic identities also have prominent historical traditions that can legitimize a violent strategy. Religious identities, however, are unique in that they also provide its believers with a metaphysical context in which one's struggle takes place.

Religion provides those who believe with an explanation of the afterlife. Each religion differs in its conception of what happens at death, but all share an emphasis on the consequences of one's actions in their earthly life. Obedience in the present life is met with rewards in the afterlife, and disobedience is often met with punishment. The starkest example of this is the Islamic suicide bombers' belief that in exchange for their lives, they and their families will be guaranteed Allah's favor and the pleasure of seventy-two virgins for eternity. Many Christian denominations also warn that if members fail to bring in new members, they may not truly be members themselves or they may be denied rewards in the afterlife. In Hinduism and Buddhism, an individual's failure to behave morally affects the next life into which the individual will be reincarnated. This focus on the afterlife adds a dimension to a conflict that would not be present without the involvement of religion, and the focus is directly associated with a greater intensity of violence than would otherwise be experienced.

Mark Juergensmeyer, a prominent sociologist and expert on religious terrorism, believes that the potency of the metaphysical worldview is a cosmic war perception that is at the heart of religious terrorism. Juergensmeyer argues that religion's metaphysical worldview places one's current situation within greater transcendental contexts that "relate to metaphysical conflicts between good and evil . . . [and] . . . transcend human experience."[8] One's actions then become more significant than simply carrying on an earthly tradition. The participants become responsible for their part in the great war between good and evil. Failure to do their part could conceivably result in a triumph of evil over good and lead to their own eternal damnation. Who could reasonably disobey given the magnitude of the consequences of these beliefs?

For religious terrorists, the world was already at war before they were ever born. If there is an ongoing war between good and evil, one (presumably believing he or she are on the side of good) is threatened by evil and must defend oneself. Violence then becomes further justified, as war demands that violence be used. This does not depend on the opposition being aware of the war, of course, as bin Laden's 1996 *fatwa* illustrates.

Included in Juergensmeyer's theory of a cosmic war perception is a demonized enemy with whom no compromise can be made. If one views the world in the context of an ongoing battle between good and evil, then one's opposition is purely evil and cannot be trusted in negotiations. There is furthermore no room for compromise, as there is no common ground between good and evil on which to meet. In a cosmic war perception, and with a demonized enemy, the only end to the conflict is the total annihilation of one side or the other.

While all five of the world's major religions have at their disposal these violent traditions and metaphysical worldviews, these are not always referenced in order to legitimize violence. In fact, some experts would argue that religion's nonviolent traditions are referenced to encourage peace much more often than religion's violent traditions are referenced to encourage war. Gandhi's nonviolent activism, based on Hindu principles, stands out as a prominent example that supports this view. In essence, religion is sometimes used to support nonviolence, and other times is used to support violence; a small number of researchers have explored this duality of religion, and their conclusions differ considerably.

Scott Appleby is the most prominent of these authors. Appleby points to the education of the believers as the most important of many factors in the determination to use religion to legitimize violence or peace. He argues that extremist religious leaders must convince their followers to ignore the religion's teachings of peace in order for the extremist movement to gain widespread support. Such leaders will be unsuccessful, however, if their followers "are well formed spiritually and informed theologically."[9] According to Appleby, those who are not "sufficiently grounded in the teachings and practices of their own tradition"[10] are followers of a folk religion. These followers are unable "to counter arguments based on scriptures and doctrines carefully chosen for their seeming endorsement of violence or ambivalence about its use"[11] and are ultimately swayed by the arguments of extremist religious leaders. In other words, Appleby argues that without a strong religious education, believers are vulnerable to the teachings of extremists in which violent traditions legitimize the use of violence. Conversely, when believers are properly educated in their faith, the violent traditions do not serve to encourage violence.

Determining the proper education of believers, however, is extraordinarily problematic for an objective observer. Who decides whether a set of followers are "well formed spiritually and informed theologically?" Very few people would argue that the al Qaeda terrorists were not well versed in Islamic teaching, nor are scholars quick to deny the Christian Crusaders' knowledge of the Bible.

If religious involvement can serve as a proxy for spiritual education, a study by Gary Marx of African Americans in the 1960s provides support for Appleby's argument.[12] Marx uses a 1964 survey of African Americans to see whether militants are more or less involved in their faith. He concludes that "the greater the religious involvement, whether measured in terms of ritual activity, orthodoxy of religious belief, subjective importance of religion, or the three taken together, the lower the degree of militancy."[13] Religious involvement, however, does not entirely measure what Appleby intended by "well formed spiritually and informed theologically." It fails to measure the level of education by measuring only the attendance and involvement of followers.

Marx provides an alternative explanation of the dual nature of religion in conflict. He argues that religion often espouses contradicting values— particularly the value placed on rewards in the afterlife or the value placed on action on behalf of a deity in the present life. When stress is put on the temporal (or this-worldly), the faithful are encouraged to do what they can for social change. On the other hand, if stress is put on the afterlife, adherents feel less of a need to try to change society. Marx's evidence from the 1964 survey of African Americans seems to support this claim, though more empirical evidence would surely be needed to accept Marx's explanation.

The discussion of the peaceful influences of religion is usually done in a normative sense in which suggestions and arguments about how religion has the capacity and should be involved in conflicts in order to bring them to a peaceful end, rather than on how that is the dominant way in which religion is involved in conflicts. What has been demonstrated repeatedly is that religious doctrine through its violent traditions and myths and metaphysical worldview legitimizes violence in a conflict by putting one's struggle in both a historical and eternal context that obligates one to obediently participate in the violence. It can also motivate the religiously faithful to join the conflict and continue to the end because of the guarantee of success in the struggle and the guarantee of rewards for one's sacrifice. In this way, religious doctrine is a powerful influence that one would expect to intensify a conflict.

Religious Organization

A religious organization also plays a role in intensifying a conflict. Its leaders, members, and communications network enhance a group in conflict by providing an existing organizational structure and personnel to the group that is necessary to sustain a prolonged violent conflict. Though many social organizations could fill this function, religious organizations are unique in the moral legitimacy they bring with them to the movement. Their endorsement of the movement is especially influential in adding to and directing the movement's membership. Thus, a religious organization plays an important role in organizing the movement and ensuring its efficiency and sustenance throughout a prolonged violent conflict.

When the leadership is supportive of a cause, they are easily co-opted as leaders of a movement. In their role of representing the community, the leaders articulate the concerns of that community and develop a theological framework for understanding the community's history. They repeat for their followers how their current circumstances should be interpreted and prescribe for them the appropriate reaction to those circumstances. Within the white supremacy movement in the United States, for instance, leaders are often co-opted from the Christian Identity[14] churches and describe for their followers how there is a conspiracy by the Jews (who are Satan's descendants) to take over the world and eliminate God's chosen people, the Aryan race. They often refer to the American government as ZOG, or the Zionist Occupied Government. This explains for its followers the erosion of power and status that many whites feel they are experiencing. In order for the Aryan race to survive, those in the white supremacy movement are obligated to stop the Jews, using whatever means necessary. If Christian Identity leaders were to remove their support from the movement and use their positions to advocate for racial tolerance and harmony, the movement would lose a piece of the foundation on which they have justified violence against Jews, and thus lose some of its influence.

Though the white supremacy illustration is an extreme example, religious leaders who become leaders in a violent conflict shape the worldviews of its members and thereby bring with them an invaluable resource. Because of the unique moral legitimacy afforded to religious leaders, they hold an unusual degree of influence over their members. Many members join the movement based on the endorsement of their leaders, adding personnel to the movement. Furthermore, these members are highly responsive to their leaders and ensure loyalty and obedience in their activities.

When a formal religious organization explicitly supports a group in conflict, the movement also benefits from the preexisting communications network that informs, educates, and coordinates the activities of a group in conflict. The web of churches, mosques, synagogues, and temples within a religious organization provide outlets for disseminating information to members of a movement. It is often in the religious buildings that theological arguments about the legitimacy of a struggle take place. It is here that new members are encouraged to join the movement and reminded of the violent traditions and cosmic war worldview that makes violence necessary.

Not only are grand theories about the legitimacy of a struggle or expected actions propagated through this web, though; information about
events are also broadcast through the various religious meeting houses. The
practical organizational elements of a group in a conflict are greatly facilitated by grafting in the preexisting structure of a religious organization.
Notices about the opposition's actions or about scheduled actions by the
group can be made in these existing meetings, where those active in the
struggle already gather on a regular basis.

Furthermore, the preexisting relationships among the clergy of a religious
organization allow a movement to coordinate its activities across a geographical area. When the movement is active in more than one location,
activities can be scheduled to coincide to have the greatest impact. These
relationships also allow for leaders to transmit information on the most effective and innovative techniques in order to create a more efficient and effective movement that achieves its goals.

Doug McAdam's influential study on the black insurgency movement in
the United States identified the role that the black churches played in providing the movement with members, leaders, and a communications network, and laid the groundwork for analyzing the role of religious
organizations in violent conflicts.[15] McAdam's study found that the leadership of the insurgency movement drew heavily on clergy and allowed
the religious organizational structure to be easily transferred to the movement. When the leaders of the churches also became involved as leaders
of the insurgency movement, they brought with them the knowledge of
how to run a complex organization, the preexisting relationships to help
run it smoothly, and the vast human and material resources of the religious group.

One of the resources available to the group through a religious organization is the membership of the religious organization. McAdam's study
found that the most active members of the churches were the most active
participants in the insurgency, largely because church membership was "re-
defined to include movement participation as a primary requisite."[16] The
moral legitimacy that is unique to a religious organization is a fundamental reason that a religious organization is an effective point of recruitment
of a group in conflict. McAdam found that the African-American insurgency movement was able to gain legitimacy by co-opting religious leaders
who "served to convey to their natural constituents the importance and legitimacy of the movement, thereby encouraging participation."[17] Religious
organizations are unique in the degree to which they can claim a moral superiority and imperative to its members, and in doing so deeply influence
their actions. In many cases, they are considered to be representatives of
God on earth and can persuade members to join and sacrifice for a cause
because of this stature among the community of believers.

McAdam's study also demonstrated how the communications network among church leaders served to make the leaders aware of both events and tactics in the movement. One example that he points out is the bus boycotts that were used to protest the segregation of blacks and whites on city buses in the southern United States. The boycott in Montgomery, Alabama, organized by Reverend Martin Luther King Jr. was inspired by a similar boycott in Baton Rogue, Louisiana, organized by King's friend, Reverend Theodore Jemison.[18] With this communications network, a movement has the potential to spread throughout a community and efficiently develop its strategies.

It is not clear when a religious group will choose to support the opposition as opposed to the status quo. As an established institution within a society, one would expect that its interest would best be served by retaining the status quo; however, as exhibited in the previous examples, religious organizations are often found in support of opposition groups. Kevin Neuhouser addresses the question of when a religious organization will support the status quo versus the opposition by evaluating the Brazilian Catholic Church.[19] He argues that the Catholic Church in Brazil began to lose members and attributed this decline to their support of the status quo. The small group of leaders who had been critical of the status quo began to gain legitimacy and was able to assert their influence on the church as a whole. As a result, the church shifted its position from supporting the status quo to opposing the status quo in order to retain or gain membership and ensure their survival.

Guenter Lewy also evaluated this question using seventeen cases of revolutions in which religion played a major part either in instigating the revolution or protecting state institutions.[20] He found that both religious doctrine and leadership were major factors in determining the stand the religion took in a conflict. He noted, however, the highly unpredictable nature of leadership, observing that "a considerable element of uniqueness that defies explanation, not to mention prediction, will remain."[21] In Lewy's study, the organizational levels of a religion did not shed any light on the religion's position in a conflict, although the organizational levels did influence a religion's ability to communicate its values and demands.

The debate about the reasons a religious group would support the opposition rather than the status quo is outside the scope of this framework. What is under consideration is not when religion will become involved but what consequence is experienced because of its involvement. Through the organizational structure of religious organizations, a group in conflict is able to benefit from the leaders, members, and communications network that strengthens the group and allows them to sustain themselves through a prolonged violent conflict. Religious organizations are uniquely ideal for this function because of the unusual moral legitimacy they garner and thus the unusual influence they hold over their members.

Religious Diaspora

As with other identities, believers are not confined within the boundaries of one state. For instance, only about 80 percent of the world's Sikhs live in the Indian province of Punjab (their historical homeland), while the remaining 20 percent live in concentrations throughout Europe and North America.[22] Those outside of a state in conflict and who share a religious identity with one of the participants in the conflict have the potential to become external participants in the conflict. Whether the diaspora simply provide a precedent that serves to inspire, or provide resources such as weapons, personnel, or finances, or even intervene to support a group militarily, the external support serves to sustain a group in conflict. Without this sustenance, the group cannot carry on a prolonged violent conflict. As such, the influence of religion on a conflict is not limited to its doctrinal or organizational qualities; it also influences a conflict by its diaspora qualities.

A group in conflict naturally looks to those in similar situations who came before them to learn how to effectively carry out their struggle and to gain inspiration. Successful revolutions have a "contagion effect" when others see how an idealistic and often weak revolutionary group overcame their oppressors and took power for themselves. A group may underestimate the costs associated with winning the fight, or may overestimate their expected payoffs from a win; either causes them to decide to initiate their own struggle. The effect of this perception is that a group takes inspiration from the success of their co-faithful.

The contagion effect of the Islamic Revolution of Iran has been much discussed since 1979. Iran became the first Islamic Republic in 1979 when Ayatollah Khomeini forced the Shah into exile. The success of the fundamentalist takeover of the country was largely seen as a victory over a corrupt and Western-dominated monarchy—a success that Khomeini urged all Islamic countries to strive for, both Sunni and Shiite. Many Islamic fundamentalists throughout the Middle East and North Africa took Khomeini's advice and followed the example of the Iranian Revolution. Groups in Algeria, Egypt, Jordan, Lebanon, Morocco, Sudan, Tunisia, Turkey, and the Israeli-occupied territories all followed Iran's example, resulting in a proliferation of fundamentalist Islamic movements by the end of the 1980s. In Algeria, in particular, fundamentalist candidates won a majority in the 1990 local elections.

Not only does a group take inspiration from the success of similar revolutionaries, but they also gain a strategy. In observing the efficiencies and inefficiencies of their predecessors, a group can develop a strategy that they believe will ensure their own success. For instance, many fundamentalist Muslims took lessons from the strategy used by Khomeini's revolutionaries in Iran. One technique used by Khomeini's revolutionaries was to hold a protest forty days after the death of protestors, because traditional Muslims would publicly mourn forty days after a family member's death. This caused an inevitable cycle of protests as the Iranian police generally opened fire and killed protestors. The technique was part of Khomeini's success in overthrowing the Shah and creating the first Islamic Republic.

A religious diaspora may also become actively involved in their co-faithful's conflict by providing material resources and political pressure. Because of the affinity between co-faithful around the world, a religious diaspora are naturally concerned for their religious relatives. When their co-faithful are involved in a violent conflict, a religious diaspora often become involved by supplying them with the resources necessary to sustain the conflict. These resources may be in the form of weapons, safe houses, and finances, fulfilling a practical need of the group in the conflict. It may also take the form of human resources or additional fighters who leave their homeland to fight for their co-religionists. Or a diaspora may indirectly support their co-faithful by pressuring their host states to intervene in the conflict with humanitarian support or political pressure on the parties to reconcile the conflict. Furthermore, a diaspora may also influence a conflict by encouraging their host state to intervene militarily. In doing so, the third party strengthens one side in the conflict and can raise their expectations for success. An increase in the expectation of success encourages the side not to compromise short of their goal and thereby prolongs a violent conflict.

The most obvious example of the diaspora effect took place in Afghanistan during the 1980s. The Afghans were faced with an invasion by the vastly larger, better-equipped, and better-trained Soviet army, who anticipated an easy acquisition of the largely tribal state. The Soviets found the Afghans much fiercer than expected, and the Muslims who came to their aid from around the world—the mujahideen—played a vital role in the eventual withdrawal of Soviet troops from the country.

The Bosnian civil war also demonstrates the importance of diaspora support, not only in terms of personnel but also in terms of material resources and finances necessary to sustain a weak movement. The Muslims in Yugoslavia were savagely repressed by the Orthodox Christian Serbs, and international attention was turned to the fragmenting former Soviet satellite state in the early 1990s; "a wave of solidarity with their newfound Balkan co-religionists swept over the Muslim world."[23] Many of the Muslim fighters who were trained and experienced in the Afghan jihad moved from Afghanistan to Bosnia to carry on the global jihad. According to Gilles Kepel, a French expert on political Islam, the Iranians violated a UN arms embargo on Bosnia and sent weapons to the fighters through Turkey and Croatia. Those weapons were supplemented by "several hundred Guardians of the Revolution (*pasdarans*) sent to train the Bosnian military."[24] Furthermore, Kepel's research indicates that the Iranians were active in indoctrinating the Bosnian Muslims, particularly through charitable networks.

The importance of a diaspora is not limited to Islam and the inspiration and material resources it supplies, nor is it limited to the vision of global revolution or jihad among its militants. The Sikh diaspora played a central role in putting political pressure on external states who then pressured the Indian government to make concessions to the Punjabis in India. As researcher Cynthia Keppley Mahmood argues: "Diaspora Sikhs have in fact been critical to the movement, and have become more so as the success of the counterinsurgency within Punjab becomes firmly established."[25] Bhabani Sen Gupta goes one step further and states that "the Sikh diaspora in the United States, Canada and the United Kingdom articulated the demand for a Sikh Homeland outside India several years before the demand was echoed by Sikh militants in Punjab."[26] Gupta points out a particular instance in which the Sikh diaspora sought U.S. intervention (in the form of sanctions) in the Punjab conflict:

> In June 1989 Khalistani lobbyists scored a success when one of their favorite Congressmen, Wally Hearger (Republican, California), moved a resolution in the House of Representatives proposing that the United States not only freeze its bilateral aid to India but also prevent international financial institutions like the World Bank from extending economic assistance to the Indian union until the Indian government stopped the violation of human rights in Punjab and abandoned its missile development program.[27]

The resolution before the U.S. Congress was ultimately unsuccessful, but received a great deal of attention, and was rejected by "a margin of a mere eight votes."[28] Without a doubt, the resolution would have never gained any attention—or in fact never would have been written—had it not been for the efforts of the Sikh diaspora in the United States.

The diaspora influence of religion is becoming an increasingly pertinent aspect of conflicts as globalization speeds the advancement of communications networks. With the advent of television, fax machines, and especially the Internet, events on one side of the world are immediately known on the other side of the world. It is now very rare that a group of people struggle in silence, without the outside world at least able to know their plight with relative ease.

Globalization has not only made it possible for external actors to be aware of a conflict by immediate communications networks, but it has also increased the affinity that the actors have with their co-faithful on the other side of the world. Scott Thomas argues that globalization "has contributed to the formation and consolidation of transnational religious groups with linkages in different countries at the national and subnational levels."[29] According to his analysis, "Globalization promotes closer links between people of similar religions in different countries. It accomplishes through technology what used to be accomplished through the expansion and consolidation of empires, albeit at a slower pace."[30]

Furthermore, globalization has made it possible for the external actors to fight in the conflict by transporting them quickly to the conflict area. While the existence of religious identities that transcend state boundaries is not new, the speed with which religious diaspora become aware of—and can become involved in—a conflict has increased the importance that these diaspora qualities of religion play in a conflict.

The effect that a diaspora has on the intensity of a conflict is not uniform, however. As illustrated in the Afghan example, the involvement of the diaspora bolstered an otherwise negligible opposition and served to extend the conflict. Had the Afghans been left to fight the Soviets on their own, one could reasonably assume that the conflict would have been over quickly and the Soviets would likely have swept through the country. Similarly, the contagion effect of the Iranian Revolution inspired like-minded opposition groups elsewhere to push on with their struggle in the hopes of their own success. However, in the Serbian example, the diaspora was a mediating voice that served to press for a resolution, not intensification, of the conflict.

Conclusion

The influence of the diaspora in combination with the influence of organization and doctrine are the three mechanisms through which religion impacts the level of violence. When one looks at a particular conflict—for example the current Sudanese crisis—and wants to know to what extent religion has caused or perpetuates the violence, one can use this framework to separate religious influences from the economic, ethnic, or other influences on the conflict. One can see how the concept of jihad has motivated the Islamic militias; how the metaphysical context of the conflict has focused fighters on rewards in the afterlife; how the religious hierarchy has lent its leaders, members, and communications network to the insurgency; and how the diaspora (of all the world's major religions) have bolstered their respective religious kin through resources, inspiration, and possibly even military intervention. This model is a useful method for breaking down the complex relationships between religion and violence.

While religion has the potential to influence the level of violence in the ways described in this model, it should be reiterated that religion's involvement will not, by necessity, always increase violence, nor is escalation the only influence religion has on violence. Rather, the model (and this chapter) limits itself to describing the potential mechanisms through which religion increases violence.

Our understanding of the complex relationship between religion and violence offers much to how we view the making of a terrorist. Delineating the mechanisms through which religion serves to encourage or discourage violence allows one to have a more complete picture of the contexts in which terrorists are bred and developed. Though hopefully we will never be able to truly empathize with the terrorist, knowing and fully understanding the motivations for their violence allows us to formulate effective strategies for diminishing the threat of terrorism.

CHAPTER 9

Terrorism and Doomsday

MICHAEL BARKUN

This chapter explores the relationship between terrorism and apocalyptic ideologies, whose shock value rests in their promise of an all-consuming doomsday. Clearly, terrorism of this sort depends upon linkages among the terrorist, his intended victim, their belief systems, and the means of violence available. The fear of doomsday increases with the likelihood that this is the terrorist's goal, that the concept of doomsday forms an important part of the victim's thinking, and that the terrorist possesses highly destructive weapons. It is thus dependent upon both external factors, such as access to weapons of mass destruction, and on internal factors, such as motivation and perception.

Exploring the Relationship between Terrorism and Doomsday

There is no natural connection between "terrorism" and "doomsday." Indeed, as brutal and disturbing as many terrorist attacks have been, most have not evoked doomsday associations. The suicide bomber may kill the innocent, random victim, and may attack in normally safe public places, but life is understood to go on despite him. Where terrorist attacks have been endemic, as in Israel and Northern Ireland, populations have shown remarkable resilience and adaptability.

The linking of terrorism with doomsday, which might once have seemed forced, does not after September 11, 2001. The collapse of the Twin Towers was as apocalyptic a scene as any in recent decades, and the associated shock compels us to examine the relationship that might exist between the two terms.

However, the connection reflects perception even more than any objective reality. To connect terrorism with doomsday is to impose a particular significance on terrorist attacks and is therefore more likely to be a connection made by victims than by perpetrators. There are certainly other ways of construing terrorism: as crime, as insurgency, as chronic violence, or as warfare. These multiple interpretations have been variously adopted by officials, scholars, journalists, and members of the public. As scholars of terrorism have also pointed out, the term terrorism itself has been defined in literally dozens of different ways by governments and academics. Terrorism-as-doomsday, therefore, is merely one among many possible understandings, although it is surely the most dramatic.

Because there are multiple definitions and interpretations of terrorism, and because terrorism-as-doomsday faces many competing ways of understanding the subject, its greatest significance lies in the very existence of the phrase. That some people have connected the two tells us much about the level of anxiety that terrorism can provoke; for to connect terrorism with doomsday is to suggest that terrorism places our collective existence at risk, even though no terrorist attack has ever caused the collapse of a major power.

"Doomsday" is not an idea that is self-evidently clear. The term itself is both precise and vague. Its origins are religious, and the religious meaning is quite specific, but doomsday has also taken on secular meanings. Its imagery, once confined to altar panels and cathedral frescoes, now more often appears in films and other forms of popular culture.

For religious believers, particularly many Christians, doomsday has a fairly exact meaning. Its religious roots lie in two complementary Christian scenarios of end-time events. In one, time will cease with God's Last Judgment, when the world will be destroyed and replaced by "a new heaven and a new earth." This appears to be the earliest meaning of doomsday in English, going back to at least the tenth century. To some believers, however, this event will be preceded by a sequence of stages, during which escalating conflict between good and evil forces will result in the final, titanic battle of Armageddon.

As a result, doomsday acquired both negative and positive associations, suggesting both destruction and regeneration. On the one hand, it stood for the elimination of the old order, whose sinful institutions would be destroyed. On the other hand, it implied that the resulting "clean slate" would be filled with something vastly superior through a messianic figure (Christ's Second Coming) and a divine salvationist purpose.

To the extent that this divine plan was thought to incorporate multiple, preparatory disasters preceding the final Day of Judgment, doomsday invites a more flexible understanding, implying the end of a particular social order rather than the ultimate conclusion of history. Such a broadened meaning can be found in nonreligious usage. Stripped of its theological trappings, secularized doomsday implies the "end of civilization as we know it"—in other words, some cataclysmic event that destroys basic social, political, and economic institutions. In this broader sense, doomsday is more often ascribed to the mischief making of humans than to the Deity, and it is this second meaning that has become linked to contemporary terrorism.

Outside of the Christian West, beliefs about a final world cataclysm may be found in a variety of cultures. They often appear, however, in popular religion—the largely oral and less visible folk beliefs that develop alongside of, and sometimes in opposition to, official orthodoxy. Apocalyptic strains may be found in Islam, in association with the appearance of a salvationist Mahdi; in the Buddhist vision of a "Buddha of the future"; and in Native American beliefs about the ancestors' return. Here, as in Christianity, the destruction of the old and corrupt implied the appearance of something new and pure. In addition, Christian religious concepts have diffused widely, not only as a result of systematic proselytizing but also through the communication channels of globalization. In any case, the symbols associated with doomsday in the West, both the religious and secular varieties, have made their way into the consciousness of societies around the world.

The most famous secular doomsday formulation, however, has nothing to do with familiar doomsday imagery or with terrorism. Rather, it is the fanciful "Doomsday Machine," advanced in 1960 as a thought experiment by the nuclear deterrence theorist, Herman Kahn. He imagined a device "whose only function is to destroy all human life."[1] Such a machine might consist of weapons capable of blanketing the earth in lethal radioactivity, automatically activated if the United States were to suffer an attack of a particular magnitude. Such an attack would extinguish the human race, both the attackers and their targets. Kahn presented this idea not as a policy proposal but as a way to illuminate problems and dangers in U.S.-Soviet nuclear deterrence. A few years later, Kahn revised the Doomsday Machine exercise in a way that made it more compatible with terrorism, although he seems not to have recognized this application. He asked what effect the cost of such a machine would have on the stability of international relations. If its cost were in only the tens or hundreds of dollars, its creation would be inevitable, unless knowledge of how to construct it were monopolized. The danger would persist even if the cost were raised to the hundreds of thousands, since "there are still enough determined men . . . willing to play games of power blackmail, and enough psychopaths with access to substantial resources to make the situation hopeless."[2] While he was merely engaged in an intellectual exercise, it is instructive that he saw the danger in terms of individual criminality or pathology rather than non-state organizations. While Kahn coined the phrase "thinking about the unthinkable," the likelihood of doomsday weapons in the hands of terrorists was clearly unthinkable to him in the 1960s.

Given a Cold War metaphor such as the "Doomsday Machine," there still seems no necessary reason why doomsday should now be associated with terrorists. Like some other forms of violence, most terrorism is small-scale. Like violent crime, guerrilla attacks, and civil unrest, most terrorist attacks involve small geographical areas and limited numbers of victims. This is, for example, the case with bombings, assassinations, and hostage-takings. As noted terrorism researcher Jonathan Tucker has pointed out, groups with specific political agendas shy away from mass-casualty attacks, since they are likely to injure rather than advance their objectives.[3] Such attacks may be shocking and repugnant, but they do not evoke doomsday associations.

However, despite this, the terrorism-doomsday linkage has grown, and not without reason. The concern has arisen in part because of the imagery of the September 11th attacks. The exploding aircraft, the collapsing towers, and the fleeing crowds resembled nothing so much as a Hollywood portrayal of world-ending calamity. However, this factor alone does not provide an adequate explanation. The intellectual roots of the connection lie in increasing fear that future attacks will use weapons of mass destruction (WMD). WMD concerns exist despite the fact that to date, all mass-casualty terrorist attacks have used relatively low-technology weapons. The September 11th attacks, while unconventional in the use of fuel-loaded aircraft, did not involve chemical, nuclear, biological, or radiological weapons, those normally categorized as weapons of mass destruction. The actual use of such weapons by nonstate actors has been exceedingly rare. The major example remains Aum Shinrikyō's release of sarin gas in the Tokyo subway in 1995. Something on the order of 2,000 people became ill, but only twelve died. The anthrax attacks in October 2001 produced twenty-three confirmed cases, with five deaths. In addition, the four categories of WMD are not identical in their potential for destruction. Nuclear and chemical weapons, for example, do not have equivalent capacities for social disorganization, nor do they have equivalent capacities to produce doomsday, whatever might be meant by that term. Thus the attribution of "doomsday weapons" to terrorists is not related to clear evidence of possession, use, or possible consequences.

Just before the start of the millennial year—2000—law enforcement agencies around the world worried about possible violence triggered by millenarian religious groups. In October 1999 the FBI was forced by press leaks to release "Project Megiddo," a report on the possibility of religiously-generated year 2000 violence. Although the report rated the danger as relatively small, the title of the report, utilizing the Hebrew name for Armageddon, sent a more disquieting message. The FBI warned that "religiously motivated extremists may initiate violent conflicts with law enforcement officials in an attempt to facilitate the onset of Armageddon, or to help fulfill a 'prophesy' [sic]."[4] A few months later, on 18 December

1999, the Canadian Security Intelligence Service (CSIS) released a report called "Doomsday Religious Movements." While CSIS was also more concerned with religious sectarians than with terrorist organizations, their connection of doomsday with issues of public security suggests how governments viewed the relationship between religion and violence. While the CSIS report did not offer an explicit definition of doomsday, the phrases employed made the point of view clear: "apocalyptic struggle," "catastrophic scenario," "eradicate enemies."[5] This suggests not so much a theologically-based conception as a worldview organized around what terrorism scholar Mark Juergensmeyer has called images of "cosmic war,"[6] where a great battle is about to commence, upon which hangs the fate of the world. The enormity of the coming conflict will make it cataclysmic for any but the victors.

Terrorism and doomsday can be linked in two different ways: by an attack which the perpetrators hope will cause doomsday, or by the potential victims' belief that doomsday will be the result of an attack. The less likely possibility is that terrorists themselves will act to produce doomsday, thereby accelerating a process of apocalyptic change. That would require not only access to potent weapons but also an appropriate eschatology (a belief system about how the end-times will occur). This is ordinarily the province of religion, although revolutionary political ideologies can possess secular "end-of-the-world" visions. In a somewhat different but related vein, the al Qaeda leader Ayman al-Zawahiri, in a message broadcast in November 2004, promised to fight Islam's enemies "until doomsday," implying not only extraordinary tenacity but eventual victory. The other, more likely connection between the two concepts is through the perceptions of persons other than the terrorists themselves—actual and potential victims, as well as onlookers. While these others may have little or no knowledge of the terrorists' intentions, they may understand an attack in terms of doomsday, based both on its intrinsic characteristics and on their own beliefs about what doomsday might be like. Again, the threat of annihilation produces a potent form of the fear that terrorists seek to inspire.

The only terrorist group that may have mounted an attack in order to bring about doomsday was Aum Shinrikyō.[7] This cannot be said with certainty, since the aims of the 1995 gas attack are still unclear. However, in the time immediately preceding that incident, Aum's guru, Shoko Asahara, came to believe that an Armageddon-like Third World War was imminent, and that only his followers would survive. One theory is that the gas attack was intended to spark this conflict. On the other hand, it simply may have been an attempt to frustrate an imminent police raid on the sect, since the trains containing the gas were converging on a station beneath police headquarters.

In any case, nonstate groups have generally not been in a position to develop or acquire such weapons of mass destruction. They have normally lacked access to trained personnel and laboratory facilities (both of which, however, Aum possessed) or the cash and contacts necessary for purchase. However, renewed fears of nuclear proliferation and revelations about networks supplying components and information suggest that nuclear weapons may no longer be so difficult for private groups to secure. Even if they were able to acquire the weapons, they might not be able to employ them effectively, a limitation particularly true of chemical and biological weapons.

Whether or not terrorists can actually acquire WMD, the concern that they might do so remains strong. To some extent, this is an artifact of the October 2001 anthrax letters and their perceived connection to the September 11th attacks. However, there is another reinforcing factor: the culturally transmitted symbolism of doomsday that is virtually universal, albeit in different forms.

The origin of doomsday symbolism in the West lies in biblical imagery, such as that found in the Book of Revelation, the final book of the Christian Bible. Two types of images predominate in Revelation, natural cataclysms and uncontrolled military violence. The emphasis upon natural disasters is especially marked, since they are beyond human agency and control, and are understood as the hand of God in history—earthquakes, eruptions, and plague, for example. This religious tradition has remained sufficiently vital so that in the months after September 11th, several American evangelists warned that the attacks signaled the beginning of history's final chapter. After the 2005 South Asian tsunami, Muslim clerics in Indonesia asserted that the disaster was God's reaction to religious laxity.[8]

Traditional doomsday speculation through the early nineteenth century sought the religious meaning of calamities, which were regarded as pointers to the imminent end-times. However, the centrality of natural disasters in end-time thinking began to decline under the pressures of science and technology. They made natural forces explicable, provided protection against them, and sometimes predicted their occurrence. In addition, technological prowess also made possible something previously unthinkable: doomsday caused by human action.

This shift in emphasis appears in European and American popular literature, where end-of-the-world stories have been a staple since the late 1800s. As W. Warren Wagar's exhaustive study of this genre reveals, prior to 1914 almost all such stories assumed that civilization would be destroyed by a natural disaster. After World War I, however, human action replaced nature, either through war or through mistakes made by scientists who could not control the powers they unleashed.[9]

The capacity of human beings to cause doomsday, either intentionally or inadvertently, began to receive significantly wider attention during the 1970s, with renewed concern about nuclear war, energy shortages, and environmental collapse. Terrorists played no role in these future scenarios. Rather, responsibility was believed to lie with the policies of major states, such as the United States and the Soviet Union. However, by the late 1990s, that picture had changed.

The Soviet Union dissolved, and in the chaotic post–Cold War world, terrorists have become the most feared malefactors. The capacity to cause mass destruction and/or mass casualties, once held almost exclusively by states, is now frequently ascribed to nonstate organizations. In part, this is due to fears about the fate of unguarded weapons of mass destruction in the former Soviet Union, as well as the activities of now-unemployed weapons scientists. In addition, chemical and biological weapons can in principle be fabricated by groups with relatively modest resources. Finally, the known weapons programs of such "rogue states" as North Korea raise the prospect of intentional sale or transfer to terrorists. Thus, features of the contemporary political landscape have made terrorists' doomsday capabilities appear plausible, and therefore the fear derived from these perceived capabilities becomes all the more potent.

The Spread of "Doomsday Culture"

Terrorism exists within numerous contexts: a political context defined by states, international organizations, and interest groups; a technological context defined by a knowledge base, skill sets, and available resources; and a cultural context defined by prevailing values, ideas, and symbolic representations. The latter is the least understood and appreciated, in large part because it manifests itself in so many ways—through religion, popular culture, and oral tradition. Yet the cultural context is essential to understanding the nexus of terrorism and doomsday, for the connection between the two depends upon largely unspoken understandings about world-ending catastrophe.

The religious beliefs about the end-times described earlier have not disappeared, although they have been modified. The Rev. Jerry Falwell, for example, believes that the "fervent heat" mentioned in a doomsday passage in the Book of Revelation actually refers to a world-ending nuclear explosion. Secular beliefs have also helped shape the current linkage of terrorism and doomsday.

These ideas have found niches in popular culture, where doomsday motifs proliferate in novels, films, and television programs. The end-of-the-world fiction already referred to was followed by disaster movies, a Hollywood staple for decades. Finally, television and the Internet have completed the media saturation with its own apocalyptic images. The imagery normally involves scenes of mass panic, destruction, and death, and it was the similarity of 9/11 pictures to earlier fictional representations that made television coverage of September 11th so chilling. However, the capacity of images to shock does not depend only upon the magnitude of destruction, a point understood by Iraqi and other terrorists who videotape beheadings of hostages. These carefully staged rituals of brutality function like the tiny images of death and suffering in the apocalyptic panels by the sixteenth-century Flemish painter Hieronymous Bosch, whose works depend upon the cumulative effect of many small but horrific scenes set beside one another. Whatever the medium, there has been less tendency to attribute doomsday to the deity or to impersonal natural forces and a greater propensity to fear conspiratorial terrorists.

This comes at a time when conspiracy beliefs have already spread widely, encompassing a range of subjects from the Kennedy and King assassinations to the 9/11 attacks. Since terrorists necessarily operate in small, clandestine groups, they constitute conspiracies. However, conspiracy *theories*, as opposed to actual conspiracies, commonly attribute to the plotters attributes which they usually do not have: for example, powers of destruction and concealment that can seem virtually superhuman. Hence the prevalence of conspiracy theories reinforces overestimations of terrorists' capabilities, including their power to bring about doomsday.

This suggests that terrorism is not merely a phenomenon that is objectively "out there"; it is also a category whose construction is facilitated by a host of cultural factors. The contextual boundaries that define the term "terrorism" and its use depend upon the attitudes and predilections of the definer and user. This is true of those with particular ideological commitments, who may quite consciously conceive terrorism in order to reinforce their policy preferences, but it is also true in the society at large, where terrorism acquires specific meanings through the accumulation of associations and images.

The current penchant for doomsday speculation by conspiracists makes the connection with terrorism seem more natural, for terrorists by necessity work secretly. As conspiracy theories about politics have spread, it has become commonplace to conceive of the enemy not as a hostile state but as a small, secret organization. This tendency is also consistent with the structure of the post–Cold War world, in which no other state approaches the military power of America. In this environment, the fantasies of popular culture have taken on a new credibility, seemingly validated by al Qaeda's devastating attacks. Terrorists now fill the "enemy vacuum" created by the collapse of the Soviet Union.

There is often a symbiotic relationship between adversaries. The enemy is feared, but its presence can confer intangible benefits on those it threatens. The existence of an enemy reinforces a sense of group identity by presenting an "other" against whom one stands in opposition. The danger the enemy poses increases group cohesion, for internal conflicts must be put aside in order to devote full energies to repelling or defeating the adversary. This mobilization enhances the sense of group purpose, conceptualized as a "war" or "crusade." To suggest that enemies perform these functions is not to suggest that the threats posed are illusory. They may be quite genuine. However, they also confer benefits on the putative victims, who now mobilize against the threat.

Religious terrorists almost reflexively oppose the secular societies they confront. In so doing, they may also extend their hostility to the technology that characterizes such societies. The final instructions for the 9/11 hijackers, found in Mohammad Atta's unchecked luggage, directed the attackers not to be intimidated by the West's technology, since it is no match for divine power.[10] The technological prowess of developed societies is inextricably bound up with many of the attributes that terrorists find distasteful—consumerism, sexuality, the mass media, and forms of popular amusement. To triumph without weapons of mass destruction would deal a double blow to the adversary, destroying it without resorting to the enemy's weapons. Yet those very weapons, especially WMD, seem most likely to achieve their desired ends. The necessary result is an ambivalence often found in movements that seek a return to a lost "golden age" (in the Islamist case, the early eighth century). The ambivalence turns on the acceptable mix of ideological purity and pragmatism.

Thus, religiously driven terrorists may feel torn between a temptation to employ what terrorism expert David Rapoport has called "weapons of the apocalypse"[11] while disdaining such weapons as the product of corrupt cultures and, in any case, unnecessary for God's elect. The elect draw upon supernatural sources of strength and consequently need not have recourse to worldly arms. During the Middle Ages, Christian chiliasts (individuals who believed that Jesus will reign on earth for 1,000 years) sometimes fought what they believed to be end-time battles with scythes and pitchforks. They were, of course, defeated, and while this was no surprise to their enemies, it came as a shock to them, since they believed fervently that God would fight for them. On the other hand, religious terrorists, lacking concrete political programs, feel no need to preserve their adversaries' world and "are prepared to resort to any weapon to destroy their enemies."[12]

It may also be possible to produce doomsday *effects* without doomsday *weapons*, a point already made by the use of box cutters on September 11th. A large conventional explosion or conflagration appropriately sited might convey the sensation of experiencing doomsday using technologically primitive means. The interdependencies that pervade modern life can spread damage far beyond the area of initial impact.

Religious belief in a doomsday, at which point normal history will end, is rarely held in isolation. Rather, it functions as part of a complex of end-times ideas. These may include the identification of the evil forces that must be defeated, as well as ways of determining how close doomsday actually is, whether through the calculation of dates or the identification of portents whose appearance signifies that apocalyptic events are imminent. The apocalyptic believer, therefore, scans the horizon for events that may be considered doomsday-related "signs of the times."

The difficulty with such scenarios is that they seem to offer no opportunity for meaningful human action, for events are to unfold according to a divine plan. However, those who anticipate doomsday may not be satisfied to wait upon events. Despite their faith in doomsday's inevitability, they often yearn to accelerate the timetable. The tension between divine inevitability and human impatience can be maintained only as long as passive and active orientations are in approximate balance. However, should frustration overcome fatalism, believers might seek to "force the end" through a catastrophic act of their own making.

Such responses have sometimes involved violence turned inward upon believers themselves rather than upon the outside world. The "revolutionary" suicide of the Jonestown community in Guyana in 1978 is perhaps the most striking case. Other, smaller instances of collective self-extinction have occurred in such smaller religious groups as the Order of the Solar Temple and Heaven's Gate, both during the 1990s. None of these organizations were terrorist-oriented, and all had either broken most ties with the larger society or lived in relative harmony with it.

However, religious terrorists might well conclude that a direct attack upon the supposed forces of evil might be necessary to spark the final transformation. By seeing themselves as instruments of divine will, they feel both mandated and empowered as the means through which doomsday will be brought about. Such behavior inevitably raises issues of rationality. To what extent may terrorists be expected to engage in means-ends calculations that others could anticipate and understand? If they do, then the acquisition and use of WMD might well follow.

However, the issue of terrorists' rationality is complex, particularly so where religiously motivated terrorists are concerned. Since it is their doomsday proclivities that concern us, the rationality problem needs to be explored further. Religious terrorism has two characteristics which, while shared with some secular terrorism, are especially pronounced: a tendency toward dramatic attacks (often against symbolic targets) and the frequent failure to claim responsibility.

The Production and Reproduction of Fear

When seeking to frighten someone, it is useful to know what one's target fears. Potential targets of terrorism have done so in part by generating constructs of doomsday, which go back centuries prior to contemporary terrorism. Doomsday, by threatening the destruction of "everything," signifies ultimate loss. As we have also seen, the originally religious conceptions of doomsday engendered countless secular variations which thrived in popular culture. These developments, too, largely predated current terrorism. More recently (and particularly in the post-9/11 era) fears have been further signaled about the means terrorists might use. Hence the uncounted academic conferences, media interviews, and government programs devoted to the potential use of WMD by terrorists, and especially the threat of bioterrorism. Here, as elsewhere in the domain of terrorism, a complex dynamic exists between objective reality and mental images, for there are both genuine external threats and fears which we project onto adversaries.

Fear thus comes from two sources: from the outside, through acts committed or threatened by terrorists, and from within, as a result of the unconscious apprehensions and conscious planning by putative victims. Each is influenced by the other. Terrorists might be tempted to threaten a doomsday attack even if they lack the means to produce one, calculating that the threat itself would destabilize their target. However, the most dangerous result would be a convergence of doomsday scenarios. Doomsday predictions can become self-fulfilling prophecies, in which expectations of worst cases produce the dreaded behavior. The danger is heightened by the tendency of many terrorists to prefer attacks that are quite literally theatrical. That is, attacks that are understood in dramaturgical terms—events constructed with the intention of being played out for audiences in ways so vivid and shocking that they cannot be ignored.

Mark Juergensmeyer characterizes the attacks by religious terrorists as "performance violence."[13] Thus the attacks presuppose audiences, a publicly visible "stage" where the attack occurs, and dramatic consequences that demand to be noticed. At the same time, they often occur without accompanying political demands and often have little or no obvious strategic value, doing little to alter the military balance between terrorists and governments. Indeed, it is in part the lack of military utility that contributes to the belief that some religious terrorists are irrational.

The rationality issue largely evaporates in light of Juergensmeyer's assertion that such attacks are not only performances but are also "performative"—acts intended to make something happen.[14] However, the connection between the performance and the consequence is often obscure to nonbelievers. An act which appears to be senseless destruction to a skeptic may seem a critical catalyst of change to the perpetrator. This is particularly so where a terrorist act arises out of religious beliefs that victims do not share. In such a case, the terrorist is likely to invoke supernatural forces that seem illusory to others. In addition, the terrorist may believe that his actions have caused changes that go far beyond visible damage and in fact may be wholly invisible to others, for the religious terrorist may think that he has unleashed a cosmic force or caused some critical change in the invisible spiritual realm which can be apprehended only with the eye of faith. The terrorist may believe he has a special knowledge, unknown to others, which identifies forces, vulnerabilities, and points of leverage that outsiders cannot see. This results in an act of destruction that seems meaningless to others, and all the more terrifying for its apparent pointlessness.

Here we need to appreciate the differing perspectives of insider and outsider. For what may make perfect sense to the one may appear irrational to the other. Where the two are separated by theology, worldview, or culture, the likelihood of such divergent understandings is particularly great. The CSIS "Doomsday" report discussed earlier asserted that "irrationality . . . underlines the threat posed by Doomsday Religious Movements."[15] The presumption is that anyone who would initiate an act of mass death and destruction necessarily lacks the capacity for reasoning, since the dead would include the innocent as well as many, perhaps all, of the perpetrators. Indeed, the logic leading to such a judgment is much the same as that which argues for the irrationality of individual suicide bombers. The suicide bomber constitutes doomsday-in-microcosm. His self-annihilating act prefigures a universe of endless destruction, consuming the destroyers themselves.

In addition, terrorists who appear to be religious or ideological "fanatics" are often capable of behaving with pragmatism and calculation. A case in point was Osama bin Laden's videotaped message to Americans just before the 2004 presidential election. He omitted most of his customary religious rhetoric, cast no aspersions on Christians or Jews, and sought to appeal to his audience on the basis of self-interest. The statement was clumsy and ineffective, but the fact that it was made at all suggests that care must be taken in making categorical statements about terrorists' irrationality.

Yet regardless of the scale of an attack, its consequences may well have been foreseen by the attackers, for whom they will make perfect sense. Acts which appear irrationally self-destructive to victims are likely to seem both inevitable and necessary to those who cause them. The reason lies in the historical "script" that forms the basis for apocalyptic terrorism. As long as the action can be seen as consistent with the religious script, its objective characteristics cease to be relevant. While a "reality principle" might eventually assert itself in the face of mounting defeats, millennialists have historically demonstrated an enormous capacity for rationalization in the face of apparent failure. Deeply held beliefs are often maintained even in the face of strong contradictory evidence. The presence of facts that raise questions about central beliefs is referred to by social psychologists as "cognitive dissonance." This dissonance might be resolved by changing beliefs, but it is more often dealt with by manipulating or editing facts to make them conform to beliefs. Thus perpetrator and victim may have radically different criteria for political success, and perpetrators may be unfazed by outcomes which victims consider failures.

Terrorists have a choice between producing fear through their choice of weapon, or producing fear through an attack's effects. A WMD might, in fact, not do much damage (as was the case with the anthrax letters) but produce disproportionate fear, anxiety, and disruption. Alternatively, an explosive or incendiary device, appropriately sited, might produce doomsday-like destruction without recourse to sophisticated weaponry.

Ultimately, however, doomsday terrorism tells us more about the perceptions of victims than about the minds of terrorists. That is because, in the end, doomsday terrorism is not a clearly identifiable category of violence. It is instead a construction placed upon groups and events. That such a concept exists at all is evidence of the shock religiously motivated terrorism has produced in potential victims. It also testifies to the escalating fear that such terrorism will be joined to weapons of mass destruction. Chemical weapons have been in the arsenals of great powers since World War I and biological and nuclear weapons since World War II. Yet for all the suffering and death they have produced, the historical record speaks to the unusual restraint governments have exercised in their use. The motives for this restraint—generally more tied to self-interest than to morality— need not detain us here. Insofar as terrorism is concerned, however, there are different expectations.

Religious terrorists are not thought to be governed by the same prudential considerations as governments, and, as we have seen, there are grounds for this belief. Hence it is less the weapons themselves that cause concern than it is the worldview attributed to those who might possess them. Defense against a doomsday attack would be greatly facilitated if it were possible to predict with reasonable accuracy the groups and individuals likely to attempt it. However, this goal appears unlikely to be realized any time soon. Indeed, after the 1995 Oklahoma City bombing and Aum Shinrikyō release of nerve gas in the Tokyo subway that same year, law-enforcement agencies and scholars made serious attempts to identify likely perpetrators of mass casualty attacks.

The difficulty in making reliable identifications before the fact is the high probability of false positives. The characteristics of individuals and groups known to have contemplated large-scale terrorist incidents turn out to be shared by large numbers of nonterrorists. Investigations after terrorist attacks have identified charismatic leadership, violent rhetoric, apocalyptic belief systems, and social isolation as possible predictors. While one or more may well be necessary conditions for a doomsday attack, they are unfortunately not conditions that are both necessary and sufficient.

One reason prediction has proven so difficult is that groups that manifest these characteristics may be nonviolent at one point in time and violent at another. That is, the groups are dynamic, so that group structure and ideology might remain relatively stable while other factors change in less visible ways: for example, perceptions of the environment, beliefs about what the group's enemies are planning, and personality changes in the leader. Consequently, evidence reliable at the time of its acquisition may not provide useful policy guidance later on. Terrorist groups need to be viewed as in constant interaction with their environments and therefore subject to transformation on the basis of that interaction.

Superimposed upon this complex of ideas are anxieties about doomsday that have developed independently of terrorism. Some, as we have seen, arose from the religious conviction that at or near the end of history, cataclysmic events would destroy much of the existing social order. In secularized form, these fears circulate in the general population, where they have become associated with a variety of catastrophe scenarios: accidental nuclear war, global warming, famines, and resource shortages, and the breakdown of complex technological systems. It requires no great conceptual leap to project such free-floating anxieties onto religious terrorists. Given trends in globalization, it is also entirely possible that terrorists themselves are familiar with these forecasts. Foreign students studying at Western universities would necessarily have acquired some familiarity with the imagery of popular culture, as well as the high level of concern such possibilities can stimulate. It may be from just such fortuitous cultural encounters that self-fulfilling prophecies are made. In that sense, to believe something is real may be to make it real.

Conclusion

The subject of terrorism and doomsday is thus a complex fabric. Its strands include the capabilities of terrorists, their motivations, and their knowledge about their targets; and we must as well take into account the victims' state of knowledge about terrorists, as well as the ambient religious and secular ideas about end-time destruction. The difficulty lies not only in grasping and properly weighing all these factors, but also in being able to separate beliefs from actual dangers. In all considerations of risk, but especially when mass casualties may be involved, those who are vulnerable cannot readily distinguish objective risks from subjective. Where the possible outcome is doomsday—potentially, the destruction of "everything"—maintaining the distinction is particularly difficult. The terrorist may therefore attack either by utilizing an arsenal of doomsday weapons (WMD or conventional) or by manipulating his target's doomsday fears.

CHAPTER 10

Fueling the Fires: The Oil Factor in Middle Eastern Terrorism

MICHAEL T. KLARE

Terrorism, as we know it, has been employed by many different groups over a long period of time and under a wide range of circumstances. At essence, it is a technique for inflicting significant pain on an adversary who may enjoy superiority in conventional military terms but is vulnerable to unconventional means of attack. In this sense, it is a universal phenomenon, disconnected from time and place. But all those who employ this technique do so with specific ends in mind, invariably derived from the distinctive circumstances in which they exist. To understand a particular outbreak of terrorism, therefore, it is necessary to identify and assess these unique circumstances. In the case of terrorism in the modern Middle East, this means, among other things, considering the catalytic role of oil.

Oil is not, of course, the only factor that must be considered in this regard. For example, any comprehensive analysis of the causes of Middle Eastern terrorism must acknowledge the enormous influence wielded by militant Islamic clerics who advocate the use of violence in protecting the Muslim world and its values against what is viewed as the unrelenting encroachment of the West. Likewise, it is necessary to appreciate the colonial past of the region and the deep sense of humiliation experienced by Middle Easterners as a result of the conspicuous and often overbearing presence of foreign troops, officials, and entrepreneurs in their sacred lands. All this being said, it is also true that oil has played a critical role in the West's encounter with the Middle East and so should be viewed as a significant factor in the equation. Indeed, the pursuit of oil has long been one of the most powerful motives for Western penetration of the region and is thus inextricably tied to other key factors.

From the extremists' perspective, the pursuit of Middle Eastern oil is but the latest chapter in a long drive by Western nations to overpower Islamic societies, occupy their lands, and extract their precious resources. Islam's long-term decline from the "golden age" following Muhammed's rise in Arabia, they believe, is the product of insufficiently zealous adherence to the literal teachings of the Koran, on one hand, and of the predatory actions of Islam's enemies, on the other. As suggested by the National Commission on Terrorist Attacks upon the United States (the 9/11 Commission), "The extreme Islamic version of history blames the decline from Islam's golden age on the rulers and people who turned away from the true path of their religion, thereby leaving Islam vulnerable to encroaching foreign powers eager to steal their land, wealth, and even their souls."[1]

What makes oil so significant in the extremists' worldview is that it figures in both sides of this equation. On one side, it has replaced slaves, spices, jewels, and other treasure as the principal lure for Western penetration of the Muslim world, precipitating an abiding frenzy of invasion and plunder. On the other, it has led to the cultivation and installation of client regimes that open their countries to foreign exploitation in return for a token share of the profits, abandoning their Islamic responsibilities in the process. For Osama bin Laden, oil is "black gold," an irresistible attraction for Western invaders and the principal source of corruption among Middle Eastern leaders.[2] "You have to realize that our enemy's biggest incentive in controlling our land is to steal our oil," bin Laden told his sympathizers in a December 2004 videotaped address. "So do not spare any effort to stop the greatest robbery in history."[3]

It is the "criminal" nature of Western oil operations, in bin Laden's view, that justifies the use of force in combating Western firms and governments. "They rip us of our wealth and of our resources and of our oil," he told a group of journalists in 1998. Under these circumstances, he argued, Muslims are fully justified in using violence—even terrorist violence—to protect their resources and way of life. Whereas terrorizing innocent people is reprehensible, he explained, "terrorizing oppressors and criminals and thieves and robbers is necessary for the safety of people and the protection of their property."[4]

For those who adhere to this worldview, it was the British and the French who initiated the theft of Middle Eastern oil resources, but it is the United States that has become the greatest culprit in this regard. Not only have U.S. firms become major actors in the extraction of Middle Eastern oil, but the United States has become the principal supporter of the pliant, corrupted regimes that currently rule Muslim societies. As noted by former CIA analyst Michael Scheuer, a major tenet of the extremist outlook is that the United States has become the "restorer . . . of nineteenth- and twentieth-century European colonialism, as the occupation of Afghanistan and Iraq and the domination of the Arabian Peninsula ensures a supply of cheap oil to the U.S.-led West."[5] For the terrorists, this means that the anticolonial struggle once waged against the French and the British must now be directed against the United States; and as it was once deemed necessary and legitimate to employ violence to dislodge the Europeans, it is equally necessary and legitimate to use force now against the Americans.[6]

This line of reasoning may not be shared by the majority of Middle Easterners, but there is no doubt that it is viewed with sympathy by many of them. For vast numbers of devout Muslims, there is a direct connection between oil and the invasive presence of Western forces in the Islamic world. Osama bin Laden may be engaging in cynical opportunism when articulating this argument, but there is no doubt that his portrayal of Western oil operations as outright plunder finds widespread resonance among the greater Muslim population, and has contributed to the growth and survival of al Qaeda.[7] This being the case, it is essential to identify and assess the links between oil, terrorism, and the American role in the greater Persian Gulf area.

In particular, it is necessary to examine three key aspects of this equation: the relationship between European colonialism and the onset of oil production in the Middle East; the nature of U.S. ties with leaders of the oil-producing nations; and the strategic role of oil infrastructure in the war between the terrorists and their opponents.

Colonialism, Oil, and Resistance

The European powers did not initially seek dominion in the Middle East for the purpose of extracting the region's oil supplies, but the discovery of petroleum in these lands and Europe's growing reliance on oil as a major source of energy certainly contributed to the tempo and vigor of imperial intervention. Great Britain, the most assertive European power in the region, originally took a significant interest in the Middle East to ensure the safety of its communications with India—long viewed as one of the crown jewels of the British empire. Following the completion of the Suez Canal in 1869, Britain sought ever-increasing control over Egypt (then a part of the Ottoman empire) to protect this vital asset, and in 1882 established a protectorate over the country. The British then extended their influence to other countries in the region, but usually were less interested in the internal affairs of these territories than in their geopolitical position with respect to vital transportation routes.[8] This outlook changed in 1908, however, when oil was discovered in Southwest Persia; from then on, the pursuit and protection of major oil concessions figured prominently in British policies and activities in the greater Gulf area.[9]

The relentless pursuit of oil altered the social, political, and economic landscape of this region in ways that set the stage for the emergence of violent anti-Western movements, the precursors to modern terrorism. Oil production by foreign, mainly British-owned, companies had this effect in several ways: by inserting a prominent foreign presence in areas occupied by conservative Muslim communities with little exposure to (or tolerance of) non-Muslim groups; by employing large numbers of local people under conditions that often bred resentment toward foreign overseers; and by prompting London to form political alliances with local monarchs who were viewed as especially receptive to British interests, thereby alienating them from the broad masses of their own peoples. All of these phenomena were to arise with particular force in Persia (Iran after 1935), the first country in the Middle East to experience intensive oil-field development.[10]

Persia began to play a significant role in British foreign policy in the years just before World War I, when the Royal Navy started the conversion of its warships from coal to oil propulsion. This process was accelerated in 1912 by Winston Churchill, then the First Lord of the Admiralty, who believed that the use of oil would provide British ships with a marked advantage over the coal-powered ships in the German Navy in any future encounter. But while oil propulsion provided Great Britain with a significant combat advantage, it also entailed a significant vulnerability: Possessing no oil of their own (the undersea fields of the North Sea would not be discovered for another sixty years), the British were entirely dependent on imported supplies from possibly unreliable providers abroad. To overcome this vulnerability, Churchill and his allies sought to establish ironclad British control over a major foreign source of supply. And the only foreign reservoir wholly owned by an English firm—a concession secured in May 1901 by William Knox D'Arcy—was located in the Khuzistan region of Southwest Persia.[11]

Like other rural areas of the Persian Gulf basin that were later found to contain oil, the Khuzistan region had experienced little prior contact with European intruders, and its people were deeply suspicious of (and often hostile to) foreigners, especially those who did not observe traditional Islamic beliefs. Indeed, the prospecting and drilling teams sent to the region by D'Arcy came under periodic assault from local tribesmen, and in 1907 he appealed to the Foreign Office for assistance. Concluding that protection of the D'Arcy concession was vital to British strategic interests, the government honored his plea and dispatched a small infantry force to the area. Although the resulting skirmishes were on a relatively small scale, they proved to be a harbinger of much more significant encounters to come.[12]

The stakes for Great Britain became much greater in 1914, when Europe edged closer to a major continental war. Fearful that the D'Arcy concession in Persia would fall into hostile hands unless placed under direct British control, Churchill persuaded the Cabinet and then Parliament to approve the acquisition of a majority government stake in the Anglo-Persian Oil Company (APOC), the firm established in 1909 to manage the Khuzistan concession. In time, APOC (later named the Anglo-Iranian Oil Company, or AIOC) grew into one of the world's major oil producers and became a significant source of revenue for the British government. This, in turn, prompted Britain to play an increasingly intrusive role in Persian politics and society, eventually assuming a dominant position in the country.[13]

The large and conspicuous British presence in Persia/Iran had a number of significant consequences that, over time, were to provoke substantial resentment and hostility. To begin with, working conditions at the APOC refinery at Abadan—for half a century the world's largest—were bound to produce anti-British sentiments. While the British managers and engineers enjoyed every imaginable luxury, the mass of Iranian workers lived in appalling poverty. "From its private Persian Club, where uniformed waiters served British executives, to the tight-packed Iranian workers' quarters and the water fountains marked 'Not for Iranians,' it was a classic colonial enclave," observed Steven Kinzer in *All the Shah's Men*.[14] APOC's arrogant and oppressive treatment of its Iranian workers was echoed in the British government's overbearing approach to the government in Tehran. In 1919, London forced the reigning monarch, Ahmad Shah, to approve the harsh Anglo-Persian Agreement, giving England effective control over Persia's army, treasury, transport system, and communications network. Subsequent attempts by Iranian leaders to ameliorate conditions at Abadan and to lighten the terms of the Anglo-Persian Agreement were unfailingly rebuffed by APOC and British officials, sparking anti-British protests and steadily eroding public support for the monarchy.[15]

Great Britain continued to occupy a dominant position in Iran during the reign of Reza Shah, a charismatic military leader who overthrew the last of the Qajar kings in 1925 and established his own dynasty, the Pahlavi. The new monarch attempted to renegotiate some of the harsher terms of the Anglo-Persian Agreement, but faced implacable British resistance and was forced to accept token changes. In 1941, with Reza Shah displaying unmistakable pro-German sympathies—an inclination motivated in part by his anger over London's intransigence—British troops occupied the southern region of Iran and forced the king to abdicate in favor of his son, Mohammed Reza. British forces were withdrawn after the war, but London, along with the AIOC, retained a significant political and economic presence in the country.[16]

Not long after World War II, the winds of radical nationalism swept through the Persian Gulf region, precipitating a mortal clash between Iranian nationalists on the one side and AIOC and its British protectors on the other. Leading the charge against Anglo-Iranian was Mohammed Mossadegh, a determined nationalist who became Prime Minister in April 1951. The details of this confrontation need not be recounted here, but what is important to highlight is the intense bitterness and fury directed at the British and the AIOC because of what was viewed as their imperious presence in Iran.[17] Popular discontent over this presence, Daniel Yergin wrote in *The Prize*, "turned the animosity against Anglo-Iranian into a national obsession."[18] Then, as later, this animosity often expressed itself in violent action of a sort that would today be characterized as terrorism. In March 1951, for example, Mossadegh's predecessor as Prime Minister, Ali Razmara, was assassinated in Tehran after delivering a speech critical of nationalization; several days later, the minister of education was also assassinated.[19] With the country becoming increasingly unstable, Mossadegh was installed as Prime Minister and the Majlis (parliament) voted to nationalize AIOC. After inconclusive negotiations between Tehran and London, the British employees of AIOC were ordered out of the country by 4 October 1951.[20]

The withdrawal of AIOC personnel from Khuzistan did not end the violence associated with the British presence in Iran. For the next two years, British officials sought to persuade Mossadegh to allow AIOC back into the country under a renegotiated contract. The Prime Minister, ever cognizant of the violent fate of his predecessor, refused any arrangement that would appear to ardent nationalists as a sign of subservience to London. Eventually, the British persuaded American leaders (who feared the rise of Communist forces in Iran) to join them in a covert drive to engineer a *coup d'état* against Mossadegh by rightist military officers and supporters of the absent Shah, Mohammed Reza Pahlavi. The coup succeeded, and the Shah returned to the country on 22 August 1953 and assumed near-dictatorial powers.[21] A few months later, he negotiated a new contract with AIOC (now known as British Petroleum) and a consortium of American, Dutch, and French companies to manage the former AIOC holdings.[22]

By portraying his regime as the modern embodiment of the ancient Persian empire, Shah Mohammed Reza muffled some of the radical nationalist fury that had been directed at earlier leaders who had been considered subservient to foreign interests. But the anti-imperial, anti-Western sentiment that had been unleashed in the struggle between Iranian nationalists and the AIOC spread to other areas of the Middle East, producing a succession of violent upheavals that has continued to this day. The Iranian struggle against Britain and the AIOC also foreshadowed another aspect of more recent developments: the active participation of Islamic clerics in anti-foreigner struggles.[23] For example, Mossadegh received considerable support in 1951 from the Ayatollah Abolqasem Kashani, an outspoken critic of imperialism who often appeared at anti-British demonstrations. "Islam warns its adherents not to submit to the foreign yoke," he thundered at one such rally.[24]

Eventually, this animosity would be directed at the United States, as discussed later in this chapter. But, for another decade or so, Great Britain remained the principal target of the militants' wrath throughout the Middle East. This was most vividly demonstrated in 1956, when President Gamal Abdel Nasser of Egypt nationalized the Suez Canal, prompting

Britain and France (in collaboration with Israel) to invade and occupy the Canal Zone. To punish the invaders and bring pressure on them to withdraw, Nasser scuttled dozens of ships in the Canal, thereby blocking the flow of oil from the Gulf to Europe. (At that time, two-thirds of Europe's oil was carried by tanker through the Canal.) Anti-British demonstrations also erupted in other parts of the Middle East, often resulting in violence. In Syria, for example, pro-Nasser forces sabotaged the Iraqi Petroleum Company's pipelines and pumping stations, further reducing the flow of oil to Europe. Furious at the Europeans' heavy-handed action and fearful of triggering anti-American upheavals in the region, President Eisenhower refused to back the British and French, who were then forced to withdraw.[25]

Anti-British sentiment next erupted in Iraq, which had been ruled since 1921 by monarchs and retainers with close ties to the British government. The first king, Faisal, had been imported from Mecca for this purpose by Great Britain after World War I (ostensibly under the terms of a mandate granted by the League of Nations), and his successors were beholden to the British government for economic and military support. From the very beginning, London sought to utilize its dominant position in Iraq to protect the oil concession held by the Iraq Petroleum Company (IPC), an amalgam of British, Dutch, French, and American companies established in 1928 to assume the assets of the defunct Turkish Petroleum Company. The country's monarchs were given a certain amount of leeway in domestic affairs, but not permitted to challenge the IPC's exclusive control over Iraqi oil production and export.[26]

Like Iran, Iraq was occupied by British forces during World War II, and British domination persisted after the war. By the mid-1950s, however, this arrangement had become increasingly untenable. As noted by Peter and Marion Farouk Sluglett of the University of Utah, "the profoundly unrepresentative nature of the government, and the close association of its leading figures with Britain, meant that its policies were out of step with the aspirations of most of the population."[27] Growing popular opposition to the monarchy finally culminated in the revolution of July 1958, which resulted in the assassination of King Faisal II and the Crown Prince, along with other figures considered close to the British.[28] The successor government, headed by General Abd al-Karim Qasim, imposed tough controls on the IPC and enacted other reforms; but even these moves did not satisfy the militant nationalists of the Baath Party (a Pan-Arab socialist party founded in 1943), which staged a second revolution in 1968 and laid the groundwork for the subsequent assumption of absolute power by Saddam Hussein.[29]

By 1968, British colonialism in the Gulf region had become a spent force, and London announced plans to withdraw its forces from "East of Suez." This, in turn, produced a turning point in America's ties with the region, leading to the insertion of an ever larger and more conspicuous U.S. presence. Before turning to a discussion of the consequences of this move, it is important to note that Britain's persistent and markedly aggressive pursuit of oil in the Persian Gulf area left a legacy of antiforeigner, anti-Western sentiment that was often coupled to radical political movements or Islamic fundamentalism.[30] It was in this seething cauldron of hostility that al Qaeda and other contemporary terrorist movements were born.

America, the Saudi Royals, and the Shah

When first becoming involved in the Persian Gulf region during and after World War II, the United States did not encounter the same sort of explosive hostility often directed toward Great Britain. Indeed, many Middle Easterners welcomed the arrival of the United States, as an antidote of sorts to the poisonous stranglehold of European colonialism. The fact that American visitors, for the most part, spurned the haughty arrogance and racial superiority of British colonial officers contributed to this welcoming environment. President Eisenhower's fateful decision to condemn rather than support the 1956 British-French invasion of Suez also helped smooth the way for a growing American presence in the region. Eventually, however, this presence began to provoke resistance from those Middle Easterners who resented the pervasive influence of the Americans and the close ties established between Washington and the ruling monarchies in the region—notably, the royal family of Saudi Arabia and the Pahlavi dynasty of Iran.

Prior to World War II, the United States perceived few geopolitical interests in the Persian Gulf region. This area was rather distant from the main foci of American strategic concern—Europe, the Western Hemisphere, and the Western Pacific—and housed no American assets comparable to the British refinery at Abadan. In addition, Great Britain had long served as the Gulf's regional gendarme, and Washington had no inclination to contest or supplement that role. However, Washington's outlook changed during the course of the war, when it became increasingly evident that the United States was rapidly exhausting its domestic petroleum inheritance—of all the barrels of oil consumed by the Allies during World War II, six out of seven were supplied by the United States—and that the center of gravity of world oil production was moving inexorably to the Persian Gulf area. This prompted the Roosevelt administration to assert a more prominent U.S. role in the Gulf and to seek dominion over some of its major petroleum reserves.[31]

During the course of the war, President Franklin D. Roosevelt and his top aides picked Saudi Arabia to be the primary site of future American oil development. The desert kingdom was selected for this role in part because an American firm—the California-Arabian Standard Oil Company

(CASOC), a joint venture of the Standard Oil Company of California and the Texaco Company—had acquired a major concession in the al-Hasa area of Saudi Arabia, and partly because the British had not established a significant presence in the country, having chosen instead to concentrate on the oil resources of Iran and Iraq. In February 1943, the Roosevelt administration extended Lend-Lease assistance to Saudi Arabia, and American financial aid soon become a major source of income for the Saudi royal family.[32] To further cement U.S. ties with the kingdom, President Roosevelt met with King Abdul Aziz of Saudi Arabia aboard the USS *Quincy* on 14 February 1945 and established a tacit alliance between the two countries.[33]

No minutes were taken of the Roosevelt–Abdul Aziz meeting, and the arrangement they forged did not carry the force of a treaty or convention, like the Anglo-Persian Agreement of 1919. Nevertheless, most observers believe that the understanding reached between President Roosevelt and King Abdul Aziz represents the cornerstone of U.S.-Saudi relations, entailing a commitment by the United States to protect the Saudi regime in return for privileged access to Saudi oil. Thus, when American troops were deployed in Saudi Arabia in August 1990 to repel a possible invasion by the Iraqi forces then occupying Kuwait, Secretary of Defense Richard Cheney told the Senate Armed Services Committee that U.S. ties to the region "hark back with respect to Saudi Arabia to 1945, when President Franklin Delano Roosevelt met with King Abdul Aziz on the USS *Quincy*, at the end of World War II, and affirmed at that time that the United States had a lasting and a continuing interest in the security of the kingdom."[34] It was on this basis that CASOC—later known as the Arabian-American Oil Company, or Aramco—invested huge sums in the development of Saudi Arabian oil fields after World War II, and the Department of Defense established a military base at Dhahran and helped modernize the Saudi armed forces.[35]

In the early years of its evolution, the U.S.-Saudi relationship did not provoke the same degree of anticolonial, antiforeigner resentment as that engendered by the British presence in Iran and Iraq. This was so because American firms and officials generally maintained a low profile in the kingdom, and because the oil fields (and the U.S. base at Dhahran) were far removed from the main centers of Saudi population and culture in Riyadh, Jiddah, Medina, and Mecca. The House of Saud also commanded far more authority and legitimacy than the monarchies in Iran and Iraq, and so its embrace of the U.S. presence helped to muffle antiforeigner sentiment. This does not mean that such sentiment did not exist—resentment toward Aramco and the American presence boiled up during labor protests in the al-Hasa oil fields in the 1940s and 1950s—only that it did not achieve the explosive scale seen in Iran in 1951 and Iraq in 1958.[36] The prospect of a major crisis was also averted when the American owners of Aramco agreed to a 50-50 split of oil revenues with the Saudi government in 1950 and later accommodated themselves to the progressive nationalization of the company's petroleum assets.[37]

Although Saudi Arabia was to remain the central focus of U.S. involvement in the Persian Gulf area, Washington took a significant interest in Iran after the rise of Mossadegh and the nationalization of AIOC in 1951. Although American officials were well aware that Mossadegh was no friend of communism and that AIOC invited nationalization through its haughty and uncompromising behavior, senior figures of the Eisenhower administration, led by Secretary of State John Foster Dulles and CIA Director Allen Dulles, feared that the political instability in Iran—largely engendered by the economic decline produced by the withdrawal of British managers and engineers from Abadan, as well as the boycott of Iranian oil orchestrated by AIOC—would result in a communist takeover and the installation of a pro-Soviet regime. To prevent this, the CIA cooperated with British intelligence agencies in organizing a *coup d'état* against Mossadegh and the installation of a strong, pro-Western regime led by Shah Mohammed Reza Pahlavi.[38] Despite some early missteps, the coup succeeded and the Shah assumed near-dictatorial rule in August, 1953.[39] Once in power, the Shah rescinded many of the reforms initiated by Mossadegh and allowed a consortium of Western firms—including the Aramco partners (SOCAL, Texaco, Exxon, and Mobil) plus Gulf—to assume day-to-day management of Iran's oil fields and the refinery at Abadan.[40] With this move, Yergin observed, "the United States was now *the* major player in the oil, and the volatile politics, of the Middle East"[41] [emphasis in the original].

As in Saudi Arabia, the U.S. presence in Iran did not initially arouse the sort of antiforeigner sentiment long directed toward the British, because the United States had not been involved in the original exploitation of Iranian oil and because its critical role in orchestrating the coup against Mossadegh was not immediately evident. For a time, American oil workers and military advisers were welcome in Iran, and the Shah became a major customer for U.S. arms and industrial goods. By 1978, there were over 8,700 U.S. military technicians working in Iran, and thousands of other American specialists were working in the country's energy, transportation, and communications sectors.[42]

As the Shah's wealth and power grew, so did his megalomaniacal tendencies. Vast amounts of oil-generated revenue were spent on military modernization, the development of a domestic arms industry, highway construction, and other infrastructure improvements. These costly initiatives stroked the Shah's ego and benefited some well-connected Iranian business interests—who often received substantial bribes from American firms seeking to do business in the country—but did little for the masses of Iranians, who suffered from high inflation and the decline of traditional markets and enterprises.[43] In response to growing rumbles of discontent, much of it emanating from the country's influential Shiite clergy, the Shah clamped down on opposition movements and jailed many prominent dissidents. Before long, his notorious and widely feared domestic security organization, Savak (the Persian acronym for the National Intelligence and Security Organization) came to be seen by the masses as the principal expression of a tyrannical and discredited regime.[44] Anti-government sentiment coalesced in mass protests in 1978 and finally precipitated the departure of the Shah on 16 January 1979.[45]

The anger that erupted in 1978 and 1979 was largely aimed at the Shah, his cronies and military officers, and the agents of Savak. But because the United States had become so closely tied to the Shah and was viewed by many in the populace as one of his principal pillars of support, some of this hostility was also directed at this country. The fact that the United States had helped engineer the coup against Mossadegh—by now, common knowledge in Iran—and that American advisers had worked closely with the military and Savak served to stoke anti-American sentiment.[46] Leading this charge was Ayatollah Ruhollah Khomeini, an outspoken critic of the Shah's regime who had been jailed and then forced into exile in Iraq. From his sanctuary in Iraq, Khomeini flooded Iran with audiocassettes denouncing the monarchy and portraying the United States as the "Great Satan" for its role in installing and pampering the Shah. Not one to mince words, Khomeini described the United States as the source of all that troubled Iran: the megalomania and authoritarianism of the Shah, the pervasive economic disorder, the rise in alcoholism and sexual promiscuity, the decline of traditional values, and so on. Only a thorough purge of all things American, including the U.S. oil companies in Abadan, could cure these ills and restore the nation's spiritual health.[47]

Khomeini returned to Iran in triumph on 1 February 1979 two weeks after the flight of the Shah, and within months his followers and associates had secured effective control over the country. The foreign consortium that had managed Iran's oil industry for the past quarter of a century was dissolved, and its mangers were driven from the country. The same fate befell the American military missions and defense contractors in Iran. Finally, in the dramatic climax to this purge, hundreds of militant Islamic students screaming "death to America" (and enjoying the Ayatollah's obvious support) seized the U.S. Embassy on 4 November 1979—supposedly to protest the Shah's admittance into the United States for medical treatment—and held fifty American diplomatic personnel hostage there for the next 444 days.[48]

Whether or not the "Hostage Crisis," as it came to be called, can be described as a classic instance of terrorism, it certainly can be seen as the first major expression of violent anti-Americanism in its contemporary, Islamic-infused form. Much of the rhetoric employed by Khomeini and his followers at the time—notably the portrayal of the United States as the principal source of the Westernizing, anti-Islamic currents flowing through the Middle East and as the major supporter of the corrupt and un-Islamic regimes populating the region—has been echoed by the other extremist movements that have arisen in the area, including those, like al Qaeda, that disdain the Shiite leadership in Iran. And because the pursuit of Middle Eastern oil was (and continues to be) seen by these forces as the driving motive for America's perfidious involvement in their midst, anything to do with foreign oil extraction has became a legitimate target of wrath.[49]

From Khomeini to Bin Laden

Although fully in control of Iran, Khomeini and his clerical associates did not consider their work done; rather, they sought to spark Islamic revolutions in other Muslim countries ruled by secular or Westernized regimes and to drive the United States (and its Jewish allies in Israel) out of the Middle East entirely. "Iran's collective perception was initially messianic: in deposing the Shah and building the Islamic Republic, it was doing God's work on Earth, and it was to spread that blessing to the rest of the Muslim world," former CIA analyst Kenneth Pollack explained in *The Persian Puzzle*. "The export of the revolution also served Iran's (and especially Khomeini's) obsessive hatred of the United States and Israel. It was a way in which Iran could lash out at the Great Satan and the Little Satan, and it could be done in ways that played to Iran's strengths and our weakness."[50] As part of this effort, Iran provided money, advice, inspirational rhetoric, and other forms of support to radical Islamic groups throughout the Middle East—in the hope, as Pollack put it, "of helping them to throw off the yoke of tyranny and realize a true Islamic society as well."[51]

The first international effects of the Iranian revolution were felt in Saudi Arabia, where militant Shia and Sunni groups rebelled against the House of Saud. In November 1979, at the time of the Hostage Crisis, Shiite oil workers in the al-Hasa region organized illegal strikes and demonstrations to protest restrictions on Shia religious practices and to express their contempt for the corrupt royal family. Carrying pictures of Khomeini, they rampaged throughout the oil region, attacking army barracks and setting fire to oil installations, until government troops flooded the area and killed dozens of protestors.[52] At approximately the same time, an armed rebellion broke out among Sunni tribesmen in western Saudi Arabia. On 20 November, the rebels seized the Grand Mosque of Mecca and occupied other key sites in the area. Identifying themselves as the Movement of the Muslim Revolutionaries of the Arabian Peninsula, the rebels demanded the end of favorable terms for foreign oil companies, the withdrawal of all foreign military advisers from the country, the elimination of government corruption, and a return to the canons of "genuine" Islam.[53] Even more than the Shiite protests in al-Hasa, the Mecca rebellion—born in the religious heartland of Saudi

Arabia—posed a critical threat to the royal family, and thus provoked an immediate and powerful response by the military. Hundreds of rebels were killed in the ensuing fighting, and 64 of their top leaders were subsequently executed.[54]

Although short-lived, the Mecca rebellion of November 1979 was to have a number of long-lasting consequences. To begin with, the United States stepped up its support for the Saudi regime and provided additional assistance to the Saudi Arabian National Guard (SANG), the paramilitary organization responsible for internal security and the protection of the royal family.[55] Soon afterward, President Ronald Reagan chose to make explicit what had long been U.S. policy: that the United States would use force if necessary to prevent the overthrow of the House of Saud. Referring to the fall of the Shah two years earlier, he told reporters on 1 October 1981 that "I will not permit [Saudi Arabia] to be an Iran."[56] While comforting to the royal family, these words and actions stirred up resentment toward the United States among those who shared the rebels' damning view of the royals and sought their replacement by a more observant and ascetic regime with fewer ties to the West.

For their part, the Saudi royals responded to the Mecca rebellion by jailing known opponents of the regime and silencing critical mullahs. But in a move that was to have important and ominous consequences later, they also made numerous concessions to the conservative clergy and provided them with abundant funds (supposedly, for educational and charity work) in order to secure their allegiance to the status quo.[57] Much of this largesse was used to support religious schools (*madrasas*) in Saudi Arabia and other Muslim countries, schools that often stressed a rigid interpretation of the Koran and preached a virulent form of anti-Americanism. Some of the charities supported by these funds were also used to recruit and support Islamic militants who shared the inflammatory views of the Mecca rebels. These militants encouraged the use of violence to purge the Islamic world of hostile Western influences, and later formed the nucleus of al Qaeda.[58]

Before addressing subsequent developments in Saudi Arabia, it is necessary to say a few more words about the international impact of the Iranian revolution. In their determination to punish the United States for its support of the Shah and to bolster the forces arrayed against Israel, Khomeini's associates extended considerable aid to militant Islamic organizations throughout the Middle East. A strong Iranian presence was established in the Bekaa Valley of Lebanon and used as a base of operations for training and arming the fighters of Hizballah and Islamic Jihad, extremist movements that gained in strength following Israel's 1982 invasion of Lebanon. Some of these fighters are thought to be responsible for the terror attacks on the U.S. Embassy in Beirut on 18 April 1983 (killing seventeen Americans and forty-six others) and on the U.S. Marine compound at the Beirut airport on 23 October 1983 (killing 241 U.S. servicemen).[59] The Iranians have also been linked to the 25 June 1996 attack on the Khobar Towers in Saudi Arabia.[60]

In none of these episodes, nor in the Mecca revolt of November 1979, can it be said that oil was a direct source of violence. By this point, the issue for the extremists had become American support for what were seen as corrupt and compliant regimes in the Muslim world. At the same time, however, it was perfectly evident to all involved that American support for these regimes was largely motivated by the pursuit of oil and a preference for governments that would ease America's access to their petroleum supplies. As President Reagan put it in 1981, "There is no way that we would stand by and see [Saudi Arabia] be taken over by anyone who would shut off the oil."[61] It is this precept that so aroused the hostility of political and religious militants in the greater Gulf area and provided the fuel for Osama bin Laden's attacks on this country.[62]

As is well known, bin Laden first identified himself with radical Islamic ideologies in the late 1980s, while working in Pakistan to assist the Arab volunteers who were serving with the Afghan mujahideen in the guerrilla war against the Soviets occupiers of Afghanistan. Among those who reportedly made the biggest impression on him was Abdullah Azzam, a Palestinian jurist and theologian who argued that all Muslims have a sacred duty to wage jihad—a holy war—against the Western and Soviet infidels seeking to invade and occupy Muslim lands.[63] Many of his ideas were derived from Sayyid Qutb, an Egyptian militant who years earlier, while in jail for the attempted assassination of Nasser, wrote an influential manifesto calling for revolutionary war against impure Muslim governments.[64] Together, Azzam and bin Laden established the Maktab al-Khidamat (Office of Services) to recruit volunteers for the anti-Soviet jihad in Afghanistan and to assist them once they arrived at guerrilla base camps in northern Pakistan. At some point, for reasons not altogether clear, bin Laden broke with Azzam and established his own support network, al Qaeda (the Base). From then on, bin Laden operated independently of other jihadist groups in Pakistan but espoused the same inflammatory rhetoric originally preached by Sayyid Qutb and Abdullah Azzam.[65]

In the fall of 1990, after the Soviets had abandoned Afghanistan and fighting had broken out among rival Afghan factions, bin Laden returned to Saudi Arabia and turned his attention to the Iraqi forces that had invaded and occupied Kuwait on 2 August of that year. Viewing Saddam Hussein as a secularizing apostate whose rule was no more legitimate than that of the Soviet-backed regime in Afghanistan, bin Laden began talking of a campaign by the "Afghan Arabs," the Arab volunteers who had fought with the Afghan mujahideen, to drive the Iraqis out of Kuwait. The same sort of jihadist struggle mounted against the Soviets in Afghanistan, he argued, could now be employed against Saddam Hussein in Kuwait. Eventually, bin Laden was invited to a meeting in Riyadh with Prince Sultan, the defense minister. According to accounts of the meeting, bin Laden presented his plan for a jihad waged by the Afghan Arabs against the Iraqis and was told in no uncertain terms that the royal family would prefer to rely on the Americans, with their superior numbers and equipment.[66]

For many analysts, this meeting proved a critical turning point in bin Laden's political evolution. Up until this time, he had considered the royal family a potential ally in the struggle to protect Islam from its enemies—after all, many princes had contributed to al Qaeda's efforts in Afghanistan—but after the meeting with Prince Sultan, he came to see the House of Saud as an obstacle to his objectives. The large American military presence in Saudi Arabia was an affront to Allah, he concluded, and those responsible for inviting them had by this very act severed their ties to Islam, and so must be swept away.[67] Bin Laden's encounter with Prince Sultan and subsequent disillusionment with the royal family "constituted a point of no return," Jonathan Randal wrote in *Osama: The Making of a Terrorist*. "He had made his mind up about the Al-Saud and about the American presence. To his thinking, they were linked; to save the Kingdom, all of the American military must be made to leave, and the Al-Saud would then be easy pickings without their infidel protectors."[68] With this in mind, bin Laden began to speak out against the royal family and to establish links with militant opponents of the regime; after refusing entreaties from Riyadh to cease these activities, he was deported in mid-1991, settling first in Sudan and then in Afghanistan.[69]

It was during these years that bin Laden and his supporters began to stress the connections between oil, the American government, and the corrupt Saudi leadership. One prominent bin Laden ally, Sheikh Safar al-Hawali, wrote that the American-led "crusaders" intended to occupy the Arabian Peninsula in order to seize its petroleum reserves. Soon bin Laden was speaking in similar terms, and calling for a holy war to dislodge the Americans.[70] "Every action has its reaction," he told Peter Arnett of CNN in 1997:

> If the American presence continues, and that is an action, then it is natural for reactions to continue against this presence. In other words, explosions and killings of the Americans would continue. These are the troops who left their country and their families and came here with all arrogance to steal our oil and disgrace us, and attack our religion.[71]

In the years that followed, bin Laden returned again and again to the view that America's primary interest in the Middle East was the extraction of oil, that the United States has consistently supported local regimes that were friendly to its petroleum interests, and that the use of terrorist violence was justified to protect the resources of the Muslim world against foreign invasion and theft. "For over seven years," he argued in 1998, the United States has been occupying the lands of Islam in the holiest of places, the Arabian Peninsula, plundering its riches, dictating to its rulers, humiliating its people, terrorizing its neighbors, and turning its bases in the Peninsula into a spearhead through which to fight the neighboring Muslim peoples.

To erase this blight on the Islamic world, he thundered, it was "an individual duty for every Muslim" to "kill the Americans" and drive their armies "out of all the lands of Islam."[72]

Oil as a Strategic Target

Aside from constituting a central feature of Muslim extremists' indictment of the major Western powers—first Great Britain and then the United States—oil is also seen by many terrorist groups as a major strategic target in the struggle between militant Islam and its enemies. This is so in part because of its symbolic importance as *the* major expression of Western intervention in the Middle East and in part because of its critical role in sustaining the West's energy-intensive economies. Attack the oil fields and pipelines, the terrorists reason, and you not only focus attention on the imperial presence of the Western powers but also deliver a blow at their most vulnerable point, their excessive dependence on cheap Middle Eastern petroleum. "Pipelines are very soft targets," Robert Ebel of the Center for Strategic and International Studies (CSIS) observed in 2003. "They're easy to go after. It doesn't take a rocket scientist to figure out where you can do the most damage, both physical and psychological, with the minimum amount of effort."[73] This outlook has governed terrorist behavior in the Middle East for some time, but has gained particular momentum in recent years with the war in Iraq and al Qaeda attacks in Saudi Arabia.

Oil facilities had often come under attack during periods of labor unrest and nationalistic fervor, as in Abadan and al-Hasa during the late 1940s and early 1950s, but sabotage and vandalism of this sort did not reflect a clearcut strategic intent. Following the 1956 British-French invasion of Suez Canal Zone, however, President Nasser and his supporters specifically targeted oil production and transport facilities as a way of bringing pressure on the invaders. The Canal itself was blocked by ships sunk at Nasser's orders, while Syrian engineers sabotaged the IPC pipeline to the Mediterranean, and sympathetic workers in Kuwait wrecked that country's supply system. Together, these actions blocked the normal route for approximately three-quarters of Europe's oil, producing significant shortages and economic hardship. When President Eisenhower refused to allow emergency shipments of American petroleum to Europe, British and French leaders saw no option but to suspend the invasion and withdraw their forces.[74]

The Suez experience highlighted the importance and vulnerability of oil-supply infrastructure, inspiring numerous other acts of violence in the years that followed. During the 1970s and 1980s, it was states that most often (or most conspicuously) attacked oil-related targets in their pursuit of strategic advantage. During the Iran-Iraq War of 1980–88, for example, both sides bombed the oil infrastructure of their opponents in an effort to diminish their economic capacity to sustain extended combat operations. When Kuwait began providing substantial loans to Iraq for the purpose of acquiring arms, moreover, Iran attacked Kuwaiti oil platforms and tankers—bringing the United States into the war as guardians of Persian Gulf oil shipping (under Operation Earnest Will, 1987–88).[75] During the opening rounds of the 1991 Gulf War, Saddam Hussein set fire to Kuwaiti oil wells, causing billions of dollars in damage.[76] More recently, various terrorist groups have viewed such actions as a centerpiece of their offensive strategy—as evident in recent developments in Iraq, Saudi Arabia, and surrounding areas.

An early expression of this strategy was the October 2002 attack on a French oil tanker, the *Limburg*, while sailing off the coast of Yemen. Reportedly, the *Limburg* was intercepted by a small boat filled with explosives that came alongside it and detonated, blowing a hole in the hull and killing one sailor (along with those aboard the small boat); almost 100,000 barrels of crude oil then spilled out into the surrounding water and burned. This attack, widely attributed to al Qaeda, was seen as the opening salvo in a new campaign to punish and weaken the West by assaulting the exposed conduits of the global oil-supply system.[77]

The targeting of exposed oil infrastructure has assumed particular significance in Iraq, where attacks on pipelines and pumping stations have become a near-daily experience. The assaults started soon after the outbreak of insurgent warfare in the summer of 2003, following the collapse of the Hussein regime. Just as Iraqi and American oil managers were set to reopen the export pipeline between Kirkuk in northern Iraq and Ceyhan in Turkey, saboteurs dynamited the line, cutting off the flow of oil.[78] Every time Iraqi engineers succeeded in repairing this vital conduit, saboteurs would strike again, preventing the export of Iraqi oil. Recurring attacks have also been conducted on other pipelines and facilities in Iraq, including offshore loading terminals in the Persian Gulf.[79] In one such assault, on 24 April 2004, suicide bombers in a small boat detonated their craft after colliding with a U.S. patrol vessel guarding the Khor al-Amaya terminal, killing three American sailors.[80] Given the frequency and sophistication of these attacks, it is evident that the insurgents are not just interested in inflicting random damage, but rather are pursuing a calculated strategy of curtailing Iraqi oil exports in order to deprive the interim government of operating funds.[81] Indeed, Iraqi officials reported in November 2004 that sabotage of Iraq's oil infrastructure had already deprived the interim government of $7 billion in lost revenue[82]—a prodigious sum for a government that is struggling to rebuild essential services and thereby win the support of the general population.

Although not as great a threat to the survival of the interim government as the war in the cities, the insurgents' campaign against Iraq's pipelines and refineries has had a significant strategic impact; it has forced the United States to shift funds away from the reconstruction effort to oil field security and to commit some of its own, overstretched forces to the pipeline protection effort. In August 2004, Ambassador John Negroponte, the top U.S. official in Iraq, announced plans to reduce funding on water, electricity, and sewer projects by $2.25 billion and to use the funds released in this manner for increased infrastructure security and oil-industry rehabilitation. While deemed necessary to prevent further damage to the oil industry (and the accompanying loss of export revenues), the shift in funds will undoubtedly harm efforts to win the support of Iraqis suffering from the breakdown in essential services.[83]

The need for greater infrastructure protection has also led to the deployment of additional U.S. troops in areas housing major refineries, pipelines, and pumping stations. In late 2003, for example, the Department of Defense revived the 327th Tiger Force, an elite component of the 101st Airborne Division, to conduct airborne surveillance of the Kirkuk-Ceyhan pipeline and quash any attempts to sabotage the line.[84] Additional U.S. forces have also been deployed in the Basra area to protect loading terminals and other key installations.[85] Obviously, troops committed to the protection of pipelines and loading facilities cannot be used to fight battles elsewhere in Iraq, and so attacks on oil infrastructure have the added attraction for the insurgents of diluting the American counteroffensive.

The strategic nature of oil terrorism is also evident in Saudi Arabia, where al Qaeda and allied groups have targeted foreign firms and technicians employed by Saudi Arabia's oil industry, presumably to damage its operating capacity. The first such assault occurred on 1 May 2004, when gunmen killed five Western oil-industry workers in Yanbu, the site of a major petrochemical complex. The workers, employees of ABB Lummus (a Houston-based subsidiary of ABB, the Swedish-Swiss engineering firm), were helping to revamp a large refinery in the area; following the attack, all foreign employees of ABB Lummuns chose to leave the country, slowing work on the refinery project.[86] A second attack of this type occurred four weeks later, on 29 May when a group of armed militants said to be allied with al Qaeda stormed a residential compound occupied by Western oil workers in Khobar, near the oil center of Dhahran. This time, twenty-two people died and scores were wounded before Saudi commandos drove off the gunmen and released the hostages they had seized.[87]

Like the earlier attack in Yanbu, the assault in Khobar was widely interpreted as part of a systemic drive by al Qaeda to drive foreign technicians out of the kingdom and disrupt Saudi oil output, thereby causing intense embarrassment for the royal family and reducing its income. As suggested by Jean-François Seznek of Columbia University, "The [29 May] attack was orchestrated to display that the royal family cannot maintain security in the heart of its own oil patch, and in that sense they succeeded."[88] Other analysts noted that foreign workers comprised only a small proportion of the Saudi oil-industry workforce, and that assaults of this sort would not significantly affect the kingdom's ability to extract and export oil.[89] Furthermore, the extremists' ability to conduct attacks of this sort is thought to have been greatly reduced by a major antiterrorist crackdown conducted by the Saudi government in the wake of the 29 May assault. Nevertheless, it appears that leaders of al Qaeda, beginning with Osama bin Laden, view attacks on Saudi Arabia's oil industry as the most effective way of undermining the regime's credibility and power and thus are likely to initiate other strikes of this sort. In fact, bin Laden explicitly endorsed such actions in a December 2004 audiotaped message, calling on Muslim militants in the Middle East to "do your best to prevent them [the United States and its allies] from stealing oil. Focus your operations on it, especially in Iraq and the Gulf."[90]

Implications for the West

Bin Laden's recent statements, coupled with the recurring attacks on petroleum facilities and personnel in the Persian Gulf area, suggest that the links between oil, Western interests, and Middle Eastern terrorism remain as strong as ever. Indeed, it appears that extremists in both Iraq and Saudi Arabia have come to view oil terrorism as a major technique in their war against the West, both because of oil's symbolic importance as the principal magnet for Western penetration of the region and because of the perceived strategic value of attacks on oil installations and supply routes. Oil will, therefore, prove to be a major "center of gravity" in the ongoing struggle between Middle Eastern terrorists and their foes in the West.

This reality is certain to prove a major challenge to the Western powers. On one hand, the United States and its allies remain deeply dependent on imports of Middle Eastern energy and will become even more so in the future as oil production in the West continues its irreversible decline and Persian Gulf output accounts for an ever-increasing share of global output.[91] (According to the U.S. Department of Energy, the share of world oil production accounted for by the major Persian Gulf producers will rise from 27 percent in 1990 to 36 percent in 2025.)[92] On the other hand, the conspicuous presence of Western oil interests in the Gulf and the continued existence of regimes linked to these interests will prove an abiding source of popular irritation and resentment, thus providing aid and comfort (and recruits) to the terrorist underground. This dynamic is not likely to change so long as the Western powers rely on Persian Gulf oil and the regimes they consort with are considered illegitimate by many in the region.

One way to mitigate the severity of this dynamic, of course, is to minimize the threat through aggressive counterterrorism efforts and enhanced protection of oil installations and personnel. And, indeed, the United States and its allies are attempting to accomplish exactly this, with some success. As recent developments in Iraq and Saudi Arabia demonstrate, however, small terrorist cells can be hard to find and destroy, and oil infrastructure can prove difficult to protect. This naturally leads to the question of whether the dynamic could or should be altered from the *other* side, by reducing Western reliance on Middle Eastern oil. This is no easy matter: Because the Gulf provides such a large share of the world's petroleum, no amount of "diversification"—increased reliance on non-Gulf suppliers like Angola, Nigeria, Russia, and Kazakhstan—or drilling in protected wilderness areas (like the Arctic National Wildlife Refuge) will provide sufficient energy to replace Middle Eastern supplies. To successfully reduce its reliance on the Gulf, Western oil consumers will have to reduce their reliance on petroleum, *period*, through increased conservation and energy-saving techniques. This is not the place to weigh the relative advantages of these approaches, except to say that any discussion of strategies for combating Middle Eastern terrorism should look at all sides of the equation, not just the obvious one of aggressive counterterrorism.[93]

Oil and violence have been linked in the Middle East since the arrival of the British in Persia some 100 years ago, and will no doubt remain interlocked for some time to come. This is not because there is something inherently sinister or evil about petroleum, but rather because most of the world's oil reserves are located in the Gulf area and because, in seeking to gain access to these supplies, outside powers have inserted themselves into communities that have long been the target of exploitation. The fact that these communities are largely devoted to an ancient religious tradition that is thought to be under attack by the West, and that the pursuers of oil are mostly adherents to a different religious tradition that is closely associated with centuries of invasion and conquest, only adds to the intensity of their hostility. Under these circumstances, it will probably take the demise of petroleum as the world's leading source of energy to sever the ties between oil and violence altogether.

CHAPTER 11

Socioeconomic and Demographic Roots of Terrorism

PAUL R. EHRLICH AND JIANGUO LIU

There is a long-standing discussion of the definition of terrorism, perhaps tracing back to the South African government's passing of an "antiterrorist" law in 1967 which basically defined terrorists as those doing anything the government did not like.[1] Definitions of terrorism are numerous; they change over time and are not agreed upon in the international community, even among different agencies within a single country—including the United States.[2] Things have been further muddled by the George W. Bush administration's announcing a "war on terrorism," which—as Zbigniew Brzezinski pointed out—was (since terrorism is a tactic) like declaring a war on "blitzkrieg" rather than on Nazi Germany. For this chapter, terrorism is defined as actions carried out by militarily weak subnational or transnational groups from developing nations against private citizens, public property, or occupying troops of militarily powerful developed nations. Its goal is to achieve political ends through intimidation produced by violence or the threat of violence (for example, beheading kidnapped hostages). It is war that, in the terms of von Clausewitz, is "simply a continuation of political intercourse, with the addition of other means."[3] In this case, it is by means available to the frustrated and relatively powerless. This restrictive definition, which for convenience is referred to as "9/11-type terrorism" in this chapter, allows us in this short essay to ignore the complexities of other forms of terrorist warfare: state terrorism, with its roots in ancient Mesopotamia,[4] and the intra national terrorism of the IRA, Basque separatists, Tamils, violent American antiabortionists, and others.

There is much talk of a long "war" on terrorism, but too little attention to what must be a critically important part of that long war—changing the

basic conditions that facilitate terrorist acts. While thoughtful people realize that those acts are connected to a variety of underlying factors, social
scientists are far from understanding exactly what circumstances trigger
them.[5] Various hypotheses and arguments have been advanced about the
origins of terrorism in general[6]—and terrorism against the West, based in
Islamic fundamentalism, in particular[7]—but an integrated framework that
considers the possible causes of terrorism in a systematic manner is still
lacking. The roots of terrorism are multifaceted and deep.[8] They extend
from the past to the present; they reside in culture, politics, psychology,
and technological changes; and they are stimulated by demographic and
socioeconomic conditions.

Technological, Geopolitical, Cultural, and Psychological Factors

One very basic social factor in establishing today's terrorist landscape is
the sharp difference in rates of cultural evolution in the technological and
political-ethical spheres.[9] The former has been especially rapid in the past
two centuries, greatly increasing the destructive forces available to individuals and small groups. Whereas terrorists in 1805 were largely restricted
to one-shot firearms, the invention of dynamite in 1867 opened the door
to widespread bombings, and technological advances combined with political missteps (such as failure to make the nuclear nonproliferation treaty
work) means that terrorists in 2005 potentially have access to a variety of
weapons of mass destruction.[10] The "other means" of von Clausewitz have
changed dramatically, while cultural evolution in the political-ethical sphere
has not made all that much progress since Plato. Indeed cultural "sticki-
ness"—the failure of groups to discard outdated ideas—is an obvious element in generating terrorism. One need only think of modern consequences
of the defeat of the Serbs in Kosovo at the "Field of Blackbirds" in 1389,
or of the existence of a Jewish state in Palestine thousands of years in the
past, to find excellent examples.

The development of technological means enabled the Oklahoma City
bombing; the Marine Barracks bombing in Beirut, Lebanon; the Tokyo subway Aum Shinrikyō sarin incident; the use of Kalashnikovs, rocket-
propelled grenades (RPGs), and plastic explosives in resistance to the U.S.
occupation of Iraq; and, of course, the 9/11 disaster. Technological progress
also makes cities increasingly vulnerable to nuclear terrorism, in the form
of either "dirty bombs" (conventional explosives that spread radioactivity)
or actual fission weapons ("suitcase bombs" or crude gun-type bombs).
That technological progress has been accompanied by an increase in attractive targets, as the population density of cities has increased, tall buildings have proliferated, and centralized systems of transport and supply of

critical goods like water and electricity have proliferated. Population growth and the development of high speed transport systems also makes societies more vulnerable to biological terrorism. Dense populations are more attractive targets than dispersed ones, and automobiles and airplanes make the quick spread of pathogens and disease-carrying individuals easy.[11] Furthermore, population growth and technological advances in agriculture have created tempting targets for bioterrorism in the form of huge mono-cultures of both crops and domestic animals. To see the potential damage that could be done by agricultural bioterrorism, one need only consider the impact of the appearance of foot-and-mouth disease in England in 2001, which required the slaughter of hundreds of thousands of cattle, sheep, and pigs.

Few can doubt that one probable factor that helps facilitate global terrorism is geopolitical: the historic behavior of Western nations in the Middle East, designed to ensure the abundant, uninterrupted flows of petroleum upon which developed nations have become dependent.[12] For example, the presence of American troops in Saudi Arabia until late 2003 enraged some Muslims, especially Osama bin Laden, but was deemed necessary for ensuring security of critical energy resources in the region. And while an energy policy giving heavy weight to conservation and renewable sources could probably reduce the threat of terrorism, it would also threaten America's love affair with gas-guzzling SUVs and the energy interests that guide much of the foreign and environmental policies of the U.S. government. Furthermore, the long time lags involved in developing and deploying alternative energy technologies make it seem likely that petroleum-related factors contributing to terrorism will persist for decades.

But U.S. attempts to maintain some control of oil sources cannot alone explain the attacks on the World Trade Center and Pentagon on September 11, 2001 (9/11). Cultural (especially religious), political, and individual (psychological) factors also contribute to terrorism, but these can be extremely difficult to measure and interpret.[13] For example, fundamentalism—including Christian, Islamic, Jewish, and Hindu—is clearly one major social background factor in global terrorism, as described in several chapters of this publication. Overall, however, social scientists are not easily able to explain the thriving of supernaturalism in the United States (and the current administration) in the face of dramatic declines in theistic belief in other developed democracies, although various theories have been advanced.[14] In short, one cannot ignore the religious factor in global terrorism. It is framed by militant Islam opposed to a militant Zionism that is supported by a militant fundamentalist Christianity.[15] The demographic trends associated with these religious fundamentalist factors thus warrant considerable scrutiny in the context of the global war on terrorism.

For two primary reasons, this chapter seeks to draw more attention to persistent demographic and socioeconomic factors that can facilitate 9/11-

type terrorism and make it easier to recruit terrorists. First, politicians rarely seem to recognize—and the press all too often ignores—these factors. Second, these variables can be relatively easily evaluated, in contrast to other variables such as religious and psychological factors.[16] Analysts who claim that (at least in the Muslim world) economic factors are primarily viewed by educated Islamists as not important for creating prosperity, but only important for gaining power to strike at what is viewed as a pernicious and materialistic Western culture,[17] may well be partially correct. But it seems clear that in much of the Muslim world popular dissatisfaction with socioeconomic conditions—themselves partly traceable to demographic variables—help create the circumstances under which educated dissidents and fundamentalists can more readily mobilize the population to the participation in (and support of) terrorist acts. And the social conditions that leave much of the education of young boys in Pakistan and Afghanistan to radical madrasas (Islamic religious schools), which graduate them with no useful skills, help provide the foot soldiers of terrorism. There and elsewhere, improving social and economic conditions *can* help mitigate the motivations that lead to terrorism,[18] but the continually rapid expansion of the number of children to be educated remains in many poor countries one barrier to such improvement.

Population Growth and Age Structure

One key demographic factor operating in relation to the 9/11 attacks is population growth in the United States, as it relates to extremely high per capita consumption of energy and other resources, which in turn leads to foreign policy decisions meant to secure access to these resources. But this pales in comparison to the important and complex relationship between demographic variables and political instability in the developing world.[19] One often-neglected issue is the age composition of populations, which interacts with poverty and other factors related to terrorism. The vast majority of terrorists are young adult males. Approximately 90 percent of the individuals on the FBI's most wanted terrorist list are males who were between twenty-two and thirty-four years old when their first alleged terrorist act took place.[20] The ages of twenty suicide terrorists discussed in one prominent terrorism study[21] were between sixteen and twenty-eight, with a mean age of 21.3. This is hardly surprising; after all, the vast majority of violent antisocial behavior is generated by young males, often unemployed or underemployed. Some 65 percent of crime in the United States is committed by people between fifteen and thirty-five, and almost 80 percent by males.[22] Data from developing countries are sparse, but in China approximately 70 percent of crime is committed by people below the age of twenty-four.[23] Furthermore, changes making the age structure of the population more youthful (i.e., increased birth rates) have effects on prices, government revenues and expenditures, and the distribution of incomes that can lead to political instability. The demand for jobs, for instance, increases while revenues permitting governments to help with job creation do not keep pace, since the number of well-established taxpayers is a shrinking proportion of the population.[24] The increase in the labor force also leads to a decline in real wages (as it has in the United States in past decades) which, combined with the need for proportionately fewer older taxpayers to provide Social Security for the elderly, is not a trend likely to increase political stability.

In the first half of this century, the proportion of young males in developing nations will continue to be substantially larger than in developed countries. Huge numbers of boys now under the age of fifteen—many in Muslim nations, acquiring a hatred for the United States—will soon enter the high-crime years, and the global effects of a youthful age composition will persist. By 2050, a projected 23 percent of the males in developing countries will be between the ages of twenty and thirty-four, while less than 17 percent of males in the developed countries will be in that range.[25] Job opportunities for the disproportionate numbers of young men in poor economies are relatively scarce now. But high population growth rates are expected to continue in many developing nations, with a projected annual growth rate for people aged twenty to thirty-four of 2.82 percent (as opposed to a rate of −0.16 percent in developed countries) during the years 2000–50.[26] In the face of such growth, job opportunities may become much rarer. And large numbers of unemployed, disaffected young men—who see the West, with its permissive lifestyle and the U.S.-Israel alliance, as the enemy of Islam—provide the cannon fodder for terrorism in the Muslim world.

The world's population is projected to increase to over 7 billion by 2010. Approximately 95 percent of this growth will take place in developing countries, where social welfare and basic municipal/public services are already strained and grossly inadequate. Furthermore, urbanization is accelerating, and about half of the global population will live in cities by 2010, compared with one-third today. Population growth, especially "youth bulge" (the growing number of people between fifteen and twenty-four), will create huge new demands for social welfare and infrastructure, such as water, energy, food, housing, waste disposal, sanitation, transportation, public health, and education. Failure to meet these demands for basic needs will likely trigger more terrorism. Among those heavily affected by population pressures are countries (such as Saudi Arabia) that hold critical geopolitical positions.

While disproportionate numbers of young males will be one result of rapid population growth in the developing world, many believe that growth itself now retards development, widening the rich-poor gap and increasing the distress of those being left behind.[27] Others, however, see issues related to population structure as more critical causes of stress in Arab societies.[28] These include migration, a growing number and higher proportion of children seeking education, gender inequities, and increasing stress on patriarchal family structures. One tension-causing factor in Saudi Arabia, in addition to economic inequity, is probably its extremely high rate of population growth. It has a total fertility rate (TFR, basically defined as completed family size) of 5.7 children, exceeded in the Arab world only by Palestine, Yemen, and Oman. That growth is unlikely to slow down much in the next couple of decades—Saudi Arabia's population of slightly over 21 million is projected to grow to 41 million in 2025 and 60 million in 2050.[29] Saudi Arabia may be able to continue to command the resources to supply the infrastructure and services required by such growth. It was a major source of the 9/11 terrorists, but it is also one of the richest developing countries. On the other hand many poorer developing nations, Muslim and non-Muslim, facing high growth rates, will not be able to keep up, thus further multiplying the ranks of the disaffected.

Disparities in population growth rates among different peoples (such as certain ethnic groups and religions) may also exacerbate the conditions that breed terrorism. For example, one element in Israeli attitudes toward Palestinians is the much more rapid population growth of the latter. The total fertility rate of Jews born in Israel is under 3, approaching replacement level, while that of Palestinians in the Gaza strip is over 7, the highest of any national-level entity.[30] On the other hand, the Jewish population has more immigrants. Overall, after taking natural growth and migration into account, the annual growth rate of the Muslim population in Israel was 6.0 percent from 1950 to 1995 while that of Jews was 3.1 percent.[31] As a result, some Jews are afraid of being overwhelmed by Arab numbers, while some Arabs see their baby boom as a weapon with which to destroy Israel.[32] To complicate matters further, the high birth rates in Israel's ultraorthodox community (a TFR of 7.6) is another cause of tension, threatening—among other things—to render the Israeli welfare system insolvent.[33] The combination of these demographic trends point to a very likely future of unrest in the Middle East.

Poverty and Inequality

Rampant poverty, inequality, and large numbers of young men facing dim economic prospects produce both a humanitarian tragedy and a serious threat to those not so afflicted. As one analyst put it, slum belts around many cities in the developing world "are living with explosive population growth . . . [placing] in the hands of revolutionary organizations, dedicated to destroying governments, legions of young women and men with few good prospects—the veritable working capital of violence."[34] Even more depressing is the overall outlook for a globalizing world wracked with inequity. Distinguished theologian John B. Cobb Jr. painted the following picture of possible events as the rulers of Earth slowly discover what technological advances and biophysical limits to growth mean in terms of the need for labor: They

> will find that a greatly reduced population would be preferable. The underclass will appear not only as superfluous but also as an impediment to the well-being of those people who are productive. If, in desperation, the underclass turns to violence, then the powers that be will have the excuse they need to eliminate many of its members.[35]

Now the underclass is turning to violence.

Some indicators of socioeconomic conditions possibly conducive to creating terrorists are summarized in Table 11.1. The sample of nations chosen for this brief analysis have citizens on the most wanted list of the U.S. Federal Bureau of Investigation[36] because of alleged terrorist activities. To these have been added Afghanistan and Iraq (where the current U.S.-led "war against terrorism" is taking place) and Pakistan (Afghanistan's largest neighboring country, armed with nuclear weapons, where many people support militant Islam). The first (PPP) column can be viewed as an index to economic status (crudely, level of development). It can be assumed that poor societies are more likely to generate terrorism (even if terrorist individuals themselves are not poor) than wealthy societies. The second (gender equity) indicates the degree of disadvantage suffered by women (economic status, literacy, independence), likely an important factor in measuring how modern, educated, and intellectually resilient a society is. Equitable societies seem less likely than inequitable ones to produce the sorts of distress associated with terrorism. The third (health and population) shows the highly correlated factors of family size and life expectancy—in modern societies, the first is small and the second high. Terrorism can have roots in the distress of individuals seeing the suffering and lack of opportunities suffered by fellow citizens. The fourth (knowledge) is another measure of the degree of development. While individual terrorists may often come from the more educated segments of their societies, again their motivation may be affected by the general state of their society. And finally, the fifth data column is included because it can be argued that more-secure societies (with higher scores) are less likely to resort to terrorism than less-secure societies.

Poverty, especially because of its severely unequal distribution among nations, is obviously one of the most important factor in this discussion of root causes of terrorism. It has been claimed that Islamic rage against the United States is caused in part by the relative failure of Islamic nations to achieve economic success.[37] As can be seen in Table 11.1, in addition to the level and distribution of income, gender equity, public health, education,

Table 11.1

Socioeconomic indicators of selected countries[1]

Nations	PPP_L10%[2]	Gender Equity[3]	Health & population[4]	Knowledge[5]	Peace and Order[6]
LESS DEVELOPED COUNTRIES					
Afghanistan	—	14	9	8	4
Comoros	—	46	24	8	40
Egypt	1522	30	45	49	78
Iraq	—	22	19	25	3
Kenya	182	39	20	14	35
Kuwait	—	27	55	52	37
Lebanon	—	40	53	59	19
Libya	—	58	36	54	40
Pakistan	763	28	21	13	17
Saudi Arabia	—	36	16	38	21
Tanzania	140	46	16	6	63
Average	652	35	29	30	32
MORE DEVELOPED COUNTRIES					
Canada	7123	66	86	95	72
France	6446	59	88	86	69
Germany	7758	66	83	85	75
Japan	12082	44	91	93	92
Italy	7700	53	87	84	79
Norway	11537	74	85	91	77
United States	5744	58	82	94	58
Average	8341	60	86	90	75

1. Larger numbers mean better conditions.
2. The average purchasing power parity (U.S. dollars) per capita in the group with lowest 10 percent share of income or consumption. PPP_L10% was calculated based on the data from World Development Report 2000/2001 of the World Bank and *2001 World Population Data Sheet* of the Population Reference Bureau. The remaining indicators were from *The Wellbeing of Nations* (Robert Prescott-Allen, 2001, Island Press).
3. The average of three unweighted indicators (gender and wealth, gender and knowledge, and gender and community).
4. The lower of a health index (healthy life expectancy at birth) and an index of population (total fertility rate).
5. The average of two weighted indicators of education (school enrollment) and communication (telephone and internet use).
6. The average of two unweighted indicators (peace and crime).

communication capabilities, and exposure to violence on average all show a substantial gap between this sample of developing countries (the vast majority with substantial Muslim populations) and developed countries, with only a very few overlaps.

In addition to poverty itself, a hotbed that breeds terrorism is warehouses for refugees. There are 12 million refugees around the world, and more than 60 percent of them have been confined to crowded refugee camps or settlements for over ten years.[38] These idle and frustrating conditions (e.g., hunger and disease) make many young male refugees very resentful and cause some of them become terrorists. For example, the refugee camps of Pakistan generated Afghanistan's Taliban movement. Because of social-political instability in some developing countries and the shortage of financial support from wealthy countries, there is no reason to believe the refugee problem will shrink in the foreseeable future.

At the very least, these interacting and largely structural factors can be important to the motivations and recruitment of terrorists, even when those terrorists are relatively prosperous individuals (for example, many of those involved in the recent attacks in the United States). Although some terrorists (especially leaders such as Osama bin Laden) were members of a disaffected elite, relatively well-educated and well-off, the socioeconomic and political conditions in their nations provided a good basis for both their moral indignation and grassroots support among the disadvantaged. And sadly, what projections can be made give little hope that this important socioeconomic gap between the developing and developed nations represented in Table 11.1 will be substantially closed in the near future. For example, projected population growth indicates that the economies of Saudi Arabia, Pakistan, Afghanistan, and Egypt will need to grow by about 100 percent, 75 percent, 70 percent, and 40 percent respectively in the next quarter century just to keep per capita purchasing power parity from falling.[39] Furthermore, while the influence of cultural factors is difficult to evaluate, at the very least it seems unlikely that some potentially important ones—such as religious fundamentalism or attitudes towards globalization[40]—will change rapidly. Indeed, the very strictness of religious fundamentalism may make it extremely resistant to change and may promote a willingness to die for beliefs, which at one time was a feature of Western religious tradition and is now a major feature of Islam.[41] Indeed, one could claim that in the Western world today, a type of cultural fundamentalism surrounds the use of automobiles and SUVs, especially in the United States.

Discussion and Conclusions

This chapter has not addressed two obvious and important questions. First, why have many countries (for example, in Latin America and Southeast

Asia) which share some socioeconomic and demographic conditions with the countries discussed here and have ample reason to harbor grievances against the United States or other Western nations not generated the same sort of terrorist threats against the rich countries as have originated in the Middle East? One answer might be that the United States' exceptional support of Israel and its oil dependency have served as triggers that are absent in other regions. Also, the active suppression of guerrilla movements, such as the Sendero Luminoso in Peru,[42] by national governments is probably significant as well. The second, and perhaps more interesting, question: Why are the vast majority of people in the nations listed in Table 11.1 not terrorists? One obvious answer is that most people, rich and poor, tend to be much more focused on their own lives and families than on political action of any kind. And the poor, in particular, are often fully involved in trying to obtain bread, and do not have the luxury of time or energy for political involvement. They may contribute overall to the motivation of terrorism, rather than participate as terrorists themselves. In addition, it is clearly not necessary for the majority of a population to become terrorists in order for there to be a very effective terrorist campaign.

To answer these two important questions definitively, however, will require a much more detailed understanding of the interactions of factors such as differences in culture, history, political organization, peer pressures, and individual personality and background. Until more is known about these interactions, it will remain difficult to demonstrate a quantitative and fully convincing causal linkage between terrorism and the socioeconomic and demographic factors discussed in this chapter. Such interactions have already been the subject of substantial debate in social psychology—the subdiscipline that deals with the relationships of people to other individuals and to groups, institutions, or all of society. The basic issue is the degree to which recruitment into terrorist activity is a result of situational issues like poverty, oppression, or state terrorism and how much is due to personality traits such as aggressiveness, empathy, or political or religious zealotry. But since those traits are difficult at best to alter, it seems more useful to concentrate efforts on addressing the roots of terrorism and changing situations that might encourage it.

Thus, the prudent course is for the United States and other developed nations to work to ameliorate poverty, inequity, and oppression while trying to unravel the complex root causes of terrorism. After all, the United States would reap many other benefits from improving conditions in developing nations, even when this does not lead directly to a significant reduction of terrorism. However, while the United States should play a much more central role in helping improve demographic and socioeconomic conditions in developing nations, it is one of the stingiest rich nations in terms of development assistance, ranking fifteenth in the list of top fifteen donor countries; the United States gives only one tenth of 1 percent of GNP as aid to developing countries, while Denmark, Netherlands, Sweden, and Norway all give more than eight times that proportion, and all but Italy give more than twice as much.[43] The United States should increase its level of international aid and carefully target that aid on efforts that would change social, economic, and demographic conditions (for example, increasing employment and helping lower fertility rates) in developing countries. Aid to education (particularly of women) and to development of labor-intensive enterprises are two examples. This effort will require innovation, care, and tough diplomacy, and cannot be done overnight.

There is a real danger that development aid which is inadequate, poorly targeted, or designed without appropriate community input can actually increase popular resentment that feeds terrorism. But properly deployed, development aid could provide economic opportunities not previously available to potential recruits, and can help create a middle class with a vested interest in suppressing terrorism.[44] Aid is a tool that can be very helpful if properly applied, but that means more awareness of the penalties of poor implementation than is usual. Foreign aid from wealthy countries to poorer nations should not be viewed just as a gift but also a moral debt, because many countries in the First World attract well-educated people from the Third World and implement unfair trade policies. The brain drain and trade inequities fuel the resentment and help generate terrorism in poorer nations against the West. Furthermore, wealthy countries such as the United States need to have more commitment for reducing refugee warehouses and accept more refugees for permanent resettlement.

Without dramatic action, the demographic and socioeconomic conditions in Islamic nations in the Middle East, South Central, and Southeast Asia could continue to support terrorism and terrorists for many decades to come. Other areas where comparable conditions exist now and seem sure to prevail for decades include sub-Saharan Africa, central Asian border areas of Russia, parts of western China with minority populations, Cambodia, Laos, and parts of Latin America such as Haiti, Guatemala, Honduras, Nicaragua, and Bolivia. Thus, some of the factors upon which 9/11-type terrorism can thrive are strongly present in a substantial portion of the world and are very unlikely to disappear soon. A contributing factor that will surely exacerbate terrorist tendencies (or at least not reduce them) is the policies of the developed nations that are designed to expand their consumption and maintain their access to cheap natural resources in less developed regions.

There is one overriding conclusion to be drawn from this discussion. The factors that are clearly within the power of the United States and its allies to alter are the economic ones. It can be argued that an all-around successful strategy today for the United States economically, environmentally, militarily, and ethically would be to assume that macroeconomic factors do help to promote terrorism, and thus the United States and other rich nations should move as rapidly as possible towards an energy-efficient economy that minimizes dependence on oil (and coal and natural gas), while putting much more effort into limiting wasteful resource consumption and closing the rich-poor gap.[45] In the process, the rich could create brand-new markets for the outputs of the new economy and speed the reduction of their own population sizes to more satisfactory and sustainable levels.[46]

Acknowledgments

This chapter is dedicated to the memory of D. Loy Bilderback, California State University, Fresno, who tragically passed away just as he was gathering information to collaborate with us on this chapter. We are indebted to Gretchen Daily, Anne Ehrlich, Gary Luck, Jai Ranganathan, and Shripad Tuljapurkar for critical comments on the manuscript. We also thank Jennifer Baca, John Holdren, and Brent Wheat for their help in providing us with some references. This chapter is partly based on Ehrlich and Liu, "Some Roots of Terrorism," *Population and Environment* 23 (2002): 183–92.

CHAPTER 12

The Intersection of Terrorism and the Drug Trade

VANDA FELBAB-BROWN

The premise of a symbiotic relationship between terrorism and illicit drug economies around the world is widely accepted among scholars and policy makers. Indeed, the term "narcoterrorism" is now a standard entry in lexicons of academics and policy analysts specializing in terrorism as well as those specializing in illicit economies. Combating the narcoterrorist threat has become one of the primary objectives in the United States' stability and reconstruction policy for Afghanistan. Further, the $3.3 billion the United States has committed to combat the production of coca in Colombia is also used for combating the leftist guerrillas of the Revolutionary Armed Forces of Colombia (FARC).

As is frequently assumed, control over some aspects of the illicit drug industry brings vast financial profits to belligerent groups. However, it brings them much more than simply money and weapons. As the analysis provided in this chapter will demonstrate, it also gives terrorist groups freedom of action and hence allows them to optimize their tactics with their overall grand strategies. And crucially, sponsorship of the illicit economy bestows political legitimacy on belligerent groups (a category which includes a wide variety of terrorist and insurgency movements), since local populations are frequently dependent on illicit crop cultivation for their basic livelihood. This chapter will also show that the extent of three types of gains belligerent groups derive from the illicit economy—financial profits, freedom of action, and political capital—is influenced by several factors: 1) the government policy toward the illicit economy; 2) the character of the illicit economy; 3) the state of the overall economy; and 4) the presence or absence of thuggish traffickers.

Although terrorists derive multifaceted gains from the drug economy, the existence of a drug economy in of itself does not give rise to terrorist organizations and other belligerent groups. In the absence of political, social, and economic frustrations, the existence of an illicit economy does give rise to criminal organizations, including large or boutique-style cartels or mafia organizations. These groups, however, need to be distinguished from politically or ideologically motivated belligerent groups, including terrorist organizations. Of course, in some cases, the root causes of the illicit economy—such as devastation of the overall economy and large-scale poverty—can be the same causes that gave rise to the terrorist organizations. Yet the presence of a drug economy does not cause the emergence of a terrorist organization. Marijuana is being cultivated in California and synthetic drugs are being produced in Seattle, for example, but neither place is known to be a spawning ground for terrorism. What the interaction of terrorist groups with drug economies does do, however, is vastly increase the staying power of the terrorist organizations by greatly strengthening their physical capabilities and political capital. Successful control of the illicit economy also compresses the time a terrorist organization needs to grow from a few individuals to a large-scale organization with wide support base.

Antidrug warriors frequently assert that there is no meaningful difference for analytical and policy purposes between drug traffickers and terrorists. These two types of actors are presumed to have shared motivations and interests, if not to have actually morphed into a singular actor, "the narcoterrorist." Again, the relationship between the terrorists and traffickers is more complex than is often assumed. As this analysis will show, both actors do share some interests, such as the preservation and growth of the illicit drug economy. Yet they also have many competing interests, such as the extent of their control over the illicit economy. Thus, although they may fight the government units together, they will also frequently fight each other. No doubt, some blurring in the membership between the two groups may occur over time. Drug traffickers may adopt political goals and join belligerent groups to evade criminal prosecution, for example. Similarly, after years of futile political and military efforts, some terrorists may continue being involved with the illicit drug economy purely for financial profits and abandon any political ambitions, thus becoming regular criminals. The scale of any such blurring, however, is highly situation-specific, and it should not be assumed *a priori* that terrorists and traffickers always have identical goals or have merged into a singular actor.

Terrorists and Drugs: The Parameters of the Issue

For the purposes of this discussion, a terrorist is defined as an individual who deliberately injures or kills noncombatants. This very general definition leads to the inclusion of a large number of diverse belligerent groups in the discussion of the intersection of terrorism and drugs. Although no doubt there are fundamental differences in the motivation, techniques, strategies, and goals of different terrorist movements, such a broad definition of a terrorist allows for a richer and more nuanced discussion of the nexus of terrorism and drugs. Moreover, most insurgencies by their very nature target civilians in order to instill fear of, and compliance with, the movement. Terrorism is thus one of the key tactics of many insurgent movements. The guerrilla organization known as Sendero Luminoso (Shining Path or SL) in Peru, for example, was notorious for their brutalization of villages in rural areas as well as for inflicting high numbers of casualties by bombing civilian targets in Lima.

The difference in the character of the terrorist movements does have practical implications for the ability of the group to penetrate the international drug trade. Territory-based organizations, such as the Taliban (which was, of course, more than just a terrorist organization), can control and tax the cultivation and processing of illicit crops. But for a loose network without a substantial territorial base, such as al Qaeda, it is extraordinarily hard to profit from cultivation and processing. It is much more likely that such groups will attempt to control some part of the international smuggling routes or some aspect of money laundering. Examples of non-state belligerent groups (whether or not classified as terrorist)[1] profiting from the drug trade include the Taliban and the Northern Alliance in Afghanistan, possibly al Qaeda,[2] the FARC, the United Self-Defense Forces of Colombia (AUC), the National Liberation Army (ELN) in Colombia, Sendero Luminoso and the Tupac Amaru Revolutionary Movement (MRTA) in Peru, the Irish Republican Army (IRA) in Great Britain, the Kosovo Liberation Army (KLA) in Yugoslavia, Hizballah in Lebanon, the Kurdistan's Workers Party (PKK) in Turkey, and possibly *Euzkadi Ta Askatasuna* (Basque Fatherland and Liberty, or ETA) in Spain.

The existence of an illicit narcotics economy does not by itself cause the emergence of a terrorist movement or broader military conflict. Such an illicit economy will likely generate the emergence of a criminal organization (unless the criminal syndicate organized the illicit economy in the first place), but will not inherently give rise to terrorists, warlords, or insurgents. The difference in motivation of individuals simply seeking profit for its own sake and those seeking profit to advance their political goals is of key importance both for analysis and policy. It is, of course, possible that in the course of a prolonged conflict, terrorists may abandon their political cause and become simply drug traffickers; the FARC in Colombia is frequently pointed to as an example of such a transformation. The reverse is also not unheard of—traffickers who were originally not driven by any political motivations, but instead purely by financial profits, come to embrace a political cause in order to elevate their status and gain political legitimacy. Colombia, once again, provides an example: Some members of the rightist AUC were originally simply drug barons who, fearing extradition to the United States under drug trafficking charges, bought themselves commander position in the AUC in order to advantageously negotiate with the Colombian government and avoid extradition.

Terrorists' Gains from Illicit Economies

Terrorist groups derive three types of gains from their involvement with the illicit economy: increased *physical capabilities* (money and weapons); increased *freedom of action* (the ability to optimize tactics and strategies); and increased *political capital* (legitimacy, relationship with the local population, the willingness of the local population to withhold intelligence on the terrorist organization from the government, and the willingness to provide intelligence about government units to the terrorist organization). In fact, the magnitude and scope of increases in the strength of the belligerent groups is frequently so large and multifaceted that the terrorist groups become entrenched and difficult to defeat and gain the potential to expand their respective conflicts if they so desire. Getting access to drugs thus vastly increases the staying power of guerrilla movements and terrorist organizations.

Physical Capabilities

The size of financial benefits is frequently in the realm of hundreds of millions of dollars. The actual magnitude of the belligerent group's financial profits depends on the extent of its involvement with the drug economy, the availability of competitors for the provision of the services of the belligerent group to the drug economy, and international market prices for the illicit commodities, in addition to the four conditions specified below. The extent of the financial profits grows as the terrorist group moves from simply taxing the producers of the illicit substances (typically peasants), to providing protection and safe airstrips to the traffickers, to taxing the smuggling of precursor agents, to getting involved with money exchange and laundering. The greater the number of other actors in the conflict capable of providing the services provided by the guerrillas, the smaller the individual group's financial profits. These profits are used to improve military capabilities by facilitating procurement, paying higher salaries to soldiers and developing better logistics.

After Sendero Luminoso took control of the drug-producing Upper Huallaga Valley (UHV) in 1986, its capabilities grew to such an extent that it was able to escalate its attacks to a level of violence that posed a serious threat to the Peruvian state.[3] At that time, Peru was the world's largest supplier of coca, and the UHV the biggest coca-production region of the world.[4] More than 200,000 families were growing coca on more than 100,000 hectares in this region.[5] Virtually 95 percent of the economic activity in the UHV was coca based. In control of the region, Sendero Luminoso's leaders eventually levied a 5 percent tax on the coca paste sold by the *campesinos* to the traffickers who exported it to Colombia. Even though—because of the illicitness of the economy—profit estimates are notoriously inaccurate and broad, it is believed that SL managed to raise around $30 million a year just from the tax on coca paste.[6] This income was later supplemented by the *traquatero barons* (drug lords) paying a facilitation fee of $10,000 to $15,000 to the guerrillas for providing safe airstrips for each takeoff by an aircraft carrying coca paste out of the Upper Huallaga Valley—this alone earned them about $75 million.[7]

The total FARC income is believed to be hundreds of millions of dollars annually.[8] Estimates of FARC's income from taxing the illicit economy fluctuate between $60 and $100 million per year. The protection rents extracted by guerrillas from narcotraffickers in 1996 amounted to $600 million, and less than $200 million annually in 1997 and 1998.[9] Representing at least 50 percent of the overall income of the FARC—and around 20 percent for another leftist guerrilla movement, the ELN—the drug profits are further supplemented with income from kidnapping and extortion of oil companies (a primary source of income for the ELN) and other large businesses.[10] The overall income of the FARC itself could thus amount to $300 million a year.[11]

The AUC's annual income from the drug economy is believed to be around $75 million annually, which is approximately 70–80 percent of the group's total income.[12] This income is supplemented by protection rents from big business, oil companies, and cattle ranchers who hire the paramilitaries for protection from the guerrillas. Together, the FARC, the paramilitaries, and the ELN are involved in more than 70–75 percent of coca grown in Colombia and 40–42 percent of the country's coca production.[13] Colombia is currently the world's principal producer and distributor of refined cocaine, generating roughly 80 percent of global production.[14] All three guerrilla movements in Colombia have increasingly begun to diversify their income portfolio to include the taxation of Colombia's production of marijuana and opium.[15]

After an initial year of religious zealousness to eradicate Afghanistan's burgeoning poppy cultivation in 1994–95, the Taliban decided that eradication was both financially unsound and politically unsustainable. Progressively, the fundamentalist religious movement shifted its attitudes to tolerating poppy cultivation, then to levying a 10–20 percent *zakat* (religious tax) on cultivation and processing, and finally to actively encouraging poppy cultivation, even teaching farmers how to achieve greater yields. The profits, estimated between $30–$200 million a year, were roughly comparable to the Taliban's profits from illegal trafficking in legal goods under the Afghan Transit Trade Agreement and constituted a major portion of the country's GDP and income. When during 2000–01, the Taliban declared poppy cultivation illegal and enforced—very successfully—its edict, in order to boost heroin prices and placate the international community (in its attempt to be recognized as a legitimate government), they had stored enough heroin to maintain their supply of money without new poppy cultivation for many years.[16] All three examples—Peru, Colombia, and Afghanistan—illustrate that illicit narcotics generate only a portion of the income of those belligerent groups that become involved with the drug trade and that belligerent groups rarely rely solely on illicit narcotics for their financing. However, once belligerent groups penetrate the illicit narcotics economy, they tend to become more and more enmeshed in it.

Financial profits have been used by belligerent groups for many purposes, most obviously to finance their military campaigns and procure weapons. For example, although dynamite stolen from mines continued to be used more often than any other weapon by Sendero Luminoso even after it tapped into Peru's drug economy, once the guerrilla group profited from drugs it could also procure weapons such as machine guns, G-3 and FAL automatic rifles, U.S.-made hand grenades, and mortars.[17] Similarly, after gaining access to the drug money, SL was able to pay salaries to its combatants, with both the amount and the numbers of persons receiving funds very large by Latin American standards, thus helping recruitment of new members.[18]

As in the case of Peru, the vast financial profits of the belligerent groups in Colombia are used for multiple purposes, including most obviously the financing of their military campaigns. Although at first dependent on the army for weapons, after the AUC tapped into the drug money it was able to independently acquire numerous aircraft, including eleven Cessna, four shipping planes, and fourteen helicopters with military equipment (some of which were Black Hawks). In addition to improved procurement, the paramilitaries also sought to expand their base by offering higher wages to their fighters than do both the FARC and the ELN.[19]

Freedom of Action

The facilitation of weapons procurement and logistics allows terrorist groups to optimize their tactics and strategies for achieving their larger goals. Terrorist groups no longer need to attack military arsenals for procurement or sit in caves making primitive explosive devices. If they choose to do so, they can concentrate on strategic, high-impact, visible targets. Having assured reliable finances and logistics thus gives the terrorist group much greater flexibility in strategy and tactics.

Participation in the illicit economy can, however, also limit the mobility and freedom of action of the belligerent group if the group needs to defend the illicit economy from governmental actions or from other nonstate belligerent groups seeking to take over the illicit economy. This argument is on occasion invoked with respect to the FARC. The ability of the belligerent group to retreat from a drug-cultivation territory, for example, can be compromised by the group's perceived need to defend the coca plantations from governmental spraying planes. However, compromising its ability to retreat is a matter of choice of the belligerent group, not a matter of necessity.

Political Gains

Belligerent groups derive significant political gains, particularly political legitimacy, from their involvement with the drug economy by protecting the local population's reliable and lucrative source of livelihood (the illicit economy) from the efforts of the government to repress the illicit economy. They also derive political capital by protecting peasants from brutal and unreliable traffickers and by bargaining with traffickers for better prices on behalf on the peasants. Prior to obtaining protection from Sendero Luminoso, for example, the Peruvian peasants were vulnerable to being killed by the drug traffickers if they failed to deliver a promised amount of coca leaves, even if the reason was the eradication of the crop by the government's antinarcotics squads.[20] The members of Sendero Luminoso put a stop to this practice and also negotiated better prices for the peasants from the traffickers.[21] In Colombia, too, the guerrillas have provided protection from both the *narcos* and the paramilitaries. They also demanded that the narcotraffickers pay better wages to the *cocaleros*. In areas in which the FARC presence is weak or nonexistent, the price of labor paid by the *narcos* is lower than in areas with the guerrillas' strong military presence.[22]

Belligerent groups also buy legitimacy by using drug profits to provide otherwise absent social services, such as clinics and infrastructure, to the local population. In Afghanistan, for example, Mullah Nasim Akhundaza, a warlord in the Helmand Valley during the late 1980s and early 1990s, admitted in an interview in 1987 that he had established hospitals, clinics, and forty madrasas with his profits from drugs.[23] The large financial resources obtained from coca production allowed Sendero Luminoso to improve the water supply, the sewage and transportation systems, and street cleaning whenever it took over a village.[24] In Colombia, the FARC has used some of its drug money to establish local clinics and organize public works, such as the construction of infrastructure and provision of means of transportation.[25] Indeed, in many municipalities, the FARC has been the sole provider of essential public services.[26] The AUC also emulates this strategy, providing social services (such as hospitals) and enforcing the rule of law, such as its restrictions on prostitution.

This approach of winning hearts and minds by providing social services is consistent with the methods of many Islamist movements (like Hamas)[27] and has been undertaken even by purely criminal syndicates without political ideologies or objectives. Before the demise of the Medelin and Cali cartels, for example, top kingpins like Pablo Escobar and Rodriguez Gacha sponsored public projects in poor neighborhoods, including the building of sports facilities, hospitals, and schools. The ability to acquire political capital by subsidizing public projects is, of course, greater if the state authority is weak and absent from the regions in which the terrorist organization operates. Terrorist groups also derive political capital from drug production by being able to claim nationalist credit if a foreign power threatens the local illicit economy. The overall political legitimacy belligerent groups obtain from their sponsorship of the illicit economy is frequently very thin, but nonetheless sufficient to motivate the local population to withhold intelligence on the group from the government if the government attempts to suppress the illicit economy.

Learning Curve and Contagion Effect

Frequently, there is a learning curve in the attitudes of belligerent groups toward the illicit economy. Insurgents and terrorist groups tend to exploit drugs opportunistically rather than starting out with drug exploitation as a central feature of their grand strategy, even though the insurgency–drug nexus may eventually become a prominent feature of the conflict. However, once a group in the conflict learns how to effectively exploit the illicit economy, the multiple forms of gains the group will derive from drugs will be so lucrative and broad that they motivate other belligerent groups in the conflict to emulate their competitors' policies toward the illicit economy. This emulation is likely to take place even if the group did not originally seek to exploit the drug economy and had "stumbled on drugs by accident." The expected emulation does not mean that new terrorist groups will emerge within the conflict, but to the extent that multiple belligerent groups are present, they will emulate the successful practices of their competitors. Accordingly, illicit substances cause a *modus operandi* contagion effect, without generating new terrorist groups.

In Peru, Sendero Luminoso did not originally actively seek to extract profits from illicit substances. It only began to turn drugs to its purposes when it was pushed into the UHV by the governmental counteroffensive in other provinces—Ayacucho, Huancavelica, and Apurimac—which until then had been the main areas of SL's operations.[28] By chance, the UHV also happened to be the main coca production region in Peru.

But even after Sendero Luminoso seized the area, it did not immediately exploit the drug windfall. In fact, its first reaction was to prohibit the "anti-Marxist" drugs, in addition to its policy of prohibiting prostitution and trying to limit the consumption of alcohol. However, the fierce reaction from the peasants made SL's leaders cave in and eventually actively encourage the production of illicit substances.[29]

It took some time for the members of Sendero Luminoso to learn how to effectively exploit the coca production in the region. At first, it simply levied a tax on coca cultivation on the peasants. Later, it discovered that it could make even more money by providing protection to the *narcos* and their coca-paste and cocaine labs and charging them an airstrip fee for each plane that took off in the area that SL controlled. Next, SL leaders used the coca gains to pay for the provision of social services. Finally, the group also branched into other phases of cocaine production and distribution. In the region of Xion, for example, it became involved in currency exchange.

Once the leaders of Sendero Luminoso figured out how to exploit the drug windfall to its advantage, it provided a modus operandi for other guerrillas operating in the country. The middle-class, urban-based Tupac Amaru Revolutionary Movement (*Movimiento Revolucionario Tupac Amaru*, or MRTA)[30] emulated SL by investing in the drug business. Although originally focusing on the cities, the MRTA expanded its activity from the center of its operations, Lima, to the UHV, following the example set by Sendero Luminoso. Its goal was not to instill fear in the population, but to obtain funds and support by providing the peasants with a profitable livelihood.[31] The competition for the drug benefits led to a military conflict between the MRTA and Sendero Luminoso, in which the drug traffickers sided with SL and which SL eventually won, substantially pushing the MRTA out of the drug business.[32] The MRTA never succeeded in gaining substantial control of the UHV and the coca production, but the significance of being involved in the illicit economy was not lost on its members.

Similarly, in Colombia, the FARC's original reaction was to oppose the cultivation of coca and marijuana, since the Marxist guerrillas considered drugs counterrevolutionary.[33] This policy, however, proved vastly unpopular with the local populace. Thus, fearing the loss of its social base, the FARC recognized that it needed to tolerate coca production.[34] At first, the FARC only tapped into the most basic component of drug production, the taxing of the coca farmers.[35] Progressively, however, the group levied new tariffs on other illegal transactions, from importing precursor agents to refining cocaine. They also demanded rents from the *narcos* for coca paste, protection of labs, and the provision of airstrips. Today, the FARC (like the AUC) protects trafficking routes inside Colombia and directly traffics in the regions of Colombia where it has completely displaced the traffickers.

The Traffickers and the Terrorists

The nature of FARC's participation in the illicit economy offers little to support the "narco-guerrilla thesis" that equates the motivations and interests of the drug dealers with those of the guerrillas and terrorists. In fact, the FARC-*narcos* relationship has been extremely problematic, and the competitive interests of the two groups led to the involvement of the paramilitaries in the drug economy. True, the drug dealers initially benefited from FARC's presence in the drug-growing regions. The guerrillas established law and order in areas of their control and ensured that the peasants delivered on their promised production. The FARC also protected the fields from the Colombian and U.S. antinarcotics squads.[36]

Over time, however, the relationship deteriorated as the FARC demanded greater rents for its services and greater prices for the peasants and began to cut out intermediaries. In reaction, the drug dealers turned to the paramilitaries to provide the services previously delivered by the FARC. By the late 1980s, the *narcos* had used the paramilitaries successfully to rid the business of guerrilla influence in areas such as Santander, Antioquia, Norte Santander, Cesar, Meta, Cauca, Casanare, Huila, Boyaca, Caqueta, Putumayo, Uraba, and Cordoba. The major areas of conflict between the FARC and the paramilitaries remain the major areas of coca production—Guaviare, Putumayo, and Caqueta—which both movements seek to dominate. In the bidding war over the coca trade, the paramilitaries pandered to the *narcos*' interests by providing less physical protection to the peasants and not supporting peasants' efforts to increase prices for the coca leaves and paste.[37] Yet in domains where bargaining with the *narcos* was not involved, the paramilitaries emulated the guerrilla strategy of paying for absent social services with the drug money.[38]

The discussion above also reveals the very uneasy alliance between the narcotraffickers and the guerrillas and terrorists. The belligerent groups provide the traffickers with a safe transportation system and protection from the government's repressive policies and ensure that drug producers (peasants) deliver the promised raw materials for the illicit commodities. In return, the drug dealers provide the belligerent groups with financial payoffs and intelligence on the government's military movements. However, the relationship is inevitably complicated by the fact that the belligerent groups have multiple audiences and interests: They also protect the population from the traffickers and bargain for greater prices on behalf of the population, and they demand significant financial payoffs from the traffickers and seek to displace the traffickers from aspects of the illicit economy. Far from having morphed into a singular actor or having identical goals, the belligerent groups and the traffickers have many competing interests and frequently problematic relations.

Conditions Influencing Terrorists' Gains

Several conditions influence the size of the gains that terrorist groups can derive from drugs:

1. the state of the overall economy of the region/country (e.g., level of poverty and alternative means of subsistence);
2. the character of the illicit economy (e.g., illicit crops vs. synthetic drugs; traffic vs. production);
3. the presence of thuggish traffickers; and
4. the government's response to the illicit economy (e.g., legalization, tacit acquiescence, eradication, or interdiction).

The State of the Overall Economy

Condition one captures the extent to which local populations are dependent on the illicit economy. Although this condition is obviously not a binary variable, it can be simplified for the purposes of this discussion into two categories: *poor*, where there is a lack of alternative means of subsistence for the local population, and *wealthy*, where there are plentiful alternative means of subsistence. All other factors being equal, a poor economy increases the terrorist group's political gains, since the population is both more dependent on the illicit economy and since the participation of the terrorist group in the illicit economy is more vital for a larger segment of the population.

The Character of the Illicit Economy

Condition two captures the extent to which the illicit economy satisfies the demands of the local population—in other words, the extent to which it generates employment with viable income. The cultivation of illicit crops and the processing of natural alkaloid-based drugs allows for the employment of a much larger segment of the population—providing a livelihood for millions of people in Burma, Afghanistan, Colombia, Bolivia, and Peru, to name but a handful of countries—than simply the trafficking in any of these substances or the production of psychotropic drugs, both of which are not particularly labor-intensive. Consequently, the sponsorship of the cultivation of illicit crops brings far greater political benefits to terrorist groups than the encouragement of amphetamine labs in the basements of some houses in Moscow.

Even so, the political gains that terrorist organizations derive from trafficking with illicit commodities do not have to be negligible. Illicit economies frequently create important local power brokers, whose tolerance (if not outright support) brings the terrorist groups significant political advantages. Moreover, the byproduct of a vibrant illicit economy is frequently the flourishing of local economies from which larger segments of the population benefit. The Taliban, for example, gained substantial political capital from being the sponsor of illicit trafficking in legal commodities under the Afghan Transit Trade Agreement. It pleased the smuggling mafia by removing unreliable and predatory warlords who de-manded very high tolls. It was also welcomed by the local population, who benefited from the economic activity surrounding the traffic.[39] Regardless of the size of the political benefits, the less labor-intensive illicit narcotics economies will still bring vast financial benefits to the guerrillas.

Presence of Thuggish Traffickers

Conditions three and four capture the extent to which the local population (and the traffickers) need protection in order to preserve the existence of the economy in a particular locale. The presence of thuggish traffickers in-creases the belligerent group's political gains by allowing the group to pro-vide security to the peasants and serve as their political and economic regulators. To the extent that thuggish traffickers are not present, these po-litical benefits will decrease. In certain areas of Colombia, for example, ei-ther the AUC or the FARC had completely displaced the local traffickers. Since then, the popularity of both groups has declined tremendously, and the population in these regions is eager to be rid of the two groups. Simi-larly, in the Helmand Valley of Afghanistan, Mullah Nasim Akhundaza's total control over the opium trade resulted in the elimination of other traf-fickers, thus making him the sole kingpin in the region. Akhundaza set pro-duction quotas, decreeing in 1989 (for example) that 50 percent of the land be sowed with poppy, and providing cash advances to peasants for poppy cultivation and opium production. Any peasant who failed to fulfill their production quotas had to pay back the difference, a policy that drove many into debt. Those who did not comply with these provisions were subject to harsh penalties, and reportedly torture and execution.[40] Akhundaza's le-gitimacy thus declined. Again, with the displacement of other traffickers, Akhundaza put himself in the position of the brutal monopolist, and while his financial profits increased, the allegiance of the population diminished.

The impact of the absence of the traffickers on the financial benefits of the belligerent group depends on their ability to fulfill the trafficking role of the traffickers: If they do this well, their financial benefits will increase; if they perform this role inadequately, the illicit economy in the region (and hence their financial profits) could plummet substantially. Seeking to aug-ment their financial benefits and to control the entire drug industry in their region, terrorist groups are frequently tempted to displace intermediaries. However, by doing so, they severely compromise the political benefits they gain by being the protectors of the illicit economy.

Government Response

A government's policies toward the illicit economy can vary from eradica-tion (compensated or not) to tacit acquiescence, to interdiction, to full or veiled legalization. Any of these policies can be accompanied by the promotion of alternative development.

Eradication will frequently have a dubious effect on the financial resources of the terrorist group. Even when carried out effectively, eradication might not bring great, if any, financial losses to the terrorist organization. Effective suppression of the production of the illicit commodity may actually increase the international market prices for the commodity to such an extent that the total revenues may be even greater (at least temporarily greater, assuming that the illicit economy was not completely liquidated). The effort to boost prices of heroin was presumably one of the Taliban's motivations to carry out its eradication campaign in 2000.

Moreover, the extent of the financial losses of the terrorists also depends on the adaptability of the terrorists, traffickers, and peasants—such as their ability to store drugs, replant after eradication, increase the number of plants per acre, shift production to areas that are not being eradicated, and use genetically-altered high-yield, high-resistance crops. Thus, although the number of acres eradicated in Colombia since 2000 has been very large—for example, according to the UN the harvest of coca leaf in Colombia fell by a record 30 percent in 2002—there has been no change in the prices of cocaine on U.S. streets, a data point indicating that the flow of cocaine to the United States has not been reduced.[41] Moreover, a Colombian government study conducted during the summer of 2004 indicates that the FARC has not yet experienced any substantial reduction in its financial income.[42]

Drug eradication policies have not been successful in bankrupting terrorists and the belligerent groups to the point of eliminating them. One of the most successful cases of drug production contraction was Burma, where "eradication" was an act of nature (a prolonged drought that affected the crops during the 1980s and 1990s) and of changing market conditions (including the rise of the Golden Crescent as the main supplier of opiates).[43] But even though Burma experienced an almost 75 percent decrease in its illicit economy, Burmese belligerent groups and the traffickers benefiting from the trade were not driven out of business. They kept their financial profits by shifting to synthetic drugs, the production of which is exceedingly difficult to detect and curtail and the consumption of which is increasingly popular in the West, and by taking advantage of a new developing market for opiates in China and a new smuggling route to the West via China.[44]

Yet, although the desired impact of eradication (to decrease the belligerent group's financial resources) is far from certain and will take place only under the most favorable circumstances, unless accompanied by a large-scale successful economic development program that eliminates wide-scale poverty, eradication will definitely increase the political benefits of the belligerents. As the population is deprived of a reliable (and frequently sole) source of livelihood by eradication, the population will all the more strongly support the belligerents and will not provide the government with intelligence. It is this support base among the wider population that is of vital importance for the survival of the terrorist group.

Tacit acquiescence to the drug economy, on the other hand, reduces the political gains of the belligerents while leaving their financial gains unaffected, thus leading to the improvement of the government's ability to generate intelligence on the terrorists. If tacit acquiescence results in a split between the traffickers and the terrorist group, such as in Peru during the 1980s, tacit acquiescence could also somewhat reduce the financial income of the terrorist group. More important, however, acquiescence to the illicit economy will generate intelligence provision by the population to the government.

The case of Peru is especially illustrative of these dynamics. Initially, when the Peruvian government started taking Sendero Luminoso seriously, it did not attempt to interfere with the drug trade.[45] The area of SL's operations was placed under a state of emergency (EMZ), and the political-military command in the area concentrated on suppression of the guerrillas and largely ignored antidrug operations. The Army general in charge of the emergency zone, Julio Carbajal D'Angelo, maintained that the coca business was in fact beneficial to the Peruvian economy, since it provided thousands of peasants with a source of livelihood and generated large foreign exchange revenues for the country.[46] He also maintained that involving the military in the fight against drugs could subject his officers and soldiers to the temptation of corruption. The general's policy of keeping the antidrug squads from carrying out their counternarcotics missions earned him significant support from the local peasants as well as the drug traffickers. Both the peasants and the traffickers provided Carbajal with intelligence that allowed him to drop platoons of soldiers along Sendero Luminoso's escape routes and throughout the region of its operations. Consequently, Carbajal was able to disperse the guerrillas' columns in 1984 and pushed them out of the UHV.[47]

The crucial role of the government's policy toward narcotics was demonstrated again in the next phase, when President Alan Garcia Perez, with encouragement from the United States, adopted stringent antidrug operations. The police resumed coca-crop eradication and coca-paste interdiction. The animosity of the local population toward the police and the military and its alienation from the government grew exponentially, despite the end of the *dirty war*.[48] The peasants stopped providing the military with intelligence on Sendero Luminoso.[49] The strategy of provoking a split between the *narcos* and SL also failed. In fact, the more aggressively the government and the U.S. Drug Enforcement Administration went after the traffickers, the greater the protection the traffickers sought from Sendero Luminoso, and the closer the cooperation between the *narcos* and the guerrillas became.

The pendulum swung once again in the other direction, as the Peruvian military reinstituted a strategy of not combating the coca trade. In April 1989, Army Brigadier General Alberto Arciniega assumed control of the EMZ. From the outset, he made it clear that he would concentrate on defeating the guerrillas and not on combating drug trafficking. He believed that gaining the cooperation of the local populace was crucial for winning the antiguerrilla war. Arciniega argued that in order to fight the SL guerillas, it was necessary "to change the situation to keep the coca growers, the group which Sendero supports in order to accomplish its goals, from being subject to harassment. If we can persuade the people to join us, the war is won."[50] Indeed, Arciniega's acquiescence to the coca trade was vastly applauded by the populace, and the general received an unprecedented level of popular support. With intelligence provided by both the peasants and the drug traffickers themselves, Arciniega was able to strike at Sendero Luminoso in successive waves, and the military appeared to be gaining the upper hand.

Although effective in terms of the overall counterinsurgency effort, the tolerant narcotics approach of the Peruvian government did not last long. As a result of information provided to the U.S. government by the Peruvian police—who strongly disliked Arciniega—the general was accused of receiving bribes from the *narcos*. Arciniega vehemently denied the charges, but because of being seen as a political liability (given the U.S. antidrug pressure) and because of the tensions in his relationship with Peru's President Fujimori, the general was removed from his post after having directed the counterinsurgency for just seven months.[51] Following his removal, the military moved closer to the position of the police and the U.S. government (that is, toward suppressing coca cultivation). But again, the public mood turned against the military.[52] Disillusioned with the government, the peasants stopped providing intelligence on the guerrillas to the military. Aware of the peasants' poor economic conditions and the absence of the economic assistance promised by Arciniega, Sendero Luminoso stepped in and made the drug traffickers pay higher prices to the peasants for coca leaves. The peasants were grateful and again embraced Sendero Luminoso, and the group's support base once again grew.

Even though Fujimori dismissed Arciniega, he quickly learned that in order to win the hearts and minds of the people, so that he could win the counterinsurgency effort, he could not continue with coca eradication. Although Fujimori and his adviser Vladimir Montesinos managed to build very good relations with the United States, eradication stopped. Virtually no coca was eradicated between 1990 and 1995, and the antidrug effort switched to interdiction.

Ultimately, Sendero Luminoso was defeated, but the eradication of coca was not a factor contributing to the victory. An intelligence operation which led to the capture of SL leader Abimael Guzman Reynoso in 1992 and his order to his troops to surrender, combined with extensive amnesty for guerrillas who turned themselves in, laid the basis for the elimination of the guerrilla movement.[53] The antidrug effort centered on interdiction, and Operation Air Bridge—which targeted the planes taking off with coca paste and cocaine to Colombia—proved very effective in disrupting the supply lines, at least until the traffickers switched to using river boats instead of airplanes, and until the bulk of coca cultivation shifted to Colombia. Eradication was only undertaken in the late 1990s, once Sendero Luminoso was defeated and the government had a good control over the territory, and then it was rather effective. A government policy that tolerated the peasants' production of coca thus generated both vital intelligence on the guerrillas and greatly weakened the guerrillas' support base.

Conclusion

To summarize, the gains terrorist groups derive from access to drug production and distribution are not simply the improvement of capabilities due to an increase in their financial resources, but also includes an expansion of strategic and tactical options, and (crucially) the improvement in relations between the terrorist movement and the local population. The extent of these three types of gains—physical capabilities, freedom of action, and political capital—depends on four conditions: 1) the state of the overall economy; 2) the character of the drug economy; 3) the presence of thuggish traffickers; and 4) the government's response to the drug economy. Governmental drug eradication policies are frequently counterproductive in the overall struggle against the belligerents. The effects of trying to reduce the guerrillas' capability by crop eradication are highly uncertain, while the alienation of the peasants from the governments is substantial. However, governmental acquiescence to drug cultivation does deprive the belligerents of popular support while encouraging the provision of intelligence by the population to the government, a crucial requirement for the defeat of terrorist group.

Although the presence of a drug economy does not by itself cause the emergence of a terrorist group, it does vastly enhance its staying capacity. Moreover, the involvement in the drug industry by one terrorist group provides other groups with a successful *modus operandi* and belligerents learn from each other how to most effectively exploit illicit substances. With time, belligerent groups attempt to penetrate and control greater aspects from the illicit industry, thus colliding with the interests of the drug traffickers. Hence, far from having morphed into a unitary actor, the belligerent groups and the drug dealers often have highly problematic relations. Given the size and scope of the benefits terrorist groups can derive from penetrating the illicit drug economy and the extraordinary difficulties governments encounter in attempting to eliminate these benefits by suppressing the drug economy, it is imperative to prevent terrorist groups from accessing the drug economy in the first place. Such preventive measures should include the economic development of drug-producing regions, the military isolation of the drug-producing regions so belligerent groups cannot penetrate them, and demand reduction for drugs in consumer countries. Without the amelioration of the root causes of both illicit economies and terrorist groups, the symbiotic relationship between terrorism and the drug trade is likely to thrive.

CHAPTER 13

Terrorism and Export Economies: The Dark Side of Free Trade

MICHAEL MOUSSEAU

"I do not think any of us has a definitive understanding," asserts a leading scholar of international relations, "of the causes and consequences of the terrorist attacks of September 11."[1] This is because the disciplines of Political Science and International Relations are poorly equipped to enlighten us on the origins of terror. Traditional realist theory is state-centric and tells us only that terror is a rational strategy of the weak. This is little help in grasping terror, however, because many weak groups, including state and nonstate actors, choose capitulation before resorting to terror. Liberal theory assumes that terror is the consequence of poverty, inequality[2] or lack of democracy.[3] These theories do not differentiate conflict from the use of terror, however; they tell us only of possible sources of grievance. A real theory of terror must do more: it must tell us not only why armed nonstate groups form, it must also tell us why some of these groups use terror. A complete accounting of terror—one that offers policymakers a strategy for ending its threat—must provide answers to the following four questions: 1) What causes militant nonstate groups to form? 2) What causes some of these groups to use terrorist tactics? 3) Why is the United States (and the West) a common target of these groups? and 4) What can the United States and its allies do about it?

This chapter offers an answer for each of these questions drawing from a single, parsimonious theory whose origins are from outside traditional scholarship in international relations. Drawing on research in anthropology, sociology, and economics, the discussion examines how industrialization affects the political culture of a nation, giving rise to the popularity of extremist antimodern ideologies. Just as industrialization in Central Europe in the first half of the twentieth century gave rise to Marxism and fascism, industrialization today in the developing world has contributed to a rise in Marxism, fascism, ethnic sectarianism, and radical Islam. Just as many millions of unemployed people during Europe's industrialization perceived certain groups (or "out-groups")—the capitalist class and Jews, among others—as enemies out to destroy them, today millions in the Islamic world perceive out-groups—Americans and other Westerners—as enemies out to destroy *them*. And just as the popularity of extremism did not end in Europe until even the poorest could find living-wage jobs on the market, today the threat of extremism will continue until most of those looking for jobs in the developing world can find them.

This chapter draws on research by economic historians to show how two distinct norms of economic integration, contracting and reciprocity, give rise to two distinct political cultures that legitimate, respectively, liberal democracy and collective authoritarianism. It is also important to recognize how a reciprocating socioeconomy is a necessary condition for the widespread support for authoritarian government and acts of terror and genocide. This is followed by an analysis of the rise of contracting civilization, beginning with sixteenth–century Europe, and the consequent rise of militant groups opposed to Europe's secularizing political culture. With globalization in recent years, such militant groups in the developing world include radical Islamists as well as more traditional ethnic nationalists and Marxists. In general, one can say that the conflict between the West and al Qaeda is the third variant of the same global conflict against liberal democracy that has been in progress for most of the twentieth century: During World War II liberal democracies were attacked by believers in fascism and ethnic sectarianism; during the Cold War, they were threatened by totalitarian communists; and in the current conflict they are being attacked by radical Islam. A review of conventional realist and liberal views on interstate trade helps us unpack the complexities of this global conflict, particularly as it relates to the spread of (and resistance to) Western economic and cultural values.

Background: Realist and Liberal Views of Global Trade

Realists and liberals have opposite views of the pacifying impact of trade among nations. The classical liberals have long argued that trade encourages peace. Their argument depends on two critical assumptions. First, they assume that there are two ways a nation can obtain wealth from other nations: plunder (with war victories) or trading. Second, they assume that these options are mutually exclusive—that warring countries do not trade with each other and thus an outbreak of war ends a trading relationship. Since trade offers gains, from these two assumptions it follows that trade interdependency among nations increases the cost of war relative to its gains.[4] In addition, the high costs and risks of war render trade a more efficient means for obtaining material goods than fighting and plundering. So with advances in technology countries learn to stop fighting and become trading partners.[5] The classical liberals are deeply entrenched in the English school of *homo economicus*, which assumes that the propensity to barter is in human nature. This view is at the core of Adam Smith's classic *The Wealth of Nations* and lies at the root of most rational choice theories of international relations. Applied to states, it is assumed that all states have as their primary objective in foreign affairs the acquisition of material goods.

Realists also have their roots in the English school of thought and agree with the claim that the propensity to barter is in human nature, only they assume that a state's primary objective in foreign affairs is not wealth but security[6] or power.[7] Afraid of each other, nations are assumed to care more about relative than absolute gains. Since security and power are obtained when others are dependent on you, nations are concerned with their relative dependency upon others. States thus seek security and power by reducing trade dependency on each other and by encouraging others to be dependent on them. In this way, trade promotes conflict, as it links nations and affects the balance of power among them.[8]

The weight of the evidence indicates that interstate trade dependency favors peace. While a small number of studies have called into question this view,[9] they have been superseded by more recent analyses that find robust support for the pacifying influence of trade interdependence.[10]

Still, it is far from clear that the classical liberal explanation for a pacifying impact of trade is the correct one: There can be all sorts of reasons that trade impacts peace. In fact, the two key assumptions in the causal logic of classical liberal theory do not appear to be correct. First, studies have shown that nations frequently trade with their enemies.[11] If this happens, then trade does not necessarily render war less cost effective. Second, the historical record is quite clear that many leaders of nations express economic views and act in ways that are quite contrary to the maximization of material gains. The classic example is the ideology of Hitler and the onset of World War II. Hitler's policy of *Lebensraum* (eastward expansion) followed the economic philosophy of *Grossraumwirtschaft*, which sees gains not in trade or industry but in the acquisition of large land areas. Deeply entrenched in the English school of *homo economicus*, the British assumed that the German leadership thought in terms of liberal rationality like the British did. As a result, the British strategy of deterrence focused on economic factors important to liberal thinkers but not valued by followers of *Grossraumwirtschaft*. British deterrence thus failed to stop Hitler, who never understood it.[12]

In fact, the English school assumption (that the propensity to barter is in human nature) does not hold true. Economic historians have shown that the propensity to barter is not universal but varies across time and place.[13] Therefore, it cannot be in human nature and must be cultural. This means that the value placed on anything varies across socioeconomic cultures, and thus rational behavior according to the English school may not be rational to individuals in other cultures.

In contrast to the English school, the German or continental school assumes that economic conditions affect how one perceives his or her utility; values are socially determined, predominantly so by economic conditions. In this view, the economy and culture are inherently linked. Classics in this school include the works of Emile Durkheim, Karl Polanyi, Joseph Schumpeter, and Max Weber.[14] The errors of the English school are not just a matter of esoteric discourse; an understanding of the nexus between economy and culture is a critical step in understanding the formation of groups that engage in terror and in grasping why some of these groups, such as al Qaeda, are keen on attacking Westerners, including Americans.

The Nexus of Economy and Culture

A first step in understanding the roots of terror is to grasp the two major forms of economic exchange in history: reciprocity and contracts. Reciprocal exchange occurs among individuals in a relationship, such as friends or those sharing a common family. In reciprocity, the terms of exchange are rarely made explicit because there is no *quid pro quo*. Instead, cooperating parties meet mutual needs, driven by the motive of friendship and common utility. Favors are expected to be reciprocated, but usually indirectly. Like most friendships, an individual who fails to reciprocate when needed places the relationship at risk; herein is the incentive to give favors to friends and family.[15]

Unlike reciprocal exchange, contractual exchange is explicitly *quid pro quo*. This means there is no necessary enduring relationship among cooperating parties. Therefore, unlike cooperation in reciprocity, through contracts strangers can cooperate. Moreover, with contracting cooperating parties act explicitly in terms of self interest: there is no necessary expression of common utility during the transaction.

Within all societies today occurs some combination of reciprocal and contractual exchange, although significant variance occurs in the balance between the two. Today in the More Developed Countries (MDCs) of Western Europe, Scandinavia, North America, Japan, Australia, and New Zealand, the majority of people obtain most of their needs and desires—including jobs, homes, and consumer goods—with contracts whose terms are influenced by the forces of supply and demand, conditioned by a market (though market prices are inevitably influenced by nonmarket forces, such as government behavior). While some element of reciprocity often occurs in consumption and production—such as off-market discounting within families and among friends—the pure *quid pro quo* contract is the prevailing mode of economic exchange. Since these countries have developed economies with complex divisions of labor, there is a great deal more exchange per capita then normally occurs in other countries, so the engagement in contract is a central aspect of the way of life. This observation is particularly true for the MDCs with social democratic governments, such as Sweden, as well as others with weaker social nets, such as the United States.

In today's Less Developed Countries (LDCs), most individuals engage in various levels of contracting but, compared to the MDCs, larger numbers are more likely to depend on favors reciprocated within groups of family and friends (often called "in-groups"). Choices available on the market—in consumer goods, homes, and jobs—are fewer compared to MDCs. Individuals are thus more likely to obtain their incomes through family and other in-group connections and, in turn, have more of their income obligated to support other in-group members. Similarly, compared to individuals in the MDCs, individuals in LDCs are more likely to consume food that involves more labor-intensive preparation at home (and thus less contracting in food consumption) and to obtain their homes off-market through inheritance or squatting. In sum, your average individual in an LDC is more likely to be dependent on favors obtained from in-group members through reciprocity, compared to your average individual in a MDC who is more likely to be dependent on the availability of goods found on the market and obtained by contracting with strangers.

Many economists, including Nobel Laureate Herbert Simon, agree that most individuals make decisions with mental shortcuts, including norms and habits.[16] That is, over time, rational economic decision making in a given environment will give rise to a related set of routines, norms, and habits. It can be argued that the distinctive routines of reciprocity (clientalism) and contracting (markets) give rise to distinctive routines in political behavior. Individuals dependent on reciprocity within an in-group will have a number of reciprocating routines, such as looking foremost to the in-group for choices and opportunities, and contributing to the in-group when able to satisfy an in-group need. This is because within the in-group is probably everyone who can be trusted to take care of one's economic and physical needs. In this way, the in-group serves as a form of social insurance, but one that is informal and depends not on the enforcement of any contract (as there is no explicit contract) but on the lasting strength of the individual's relationship with the group, as well as on the fortunes of the group. The individual member thus has a strong incentive to share the values and beliefs of the group and do whatever he or she can do to strengthen its power. Routinized over time (and in most cases since childhood), this in-group orientation should render the in-group fortunes and identity, including its values and beliefs, more important than the fortunes, identities, beliefs, and the interests of members of out-groups.

The immediate family is the core unit of reciprocating groups in contractual and reciprocating socioeconomies. In the latter, however, dependency on the in-group causes the family to be a much stronger and cohesive unit. Depending on the degree to which a socioeconomy is integrated with reciprocity, the family unit can be a part of larger in-groups, even layers of them. Traditional examples of larger reciprocating in-groups include extended families, feudal systems, clans, and tribes; less traditional examples include criminal gangs, mafias, and sometimes guilds, labor unions, and political parties. Within larger reciprocating networks, hierarchies emerge as some individuals have more to give (and thus more power) than others. Often these individuals are older, or have inherited the favors banked by an elder, and thus have more influence than others. In this way, reciprocating communities are organized on a cliental basis, and patrons—such as lords, dons, and uncles—receive favors from clients as expressions of loyalty in exchange for life-long protection.

Since the routine is to obtain economic and physical security within the group, support for the in-group—including the in-group's leaders and its beliefs and values—is a more rational strategy for obtaining security than loyalty to abstract state laws and institutions. Two consequences are the practice of inherited leadership in the developing world and the persistent phenomena in these countries of weak states, periodic rebellions, clientage, substate (in-group) identities, militant ideologies, and enduring mafias.

A typical individual in an MDC, in contrast, faces quite a different set of economic routines. Opportunities are normally found not from an in-group of friends and family but in a market of strangers. The individual is thus less dependent on favors exchanged within an in-group than on strangers fulfilling the terms of contract. This reduces the importance of any in-group. More importantly, it imposes on the individual a direct interest in the existence of a strong state that enforces contracts fairly and equally. The routine of contracting also makes explicit the individual assertion of self-interest. The consequence is that contractual socioeconomies have routines of respecting the choices of individuals, the equal rights of strangers, and secular government—the core values that legitimate the liberal democratic state.

In sum, comparatively speaking, individuals in the developing world are more likely to be economically dependent on in-groups integrated with reciprocity; individuals in the developed world are more likely to be economically dependent on strangers in a society integrated with contracts. These distinctive economic conditions form routines and habits that promote distinctive political habits. Social integration with contracts promotes respect for individual choice, the equal rights of strangers, and religious and cultural tolerance—the norms that stabilize the liberal democratic state. Social integration with reciprocity promotes acceptance of in-group beliefs and values, loyalty to in-group leaders, and distrust of outsiders—the norms that support authoritarianism and sectarianism.

This view has been shown to offer a novel accounting for a wide range of phenomena, including the association of economic development with democracy[17] and the state of peace among the more developed, contract-integrated democracies.[18] It also faces few historical anomalies and coincides with a wide range of established research. Sociologists and economic historians have long documented the association of clientalist and contacting norms with, respectively, collectivist and individualist value orientations.[19] Many anthropologists and archaeologists have long considered economic conditions a leading influence on cultural mores and institutional structures.[20] There is a great deal of direct evidence linking contract-integrated development with individualist values and trust among strangers.[21] It is well established that economic development fosters and stabilizes liberal democracy,[22] and most scholars of democracy agree that stable democracy requires a liberal political culture.[23]

The Rise of Market Civilization

The roots of the contracting socioeconomic norms of our age can be traced back to northwestern Europe in the sixteenth century, but earlier societies also experienced contracting. In the fifth century B.C., Athens had a vibrant contracting society and was the center of eastern Mediterranean trade.[24] Contracting was also common in thirteenth-century Egypt as well as seventh-century Mecca at the time of Muhammad.[25] Later, contracting emerged as a common form of economic cooperation in the thirteenth-century Italian city-states of Venice and Genoa.[26] In all of these cases, the rise of contracting was associated with a cultural change toward a propensity to barter, and consequent institutional change toward more equal rights and democratic government. The Greeks had direct democracy, while the Arabian peninsula saw the emergence of Islam, which preaches equal relations with God and tolerance of outsiders and offers religious codification of the norms of contract (indeed, Muhammad himself was a business agent before his religious experience). In Venice and Genoa, a "spirit" of modern capitalism emerged[27] accompanied by a rise in the value of equal law codified in the communes.[28]

Like most reciprocating cultures, in feudal (precontracting) Europe smatterings of contractual exchange regularly occurred, such as weekly markets in towns.[29] For a variety of reasons—including the Spanish acquisition of gold bullion from the New World and their use of it to purchase goods, in the form of contracts, from manufacturers in England and Holland—starting in the sixteenth century the economies of northwestern Europe began a slow transition towards contract-integrated development. Yet until the turn of the twentieth century, the majority of Western Europeans were still not actively engaged in the market. Most socioeconomic transformations until then were limited to a minority class that dominated government decision-making. While contracting as a socioeconomic norm in mass society started early in North America,[30] viewed by some as the basis for early democracy in the United States, it was only with mass industrialization around the turn of the twentieth century that the majority of Western Europeans were able to find fair-paying jobs, homes, and food on the market. Thus, only then were the countries of Western Europe and Scandinavia able to form stable liberal democracies.

Socioeconomic changes in West Germany, Japan, Italy, and Spain after World War II also brought the majorities of citizens in these countries into the routines of contracting. The consequence today is the condition of stable peace and secular democracy among the contracting socioeconomies of Western Europe, North America, Japan, Australia, and New Zealand (and in recent years, South Korea, Taiwan, and Singapore seem to have joined this club as well). The rise of market civilization during the twentieth century was not easy, however, as it involved several antimodern revolutions, two world wars, and the mass murder of millions. Today, a third major global conflict is in progress, one that also involves antimodern extremism and terror.

The Socioeconomy of Terror and Genocide

Most scholars agree that the use of terror involves more than simply a particular set of strategic inputs: It requires a set of values beyond what is normally found in the developed democracies.[31] This is because the use of terror is not just the use of violence: It is the employment of violence that does not discriminate civilian noncombatants from military or government personnel. In this way, an act of terror is similar to genocide, as both involve the killing of innocents. The difference in the two forms of violence is in the motive—in terror, the motive is political and the act is largely symbolic; in genocide, the killing of noncombatants is the end itself.

In societies steeped in contracting, it is difficult to comprehend how anyone can engage in mass murder, whether the motive is genocide or terror. Individuals in such societies have accepted the notion that each person is responsible only for his or her own actions—a responsibility reflected in contracts. Individuals habitually respect the equal rights of others, including the right to not be unfairly targeted with violence. In contracting socioeconomies, it is thus highly immoral to murder or kidnap people, even if the victims are from other societies. This is why international human rights are a concern promoted mostly by the contracting societies of Western Europe, Scandinavia, North America, Japan, Australia, and New Zealand.

In societies highly integrated with reciprocity, however, there is no accepted notion of individual innocence. All in-group members are responsible to the group, and share responsibility for the actions of others within it. If followers do not support their leaders then they are betraying the entire in-group. Thus, all in-group members are privileged over all out-group members, and the latter are not to be trusted and are less worthy of empathy. If there is conflict, all members of the out-group are enemies worthy of discrimination. In this way, the leaders of al Qaeda can announce their intention to kill any Americans they find anywhere and gain popularity in some circles for doing so.

More importantly, within reciprocating in-groups, loyalty to the group—meaning the views and actions of its leaders—is the key strategy for securing an increase in status within the group. When needed, the ultimate sacrifice for the group (suicide) assures the individual's family an increase in status and economic support. In addition, in reciprocating socioeconomies the individual is expected to accept as true whatever the leader says is true. If the leader says God wants you to engage in suicidal mass murder, and doing so will protect your family, attest your loyalty to the group, and put you in paradise, your expected response is to accept these statements as true. If you refuse to follow the order of a leader you may be reduced in status, accused of betrayal, banished, or even killed. Since the group contains everyone who loves and cares for the individual in life, banishment may be a punishment worse than death. In these ways, a socioeconomy of reciprocity is a necessary condition for an outbreak of genocide, suicidal terror and social support for acts of terror.

Marxism, Fascism and Radical Islam

There is no single path in the shift from cliental to contract-integrated socioeconomy. The settler countries of the United States (the northern states), Canada, Australia, and New Zealand experienced relatively easy adaptations to contracting, as settlers left cliental in-groups in Europe and most found incomes with contracting upon arrival. For the nations of Europe, the socioeconomic change was complicated by the persistence of reciprocating norms and the simultaneous problems of industrialization, the latter inevitably associated with large population increases. This problem is particularly acute for nations with sizeable rural populations. Consequently, the first-comers and smaller nations of Holland, England, France, and Scandinavia experienced various political upheavals against the old reciprocating order, but their economic shifts to contracting were gradual and facilitated by the export of jobless rural peasants to the settler countries. The bigger second-comers, however, including Austria-Hungary, Italy, Germany, Japan, and Russia, mostly lacked colonies and had too many urban jobless to export. For this reason these countries were not able to complete the socioeconomic change to contracting short of war, revolution, and genocide.

Like most developing countries today, the second wave of industrialization in Europe was actively pursued by national governments as they sought to emulate the first industrializers. If a state actively pursues rapid industrialization, however, then the state becomes a source of income in the society. If a nation has a strong contracting culture, it is likely that jobs and contracts with the state are obtained on merit determined by the forces of supply and demand in a market (an example is Swedish social democracy). If a nation has a reciprocating culture, however, state-led industrialization will likely lead to an industrial state integrated with reciprocity. This is because the state, in its active pursuit of industrialization, simply emerges as a new in-group of in-groups. Since the state has a lot of resources to dole out, competition among in-groups over access to state funds can be fierce. In the absence of a strong authoritarian state the result can be a winner-take-all political environment.

In most cases, industrialization is associated with internal migration to the cities, a steep rise in urban joblessness, and an increase in contracting as an economic norm. Thus, associated with contracting, industrialization (and the emergence of winner-take-all politics) contributes to an increasing feeling of insecurity by the many migrants who lose the protections of traditional in-groups as they seek refuge in the cities. In this setting, political entrepreneurs—seeking support from the urban poor—offer ideologies that fit with their reciprocating in-group norms. To show that they can provide physical security, political entrepreneurs seek to appear strong by taking a militant approach to outsiders whom they blame for their insecurities. To provide economic security, in-groups offer financial incentives such as foodstuffs, clothing, and health care.

In Central Europe in the first half of the twentieth century, popular in-group ideologies were Marxism and fascism. Each identified an enemy outgroup as responsible for the increasing insecurities: The Marxists blamed a capitalist class; the fascists blamed other ethnic groups, particularly Jews. Today in the Muslim world Marxism has weak appeal because of its atheism, and in many countries secular fascism—such as the ideology of the Baath parties in the Arab world—long ago wore itself out in popularity. Instead, we have seen the rise of radical Islam among the masses of urban jobless. As a religion, Islam is organized so that leaders compete for followers in the appeal of their sermons. This facet of Islam has encouraged many religious leaders to tune their message to the everyday realities and perspectives of the urban poor. The consequence has been a popular reinterpretation of Islam as an antimodern ideology for the urban poor and the emergence of some Imams as leaders of in-groups offering economic and physical securities. By associating industrialization, increasing insecurities, and the rise of contracting with the omnipresence of America and the West, leaders of the new radical Islam offer social services to the poor and preach a militant message, antithetical to the West, to impress followers with their physical prowess.

The consequence has been a decline in tribal or national identity throughout the Islamic world and an increase in Islamic identity. Perhaps this is why in recent years the popular cultures in countries as diverse as Indonesia, Pakistan, and Saudi Arabia have expressed new sympathies and shared identities with Muslims in conflict anywhere (and particularly the Israeli-occupied Palestinian Territories). This is why popular culture throughout the Muslim world links the conflicts in Somalia, Bosnia, Palestine, Chechnya, and elsewhere as confirmations of a common out-group conspiracy against Islam. From the in-group perspective, all members of out-groups have interests different from that of the in-group and are not to be trusted. The consequence is that all acts of the United States and other Western governments and people, no matter how benevolent some of them may be, are widely perceived as being motivated by pure self-interest and in opposition to their own interests. By extension, because all members of an out-group are responsible for the out-group's actions, all Americans and other Westerners are perceived by members of the in-group as guilty in the global conspiracy against them. Therefore, for many (particularly the urban poor), terror against Americans and other Westerners is perceived as right and proper.

The new radical Islam should not be confused with traditional Islam. The great irony of our age is that Islam itself originated at a time of intense contracting in Mecca, and the Koran offers a number of rules to facilitate contracting, including the principles of equity and tolerance of outsiders. Thus, the new radical Islam is a deviation from traditional Islam, and the Islamic world today is in the midst of internal cultural and religious conflict. The center of gravity in this conflict is in the socioeconomy.

The Dark Side of Freer Trade

Beyond the association of Westernization with the deterioration of non-Western societies (through industrialization), there are several additional ways that globalization has contributed to exacerbating conflict between the developed and developing worlds. First, freer trade means the arrival of American, Western, and Japanese retail chains, banks, cars, and other products, and consequent mass advertising—mass contractual offerings—of Western products. In this way, not only is Westernization associated with the insecurities of industrialization, but also with chain retailing and contracting. Only the new rich and middle classes can consume many of these foreign products, however. Because wealth indicates higher ranking in the hierarchy, the new rich have an incentive to flaunt their foreign products—such as cars and clothes—to show others, particularly nearby policemen who might be inclined to enforce the law equally, that they are above it. For the masses of powerless urban poor, the status of the new rich is not justified according to their in-group norms, whether these are traditional, communist, fascist, or radical Islamic. Since the new rich often appear Western in lifestyles, their perceived illegitimate status reinforces the underlying anti-Western and anti-American sentiments among the urban poor and others in society distressed over the socioeconomic changes associated with industrialization.

Exacerbating matters, foreign corporations that appear to many in the developing world to be corrupting their societies often build haughty towers in the centers of the cities, towers that are often visible in the poorer neighborhoods. Such visible symbols of Western power and influence in the non-Western world can become targets of enraged radicals. Other symbols of Western culture are also potential targets, including embassies, resort areas in Islamic countries frequented by Western tourists, and "the World Bank, the International Monetary Fund, and the headquarters of major corporations or their affiliates in terrorist-producing countries."[32] Indeed, one should not be all that surprised with the al Qaeda attacks in Istanbul in late 2003, which included the tower of a foreign bank, and revelations in 2004 of al Qaeda surveillance of the buildings of the World Bank, the International Monetary Fund, and the headquarters of several major corporations.[33] Overall, the nature of foreign direct investment can contribute to an identification of the problems of industrialization with the West, reinforcing resentment of all things Western.

Also contributing to widespread support for acts of terror against the West is the peculiar foreign economic philosophy of U.S. leaders in recent years. Since the Reagan Administration, the United States has used its influence over LDC economies to encourage deregulation and less state support for the poor. As expressed by U.S. leaders, this view is based on the belief that the propensity to barter is in human nature, and thus a reduced state will allow the "invisible hand" to create economic growth and foster personal initiative. As discussed earlier, this view is deeply rooted in the English school, and it is not supported with historical evidence. In fact, over the past two centuries economic development in the West has been strongly associated with active state intervention.[34] Nevertheless, as a consequence of U.S. influence in recent years, numerous governments in the developing world have reduced or ended subsidies to their urban poor (including foodstuffs, transportation, and job creation programs). The result has been a worsening of conditions for many of the world's poorest. Because worsening economic conditions lead to increased reliance on entrepreneurial in-groups that preach militant antimodern and anti-Western ideologies, U.S. success in promoting less government assistance to the poor in developing countries has contributed to a rise in antimodern and anti-Western feeling, and thus increased social support for acts of terror.

Lastly, as discussed above, classical economic theory of the English school assumes that the propensity to barter is universal. Thus liberals believe that freer trade benefits everyone. However, the propensity to barter is cultural and learned. With the right economic conditions and a state that encourages it, a society can learn the logic and habits of contracting. Without these habits, however, as in many LDCs today, an increase in foreign trade with an MDC may not necessarily benefit both countries. With a dearth of a propensity to barter in reciprocating culture, those who seek wealth typically do so with political means by building connections with the state and powerful in-groups. Those who seek wealth without connections—that is, in the true spirit of free enterprise—are likely to find their way blocked by competitors who have connections with the state or other powerful in-groups. In this environment, freer interstate trade in goods and finance gives foreign firms a distinct advantage in the local economy: not only are there very few local entrepreneurs seeking to compete with them, but the deep pockets and foreign prestige of Western firms gives them an advantage in accessing the centers of power and acquiring oligarchic and monopolistic dominance. In this way, freer trade between the developed and developing world can hurt the local economy and worsen the conditions of the urban jobless—increasing the dependency of millions on extremist in-groups who blame the foreigners for their conditions.

Implications and Conclusion

A proper theory of terror must tell us not only why militant substate groups form, it must also tell us why some of these groups are antagonistic to the United States and other Western countries and why some of them use terrorist tactics. This chapter has examined why militant in-groups tend to form in developing countries, why many of them hold anti-American and anti-Western ideologies, and why some in these countries support the mass murder of Americans and other Westerners. In brief, to comprehend terror we must start by recognizing two fundamentally distinctive norms of economic integration in history: reciprocity and contracting. Social integration with contracts promotes respect for individual choice, the equal rights of strangers, and religious and cultural tolerance: the cultural basis of the liberal democratic state. Social integration with reciprocity promotes acceptance of in-group beliefs and values, loyalty to in-group leaders, and distrust of outsiders: the cultural basis of the authoritarianism and sectarianism. In this way, a socioeconomy of reciprocity is a necessary condition for the resort to terror and genocide and a leading cause of illiberal democracy, ethnic separatism, and weak and failed states in the developing world. The socioeconomy of contracting is the root basis for market-oriented economic development, stable, functional, and liberal democracy, and the condition of peace within and among today's developed democratic nations.

As described earlier, the rise of contracting impacted cultural and institutional change in Western Europe and facilitated the emergence of stable and liberal democracy in Western Europe, Scandinavia, and the European settler countries. Subsequent countries, such as Germany, Russia, and Japan, sought to emulate the successes of the first industrializers, but state-led industrialization leads to an industrial economy integrated with reciprocity, not contracts. Moreover, the second-comers generally lacked colonies to export their excess numbers of urban jobless, who desperately seek new in-groups that offer them security. For the second-comers in Europe, the successful in-group ideologies were Marxism, which equated industrialization and contracting with capitalism, and Fascism, which equated industrialization and contracting with Judaism.

Americans and Westerners today have taken a similar role as the Jews of Europe did in the developing countries of Central Europe several generations ago: It is the perception of our values that is fiercely detested. American and Western contracting norms are omnipresent on television the world over; many industrial firms and retail chains in the developing world are owned by Western corporations with Western names. The new rich in developing countries typically wear Western clothes and adopt Western lifestyles. With deeply entrenched reciprocating routines, many in developing countries—particularly the massive numbers of underemployed—perceive the West as an enemy out-group intent on attacking their societies. In this way, we can say that the conflict between the West and al Qaeda is a variant of the same conflict that has been in progress for most of the twentieth century: fascist, communist, and radical Islamic anger at the "West" originates from the same great social change of industrialization and the desperation of the millions of jobless who, with deeply entrenched reciprocating norms, seek new ideologies from in-groups that can give them physical and economic security.

Once understood, the vital part of any successful strategy in resolving the threat of terror is relatively simple: the creation of jobs. Several major U.S. foreign policy changes are necessary. First, the United States must stop discouraging the governments of LDCs from providing subsidies to their urban poor. Decreased dependency on the state means increased dependency on extremist groups. Second, economic assistance from the MDCs should be increased and used to subsidize local private enterprises, with the specific goal that most urban jobless can find jobs with living wages on the market in the form of contracts (with choice). Once contracting becomes a way of life, as it did in post–World War II West Germany and Japan, economic assistance will no longer be needed: Such countries will be stable, liberal democracies. Third, the MDCs should reduce agricultural subsidies to their own farmers, so farmers in the LDCs can have a vastly larger market to sell their produce in the form of contracting—just as the Spanish acquisition of manufactured goods in Holland and England in the sixteenth century began the process of transforming these economies towards contracting. Fourth, the United States can reduce support for al Qaeda in the Islamic world with subtle propaganda that shows the cosmopolitan trading roots of Islam, and makes clear that radical Islam is a deviation of traditional Islam. Lastly, in high-risk places like Afghanistan, Pakistan, and Iraq today, U.S. assistance should be used to put the millions of jobless immediately to work.

Many scholars agree intuitively that, at least in part, the attack on the World Trade Center and the Pentagon on September 11, 2001, was an attack on "values" of some kind.[35] It is also commonly argued that terrorists hate us because we have democracy and freedom. This intuition is only partly right: The war on terror is at its core a clash of values, but they hate us not because we have democracy. They hate us because they view outsiders (us) as untrustworthy, and they incorrectly perceive our values as selfish and antagonistic. Just as the British failed to deter Hitler because they believed Hitler thought in terms of liberal rationality, today we can fail to win the war on terror if we attribute the actions of al Qaeda, after the fact, as tactics in some rational strategy to achieve greater material wealth, power, or security. Once we abandon our English school–based theoretical assumptions and allow preferences to vary according to socioeconomic conditions, we can see why militant groups form, why terrorism is used by these groups, why they detest the West and, most importantly, what we can do to end the threat of terror.

PART III

ALTERNATIVE VIEWS ON ROOT CAUSES OF TERRORISM

CHAPTER 14

Terrorism, Interdependence, and Democracy

BENJAMIN R. BARBER

Terrorism has a long history, but its modern trajectory may be said to have begun on September 11, 2001 with the fearsomely unprecedented and altogether astonishing assault on the temple of free enterprise in New York City and the cathedral of American military might in Washington, D.C. This event reflected in dramatic fashion the collision between two forces: one, the disintegral tribalism and reactionary fundamentalism, which I have called Jihad (Islam is not the issue);[1] and the other, integrative modernization and aggressive economic and cultural globalization, which I have called McWorld. This collision between Jihad and McWorld (for which America is not solely responsible) has been brutally exacerbated by the dialectical interdependence of these two seemingly oppositional sets of forces. In bringing down the twin towers of the World Trade Center and destroying a section of the Pentagon with diabolically contrived human bombs, Jihadic warriors reversed the momentum in the struggle between Jihad and McWorld, writing a new page in an ongoing story. Until that day, history's seemingly ineluctable march into a complacent post-modernity had appeared to favor McWorld's ultimate triumph—a historical victory for free-market institutions and McWorld's assiduously commercialized and ambitiously secularist materialism.

In *Jihad vs. McWorld*, written over ten years ago in 1995, I warned that democracy was caught between a clash of movements, each of which for its own reasons seems indifferent to freedom's fate and might suffer grievously.[2] It is now apparent, as we mount a new military offense against Jihad (understood not as Islam but as militant fundamentalism) that the very democracy in whose name the battle is waged may become the principal victim of the battle currently being waged.

Today, the outcome of the confrontation between the global future embedded in McWorld's global, but anarchic, markets and the radical reaction to it represented by reactionary Jihad seems far less certain. Democracy itself is in the balance. As the world enters a novel stage of shadowed warfare against an invisible enemy, the clash between Jihad and McWorld is again poignantly relevant in understanding why the modern response to terror cannot be exclusively military or tactical but rather must entail a commitment to democracy and justice even when they are in tension with the commitment to cultural expansionism and global markets. The war against terrorism also will have to be a war for justice if it is to succeed. The struggle for democracy will have to do more than overthrow tyranny or vanquish rogue states to be effective.

The new context for the struggle against terror and the struggle for liberty and democracy is interdependence. In his Second Inaugural address, President Bush observed that "the security of liberty in our land increasingly depends on the success of liberty in other lands." As once Trotsky insisted there could be no socialism in one country alone, today we can see clearly that there can be neither liberty nor justice nor security in one country alone. That is the powerful mandate of interdependence, whose agenda has been advanced by the failure of its sovereigntist alternatives over the last years. Nations simply cannot defeat global enemies—whether global poverty, global injustice, or global terrorism—by themselves.

Back in 2001, just a week after the trauma of the first large-scale assault on the American homeland by foreign terrorists, an attack that was more successful than even its scheming perpetrators could possibly have hoped for, the President joined the abruptly renewed combat with Jihadic terrorists by deploying a sovereigntist rhetoric of retributive justice: "We will bring the terrorists to justice," he said gravely to a joint session of Congress, "or we will bring justice to the terrorists." The language of justice was surely the appropriate context for the American response, but it will remain appropriate in the second Bush administration and beyond only if the compass of its meaning is extended from retributive to distributive justice. Moreover, the emphasis on what "we" (Americans) would do stood in stark contradiction to the realities of interdependence, which seemed to demand multilateral action and common solutions.

Only the globalization of civic and democratic institutions is likely to offer a way out of the global war between Jihad and McWorld—an option that will be explored in some detail at the end of this chapter. A new understanding of global democratic interdependence responds directly to the resentments and spiritual unease of those for whom the trivialization and homogenization of values is an affront to cultural diversity and spiritual and moral seriousness. But it also answers the complaints of those mired in poverty and despair as a consequence of unregulated global markets and of capitalism run wild because it has been uprooted from the humanizing constraints of the democratic nation-state. By extending the compass of democracy to the global market sector, civic globalization can promise opportunities for accountability, participation, and governance to those wishing to join the modern world and take advantage of its economic blessings; by securing cultural diversity and a place for worship and faith insulated from the shallow orthodoxies of McWorld's cultural monism, it can address the anxieties of those who fear secularist materialism and are fiercely committed to preserving their cultural and religious distinctiveness. The outcome of the cruel battle between Jihad and McWorld will depend on the capacity of modern institutions to make the world safe for women and men in search of both justice and faith and can be won only if democracy is the victor.

The Democracy Imperative

If democracy is to be the instrument by which the world avoids the stark choice between a sterile cultural monism (McWorld) and raging cultural fundamentalism (Jihad), neither of which services diversity or civic liberty, then America, Britain, and their allies will have to open a crucial second civic and democratic front aimed not against terrorism per se but against the anarchism and social chaos—the economic reductionism and its commercializing homogeneity—that have created the climate of despair and hopelessness that terrorism has so effectively exploited. A second democratic front will be advanced not only in the name of retributive justice and secularist interests, but in the name of distributive justice and religious pluralism. Exactly how this democratic front can be made to succeed remains controversial, however. The Bush administration has depended on a military strategy against rogue states like Iraq, and some believe that this has actually enhanced the appeal of terrorists.[3]

The democratic front in the war on terrorism, whether military, economic, or civic, is not of course a battle to dissuade terrorists from their campaigns of annihilation. Their deeds are unspeakable, and their purposes can be neither rationalized nor negotiated. When they hijacked innocents and turned civilian aircrafts into lethal weapons, these self-proclaimed "martyrs of faith" in truth subjected others to a compulsory martyrdom indistinguishable from mass murder. The terrorists offer no terms and can be given none in exchange. When Jihad turns nihilistic, bringing it to justice can only take the form of complete extirpation—root, trunk, and branch. Eliminating terrorists will depend on professional, military, intelligence, and diplomatic resources whose deployment will leave the greater number of citizens in America and throughout the world sitting on the sidelines, anxious spectators to a battle in which they cannot participate, a battle in which the nausea that accompanies fear will dull the appetite for revenge. The second front, however, engages every citizen with a stake in democracy and social justice, both within nation-states and in the relations between them. It transforms anxious and passive spectators into determined and engaged participants—the perfect antidote to fear.

The first military front had to be prosecuted, both because an outraged and wounded American nation demanded it and because terrorists bent on annihilation will not yield to blandishments or inducements. They are not looking for bargains but for oblivion. Yet to be the successful prosecution, the military front—so successful when multilaterally prosecuted in Afghanistan, much less so in the multilateral intervention in Iraq—needs to be accompanied by a second civic front, one that focuses not on imposing democracy from the outside top down, but in encouraging it from the inside, bottom up. The struggle against terrorism on the civic front will, also in President Bush's words, be a war for justice, but a war defined by a new commitment to distributive justice: a readjudication of North-South responsibilities, a redefinition of the obligations of global capital to include global justice and comity, a repositioning of democratic institutions as they follow markets from the domestic to the international sector, a new recognition of the place and requirements of faith in an aggressively secular market society. The war against Jihad will not, in other words, succeed unless McWorld is also addressed. International anarchism breeds injustice, whether it is fomenting crime and terrorism or catalyzing "wild" capitalism and predatory market practices.

To be sure, democratizing globalism and rendering McWorld less homogenizing and trivializing to religion and its accompanying ethical and spiritual values will not appease the terrorists, who are scarcely students of globalization's contractual insufficiencies. Jihadic warriors offer no quarter, whether they are the children of Islam, Christianity, or some blood tribalism, and they should be given none. These warriors have been described as people who detest modernity[4]—the secular, scientific, rational, and commercial civilization created by the Enlightenment as it is defined by both its virtues (freedom, democracy, tolerance, diversity) and its vices (inequality, hegemony, cultural imperialism, and materialism). What can these enemies of the modern do but seek to recover the dead past by annihilating the living present?

Terrorists, then, cannot themselves be the object of democratic struggle. They swim in a sea of tacit popular support and resentful acquiescence, however, and these waters—roiling with anger, resentment, and humiliation—prove buoyant to ideologies of violence and mayhem.[5] Americans were themselves first enraged and then deeply puzzled by scenes from Islamic cities where ordinary men, women, and children who could hardly be counted as terrorists nonetheless manifested a kind of perverse jubilation in contemplating the wanton slaughter of American innocents. How could anyone cheer such acts? Yet an environment of despairing rage exists in too many places in the third world—as well as in too many third-world neighborhoods of first-world cities—enabling terrorism by endowing it with a kind of quasi-legitimacy it does not deserve. More recently we have seen an insurgency in Iraq that threatens to spoil the democratization that was supposed to ensue from the American intervention there, proving once again that democracy cannot be imposed from the outside or produced by force of arms. It is not terrorism itself but this facilitating environment of resentment and insurgency against which the second-front battle to address the background causes of resentment is directed. Its constituents are not terrorists, for they are terrified by modernity and its costs and, consequently, vulnerable to ameliorative actions if those who embrace democracy find the will to take such actions. They are only tacit terrorist supporters by default, because they do not believe they have alternatives. What they seek is justice, not vengeance. Their quarrel is not with modernity but with the aggressive neoliberal ideology that has been prosecuted in its name in pursuit of the global market society more conducive to profits for some than to justice for all. They are not even particularly anti-American; rather, they suspect that what Americans take to be a kind of cynical aloofness is really self-absorbed isolationism, and that what Americans think of as pragmatic alliances with tyrannical rulers in Islamic nations (such as Saudi Arabia and Pakistan) are really a betrayal of the democratic principles to which Americans claim to subscribe.[6] They know Americans preach democracy, but cannot always believe that American intervention in the name of democracy is not in truth a cover for imperial ambition, oil adventures, and power politics. The war in Iraq has unfortunately done little to address such concerns. Quite the contrary.

Terror and Rage in a Liberated Country

The pictures of mutilated American corpses hanging from a bridge in Fallujah told a terrible but revealing story. On its face, it was another episode in the daunting story of evil begun on 9/11, but put in context it was also a story about why, although we have won the war against rogue states and are making progress in the war on individual terrorists, we may be losing the overall war on terrorism. What was most disturbing in the pictures from Fallujah was what was most disturbing in the pictures broadcast from much of the Muslim world after 9/11 of ordinary people reveling in the extraordinary destruction unleashed against innocent American civilians.

It was possible to imagine how a small sect of evil men might wish annihilation on us. But how could men, women, and children—who themselves would never engage in acts of terrorism—celebrate such heinous assaults on the innocent? The question was then, as it was in Somalia and is today in Fallujah, why do they hate us so? Not the few who kill but the many who shout for joy at the killings? Did we not come to liberate and democratize them? And yet they wish upon us only gruesome death?

This is the enduring puzzle of the war on terrorism, not the terrorists themselves, but these people whose motives we do not understand and whose antagonism we have not even begun to measure, let alone address. These are the tacit terrorists who create safe zones for the active killers, the people whose hatreds and resentments fuel the wars against America, the population from whom the actual fighters and suicide bombers are drawn. They are why we cannot "decapitate" terrorism by removing leaders or arresting individual evil-doers. They are why Sharon's mailed fist pummels Palestinian terrorism without destroying it, whereas his reaching out to Palestine's new Prime Minster Abbas, who won Palestine's first democratic election in the post-Arafat era, may reap better results for Israeli security.

If Abu Musab al-Zarqawi operated alone with a tiny cell of supporters in Iraq, he would have been caught long ago. If Osama bin Laden was a solitary mass murderer, he would have nowhere to hide. But these active terrorists have made vast safe houses out of their tacit support base, turning whole regions into "safe provinces" in Afghanistan and "safe cities" in Iraq that thwart decisive American victories in both countries. The logic of the war on terrorism advanced by the Bush administration has been that a tiny coterie of evil zealots were responsible for the horrendous deeds of 9/11, for the subsequent evils in Casablanca and Bali and Istanbul and Madrid, and for the civil unrest and the ongoing assaults against civilians in Iraq. But the harsh reality is that such deeds are not possible in the absence of a wider sea of support that protects and nourishes the evil-doers.

Mao Tse-Tung, the architect of modern guerrilla war, understood that his insurgents fighting the Kuomintang Nationalist Government in China could swim only when buoyed up by the sea of "the people." Terrorism flourishes and reproduces itself, despite America's overwhelming military and intelligence capabilities, because it has a far wider constituency than we are willing to acknowledge. For to acknowledge it would be to acknowledge that terrorism is a symptom of global systemic disorders, and that until those disorders are addressed (whether or not America is their cause), America will not be greeted as a liberator anywhere, and the horrors visited on individual Americans and other allied innocents will continue.

Elections or no, there will be no democracy in Iraq as long as tacit terrorists there prefer chaos to the American occupation. There will be no peace in Afghanistan as long as tacit terrorists there and in Pakistan provide Mullah Omar and Osama safe passage. The United States is winning the war against rogue states and active terrorist cells, but it is losing the struggle—it is barely engaging in the struggle—against the tacit terrorists. They will not be vanquished by war and occupation, for their deep hatreds arise not out of fundamentalist zealotry but out of grievances rooted in humiliation, poverty, hopelessness, and cultural resentment.

These forces produce far more intractable enemies than teens wearing explosive belts and terrorist cells planning urban mayhem. We need not sympathize with those who revel in our misfortune, but we need to understand them and address the toxic combination of powerlessness, resentment, and humiliation that drives them. The axis of evil can be overcome by prudent intelligence and brute force. The axis of anger—far more encompassing—is difficult to fathom and still harder to address. But until we begin to do so, our courageous troops and billions of dollars notwithstanding, the hatred will abide, the gruesome scenes of carnage will multiply and the war on terrorism will find no resolution.

Reframing the Global Conflict

With these realities in mind, we can confront the language of exceptionalism and morals used both by the protagonists in the struggle, like President Bush, and by observers like Samuel Huntington. Hyperbolic commentators such as Huntington have described the current divide in the world as a global clash of civilizations, and warn of a cultural war between democracy and Islam, perhaps even between "the West and the rest." But this is to ape the messianic rhetoric of Osama bin Laden, who has called for precisely such a war. The difference between bin Laden's terrorists and the poverty-stricken Third-World constituents he tries to call to arms, however, is the difference between radical Jihadic fundamentalists and ordinary men and women whose main concerns include feeding their children and nurturing their religious communities. Fundamentalists can be found in every religious sect and represent a tiny, aggravated minority whose ideology contradicts the very religions in whose names they act.[7] The remarkable comments of the American fundamentalist preacher Jerry Falwell, interpreting the attacks on New York and Washington as the wrath of God being vented on abortionists, homosexuals, and the American Civil Liberties Union, no more defines Protestantism than the Taliban defines Islam. Moral messianism and Manichean rhetoric are appropriate neither for America nor for the mullah who lead Islam throughout the world.

What I have called the struggle of Jihad against McWorld is not a clash of civilizations but a dialectical expression of tensions built into a single global civilization as it emerges against a backdrop of traditional ethnic and religious divisions, many of which are actually created by McWorld and its infotainment industries and technological innovations. Imagine bin Laden without modern media: He would be an unknown desert rat. Imagine terrorism without its reliance on credit cards, global financial systems, modern technology, and the Internet: Terrorists would be reduced to throwing stones at local government and community leaders. It is my argument that what we face is not a war between civilizations but a war within civilization, a struggle that expresses the ambivalence within each individual juggling the obvious benefits of modernity with its equally obvious costs. Thus, even as the United States confronts both terrorism and rogue states frontally, seeing in them signs of an intolerable global anarchy, protesters confront what they regard as the intolerable anarchy of global markets and international financial capital.

From Seattle to Prague to Stockholm and Genoa, street demonstrators have been protesting the costs of this other form of malevolent interdependence—anarchic globalization. A hundred thousand protestors do not take to the streets unless something is amiss, although they have mostly been written off as anarchists or know-nothings. More media attention has been paid to their theatrics than to the deep problems those theatrics are intended to highlight. After September 11, some critics even tried to lump the antiglobalization protestors in with the terrorists, casting them as irresponsible destablizers of world order. But the protestors mostly are the children of McWorld, and their objections are not Jihadic but merely democratic. Their grievances concern not world order but world disorder, and if the young demonstrators are a little foolish in their politics, a little naive in their analyses, and a little short on viable solutions, they understand with a sophistication their leaders apparently lack that globalization's current architecture breeds anarchy, nihilism, and violence. They know too that many of those in the Third World who seem to welcome American suffering are at worst reluctant adversaries whose principal aim is to make clear that they too suffer from violence, even if it is less visible and destroys with greater stealth and over a longer period of time than the most murderous schemes of the terrorists. They want not to belittle American suffering but to use its horrors to draw attention to their own. How many of these "enemies of McWorld," given the chance, would prefer to enjoy modernity and its blessings if they were not so often the victims of modernity's unevenly distributed costs? How many are really fanatic anarchists themselves and how many are merely instinctive guardians of fairness who resent not capitalism's productivity but its own anarchy—the claim that, in the absence of global regulation and the democratic rule of law, capitalism can serve them? It is finally hypocrisy rather than democracy that is the target of their rage, something the Bush administration, with all its fine Second Inaugural rhetoric about liberty, seems not to appreciate.

Too often for those living in the Second and Third Worlds south of the United States, Europe, and Japan, the discourse of liberty and globalization looks like a cover for an imperious strategy of a predominantly American economic behemoth. Too often what we understand as the market-driven opportunities to secure liberty and prosperity at home seems to others not sincere but a rationalization for exploitation and oppression in the international sphere; too often what we call the international order is for them an international disorder. Our neoliberal antagonism to all political regulation in the global sector and to all institutions of legal and political oversight, as well as to all attempts at democratizing globalization and institutionalizing economic justice, looks to them like brute indifference to their welfare and their claims for justice. Western beneficiaries of McWorld celebrate liberal market ideology, with its commitment to the privatization of all things public and the commercialization of all things private, including now Social Security, and consequently insist on total freedom from government interference in the global economic sector (laissez-faire). Yet total freedom from interference—the rule of private power over public goods—is another name for anarchy. And terror is merely one of the many contagious diseases that anarchy spawns.

What was evident to those who, before September 11, suffered the economic consequences of an undemocratic sovereignty was that while many in the First World benefit from free markets in capital, labor, and goods, these same anarchic markets leave ordinary people in the Third World largely unprotected. What has become apparent to the rest of us after September 11 is that the same deregulated disorder from which financial and trade institutions imagine they benefit is the very disorder on which terrorism depends. Markets and globalized financial institutions, whether multinational corporations or individual currency speculators, are deeply averse to oversight by nation-states. McWorld seeks to overcome sovereignty and make its impact global. Jihad, too, makes war on sovereignty, using the interdependence of transportation, communication, and other modern technological systems to render borders unimportant and sovereign oversight irrelevant. Just as jobs defy borders, hemorrhaging from one country to another in a wage race to the bottom, and just as safety, health, and environmental standards lack an international benchmark against which states and regions might organize their employment, so too anarchistic terrorists loyal to no state and accountable to no people range freely across the world, knowing that no borders can detain them, no united global opinion can isolate them, no international police or juridical instructions can interdict them. Both Jihad and McWorld undermine the sovereignty of nation-states, dismantling the democratic institutions that have been their finest achievement without discovering ways to extend democracy either downward to the subnational religious and ethnic entities that now lay claim to people's loyalty or upward to the international sector in which McWorld's pop culture and commercial markets operate without sovereign restraints.

Unlike America, which aspires to retain the sovereign independence that defined its earlier history, the terrorists acknowledge and exploit the actual interdependence that characterizes human relationships in the twenty-first century. Theirs, however, is a perverse and malevolent interdependence, one in which they have learned to use McWorld's weight jujitsu-style against its massive power. Ironically, even as the United States fosters an anarchic absence of sovereignty at the global level, it has resisted even the slightest compromise of its national sovereignty at home. America has complained bitterly in recent years about the prospect of surrendering a tiny fraction of its own sovereignty, whether to NATO commanders, to supranational institutions such as the International Criminal Tribunal, or to international treaties such as those banning land mines or regulating emissions.

The challenge today is then to construct institutions of benevolent interdependence that can address the challenges of malevolent interdependence. We must learn to contain and regulate the anarchy that foments both the destructiveness of terrorists and the injustices of global capital. Citizens need not await Presidents or governments to embrace interdependence and work to construct this new civic architecture of global cooperation, however. Indeed, they cannot wait. For the challenge is how to get "sovereign" political policy to catch up to global realities. The lessons of the above tutorial suggest that global governance must be built bottom up, not top down, and that it is more likely to come from transnational civic cooperation and the work of NGOs and economic organizations than from states. This is in any case how democracy is ideally constructed: Create a foundation in education, free institutions and citizenship, and build a political edifice on top of that foundation once it is secure. In other words, the continuing reluctance of governments to commit in practice to the global governance ideals to which they are committed in theory need not prevent citizens from working towards greater international cooperation.

Global governance will depend in the first instance on global citizenship, which in turn will have to rest on the fashioning of a global civil society and global civic education. For citizens—whether local or global—are made not born, educated and socialized into their roles rather than natural inhabitants of those roles. That was the lesson taught by the American founders when Thomas Jefferson and John Adams both recognized that without educated citizens the experimental new constitution would never work. By the same token, in James Madison's words, a bill of rights and a constitution were not worth the parchment on which they were written in the absence of educated citizens who could make those documents work in practice.

The challenge today is then to create the foundations for global governance before trying establish anything resembling a global government. The natural stepping stones between national and global institutions are regional associations, for which the European Union is the paradigm. The African Union, the North American Free Trade Association and the Arab League, however narrowly constituted today, can become instruments of regional cooperation and eventually of new forms of "pooled sovereignty," teaching individual nations that by sharing their powers they do more to retain the self-government associated with sovereignty than by insisting on its traditional insular expression.

The traditional UN system (above all the special transnational agencies—such as the United Nations Educational, Scientific and Cultural Organization, the World Health Organization, and the International Labor Organization—that are associated with it) holds out some promise for international governance, although the United Nations is ultimately a state-based establishment limited by its origins. Minimally, the UN General Assembly could be the basis for a global Senate representing member states, if it were complemented by a Global Parliament directly representing people. The Bretton Woods system of international financial institutions, including today the World Bank, the International Monetary Fund, and the World Trade Organization, has the reputation of being the handmaiden of global capitalism and anarchic free markets, but inasmuch as these organizations are in fact dominated by democratic nation-states (the G-8 and to a degree the G-20), they are more transparent, accountable, and susceptible (via their constituent democratic states) to democratic control and use than, say, nongovernmental organizations (NGOs). For while NGOs, though often global and noble in their aspirations, are neither democratic nor accountable nor even transparent in their organizational structures, the international financial institutions (IFIs) can potentially become tools of global economic reform, regulation, and oversight, and can be instrumentalities of global democratic consciousness.

Among the tools that might facilitate transnational forms of governance are technologies like the Internet (already being used by malevolent NGOs such as al Qaeda and international right-wing movements like the Nazis) and the multiplying NGOs of the world. These NGOs (like Doctors Without Frontiers, Transparency International, Human Rights Watch, the International Red Cross, and Red Crescent) ignore frontiers in order to conduct business globally. Their influence is in turn enhanced by organizations like CIVICUS (an NGO clearinghouse and umbrella organization) and the World Social Forum (The Davos World Economic Forum civic counterpart that has met regularly at Porto Allegre in recent years),[8] as well as by such social and dissident movements as Attac. There are myriad other groups that include the Community of Democracies (a U.S.-led coalition of Democratic Nations and NGOs that meet biannually), the Club of Madrid (several dozen ex-Presidents including Bill Clinton, Mikhail Gorbachev, Mary Robison, Kim Phillips, and Fernando Cardoso), Compact 400 (socially responsible corporations meeting under the auspices of the United Nations) and both the Jubilee 2000 campaign—which managed to erase nearly one-half of the third world's debt—and the Millennium Goals (asking developed nations to devote 0.7 percent of GNP to foreign aid rather than the 0.2 percent or less that is the norm in North America and Europe today).[9]

Global Interdependence: A New Understanding

In short, one need not dream of global governance as some utopian ideal. There are many different ways in which the journey to transnational governance is already under way and thus many ways in which individuals can support it. The spirit of the movement is expressed in the new Declaration of Interdependence, promulgated in 2003 and celebrated in a first "Interdependence Day" festival in Philadelphia and Budapest on 12 September 2003 and celebrated again in 2004 in Rome and many other world cities. In 2005 and beyond, celebrations are slated for a half-dozen or more major cities including Istanbul, Paris, Fez, and Sao Paulo.[10] The Declaration of Interdependence, accessible online at the Citizen's Campaign for Democracy website (http://civworld.org/declaration.cfm), captures the spirit of civic globalism by mimicking the language of the Declaration of Independence:

Declaration of Interdependence

We the people of the world do herewith declare our interdependence both as individuals and legal persons and as peoples—members of distinct communities and nations. We do pledge ourselves citizens of one CivWorld, civic, civil and civilized. Without prejudice to the goods and interests of our national and regional identities, we recognize our responsibilities to the common goods and liberties of humankind as a whole.

We do therefore pledge to work both directly and through the nations and communities of which we are also citizens:

To establish democratic forms of global civil and legal governance through which our common rights can be secured and our common ends realized;

To guarantee justice and equality for all by establishing on a firm basis the human rights of every person on the planet, ensuring that the least among us may enjoy the same liberties as the prominent and the powerful;

To forge a safe and sustainable global environment for all—which is the condition of human survival—at a cost to peoples based on their current share in the world's wealth;

To offer children, our common human future, special attention and protection in distributing our common goods, above all those upon which health and education depend; and

To foster democratic policies and institutions expressing and protecting our human commonality;

and still at the same time,

To nurture free spaces in which our distinctive religious, ethnic and cultural identities may flourish and our equally worthy lives may be lived in dignity, protected from political, economic and cultural hegemony of every kind.

Interdependence Day and the Declaration of Interdependence whose promulgation it marks allow new global citizens to move beyond both the horrors of 9/11 and the uncertainties of the war in Iraq and affirm the creative potential of what is for now merely a grim reality. In a world where there are both doctors without frontiers and health plagues without frontiers, workers without frontiers and warming without frontiers, markets without frontiers and munitions without frontiers, surely it is time for citizens without frontiers. Not as a hope of wistful idealism but as a mandate of uncomfortable realism. The simple fact is that no American child will ever again sleep safely in his or her bed if children in Baghdad or Karachi or Nairobi are not secure in theirs, that Europeans will not be permitted to feel proud of liberty if people elsewhere feel humiliated by servitude. This is not because America is responsible for everything that has happened to others or because Europe was once the imperial colonizer of the world, but because in a world of interdependence the consequences of misery and injustice for some will be suffered by all, because to be powerful is not only to impact the whole earth, like it or not, but to reap the consequences, like it or not.

Once upon a time, there was no plausible alternative to national sovereignty. Today there is no feasible alternative to global governance. The only question is how best to get there without destroying ourselves along the way.

CHAPTER 15

Human Security and Good Governance: A Living Systems Approach to Understanding and Combating Terrorism

MADELFIA A. ABB AND CINDY R. JEBB

Human kind has not woven the web of life.
We are but one thread within it.
Whatever we do to the web, we do to ourselves.
All things are bound together.
All things connect.

—*Chief Seattle*[1]

Introduction

The tragedy of 9/11 revealed to the United States what most of the developing world has realized for some time: Terrorism is a real threat to security on many levels. U.S. policymakers have been left to cope and to manage security policy in the absence of good theory and in the midst of shattered paradigms. Stephen M. Walt explains that "there is an inescapable link between the abstract world of theory and the real world of policy. We need theories to make sense of the blizzard of information that bombards us daily."[2] Unfortunately, reality appears to have outpaced theory, to the detriment of both policymakers and academics. This chapter offers a new way to view security, using the living systems theory approach to better understand the significance of addressing human security issues and their link to combating terrorism. In other words, viewing human security and its relationship to the human system, political system, and the terrorist system may enable us to better address terrorist threats now and in the future. This chapter does not offer a predictive model; however, the living systems approach highlights the connections between human insecurities and the human, political, and terrorist systems, thus revealing important patterns and insights concerning global terrorism.

This chapter begins with discussions on human security and the living systems theory to illuminate definitions and concepts that are then applied to the human, political, and terrorist systems. This analysis helps us better understand these as living systems. The next section discusses the international system and the rise of failed states as important phenomena that impact security at the individual level. It discusses how the process of globalization and failed states create, sever, and influence the interconnectedness of the three living systems. Examples from the Horn of Africa illuminate the impact of human insecurities and their effect on governance and global terrorism. In sum, by framing the challenge of terrorism through the living systems theory, policy makers may better understand the significance of human security in the fight against terrorism.

Human Security

Human security is a term that acknowledges the individual level of security. If people are insecure, then that insecurity can quickly spread throughout a state, the region, and the globe. In other words, human security is really a bottom-up approach towards national and international security. The United Nations recognized this approach in a 1994 report:

> The concept of security has far too long been interpreted narrowly: as security of territory from external aggression, or as protection of national interests in foreign policy or as global security from the threat of nuclear holocaust. It has been related to nation-states more than people. . . . Forgotten were the legitimate concerns of ordinary people who sought security in their daily lives. For many of them, security symbolized protection from the threat of disease, hunger, unemployment, crime [or terrorism], social conflict, political repression and environmental hazards. With the dark shadows of the Cold War receding, one can see that many conflicts are within nations rather than between nations.[3]

Human insecurities are derived from those threats that target the survival of human beings and which states cannot, will not, or are unable to deter or prevent. Such threats include disease, famine, poverty, political oppression, lack of housing, etc. The European Union's *A Human Security Doctrine for Europe* further defines human security as

> individual freedom from basic insecurities . . . genocide, widespread or systematic torture, inhuman and degrading treatment, disappearances, slavery, and crimes against humanity and grave violations of the laws of war as defined in the Statute of the International Criminal Court (ICC).[4]

These insecurities, in one form or another, have always been present in the developing world. They cross state borders, affect the physical environment, put enormous pressure on political systems and societies—especially those within a region of weak states—and present vulnerabilities for criminal and terrorist organizations to exploit. The Horn of Africa is a region of such weak and—as in the case of Somalia—failed states. The people of this region experience these insecurities, such as famine, poverty, disease, and—as in the case of the Sudan—genocide. The urgency of a new approach is clear: due to the forces of globalization, these insecurities can no longer be contained, and they have far-reaching consequences. These consequences can be best understood through the lens of the living systems theory.

Living Systems Perspective: Human, Political, and Terrorist Systems

The living systems theory offers a nonlinear and holistic framework by which to understand human insecurities and their influence on the security environment, particularly terrorism. It views the world as a living system consisting of multiple systems within systems with an almost infinite number of relationships and connections among all systems, living and nonliving.[5] While it is important to recognize the influential nature of all systems, this study focuses on the human, political, and terrorist organizations as living systems in order to address issues of human security and good governance. There are two reasons for choosing these systems. First, it is virtually impossible to explore all systems, particularly in one chapter. Second, legitimacy is central to the current fight against terrorism. These three living systems take center stage in our study because their relationships and connections reflect the phenomena of legitimacy. Terrorists want to delegitimize local governments (the political systems) in the eyes of the people; governments want to bolster their legitimacy among the people (the human systems); and the people reside at the center of this fight for legitimacy. Without societal support, the terrorist system cannot expand or capture power, while the government—if it does not fail—will rule miserably.

According to Fritjof Capra, a noted physicist and systems theorist, a living system possesses form, matter, process, and meaning.[6] These four criteria of living coexist and enable living systems to adapt, survive, create, and propagate through time. Capra's following example helps illustrate the explanatory power of the living systems approach:[7] When you kick a nonliving system called a rock, the rock will move in the direction of the kick. But when you kick a living system called a dog, the dog can respond in many ways. The dog can do nothing, bite, move, growl, yelp, run away, etc. The dog will decide what it will do. The act of kicking does not direct the dog towards one particular response. The dog decides. In turn, human, political, and terrorist organizations are living systems, for each possesses these four criteria. Attempting to direct any one of these systems in a particular direction may result in unintended consequences. Each system, through its interactions with other systems, will adapt, create, and ultimately choose its own path. To fully understand why these systems are living systems, the next sections of this discussion will explain and apply each criteria.

Form

The criterion of form describes the pattern of organization and the interrelationships among the system's components.[8] Both living and nonliving systems have form, but only a living system has an autopoietic form—a "networked pattern in which the function of each component is to participate in the production or transformation of other components in the network."[9] This is a characteristic which nonliving systems do not have—the ability to self-bound, self-organize, self-generate, and self-perpetuate.[10]

Human, terrorist, and political systems are each made of patterned networks that enable them to self-generate. The complexity of form increases as the intricacies of the networks increase. For example, the human being is a living system that is more complex than a simple biological cell. The form of a human being consists of a head, arms, legs, body, hands, neck, feet, and so on. Through the process of human reproduction, human beings (as a network of components) self-generate and create babies who grow up into adults. Children carry the same form or pattern of networks to give them the capability to create future generations. Groups of human beings make up a human system. For the purposes of this chapter, society can also be viewed as a subset of the human system. The societal, political, and terrorist systems each possess humans as components, and more significantly, the ways in which these components organize themselves form the basis of the connections among the three systems of interest. In other words, an individual component (i.e., a human being) may connect societal, political, and terrorist systems through family, religion, ethnicity, loyalties, and other ties.

A society is composed of subsystems, such as ethnic groups, religious groups, professional groups, families, and other components.[11] It can organize along different groupings based on changes in the environment. For example, if famine occurs, and the state cannot provide food, the society may reorganize along ethnic groups because these types of system components may be better able to provide for their members; some groups may even leave the country. A society's components may be defined in terms of an urban-rural split based on economic imperatives. In sum, based on a variety of factors, a society may self-organize into a variety of different patterns and groupings.

Like the human and societal systems, a terrorist system may also be defined in terms of how it is organized—in particular, how its members, supporters, ideology, financial resources, technology, and other components enable it to self-generate. In some instances, leaders are critical to a terrorist group's survival, and the organization may be hierarchical to reflect a leader's preeminence. If a terrorist group is hunted, it may need to go underground, and some of the after-effects may include different recruitment techniques, changed ideology, and, therefore, a different form.

A political system, which is composed of the ruling elites and governmental institutions, provides society with the distribution of power, resources, political identity, and collective security. The arrangement of these institutions can change and self-generate based on numerous factors. Such changes may be reflected in power-sharing arrangements, electoral rules, interest group configurations, political parties, and so forth. Each of these living systems possesses the ability to self-generate and take on different forms.

Matter

The second criterion, matter, reflects a living system's ability to interact with its environment.[12] A living system is organizationally closed, but unlike a nonliving system, it is structurally open to the flow of energy and matter.[13] A living system's structure allows it to interact with its environment in order to obtain both the energy and resources necessary to sustain self-making and self-organizing processes.[14] Human beings must eat in order to have the energy to survive and propagate. A human system thus interacts with other living systems like the animals, plants, and earth. Furthermore, the interactions between living systems can be either good or bad—for example, humans create pollution, which impacts the atmosphere, which in turn impacts the animals and plants of the earth, and in the end impacts the humans who need these animals and plants to survive. This circular pattern is an example of the relationship between living systems.

Societal, terrorist, and political systems also share this interdependence, given that the most significant component of their network is their human system. These systems are also organizationally closed but allow matter within their structure in order to sustain their self-generating, self-bounding, and self-organizing forms of networks. Living systems interact between and among other systems and the environment, and thus may create new connections or sever old ones. They may even create new structures.[15] Whatever the new structure is, there are remnants and components from the old structure that are preserved; thus, living systems are historical beings and as such are learning systems.[16] Learning systems have the capacity to know and adapt to ensure their survival and anticipate crises.[17] Living systems can also create new connections with other systems. These connections are vital in order to live.

From a societal perspective, it is clear that some societies are open and some are closed. Generally, closed societies do not last very long. One can argue, from a post–Cold War perspective, that the Soviet communist society was an example of a closed society that eventually died. Terrorist systems rely on recruitment, ideological support, financial support, global safe havens, and other forms of energy and matter in order to exist. Political systems that respond to society's needs, allow for information flows, and so on, are primarily more effective and legitimate; these political systems do well. Those political systems that try to stifle society and prohibit information have to work extra hard to maintain power, and generally they are unstable systems.

These examples highlight the connections and interdependence of living systems. Their interactions may even create new structures or networks.[18] Examples of such interactions may include cultural exchanges in a social context or alliances in a political and terrorist context. Al Qaeda found it beneficial to join with the Taliban in Afghanistan during the 1990s. In doing so, al Qaeda found a safe haven and a base of operations for its leaders and training cells. The financial gain the Taliban received from this union helped them in their cause against the Northern Alliance and sustained their way of life. This criterion of matter highlights the significance of connectedness, interrelationships, and interdependence among living systems.

Process

How living systems will respond—whether to regenerate into new structures, to establish new networks, or to respond unpredictably—depends on their cognitive process, the third criterion.[19] This criterion establishes the nonlinear nature of the living systems approach. Cognition refers to a system's ability to know and adapt.[20] A living system perceives and relates with its environment and is, therefore, able to self-generate (the first criterion). Cognition is the very process of life[21]—a process that describes and guides the interactions and adaptation between the plants, animals, humans, and environmental systems. Their interactions and self-organizations occur simultaneously. A living system determines its spontaneous response, given the existing interactions and conditions of its environment.[22] How a living system responds may or may not be predictable. What is predictable and can be anticipated is that its response is emergent (meaning spontaneous) and novel (meaning unique and creative).[23] The cognitive process highlights the fact that the responsibility of learning, adapting, and changing to ensure survival and propagation lies within a living system (recall Capra's earlier example of the dog).[24]

A system's ability to self-generate and self-organize stems from the process of cognition. A simplistic example is how the U.S. government responded to 9/11. It created the new Department of Homeland Security, changed its foreign policy, and implemented new legislation. This criterion of process highlights the complexity and unpredictable nature of living systems. Did Osama bin Laden expect the United States to invade Afghanistan and/or Iraq? The key to the survival and prosperity of all living systems lies in the interconnectedness and interrelationships of all these systems, influenced by their respective cognitive processes.

Meaning

Meaning, the fourth criterion, refers to the human and social domains of living systems.[25] It reflects the rules of behavior, values, intentions, goals, strategies, designs, and power relations that are essential to human social life.[26] In essence, meaning refers to the unique perspective or view of the world that a system has, based on its unique qualities. For the purpose of this discussion, this criterion can be considered a system's mental map. For example, while the United States may regard al Qaeda members as terrorists, al Qaeda members view themselves as martyrs. Different societies, based on their unique historical experiences, culture, and norms, have different perspectives on the world and view world events differently. For example, the United States saw 9/11 as a marked shift in the international system. Many other countries view subsequent U.S. actions as the global systemic shift.

In sum, this analysis enables one to understand how societal, political, and terrorist systems can be considered living systems, as summarized in Table 15.1. History provides a record of how these systems have lived through the years. Those that have survived and prospered reflect their enduring legacy of self-generation, interdependence, cognitive process, and fundamental beliefs. The quality and quantity of relationships and connections that the components of these systems create between and among each other, as guided by their way of life and beliefs, allow them to live through crises. At the helm of modern-day systemic connections is the crisis of global terrorism. Viewing human security through the lens of living systems theory and its relationship to the overall security environment reveals its interrelationship with the terrorist system as well. This framework helps to better anticipate these systems' behaviors, thereby providing policy makers with a useful tool for thinking about and crafting strategy and policy. As the next section of this chapter will elaborate, the interconnections among the three systems in question—and their interactions with the global environment and responses to human insecurities—are enlightening.

Living Systems Responses to Globalization and Crises of Legitimacy[27]

As Benjamin Barber and other noted scholars have illustrated, globalization brings to the forefront the complexity and chaotic nature of life and

Table 15.1

Summary of a Living Systems Perspective

Criteria	Societal	Political	Terrorist
Form (or Pattern of Organization)	ethnic groups class divisions urban/rural splits occupation civil society	political parties military electoral system ruling elites local, municipal, county, state, federal executive, legislative, judicial	leaders recruiters trainers finance logistics perpetrators/ executors intelligence
Matter (or Dissipative Structure)	information environmental factors	information neighboring states openness to ruling elites	money new recruits information technology
Process (or Cognitive Process)	changes in social groupings political and group identities	changes in electoral process distribution of power and resources policy governance	indoctrination religious/other ideology recruitment alignment, alliances
Meaning	culture religion way of life norms world view political identities	beliefs ideology values political identity national identity	ideology common belief martyrdom

our world.[28] Clearly, the effects of globalization appear numerous as well as the interpretations, both normative and empirical. According to Hans-Henrik Holm and Georg Sorensen, the unevenness of globalization causes variations among regions:

> We need to study the effects of uneven globalization . . . as they are "filtered through" different regions. It is . . . the combined effect of uneven globalization and the end of the Cold War [that causes] increased variation, not only between North and South but also among different regions of the world.[29]

Some of globalization's manifestations include advanced technology, communications, mass transportation, and other human inventions that provide various societal and political systems the opportunities to decide whether or not to join a global network. Unfortunately, there are societal and political systems that are unable to join due to their lack of awareness or just simply the lack of capacities. These living systems tend to reside in the underdeveloped areas of the world. In the case of some African nations, like those in the Horn of Africa, members of these systems are dealing with human insecurities of aids, poverty, hunger, famine, and genocide on a daily basis. Both globalization and human insecurities are conditions that affect living systems' capacities and choices.

Not only does globalization provide the opportunity for political systems to decide between action and inaction, but the same opportunity exists at the individual human level. "Globalization increases risks and opportunities for individuals, who become both objects and participants in global processes, and individual actions may have dramatic consequences for international relations."[30] On the one hand, individuals can make a huge impact, for both good and bad. On the other hand, individuals are very much the victims of transnational threats and certainly of human insecurities. Notably, human security's focus on a bottom-up approach acknowledges the importance of the individual in the overall schema.

Harvard University researcher Jessica Mathews argues that indeed, globalization has changed the character of the significant players in the international system. She argues that there has been a "power shift" away from nation-states and towards nonstate actors. The increased accessibility and sophistication of information technologies has displaced the government's monopoly on information. Mathew's insights illustrate the decisions and chosen responses of living systems to the information revolution. Some living systems decide to change communal relations, evolve into new groups, alter state-societal relations, and/or establish new communal connections across state borders.[31] Global reach is available to almost any system. Terrorist systems have access to low-tech gadgets as well as the materials, technologies, and experts required for acquiring and using weapons of mass destruction.[32] In the early 1990s, terrorism expert Bruce Hoffman predicted that the end of the Cold War era would unleash forces "long held in check or kept dormant by the cold war [that] may erupt to produce even greater levels of nonstate violence."[33] These nonstate actors, primarily terrorists, leveraged these forces to develop their capacity for innovation. Equally disturbing is the fact that there are other dangerous living systems that may emerge. Even before 9/11, the U.S. National Security Strategy described a list of transnational threats that affect living systems and impact the individual level of security:

[These are transnational] threats that do not respect national borders and which often arise from non-state actors, such as terrorists and criminal organizations. . . . Examples include terrorism, drug trafficking and other international crime, illicit arms trafficking, uncontrolled refugee migration, and trafficking in human beings. . . . We also face threats to infrastructures, which increasingly take the form of cyber-attack in addition to physical attack or sabotage.[34]

Moreover, with the end of the Cold War, there appeared to be no ideological competitor to democracy. The dialogue of competition between democracy and communism had been secular. However, the end of communism as a viable alternative to democracy seemed to bolster religion as a political solution.[35] Furthermore, democracy and other secular forms of governing have not been effective everywhere. Many Western institutions and experiments with democracy proved disastrous in the Third World, and particularly in Africa. In short, many political systems were operating without a coherent and workable ideology or meaning, and, combined with their ineffectiveness, these systems proved to be illegitimate.

As a result of corruption, bankrupt ideologies, and political and economic underdevelopment, the conditions for failing states have been on the rise. It is more than ineffectiveness; it is a loss of legitimacy. Many perceive secular nationalism as a failure. They no longer believe in its institutions, and more importantly, they no longer "believe in it [nationalism]. In their own way they are experiencing what Jurgen Habermas has dubbed a modern 'crisis of legitimation,' in which people's respect for political and social institutions has been deflated throughout the world."[36] When a human system faces a crisis of legitimacy, it can respond in many ways, to include changing its view of the world. In these circumstances, religion has emerged as a powerful, transnational, and alternative force. It has a built-in organization that crosses boundaries (form and matter); it is a ready-made force that, when used by extremists, can motivate members, mobilize resources, and marshal recruits (process), provide moral justification for increasingly lethal acts of violence (meaning), and become what Bruce Hoffman describes as a political movement.[37] When terrorist systems exploit religion to fill a legitimacy vacuum, they become a formidable force in the fight for legitimacy *vis-à-vis* political systems, especially in weak and/or failing states.

Interestingly, the political systems of Africa have also been in search of legitimacy, and this search has been a struggle. It is much easier to point out the failures, but there has been some positive progress. As African scholar Ebere Onwudiwe observes, "for every horrific political story in Africa, there is another story of courageous and creative enterprise accomplished under circumstances that those who live and vote in developed democracies could not even begin to imagine."[38] However, not only have the political systems in Africa had to cope with the struggle for legitimacy—and, as discussed earlier, the unevenness of globalization—they have also been experiencing global terrorism.[39] Some have been able to stay on the democratizing course while fighting terrorism, but it is the ideological movement that is so dangerous to newly transforming states; particularly, religious-based ideological movements.

How do developing political systems learn and adapt in this environment? Not only do the people need to believe that the political leaders have the right to rule, but they also need to know that their basic needs will be fulfilled. In other words, political systems need to provide good governance—that is, legitimacy and effectiveness. Throughout Africa, the development of democracy has not been quick, and perhaps the Western expectation of quick results is the wrong measure. It is also evident—and Nigeria is a great illustration—that Western institutions do not necessarily bring democracy. Successful implementation of the meaning of democratic values, such as equal opportunity, freedom, human empowerment, civil liberty, and rule of law, requires the right connections between society and the state. Much of the literature on democratization acknowledges that it is a nonlinear process, requiring congruence between society and the state. In other words, each society and political system has its own history, political culture, physical environment, economic conditions, and other significant aspects—all of which must be considered when crafting political institutions. There is no one-size-fits-all.

Sometimes a state requires a period of one-party rule and various interest groups to help socialize and foster unity. Kenya, once a one-party state, now boasts many political parties. For some, a presidential system is best, so that there is a symbol of unity in the office of the presidency. For other societies, a parliamentary system is best, so that representation of different societal groups is immediately apparent. For some, power-sharing arrangements are key, in order to demonstrate the importance of representation and to ensure that no one minority or tribe is locked out of government. These political systems have chosen many permutations as they responded to the security environment, society, effects of terrorist threats, and their own political institutions.

This struggle to adapt in a vacuum of legitimacy changed the interrelationships between terrorist and political systems. Interestingly, noted political scientist Louise Richardson argues for a re-examination of the relationship between states and nonstate actors, primarily terrorist groups.[40] For example, there are new relationships between terrorist groups and their state-sponsors to consider. In her research, Richardson describes a five-part continuum of possible relationships. First, there is total state control *vis-à-vis* the terrorist group, where the state directs the killing of dissidents. The second stage describes the state's recruitment and training responsibilities of the group for particular missions. The third stage also reflects state control through its direct instructions concerning the group's activities. In the fourth stage, the terrorist group is seen as having operational autonomy, but still receives a state's financial, training, and safe-haven support. Finally, in the fifth stage, state sponsorship of the terrorist group still occurs, but the state's expectations are only based on common diffuse interests. For example, Libya supported the IRA, not because of Muammar al-Qaddafi's specific interest concerning the situation in Northern Ireland, but due to the IRA's efforts against Britain.[41]

At an extreme opposite end of the spectrum Afghanistan can possible be considered to have been a terrorism-sponsored state in its recent history. Indeed, one could argue that without the finances of al Qaeda, as well as the organization's constant influx of young, energetic Muslims, the Taliban's ability to rule Afghanistan would have been considerably weakened. In this case, the terrorist system appears to support the political system. Another worrisome case is Somalia, officially considered a failed state, where the danger is that conditions are perfect for providing terrorists with a safe haven and the ability to create a terrorist-sponsored state similar to what happened in Afghanistan.[42] This connection between living systems turns the whole idea of the international system of states on its head. It truly speaks to the influences of viable and aggressive networks of living terrorist systems.

Another global trend that must be addressed is what Harvard professor Jessica Stern refers to as the "protean nature" of terrorist groups.[43] Terrorist systems change and adapt in order to survive. In fact, they learn to change and adapt faster than their adversaries. Terrorist systems will even change their missions and forge unlikely connections or alignments. For example, there is evidence that al Qaeda—a Sunni-based Islamic group—has ties with Hizballah, a Shia group.[44] These emergent and novel innovations and adaptations, along with the counterintuitive quality and scope of networks or alignments, require close scrutiny in the post-9/11 world. If one considers the confluence of networking, accessibility to information and technologies (including weapons of mass destruction), and religious ideology, then the trend can only be one of increased lethality. Perhaps even more dangerous is how a terrorist organization's ideology can foment other groups. So, while al Qaeda may have to go underground due to the world's hunt for its members, other groups have been spawned to address more local concerns or human insecurities of society. This highlights the fact that at the end of the day, the terrorist requires public support. The fight for legitimacy within and across societies is central between political and terrorist systems.

For a political system to achieve legitimacy, at the very least, it must be attuned to human security. In other words, it must fulfill basic needs and provide security at the individual level. The complexity of the relationship of the political system and society can make achieving human security a daunting task. For example, in an ethnically cleavaged society or one that experiences class divisions, or even an urban-rural split, there may be issues of uneven distribution of goods, including security at the individual level. The most challenging society for a polity to rule is one that has reinforcing cleavages such that loyalties to a group or tribe supercede loyalties to the state or the political system. How a political system interacts with a society will determine if it can overcome these divisions. Some states have created interest groups to help provide a mechanism for societal matters to be heard. Interest groups also can serve to cross-cut divisions and build identities on various issues. Some political systems use various socialization agents, such as schools, to help build state loyalties. If a political system can demonstrate its ability to at least provide its society with basic needs, then people may start believing in the political system and do not have to look elsewhere for such provisions. And if people feel that they are represented, then they may start to feel that they have a stake in the success of the political system. In essence, a political system must have the capacity to provide basic needs as well as the vehicles for political participation. If neither exists, then people look elsewhere, and if there are no political means for expression, people may look outside the polity to be heard; this can lead to all forms of political violence.

How well political systems adapt is hard to measure. The living systems approach prompts us to look at the relationship between the political and societal systems. Does society have allegiance towards the political system? Who are the political elites? Do they come from all segments of society? How does society grow political elites? How do people in society identify themselves? How does the political system handle terrorist organizations? Does it have rule of law, or are all opposition groups oppressed? The answers to these questions reflect a political system's legitimacy.

To evaluate society as a living system, it is especially important to understand it within context of the physical environment. What kinds of resources are available or unavailable? What kind of climate? How do people make their livelihood? These questions are critical especially in the underdeveloped world where climates are harsh, food is scarce, and the population exposed to disease. In such societies, the ability for a state to provide basic necessities is a life-or-death matter. If it cannot, then people will turn to their tribe, or sect, or clan, or any other entity that is perceived to have this capability—including terrorists and insurgent groups. Such societies have the potential for conflict, as competition for scarce resources can become fierce. How does a state forge a national identity under these circumstances? And, unfortunately, it is these circumstances that invite terrorist organizations to demonstrate an alternative to the state. Terrorist organizations can easily work the seams of such a cleavaged society and cause havoc for a struggling political system.

In societies that have some development opportunities, new interests arise. Some of these interests may be expressed as interest groups. Mechanisms for political participation evolve, and as education develops, people learn how to participate in the political system. Other points of connection between society and the political system include elected leaders, informal leaders, and political parties, as well as daily contact with the bureaucracy, such as the police, tax collectors, and others. Society, through education and civic groups, grows political elites. Values in the society become focused on such matters as rule of law, equal opportunity, freedom, and human development. All these points imply a study beyond the scope of this chapter, but it is important to understand that society can either embrace legitimacy for the political system or look for an alternative. What these connections imply, however, is the tremendous influence at the human level. If people must constantly worry about basic survival, a political system cannot survive.

Moreover, if people feel that they cannot trust the political system, then they will turn their allegiance elsewhere, which reflects a level of legitimacy concerning the political system versus perhaps a competing system. They may identify with a tribe that straddles a state border, a sect, or other such group. Clearly, the level of legitimacy affects a system's "meaning." In other words, a political system that has legitimacy views the world differently than one that constantly struggles. Legitimacy also reflects the political system's ideology. Ideology provides meaning and purpose as well as outlook, and this holds true for the terrorist system. An ideology reflects the terrorist system's world view and how it sees itself in that world. For example, society derives meaning from its culture, history, political system, terrorist system, and all of them at once.

And for those people who are either involved in a conflict, without food, or without a livelihood, leaving the polity becomes a viable alternative. Refugee flows or internally displaced people put pressure on political systems and neighboring political systems, and they offer vulnerabilities for terrorist systems to exploit. Returning to the earlier focus of this chapter on the forces within the global security environment, it is evident that what happens to people in the Horn of Africa has significant implications for the security of people across the globe.

Case Study: Horn of Africa

The Horn of Africa (HOA) is the perfect case for a living systems approach towards understanding how best to view human security. It is a region comprised of weak states, porous borders, and, for now, one failing state: Somalia. It has all the elements of the societal, political, and terrorist systems. And the activities in HOA reach not only to its immediate regional neighbor, the Middle East, but worldwide as well. The region has a rich mosaic of cultures, tribes, and religions that know no boundaries. Unfortunately, it also experiences all the hardships of human insecurities, from disease to famine to conflict and terrorism. Political systems throughout the region are struggling to gain legitimacy and capacity. Terrorist organizations are adapting to the local realities and are vying for that same legitimacy.

The Sudan crisis provides a clear example of the interactions of systems, where a terrorist system exploited human insecurities and a weak political system. The actions of an emergent terrorist system took advantage of a vulnerable society and illegitimate political system. Over the years since independence, the weak political system of Sudan has relied on militant Islam as a means to bolster its military regime. A key figure in the story of the Sudan is Hassan al-Turabi, whose version of Islamist ideology, in varying degrees over the last decades, served as a ruling ideology. He joined the Muslim Brotherhood in the Sudan during the 1950s, and by the late 1980s, he had established the National Islamic Front (NIF), which was an umbrella party for Islamic parties dominated by the Muslim Brotherhood. Al-Turabi extended his network throughout his career. He was a mentor for Ayman al-Zawahiri, who founded the Egyptian Islamic Jihad. This group later merged with Osama bin Laden's al Qaeda, and al-Zawahiri is now bin Laden's second in command. Sudan reflects an alliance between a state and terrorist organization that preyed on a vulnerable society. Sudan's government tried to delegitimize democratic opposition and employed "divide and rule" tactics among the ethnically divided society. Clearly, what happened in Sudan had reverberations throughout the region and beyond.[45]

In Kenya, there was evidence that al Qaeda was operating within its borders. Unfortunately, it took five years to acknowledge the local presence of al Qaeda even after the 1998 embassy bombing in Nairobi.[46] Interestingly, al Qaeda's presence reflected its assimilation within local cultures and peoples. The operatives easily slipped through borders and porous security systems and recruited Kenyans. In 2002, a suicide car bomber destroyed the Israeli-owned Paradise Hotel in Mombassa, killing twelve and wounding eighty, while another group of terrorists attempted to blow up an Arkia Airlines plane with two shoulder-launched missiles as it departed Mombasa Airport for Tel Aviv (both missiles narrowly missed the plane). It was clear that there was a Kenyan terrorist movement afoot.[47] The good news is that Kenya's ability to grow a multiparty democracy has helped to mitigate and stem the growth of these local Islamic militants, but much work remains.[48]

After 1991, with the collapse of the government of Somalia, al Itihaad al Islaiya (AIAI or Islamic Union) became the emergent militant Islamic force that presented challenges to the region. Some U.S. officials claim that AIAI became an ally of al Qaeda in common effort against the U.S. presence in Somalia in 1993. Reports indicate that AIAI was responsible for logistical support in al Qaeda's bombing of the U.S. Embassy in Nairobi in 1998 and al Qaeda's 2002 attacks on an Israeli airliner and hotel near Mombassa, Kenya. AIAI's activities extend into Kenya's North Eastern province in an effort to create a "pan-Somali Islamic Caliphate." Interestingly, AIAI has established "Islamic Courts" and penetrated the security and judicial systems of the transitional national government that sits in Mogadishu.[49]

Another Islamic extremist group, the Eritrean Islamic Jihad (EIJ), has emerged in Eritrea, calling for the establishment of an Islamic state. It is also a member of a larger network, the Eritrean National Alliance, which opposes President Isaias Afwerki and his government. Over the years, the National Islamic Front in Sudan and al Qaeda have supported EIJ.[50]

This brief description of the conditions in the region of HOA provides just some examples of how the terrorist system has adapted and interacted with the political and societal systems in the Horn of Africa. How should legitimate political systems fight these terrorist systems? What tools are available? How should the international community engage in the fight? If we assume that the struggle is political, then winning the fight for legitimacy with the people is key. The danger of the terrorist ideology sparking a political movement among the populations of the Horn of Africa is enormous. To prevent this situation, the societies of Africa must be presented with a viable alternative by their own governments.

Policy Implications

The patterns and insights revealed from the application of the living systems theory offer considerations for policy makers. A key discovery is the recognition of the interrelationships and connections among the systems in the HOA. It highlights the value of addressing human insecurities as a means towards combating terrorism. By addressing the issues of basic survival at the individual level, as opposed to addressing security at the traditional state level, it is clear that these efforts can have rippling effects on society, governments, and terrorist organizations. Security policy requires a holistic approach that views human security as a critical lynch pin.

Furthermore, legitimacy as a form of interdependence and interconnection between political systems and societies is central to fostering good governance. This awareness provides the foundation for understanding how best to craft a patient, long term approach in the fight against terrorism. A policy that builds legitimacy internal to the target nation as well as external to the region and to the international actors assisting in the effort is critical.[51]

Not only must policy makers understand how best to cultivate legitimacy, they must also understand that the terrorists are trying to accomplish the same goal. We have already seen that al Qaeda recognizes the importance of adapting to the local situation and grievances. It is important for policy makers to also understand the local nature of the complex security situation. In other words, if winning hearts and minds is the goal, then policy makers must understand those hearts and minds in terms of the local culture, history, physical environment, and informal and formal governing institutions, to name just a few critical pieces of knowledge. Terrorism is not monolithic. Local terrorists groups have specific goals and ideologies that must be understood within the context of a specific region. The global war on terrorism can only be won at the local level. That is where it counts; that is where the hearts and minds reside; that is where policy makers can make a difference in people's lives.

Another aspect of this type of "war" is that it is long term. Attacking the terrorist system by addressing human insecurities can be effective, though it may take time and results may not be immediate. Policy makers need to change their concept of time when fighting terrorism. Terrorists enjoy the fact that time is on their side. The time between terrorist attacks can be long. How does one measure success and incorporate strategic patience? Moreover, the living systems approach highlights the complexity of system interaction. This is an important idea as policy makers try to anticipate second- and third-order effects of their actions. There will be unintended consequences, but understanding these complexities may help create more adaptable and flexible strategies. For the United States, the global war on terrorism requires political and societal support. U.S. politicians need to be able to articulate long-term policy in order to garner support from U.S. society and from allies. And they must prepare society and allies for the inevitable shifts in strategy required to win. This will not be easy.

Finally, recalling the analogy of the dog, policy makers must also realize that they cannot make choices for other living systems. This is an important insight gained from the living systems approach. The dog's reaction to a kick is the dog's choice. For example, though the United States recognizes the vulnerability of the Horn of Africa to terrorist influences, the United States must also recognize that it cannot force its desired end state on the HOA. In the end the HOA must decide its future for itself. Similarly, the United States cannot dictate the type of government Iraq will have; the people of Iraq must make that choice. Indeed, policy makers can at best create conditions that will help other systems make good choices; understanding this point is critical as the international community engages in stabilization efforts across the globe.

The fight against terrorism is a multidimensional fight. It requires a unified interagency and international effort. Human security provides a focus for such an effort. It presents an opportunity to seize the initiative to help societies survive and prosper, while offering an alternative to extremist ideology. More effort must be made to work with allies and coalition partners. Terrorists know no boundaries; the international community must afford itself the same opportunities for developing networks across countries and agencies that adapt, innovate, and create.

Acknowledgments

The views expressed herein are those of the authors and do not purport to reflect the position of the United States Military Academy, the School for Command Preparation, the Department of the Army, or the Department of Defense.

CHAPTER 16

Terrorism and the State: The Logic of Killing Civilians

CLARK R. McCAULEY

"Kill one man, frighten a thousand." This Chinese maxim is perhaps the most succinct definition of terrorism, a definition that recognizes terrorism as a strategy of coercion. Between individuals and between groups, the strategy is the same: to make others do what they would not do willingly by punishing those who resist. The value of this strategy is not limited to those punished; it coerces also those observers who might otherwise be tempted to resist.

Violence as coercion is as old as history. The terrorism we refer to most often today is violence from below—violence against civilians by nonstate actors, for political purposes. The shock value of this kind of terrorism comes from its attack on civilians, especially women and children. Historically, however, terrorism has more often been violence from above—violence against civilians by states. Terrorism is principally a state strategy because the state usually has the predominant power of violence. States use terror to extract men and resources from territory controlled by the state and to gain new territory.

Warfare is the case of coercion of one state against another. Sometimes, whether for revenge or for warning, warfare extends to eliminating an entire population in the kind of killing we now call genocide. For example, the Romans leveled Carthage in 146 B.C. (leaving 200,000 dead). Genghis Khan annihilated everyone in the city of Herat after the city revolted against him in 1220 (300,000 dead).[1] But modern war has been generally understood to be war against enemy armed forces. Napoleonic war, the paradigm of modern war, was aimed at defeating the enemy army and occupying the enemy's country. Von Clausewitz developed his famous treatise *On War* from the evidence of Napoleonic campaigns: "To sum up: of all the possible aims in war, the destruction of the enemy's armed forces always appears as the highest."[2] This perspective permitted and encouraged a clear distinction between combatants (people in uniform) and noncombatant civilians.

This chapter argues that the rise of the modern nation-state that began with the French Revolution has been accompanied by slow but steady erosion of the distinction between soldiers and civilians. After reviewing some indications of this trend, this discussion concludes with an examination of the dynamic relation between state terrorism and nonstate terrorism.

The Citizen-Soldier and Interstate War

Modern nationalism is often said to begin with the French Revolution. Whether states make nations or nations make states, the result has been a more centralized state with a new understanding of citizenship and a new political morality.

The French Revolution and the Development of the Nation-State

In the early 1800s, other European states had to come to terms with the new power of the French state. The French Revolution brought a new legitimacy to the state, a new fervor in citizens' attachment to the state, and a new army that drew on these. With the *levee en masse* (a military draft) initiated in 1793, the French army grew to over 600,000 men, far larger than the armies of France's enemies.[3] To support this new army, the civilian population was mobilized to forge arms and manufacture gunpowder, to sew uniforms and cobble boots. Carts and wagons, horses and drivers were recruited for army service; food was requisitioned and stockpiled. These state-led industries were, no less than the new recruits, essential to the success of the new model army. The *levee en masse* and all that came with it marked the beginning of the modern nation-state.

Psychologically the Revolution offered a new form of political identification; morally it offered a new principle of political legitimacy. These were combined in the shift from "*Vive le roi*" (long live the king) to "*Vive la nation*" (long live the nation). The sovereign nation included all its citizens (understood to exclude former aristocracy and clergy), and all citizens were equally subject to the obligations of citizenship. The army and the civilian mobilization that accompanied it were the expression of this national consciousness. The army taught men to speak French rather than their local dialects. The army and later the French school system taught that a person's attachment to the nation should replace village or regional attachments.

With the new understanding of what it meant to be French came a new understanding of the enemies of France. If the nation is endangered, and the nation is all its citizens, then the state that threatens the nation is the enemy and the enemy includes all the citizens of that state. If the German army threatens Paris, it is not just the army but "Germans" who are the enemy. The wars of nation-states depend upon mobilization of "imagined communities" of citizen soldiers.[4] The implications of community against community were not long in coming.

Killing Civilians in the Franco-Prussian War

The power of the citizen-soldier was expressed in a new form in the Franco-Prussian war of 1870. The Prussians had reformed their army on the French model, including a variant of universal military service, but saw their army as the bulwark of monarchial order against the threat of French-style revolution. The reformed Prussian Army defeated the French army, but then found itself harassed by irregular French units as it approached Paris. These *francs-tireurs* (free shooters), with or without vestigial uniforms, were seen by the Prussian army as outlaw murderers. They and their villages were subject to harsh reprisals, including hundreds of executions. The *francs-tireurs* killed perhaps a thousand Prussians, but their greater success was in the fact that about a quarter of Prussian troops in France had to be devoted to guarding communications lines.[5]

This early example of irregular or guerrilla warfare brought into focus two different visions of a nation at war: a nation represented by a regular army versus a people rising up to defend their nation. The first rested on a clear distinction between combatants and noncombatants; the second denied this distinction. As often happens when previously clear boundaries are blurred and contested, there was a considerable effort in the years between 1871 and 1914 to define who was entitled to treatment as a lawful combatant. In general the larger countries wanted tighter definitions of combatants as regularly organized units under state control, whereas the smaller countries preferred to reserve the right of citizens to take up arms against an invader.

In the Brussels conference of 1874, the following was agreed (and remained unchanged in the Hague Conventions of 1899): "The population of a non-occupied territory who, on the approach of the enemy, of their own accord take up arms to resist the invading troops, without having had time to organize themselves . . . shall be considered belligerents, if they respect the laws and customs of war."[6]

The status of those taking up arms against an occupying army—including definition of when an invading army becomes an occupying army—was left undetermined. As noted later in this chapter, issues of status and definition emerge with new importance in discussions of insurgency and the terrorism of nonstate actors.

The treatment of civilians in World War I was in one instance a replay of the Franco-Prussian War. When the German army invaded Belgium and France in 1914, it nervously expected more of what it had suffered from the *francs-tireurs* in 1870. Although there was in fact no serious resistance to German occupation, the Germans took firm action to repress and intimidate the civilian populations occupied. In August 1914, the German Army in France and Belgium burned 20,000 buildings and executed 6,000 civilians.

Bombing Civilian Targets in Interstate War: Twentieth Century Theory and Practice

The development of strategic bombing, as described in Robert Pape's *Bombing to Win*, offers a convenient window on the developing understanding of the distinction between combatants and noncombatants.[7] For the analysis presented in this chapter, Pape's distinctions among bombing strategies can be represented in terms of three kinds of bombing target: military, military-industrial, and civilian. The first of these aims to reduce enemy military capacity by bombing military forces, installations, communications, and transportation in and behind the lines of battle. The second aims to reduce enemy military capacity by attacking crucial nodes in the industrial web that supports both military and civilian capacity—rail yards, electric power plants and dams, petroleum production and distribution, military plants (such as those producing aircraft and tanks), and civilian manufacturing plants that produce crucial materials such as ball bearings for both civilian and military purposes. The third kind of bombing target aims to hurt civilians enough that they pressure their government to stop fighting. The hurt can be direct, by bombing population centers, or indirect, by destroying water, power, transportation, and communication systems that will leave civilians suffering from cold, hunger, and disease.

Thus, of the three kinds of bombing targets, the first aims to avoid civilian casualties, the second accepts civilian casualties for workers in crucial industries, and the third aims to maximize civilian casualties.

Bombings during World War I

World War I greatly expanded the use of military aircraft, and the targeting of civilians began with the German air offensive of 1917. German hopes of quick victory on the battlefield had bogged down in trench warfare, and an air war was undertaken in an effort to undermine British support for the war. Theoretically, significant and concentrated damage to London would produce a weakening of civilian support for the war. In fact, 9,000

German bombs (totaling 280 tons of explosive) killed 1,400 and wounded 3,400, but British public support for the war remained undiminished.

Indeed, the British were confident that they could stand up under bombing better than the Germans. In 1918, they undertook their own air war against German cities, and were planning an expansion of counter-city bombing for 1919 when the Germans surrendered.

Between the Wars

Originally a counsel of desperation, bombing enemy civilians to break enemy morale was advanced after World War I as an explicit strategy by theorists in both the British and U.S. air forces. The British saw some success in bombing Iraqi and Afghan tribesmen into submission to British authority in the 1920s. The United States similarly surprised Sandino rebels in Nicaragua in the 1920s. Japanese warplanes bombed a working district in Shanghai, China, in 1932. Italian forces subjugated Ethiopia in 1936 with an offensive that included air attacks, using both bombs and poison gas on Ethiopian towns; civilian casualties may have reached 225,000 or two percent of the Ethiopian population.

The German Condor Legion infamously bombed Guernica in 1937 during the Spanish Civil War; high explosives and incendiaries killed about 1,000 civilians. Guernica was the cultural capital of the Basques, but Basque resistance to Franco and the Germans was undiminished. Less celebrated were the bombings of Spanish cities carried out by both Nationalists and Loyalists in 1936; both sides noticed that enemy morale was undented, and they moved to focus more on military targets.[8]

City Bombing by Germans in World War II

With the lessons of Spain fresh in mind, the Luftwaffe preferred military targets in their bombing strategies. Nevertheless, the Germans bombed Warsaw for ten days in September 1939 and killed 25,000 civilians before the city surrendered. After a breakdown of surrender negotiations with the Dutch in May 1940, the Germans bombed the business district of Rotterdam and killed at least 1,000 civilians. The Germans threatened to bomb Utrecht next, and all Dutch forces surrendered.

The Germans initially attacked only military targets in Great Britain, with particular success against British airfields. In response, the British sent bombers to Berlin. Hitler was incensed, overruled the Luftwaffe's focus on military targets, and ordered the Blitz—the terror bombing that was expected to break British morale. In 1940–41, the German air force attacked London and other major British cities, killing 44,000 and injuring 143,000. Ironically, the German shift from military to civilian targets saved the Royal Air Force and saved Great Britain from invasion.

Despite the failure of what can be called "terror bombing" of Great Britain in 1940–41, Hitler ordered terror bombing of Belgrade in April 1941 to reverse a coup that blocked Serbia's alliance with the Nazis. The deaths from the campaign in Belgrade were about 17,000, after which the Nazis easily took control of the city.

It is important to note that, from the German perspective, the results of city bombing were not entirely negative. Terror bombing failed in Great Britain and Spain, but brought quick surrenders in Warsaw, Rotterdam, and Belgrade.

British and U.S. Bombing of German Cities in World War II

At the beginning of World War II there were important differences in the details of strategic bombing theories in the United States and Great Britain. The British expected direct attacks on enemy civilians to disorganize industrial production, break civilian morale, and bring the enemy quickly to surrender. British experience triumphing over this theory in World War I did not interfere with British thinking, perhaps because other populations were thought to be more skittish than the British. Direct targeting of civilians had the practical advantage of requiring only area bombing rather than precision bombing; area bombing could be accomplished in the relative safety of nighttime sorties.

In contrast, the Americans had a theory of the modern industrial society as a fragile web, easily disrupted by targeted attacks on crucial nodes of production and distribution. The most famous expression of this theory was the 1943–44 campaign of U.S. attacks on Schweinfurt, where much of Germany's production of ball bearings—crucial for a mechanized economy—was located. Bombing from 25,000 feet necessarily implied some inaccuracy, and hundreds of civilians died in the bombings despite German bomb shelters. Although the factories were badly damaged and production was substantially if temporarily reduced, the bombing had little impact on the war. The Germans had earlier recognized the importance of ball bearings and had stockpiled sizeable quantities. Two additional air bombing campaigns are worth noting for this discussion: the Hamburg air offensive, and the Dresden air offensive.

Hamburg Air Offensive. A series of British and U.S. bomber attacks on Hamburg were conducted between 29 July and 3 August 1943. Hamburg was a major industrial center, the largest seaport in Europe and home to U-boat factories and yards. Its population was about 2 million; about 40,000 died, including 8,000 children and 21,000 women. Having earlier given up on military-industrial bombing, the British targeted civilian areas with explosives and incendiaries in night attacks. The Americans bombed in daylight and aimed for military-industrial targets such as rail yards and factories.

Dresden Air Offensive.   On 14 and 15 February 1945, U.S. and British bombers dropped bombs on the city of Dresden, which normally had a population around 600,000 but was swollen with refugees from the Red Army advancing on Germany from the East. The bombing technique was designed to produce widespread fire: first, high explosives were used to blow the roofs off of houses and expose frame timbers, then incendiary bombs were dropped to ignite the beams, then more high explosives were used to hamper fire services. The result was a firestorm in which super-heated air (1,000 degrees Fahrenheit) rising at the center of the fire sucked in cool air from around the base of the fire; the cool air rushing in had the velocity of a tornado (150 mph) and could pull people into the fire. The resulting deaths were between 35,000 and 45,000, almost all of them civilians and mostly working class or refugees.

Total German Casualties.   The Summary Report of *The U.S. Strategic Bombing Survey* offers an overview of allied bombing of Germany:

> In the wake of these attacks there are great paths of destruction. In Germany, 3.6 million dwelling units, approximately 20% of the total, were destroyed or heavily damaged. Survey estimates show some 300,000 civilians killed and 780,000 wounded. The number made homeless aggregates 7.5 million. The principal German cities have been largely reduced to hollow walls and piles of rubble. German industry is bruised and temporarily paralyzed. These are the scars across the face of the enemy, the preface to the victory that followed.[9]

U.S. Bombing of Japanese Cities

As in Europe, U.S. bombing in the Pacific began with an interdiction strategy that targeted military industries, especially aircraft manufacturing, and the raw materials required for these industries. Long-range bombing with relatively small payloads and generally unimpressive results led toward a shift to area bombing of Japanese cities. The explicit goal was to produce the economic, administrative, and psychological collapse of Japanese society that would end the war without need for a U.S. invasion of Japan.

The extent and impact of the terror bombing of Japan is not generally recognized today. Beginning with the raid on Tokyo in March 1945 that killed 84,000, the mostly wood buildings of Japanese cities were attacked with incendiaries. The six largest cities—Tokyo, Nagoya, Kobe, Osaka, Yokohama, Kawasaki—were attacked multiple times. Attention then turned to smaller cities. Of sixty-two cities with a population over 100,000, fifty-eight were firebombed. By the end of the U.S. bombing campaign, 40 percent of the urban area of the sixty-six cities attacked had been reduced to cinders, 22 million had lost their homes, 900,000 were dead and 1.3 million were injured.[10]

Compared with the firebombing, the damage produced by atom bombs in August 1945 was relatively small. In Hiroshima, 45,000 died the first day and 19,000 over the next four months from radiation and other injuries. In Nagasaki, 22,000 died the first day and 19,000 in the following months. Thus, neither atom bomb killed as many as the 84,000 killed by the firebombing of Tokyo in March 1945.

Other Civilian Casualties in Interstate War

Bombing is not the only form of military action that kills civilians. Attacking enemy merchant ships has long been a part of war, and even carefully focused attacks on military targets often produce civilian casualties.

Sinking Merchant Ships in World War I and World War II

During World War I, German submarines sank more than 5,000 merchant vessels, resulting in the loss of 15,000 lives.[11] Enemy merchant ships were targeted by both sides in World War II, mostly by submarine attacks. The United States lost 1,500 merchant ships, with 9,300 sailors killed and 12,000 wounded.[12] The United Kingdom lost 2,100 merchant vessels, with 30,000 people killed.[13] Japan lost 1,300 merchant vessels to U.S. attacks during World War II.[14]

Merchant ships are not military vessels and their crews, in great majority, are civilian rather than navy personnel. But a declaration of war can make a civilian sailor into something very much like a navy man; merchant vessels become in war a "merchant marine" or a "merchant navy." The extent to which their reality remains civilian was made evident in World War II for British seamen whose vessels were sunk; their pay stopped from the day the ship went down.[15]

Collateral Damage: Some Recent Examples

Unintended civilian casualties resulting from military action are often referred to as *collateral damage*. Despite the best efforts of military planners, such casualties are far from rare. The U.S. military, even with the most accurate weapons in the world and strong motivation to avoid civilian casualties, continues to produce significant numbers of unintended deaths.

The U.S. bombing campaigns in North Vietnam were aimed at military and industrial targets and avoided civilian population areas. Nevertheless, in the course of bombing rail yards and bridges, as well as steel, cement, explosives, and chemical plants, approximately 52,000 civilians were killed between 1965 and 1968. The 1972 bombing campaign against North Vietnam killed about 13,000, including many civilians.[16] Other examples include:

- The U.S. invasion of Panama in 1989 killed 300 civilians and injured 3,000.[17]
- The U.S. war to evict Saddam Hussein from Kuwait in 1991 killed 5,000 civilians.[18]
- NATO bombing of Milosevic's Serbia from March to June 1999 killed at least 500 civilians.[19]
- The U.S. war against the Taliban and al Qaeda in Afghanistan killed about 1,000 civilians between October 2001 and February 2002.[20]
- The U.S. war to oust Saddam Hussein from Iraq in 2003 killed 5,000–10,000 Iraqi civilians.[21]

Even when military forces incur serious risks to avoid civilian casualties, and even when such casualties are minimal by historical standards, those who suffer these casualties are likely to focus more on their losses than on the efforts that kept their losses low.

Embargo

A special case of collateral damage is the impact of an embargo, which cuts off supplies to the enemy; its direct intent is not to kill (except perhaps when planes and ships are enforcing the embargo against violators). As a means of influencing a state's behavior, an embargo thus seems to offer an appealingly nonviolent form of coercion.

In practice, however, an embargo often works on the same principle as terror bombing: to hurt enemy civilians enough that they pressure their government to satisfy the demands behind the embargo, or even remove the government from power altogether. When the target of an embargo is an industrial nation, the same combination of military and civilian significance that leads to strategic bombing leads to civilian suffering under the embargo. If the embargo lasts long enough, civilian suffering can include a significant death toll, especially for children and the elderly. After the 1991 war, the UN embargo of Iraq was associated with a doubling of the mortality rate for children under five. UNICEF concluded that if the mortality rates of the 1980s had continued through the 1990s, "there would have been half a million fewer deaths of children under five in the country as a whole during the eight-year period 1991 to 1998."[22]

Civilian Killing by the Police Power of the State

The distinction between combatants and noncombatants is usually an issue in relation to the operations of regular armed forces in interstate conflict. Nevertheless, it must also be observed that the greatest killing of civilians occurs not between states but within states, and not by military power but by police power. In his recent book *Death by Government*, Rudolph Rummel offers perhaps the most complete accounting of this kind of killing during the twentieth century.[23] He begins with the distinction between military deaths and civilian deaths: 34 million combatants killed in interstate and civil wars; 169 million noncombatants killed in war and peace. Of the 169 million civilian deaths, enemy civilians killed during war amount to 39 million; these are the kinds of casualties cited above in discussing the bombing of civilians. This is horrific killing, but small in comparison with the killing of civilians by their own governments: 130 million. Notice that in this categorization, 200,000 German Jews killed by the Nazis are counted in the 130 million whereas 5 million non-German Jews killed by the Nazis are counted in the 39 million.

Sometimes civilians killed by the government were members of a particular minority group—Armenians, Kulaks, Jews, Tutsi—and the killing can be described as genocide. Sometimes the victims were defined as enemies of the state by their political opposition to (or lack of fervor for) the state—Communists and Nationalists in China, or "Cambodians with Vietnamese minds" in Pol Pot's Cambodia—and Rummel refers to this killing as *politicide*. Whether by direct execution, by starvation, by overwork, by expulsion and exposure, or by some combination of these, killing by category requires the power of the state. Individual motives of anger, hatred, revenge, or booty can produce deadly riots, but big killing requires organization, division of labor, routinization, and bureaucratic incentives. In short, big killing is government work.[24]

Police and militias are often closer to the killing than regular military forces. But the police power of the state is in the end backed by the state's military power. This dependence is made evident when regular troops are called in to deal with riots and disasters that are seen as beyond the capabilities of local police. To the extent that military forces support the state and its monopoly of violence, the military are indirectly responsible for genocide and politicide even when the killing is more directly the work of police or militias.

Compared with government killing, nonstate violence is weak. Rummel estimates that 518,000 civilians were killed in the twentieth century by nonstate groups such as domestic guerrillas and international terrorists. Half a million killed by nonstate actors is less than half a percent of the 130 million civilians killed by state police power.

Theory and Practice of Insurgency War

Recent theorizing about war has focused on guerrilla war, low-intensity war,[25] asymmetric war, insurgency war, or fourth-generation war.[26] This is the warfare of the weak against the strong, a warfare that aims not at destroying the enemy's military power but at convincing enemy decision makers that victory is impossible or too expensive. The insurgents win when the enemy's political will is broken, an outcome that may be more likely when the enemy is a democratic state with short patience for foreign wars.

Insurgency war is often traced to Mao Tse-Tung's three-part strategy of People's War that brought the Communists from mountain hideouts to control of China after World War II.[27] Phase I concentrates on building political support for insurgents, with a few assassinations or armed attacks conducted for political and propaganda purposes. Phase II takes control of civil administration in some areas and conducts attacks to capture arms and wear down the enemy. Finally, in Phase III the insurgents commit regular military forces, carefully preserved to this point, in a final offensive against the enemy.

Reverses at Phases II or III can be answered with reversion to an earlier stage. Even Phase I insurgency (and especially Phase II insurgency) imposes a major cost to the enemy trying to control an area. Insurgency war need not be decisive to win; it need only persevere beyond the enemy's tolerance. Mao fought the People's War for twenty-seven years; the Vietnamese fought first the French and then the Americans for thirty years; the Sandinistas fought Samoza for sixteen years; and the Afghans fought the Soviets for ten years.

The foundation of insurgency war is political rather than military power. So long as cadres for the insurgency can be raised from among its sympathizers, it can recover from any level of military reversal. Thus, despite many successes, the Israelis have not succeeded in pacifying the Palestinians, the Russians have not succeeded in pacifying the Chechens, and the United States has not brought peace to Haiti or installed democracy in Afghanistan or Iraq.

Insurgency war is political in another sense as well: Success often depends on the sympathies of bystander states and peoples. Mao profited, at least at the beginning of his revolution, from Soviet support; Afghan resistance to the Russians was supported by the United States and by Arab oil states; and Nicaragua's Sandinistas were supported by U.S. liberals and church groups in their insurgency against the Samoza government.

As historian Arthur Waldron points out, the ideals if not the practice of the Chinese People's War go back to the *levee en masse* of the French Revolution.[28] The distinction between civilian and soldier was blurred in the levee and nearly eliminated in the case of the *francs tireurs* of the Franco-Prussian War. As the logic of war against industrial nation-states leads to attacks on civilians, so does the logic of war against insurgency. As the Prussians were moved to reprisals and executions against villages in the vicinity of the *francs tireurs*, so modern armies are moved to attack the civilian base that insurgents come from and hide within.

An early example of the kind of military tactic that can succeed against insurgency was provided in the Boer War, 1899–1902, in which 450,000 British troops finally prevailed over 50,000 Boer irregulars. The British success was based on burning Boer farms, killing Boer livestock, and collecting Boer women and children into camps. Epidemic diseases and malnutrition in the camps killed 27,000 of approximately 100,000 white inmates.[29]

A more recent and extreme example of scorched-earth strategy against insurgency is the experience of the Soviet Union in Afghanistan between 1979 and 1989. Although unsuccessful politically, Soviet bombs and mines did succeed in killing a million Afghans and pushing another five million as refugees into surrounding countries. The Islamic government of Sudan has similarly attacked villages associated with Christian and animist insurgents in the south of the country; bombs and starvation have killed nearly 2 million and created half a million refugees.

Thus, while there are many differences between interstate war and insurgency war, there is one striking commonality: use of violence against civilians. Whether the enemy is an industrial state, a tribal people, or something in between (as in the Boer War), the distinction between combatants and noncombatants is evidently difficult to maintain. Why is this so?

In any given case, one is tempted to attribute the killing of civilians to the personal pathology of the killers, to the triumph of anger and hatred over reason and compassion, or to some inhuman ideology. But this kind of piece-meal interpretation does not seem adequate to account for the broad pattern of state killing of civilians that has evolved since the French Revolution. More democratic and liberal states kill fewer, and more authoritarian states kill more, but, as noted above, even the United States and Great Britain have justified killing enemy civilians under some circumstances.

The pattern makes more sense if it is seen, not as an episodic failure of morality, but as the consistent expression of a distinctive moral vision. State killing of civilians expresses the logic and morality of the modern state, in which citizen and soldier are joined and the state and its military represent a whole people, a nation. The same logic, applied outward, makes the enemy larger than its military: The enemy is also a whole nation. The more enemy violence is seen to depend on civilian support and mobilization, the more enemy civilians are to be held responsible. Whether as the base of an industrial state or as the base of an insurgency, civilians are targets because, when the people are sovereign, the people are responsible.

This is, of course, precisely the logic of terrorism from below, the logic of nonstate violence against civilians of the state that is seen as the enemy. Nonstate terrorists accept the premise of the nation-state; they agree that the enemy is not just a military force but the whole population the military emerges out of and represents.

Terrorism as Insurgency

Implied in the previous section of this discussion is a strong relation between nonstate terrorism and insurgency. Some familiar examples of insurgency have also been described as terrorism: the FLN against the French in Algeria, the Viet Cong against the United States in South Vietnam, the Chechens against the Russians, the Palestinians against Israeli Jews, and al Qaeda against the United States. The implication of such examples is that terrorism from below is a form of insurgency. From this point it makes sense to talk about terrorism from below, nonstate terror, simply as terrorism.

Terrorism can be identified with Phase I of People's War, in which political mobilization is the focus, with only a few assassinations or attacks for propaganda purposes. In Phase I, insurgents do not usually control territory or administration, at least not in the area in which they are operating in this phase. Like Phase I insurgency, terrorism is the warfare of the weak; the terrorists cannot stand against regular military units. Like insurgency, terrorism is often of long duration. A review of seventy-seven terrorist groups active after World War II found that forty-one were active for ten years or more.[30] Notably, terrorism and insurgency both depend more on political than on military power.

Like the military forces of a nation-state, terrorists are only the apex of a pyramid of supporters and sympathizers.[31] The base of the pyramid are all those who agree with the political goals of the terrorists, even if they do not agree with terrorist attacks on civilians as the means to those goals. Higher layers of the pyramid are associated with smaller numbers but more support for terrorist tactics and more commitment and risk taking for the terrorist cause. In Northern Ireland in the 1980s and 1990s, for instance, the IRA seldom had more than 200 individuals on "active service," but the base of IRA support included all those who agreed with the IRA objective: "Brits out."

Insurgents and terrorists depend upon their civilian base of sympathizers and supporters. The terrorist apex cannot survive long without cover, information, money, supplies, expertise, and, especially, recruits from lower in the pyramid. Insurgents and terrorists cannot be beaten so long as they can disappear into and recruit from the pyramid that supports them.

It is not news that terrorism can be thought of as a form of insurgency. The value of focusing attention on this relation is that theorizing of insurgency and theorizing of terrorism suffer from the same disproportion: Attention to the impact of nonstate terrorism on the political will of those attacked has suppressed attention to the impact of state violence in creating sympathy and support for nonstate violence.[32] For insurgents and terrorists, in-group sympathy and mobilization are issues of survival.

Terrorists versus the State: It's Politics

What do terrorists want? In the short term they want to be and to appear to be powerful. The warfare of the weak must fight initially against the perception that nothing can be done, that the enemy is too powerful to fight against. In the medium term they want to mobilize more of their base of sympathizers to active commitment and support. In the long term they want to succeed in whatever their cause is: independence, status, power, respect. That is, they want to hurt the enemy in ways that are public and important; they want to be recognized as the leaders of the movement that expresses and accomplishes the goals of their people; and they want to break the enemy's political will to resist.

The three phases of the People's War correspond roughly to these three levels of terrorist success. Phase I shows power to survive and hurt the enemy, Phase II shows power to administer and defend an area, at least for a time, and Phase III shows dominating military power.

Phase I depends, for terrorists and insurgents, on a kind of jujitsu strategy—using the enemy's strength against him. The strategy is to attack the enemy in ways that will elicit a response that does for the terrorists what they cannot do for themselves—mobilize their sympathizers into commitment and risk taking under terrorist leadership. The psychology of this strategy is powerful and reliable: an external threat increases in-group cohesion and produces changes in in-group psychology that have been called "the authoritarian triad."[33] The external threat produces increased respect for in-group leaders, idealization of in-group values, and increased sanctions against in-group deviates. (Americans saw this psychology at work for themselves after September 11, 2001.)

Thus, a crucial strategy of terrorists and insurgents is to elicit a state response that will mobilize terrorist sympathizers.[34] The foundation of this strategy is apparent in Mao's "Six Main Points for Attention" in the Red Army: "Soldiers were urged to replace straw bedding and wooden bedboards after staying at peasant homes overnight, to return whatever they borrowed; to pay for anything they damaged, to be courteous; to be fair in business dealings; and to treat prisoners humanely."[35] Mao was concerned here that the Red Army should provide a positive contrast to the depredations of the Nationalists, who often plundered the peasants they encountered. The behavior of the Nationalists would mobilize the peasants for the Communists.

The Sandinistas relied on the power of jujitsu both to recruit peasant sympathies against the Samoza government and to recruit foreign sympathizers: "The Western media were invited to Nicaragua to visit with the Sandinistas and report on the atrocities committed by the National Guard. The Sandinistas could count on the Guard committing atrocities virtually every time they operated against the guerillas. . . . During this period, they invited numerous members of U.S. congregations to visit Nicaragua and witness for themselves the brutality of the government and the moderate approach of the coalition."[36]

A more recent example can be seen in the rhetoric of jujitsu from bin

Laden, particularly in the tape released just before the 2004 U.S. presidential election:

> The events that affected my soul in a direct way started in 1982 when America permitted the Israelis to invade Lebanon and the American Sixth Fleet helped them in that. This bombardment began and many were killed and injured and others were terrorized and displaced. . . . And as I looked at those demolished towers in Lebanon, it entered my mind that we should punish the oppressor in kind and that we should destroy towers in America in order that they taste some of what we tasted and so that they be deterred from killing our women and children.
>
> And that day, it was confirmed to me that oppression and the intentional killing of innocent women and children is a deliberate American policy. Destruction is freedom and democracy, while resistance is terrorism and intolerance. This means the oppressing and embargoing to death of millions as Bush Sr. did in Iraq in the greatest mass slaughter of children mankind has ever known, and it means the throwing of millions of pounds of bombs and explosives at millions of children—also in Iraq—as Bush Jr. did, in order to remove an old agent and replace him with a new puppet to assist in the pilfering of Iraq's oil and other outrages.[37]

The United States must contest this rhetorical construction in order to cut al Qaeda off from its base of sympathy in the Muslim world. To ignore bin Laden's claims with an assumption of moral superiority because terrorists attack civilians cannot succeed against the record of state killing of civilians. More precisely, stonewalling can work at home in the United States but not with a billion Muslims worldwide, and, increasingly, not with Europeans, either.

Terrorists recognize that they are in a political contest with the state they attack. The contest is for the sympathies of those the terrorists claim to represent, for the sympathies of the public and the decision makers of the state attacked, and for the sympathies of bystander peoples and states. The terrorist advantage is to see a political contest where the state sees only crazies and criminals. State failure to see terrorism as a political contest is indicated by a surprising fact about the study of terrorism: There are many databases recording terrorist attacks but not one that records on the same time scale the state responses to terrorist attacks. The contest between David and Goliath cannot be understood by watching only David.

Conclusion

In Europe before the French Revolution, civilians were not a threat in time of war. Their local loyalties were no threat either to professional soldiers or to the elites who controlled these soldiers. As armies passed through a landscape, civilians could be pillaged for supplies and booty, and their women could be raped. Absent revenge or a lesson against rebels, however, there was no reason to kill people who were valuable as producers and tax-payers for whatever state controlled them.

The *levee en masse* of the French Revolution blurred the distinction between citizen and soldier in a way that raised French power even as it broadened the definition of the enemy. By the end of World War I, the nation-state had everywhere triumphed in Europe, and war between states was recognized as a contest between two industrial systems that depend as much on civilians as soldiers. Insurgency wars and People's War have blurred still further the line between civilian and soldier: The insurgent and the terrorist rise out of civilian populations and politics, and return to these as often as necessary.

In war against other states, the modern state has recognized the power of civilian mobilization in an industrial state to justify attacks that kill enemy civilians. Such attacks killed 39 million in the twentieth century. In war against internal enemies, the modern state has recognized the threat to its own power to justify killing disaffected ethnic and political categories among its own civilians. Such attacks have killed 130 million in the twentieth century.

Against this state killing can be measured the killing by guerrillas and terrorists: approximately half a million civilians killed in the twentieth century. Both state and nonstate killing are evidence of the blurred boundary between civilian and combatant, but the numbers suggest that the terrorists should not be the first target of those concerned about civilian deaths.

Of course it is possible to argue that states killing civilians has nothing to do with the motivation or the morality of nonstate actors killing civilians. But if terrorism is like insurgency in its dependence on a political base, then the contest between state and terrorist is a political contest. As the terrorists aim at the political will of the state and its civilian population, so the state must aim for the political will of the pyramid of terrorist sympathizers. In this contest, it will avail the state little to pretend that its own killing of civilians is irrelevant to the morality of terrorism.

Acknowledgments

The author is grateful for support for this work from the Andrew W. Mellon Foundation, the Solomon Asch Center for Study of Ethnopolitical Conflict, and Bryn Mawr College.

CHAPTER 17

Digging Deep: Environment and Geography as Root Influences for Terrorism

P. H. LIOTTA AND JAMES F. MISKEL

While the focus of most chapters in this volume has centered on root causes of terrorism, this chapter stresses that the environment and geography—specifically the physical landscape in which terrorists live—are influences, important ones to be sure, but not causes. Environment and geography are part of the complex, intertwined dynamics that provide the conditions for the recruitment and training of terrorists, and growth of terrorist organizations. Specifically, we argue that environment and geography provide both context and opportunity for the making of a terrorist. The context springs from the objective conditions that shape the strategies and tactics that are employed in terrorist operations. The opportunity consists of objective conditions that permit the organization, recruitment, and training of terrorists and the continuous functioning of networks of logistics and intelligence support.

An opportunity is not a cause. Poverty, for example, does not necessarily lead to terrorism, just as resource scarcity does not directly lead to individual or group acts of terrorism. Profiles of al Qaeda members compiled by a former CIA analyst, for example, demonstrate that many members of terrorist groups are from reasonably well-off families.[1] Further, most September 11 suicide-hijackers were from upper-middle-class Saudi families. As conditions, environment and geography simply provide the space (and sometimes, part of the motivations) for violent behavior.

As it has evolved in both its natural rural state and its man-made urban state, the physical landscape has generated a variety of troubling effects that increase the space for terrorism to prosper. There are specific physical landscapes in which terrorism is most likely to germinate: the rapidly urbanizing cities of what we term the Lagos-Cairo-Karachi-Jakarta Arc, the undergoverned rural provinces within functioning but troubled states, and "feral" zones within major cities. All are linked to the broader world through globalization which, for all its positive effects, has greatly facilitated the cross-border transfer of people, information, weapons, money, electrons, and disease. Because globalization is so intricately entwined into the world economy, it has become virtually impossible to quarantine these spaces off from the rest of the world. Thus, the threats that emerge from these spaces will, by virtue of globalization, have "reach."

Environment and geography act as influences for terrorism and terrorist opportunities. Too much of our thinking about security has, until recently, reflected the anecdote about the drunk who loses his keys in the dark and only looks for them under the streetlight because that's the only place where he can see. Afghanistan has taught us to start thinking differently about the places where the streetlights do not shine, the darkened zones of the earth where there is no electricity.[2] Even as the world population and economy grow, in some parts of the globe darkened zones will only proliferate. This is due in large part to rapid urbanization, which drains the countryside of population and at the same time so drastically strains some national governments that they cease attempting to manage both the city and the country and instead leave remote rural areas to their own devices.

Taking Advantage of the Context

In a variety of ways, the physical landscape—the space in which terrorists operate—directly affects the strategy and tactics of both the terrorists and antiterrorist forces, whether military or police. Because terrorists are almost always operating from a position of comparative weakness relative to opposing military forces (law enforcement forces are another matter), terrorist organizations have an incentive to use geography in ways that compensate for their weaknesses. Consequently, terrorists have developed effective techniques for blending into their environment, like chameleons who camouflage through skin coloration, physically relocating (like amphibians) from one environment to another and segmenting their operational structures so that the body as a whole can regenerate a lost unit, much like a frog can regrow a severed limb. This is, in fact, the story behind the story of September 11, 2001, just as it is the story behind the story of how al Qaeda has continued to function after the downfall of its patrons in Afghanistan. The September 11 terrorists blended themselves into the environment of several American and European cities; both before and after September 11, al Qaeda physically relocated its "headquarters," and the organization has survived the loss of numerous appendages, such as the cells of activists in Hamburg and the midlevel leaders that were captured in Afghanistan.

In the future, terrorists will rely on the environment and geography for both attack and retreat. Terrorists may also abuse "root influences" of environment and geography in the following ways:

- relying or forcing critical infrastructure degradation or collapse, to include not only physical systems and structures, but also contamination of food supplies or resources in ways difficult or impossible to detect;
- using infectious disease that cannot be controlled, whether or not through the use of biological agents;
- operating in conditions of intrastate and/or interethnic conflict in failed or failing states;
- using to advantage conditions where environmental stress, resource scarcity, and depletion occur;
- the trafficking of drugs, small arms, and inhumane weapons, often coupled with conflicts that are claimed as insurgencies.

While none of these aspects is necessarily new, the capacity to induce chaos is greater today than ever before. We know, for example, that the Soviets experimented with strategic biological weapons, such as smallpox that could be delivered with ICBMs.[3] Soviet weapon experts recognized, however, that smallpox could be released far more secretively on enemy territory; thus, in an age of globalization where disease knows no borders, chaos strategists recognize this advantage as well.

Terrorist groups have disparate objectives, and in some cases their stated political objectives are window dressing for seamier or nihilistic purposes. One can say, however, that a tactical goal of all terrorist groups is to prevent intervening military forces from achieving complete success at restoring stability and suppressing terrorist activity. With respect to this tactical goal, it is clear that terrorists have experienced considerable success in places like Somalia, Iraq, and Afghanistan. They have been able to achieve this success by effectively and creatively taking advantage of the physical landscape.

In American warfighter terminology, deception and surprise are standard checklist items in thinking about war. But American intelligence assets, in terms of technology and capabilities the most superior in history, fall short when it comes to the unclear art of human intelligence and human unpredictability. In truth, despite all our progress with conventional and unconventional war since the American experience in Southeast Asia, there still rings an identifiable empathy with how the debacle of Somalia was, in some respects, not different from the debacle of Vietnam: "If only the little bastards would just come out . . . and fight like men, we'd cream them."

The frustration inherent in these remarks, of course, also explains why terrorists will continue to rely on environment and geography as factors of advantage in confronting more traditional adversaries. Further, there are distinct differences from terrorists and traditional security forces. Arthur Waldron of the University of Pennsylvania has in the past described war in the ideal type as having three distinct phases: engagement, chaos, and chopping of heads (*jiaofeng*, *luan*, and *zhan*).[4] The master of this "intellectual" approach to warfare, of course, is Sun Tzu, who employs *jiaofeng*, *luan*, and *zhan* through instantaneous, differential shock-wave application. Yet when American warfighters speak of "cutting off and killing" an enemy, they mean "to chop heads" in the metaphorical sense; when the terrorist speaks of *zhan*, or its linguistic equivalent in a different culture, he is being literal. That said, new operational concepts and force employment *did* produce an advantage in crushing the Taliban and al Qaeda forces in 2001—through a network of unmanned aircraft that led to increased battlefield awareness, special operations forces used as forward spotters, motivated indigenous forces, precision major fires delivered by various means, and rapid maneuver to cause the enemy to break. This led to battlefield success, though not necessarily to strategic victory. Moreover, the Taliban and al Qaeda made a classic mistake in Afghanistan: They were stupid enough to fight back. That is to say, they failed to understand that geography and the environment were suddenly less advantageous due to American co-option of Northern Alliance forces that were equally well adapted to the geography and new tactics for dealing with the landscape of Afghanistan. These new tactics included forward positioned Special Forces units who blended into the environment and could physically relocate in a functional way by calling in precise air strikes instead of attacking the targets on the ground.

It seems worth recalling that five decades ago, Roger Trinquier claimed that contemporary war is an interlocking system of political, economic, psychological, and military actions and conflicts.[5] Trinquier argued that armies tend to fight traditional warfare and that in modern war they are doomed to failure despite overwhelming firepower. Afghanistan suggests that with the advent of network warfare and remarkable advances in military technology, Trinquier's gloomy prophecy may not be as set in stone as some once believed when engaging with terrorists using environment and geography to their advantage. At the same time, in view of the incredible American military successes since the end of the Cold War, one might reasonably ask why we are pushing so hard and fast toward military transformation when there are clear and present vulnerabilities that transformation does not affect, yet which terrorists will likely target.

Even as the United States has the capacity to bring massive firepower on the battlefield—along with an increasingly sophisticated network of intelligence systems, information architecture, unmanned systems, and joint and combined force operations—we should expect to see terrorists increasingly employ environment and geography to advantage in future engagements.

Every single military engagement since the end of the Cold War suggests that we have dispatched our adversaries with ease on battlefields and in direct engagements. This would seem to be an argument *against* rapid transformation of the armed forces. Why bother, after all, to change the military when no one else can stand up to it? Increased battlefield awareness, the likely increased future use of special operations forces and indigenous forces, precision major fires delivered by various means, and rapid maneuver to cause the enemy to break, as well as what one observer has called the phenomenon of "marines turned soldiers," have all fundamentally altered how we fight. But the arguments suggesting that limited resources and the dictates of the political economy are what most constrain transformation seem to miss the mark completely. What may well be lacking is the need to recognize "closework." As Larry K. Smith phrases it:

> Overwhelming force implies, almost by definition, a lack of precision. That won't work now. What we're going to need is a much greater emphasis on the concentrated application of street smarts. I call these sorts of operations "closework." They are extremely precise missions that are used when the results are absolutely crucial. They demand the very highest standards of intelligence, of training, of preparation, of timing and execution. We haven't been particularly good at this in the past.[6]

Closework also suggests that urban warfare and often brutal forms of engagement (such as was undertaken in late 2004 in Fallujah, Iraq) will be likely in the future. Rather than relying more on distance warfare and precision engagement, we may fundamentally turn in a new direction. If it is true, for example, that one of two people on the face of the earth will live in urban environments and one of two people will live in "water-stressed" areas at some point within the next two decades, then the complexity of intersecting forces can bring about profound and often vicious consequences. These consequences might include—but certainly not be limited to—critical infrastructure collapse, the outbreak of infectious disease that cannot be controlled, and intrastate as well as interethnic conflict related to resource scarcities (such as water) and environmental stress. We must prepare for the wars we may find it necessary to fight, not plan for the wars we want to fight.

Taking Advantage of the Opportunity

For the United States of America, at least, the events of 11 September 2001 proved pivotal. On that day, the United States joined numerous other nations in the so-called "developed" world in recognizing that non-state actors—terrorist organizations—could seriously harm powerful states.

Equally, there came a recognition that U.S. citizens, their way of life, and the specific liberties that they had been accustomed to were now vulnerable and at risk. Simultaneously, there grew the disturbing awareness that this new and deadly threat did not come from a specific enemy whose identity and capabilities were clear because they were "in the light." There now seems to be an emerging understanding that aspects of non traditional security issues that have long plagued the so-called "developing world"—or, more appropriately, the emerging world—could increasingly affect the policy decisions and future choices of powerful developed states. It is this rising awareness that this chapter seeks to enhance: Terrorists will use environment and geography to their advantage in a variety of ways, but most importantly as recruiting grounds and bases of operation.

Our concern is that while the military is wrestling with (and apparently succeeding at) the challenge of developing ever more impressive means of deterring and defeating "in the light" threats as well as defeating individual terrorist cells, no agency of government at the state or multistate level (including the military) is doing enough to understand and reduce the opportunities that the evolving geography and environment trends described in this chapter will offer to terrorists. The "new" environment and geography has multiple identities: gross overcrowding of certain cities, anarchy, governmental collapse, ethnic rivalry, cultural grievance, religious-ideological extremism, environmental degradation, natural resource depletion, competition for economic resources, drugs, alliances between criminal enterprises of all sorts and terrorists, the proliferation of "inhumane weapons," cyber war, and disease. As disparate as these non traditional security realities are, they all will increasingly affect states and regions within them.

Undeniably, the increased movement to urban areas in the Lagos-Cairo-Karachi-Jakarta Arc will have a profound effect on *all* states in the future, as well as on lawless or feral urban and rural zones inside functioning states, and displaced groups of people (to include concentrations of refugees, internal migrants, and guest workers). Most of the states in the Middle East are already experiencing water scarcity (some have per capita water availability rates that are significantly lower than minimums recommended by the World Health Organization) and water resources will obviously be stressed even further as the population surges.[7] The combination of indigenous population growth, the return of guest workers sent home by European and other Middle Eastern states due to fears of terrorism, and urbanization with water scarcity will undoubtedly lead to dramatic pressures on the states of the Middle East. The return of guest workers will have at least two complementary, but negative effects. It will eliminate remittances (for some countries, the value of remittances from overseas workers is greater than the amount of the state's foreign aid receipts), and it will increase the number of individuals who will draw upon the government's already limited resources. These returning individuals may also bring with them higher expectations of government that were acquired overseas. The inability of strained local governments to satisfy these expectations is likely to increase the proportion of the population that is disaffected, impatient, and potentially ripe for recruitment by terrorist organizations and insurgent groups.

The Resource Dimension

Water is not the only resource whose scarcity may be destabilizing and may contribute to intrastate tensions, but it is by far the most important because it is directly essential to human life. Water also obviously has critical agricultural and industrial uses; without it farms cannot grow crops or feed livestock and industries cannot operate factories. Other resources may be scarce in a different sense: Oil is scarce relative to the needs of a growing worldwide economy. The higher prices caused by oil's relative global scarcity will unquestionably further strain governments of oil-importing states and thus contribute to the kind of inadequate internal governance that creates niches for terrorists. Relative scarcity could also lead to tensions between states, much as did nationalistic economic policies in Europe and the United States during the Great Depression. However, there is no absolute oil scarcity inside oil-producing states. Water, on the other hand, is absolutely scarce inside many states and is becoming relatively scarce globally.

For certain resources, abundance may contribute more to terrorism than scarcity. Diamonds and drugs are abundant in certain locations and may be scarce relative to global demand, but it is their abundance particularly in the dark and dim zones of the earth, in conjunction with the inability of stressed governments to assert control over these areas, that has enabled groups to exploit these resources to fund terrorist operations. In a way, this is also true for oil, except that oil-production has been kept under state control and it is the profits that private individuals earn from this state controlled industry that have been used to finance terrorist groups.

Reliance upon the absolute abundance of a single domestic natural resource may also be destabilizing in the sense that single-resource economies are more sensitive to global price swings. Sharp downturns in the export prices of the resource can quickly undermine state budgets and lead to the kind of undergovernance of which terrorist groups can take advantage.

The Megacity

Truly cataclysmic demographic changes will occur in a ring of cities across the Lagos-Cairo-Karachi-Jakarta Arc, where there will be astounding shifts in the global landscape that hinge on the "flocking" of populations to urban centers. According to a recent National Intelligence Council report,[8] as well as from data compiled by the National Geographic Society[9] and the United Nations Population Division[10] (in the 2001 revision), the world's population in 2015 will be 7.2 billion, and most will tend to live longer than they do today. Roughly 95 percent of the increase will take place in "emerging" countries, and nearly all this population growth will happen in rapidly expanding urban areas. Consider, for example, the difference between growth in the emerging world versus growth in the so-called developed world from 1950 to projected figures for 2015: New York City will shift from 12 million inhabitants in 1950 to 17 million in 2015, while Lagos will grow from 1 million to 24.4 million; Los Angeles will shift from 4 million to 14.2 million, while Karachi will explode from 1.1 million to 20.6 million; and, while Tokyo will admittedly mushroom from 6.2 million to 28.7, it will likely be far better equipped and able to handle the infrastructure requirements of the future "megacity," unlike many cities in the emerging world.[11]

The real concerns, therefore, lie in the "population belt" from Lagos to Jakarta. Yet, it should be stressed that urbanization itself is value neutral—neither a good nor a bad thing. Urbanization, therefore, does not have to suddenly become a security issue or a threat. While Tokyo, for example, will remain the world's most densely populated city, in many ways Japan has already accommodated for its urbanized existence. Nearly 72 percent of Japanese today already live in cities. It is unclear, however, whether Lagos or Dhaka or Tehran can sustain growth rates such as those projected above. Indeed, it is not even clear if many cities in *developed states* could sustain such rates. After all, Dhaka's projected growth rate from 1950 to 2015, compared to New York City's growth over the same timeframe, suggests that, were New York City to grow at an equivalent rate, the Big Apple (*really* Big Apple) in 2015 would have a population just shy of 600 million people—or more than twice the current population of the United States.[12] As it seems unlikely that advanced polities such as New York City and State would be able to sustain such rapid growth, how can we assume that Bangladesh—already one of the most impoverished states on the face of the earth—could possibly accommodate a dramatic surge in the population of its capital city?

The real effect of urbanization, and where it will most rapidly take place, reveals itself in the projection for the year 2015, where the number of cities with a population of over five million will skyrocket from eight (in 1950) to fifty-eight. Additionally, various population studies suggest that it could be possible to see more than 600 cities worldwide with populations in excess of one million inhabitants by 2015; in 1950, by contrast, there were only eighty-six such cities on the planet.

Our concern is not so much with megacities in Western Europe, Japan, or the United States; rather, it is in areas where shifts are occurring at a dramatically swift pace and where the infrastructures are already stressed. These shifts are most ominous in the arc from Lagos in West Africa to Jakarta in Southeast Asia. As Richard J. Norton observed, many of the burgeoning cities of the future risk becoming Petri dishes for instability, disease, and terrorism.[13] In other words, at least some of these cities will grow far beyond the "natural" carrying capacity of their respective national governments, with the result that the infrastructures of governance and public services will be stretched past the breaking point. Cities in this condition will pose a particularly serious security threat because they will have *both* substantial pockets of darkness within their municipal boundaries (concentrations of disaffected citizens without jobs or access to government services and in neighborhoods where law enforcement agencies have limited presence) and extensive commercial, communications, and transportation links to the rest of the world. In other words, it will be easy for groups in the urban pockets of darkness to export instability.

Thus surging urban populations in less developed parts of the world will create two types of dark zones whose geographies will create opportunities for terrorists to recruit and organize: lawless sections of the city and, by draining the countryside of its residents, ungoverned remote, rural areas.

The Ungoverned Rural Zone

The concept of state failure became popular in the 1990s, partially as a result of scholars like Robert Kaplan.[14] At that time, there was a sense of increasing instability and collapse of governance in many parts of the world following the end of the Cold War. Policymakers hoped that research into state failure might provide insights into the causes of state failure and indicators that could be monitored to identify states that were nearing failure. The premise was that early intervention (through concentrated foreign aid, etc.) by the international community might be able to stave off failure and thus avoid greater costs in the future in the form of regional disorder and military intervention and peacekeeping. In response, the Central Intelligence Agency established the State Failure Task Force, to conduct a comprehensive examination of why states fail. The task force developed a model for predicting failure in 1999, and since then there have been numerous examinations of the failed state phenomenon, most of which consider failed states as providing a geography and environment suitable for terrorist recruitment and organization.

Yet, events of the past few years illustrate that there are other geographies and environments that are at least as hospitable from the terrorists' point of view as failed states. Examples include eastern Colombia, where narcoterrorists have operated for years inside remote valleys; the "lawless" triangle near the Brazil-Paraguay-Argentina border, where Hizballah, arms dealers, and smugglers conduct business freely;[15] the easternmost hinterlands of the Democratic Republic of Congo, where the government had so little control that rival ethnic groups, criminal gangs, and cross-border raiders from Uganda and Rwanda fought with each other and pillaged the area of its natural resources (diamonds, and timber, predominately); and Afghanistan, beyond the outskirts of Kabul and Kandahar.

The threat that most failed states pose is usually localized. Of course, they pose a threat to their own citizens, who suffer directly from the anarchy and economic deprivation that failure entails. They also pose a threat of sorts to adjoining states that suddenly find themselves being compelled by circumstance (if not altruism) to host large numbers of migrants in temporary refugee camps that too often are temporary only in name and occasionally become bases of operation for violent groups that can destabilize nearby provinces. In sum, the spillover effects from failure rarely pose a direct threat outside the immediate vicinity of the failed state.

It is inevitable that feral zones in both the wild outback and inside city limits will emerge in numerous locations across the Lagos-Cairo-Karachi-Jakarta Arc of megacities. Further compounding the issue of rapid urban population growth is the "youth bulge" phenomenon. Although the growing number of Chechen and Palestinian suicide bombings by women suggests that gender changes are in the wind, most violence is committed by young men, usually between the ages of fifteen and twenty-nine. As the overall population grows, so, too, will the population of young men looking to the municipality to provide job opportunities and educational services. If, as seems likely in many emerging megacities on the arc, the jobs and educational opportunities are not available, discontent, crime, and urban instability will result, and if the city is unable to effectively administer neighborhoods where there are high levels of discontent, crime, and instability, festering pockets of darkness will sprout.

Other pockets of darkness are also likely to form around semi-urbanized collections of "displaced" populations. There are, for example, tens of millions of refugees who have been forced to live in slums that are evolving over time into zombie-like para-states with swelling populations. They, too, stumble, despite international support, failing to provide the opportunities and services that their growing populations demand, and create fertile ground for instability. The only saving grace is that displaced people are typically not as well connected by road, rail, or air to the rest of the world and thus will be less efficient exporters of violence to distant locations.

Finding a Way Out

In a globalized economy, it is a practical impossibility to redraw the map of the future into "green" and "red" zones, the latter being virtual No Man's Lands where hope is abandoned. Rather, many of the states that will be most affected by the trends discussed here are heavily linked to globalization and simply cannot be abandoned or even avoided. Egypt, Pakistan, and Indonesia all fall into this category of feeble—though not failed—states.

But to assume that military forces will increasingly take on the contradictory roles of regime change in preemptive wars and then assume the immense task of state and nation building in sustained "governance stability operations"—in essence "kicking the door in" and then "putting the door back on"—does seem a bit of a stretch. But this stretch is exactly what seems to be expected in our prevailing, if implicit, current mental map of the future, where terrorists can employ environment and geography to advantage.

More focus must fall on internal public sector reform and public security improvements in states where governance is currently failing to keep the lights lit or where urban population growth is likely to induce failure at the municipal level or invite government withdrawal from remote rural areas. Just as we have recognized after September 11 that homeland security requires domestic and international action, so, too, we must work with other members of the international community to develop a global consensus about the need to address foreign threats and domestic governance shortcomings as potentially related. By virtue of its own inefficiency, the divergent agenda of its leading members and its orientation towards state-level solutions, the United Nations is likely not up to the task of effectively promoting public sector reform and has been marginalized even in many of its traditional venues. More flexible and effective approaches should be considered to better organize the collective efforts of all of the actors and efforts in the international community: governments, international organizations, international nongovernment organizations, national civil society organizations, and for-profit corporations. Jonathan Lash, president of World Resources Institute, has aptly described this as a "shift from the stiff formal waltz of traditional diplomacy to the jazzier dance" of issue-based networks and creative partnerships.[16]

Further, there are basic issues that everyone both acknowledges and ignores. Future strategies must move beyond policing actions and military interventions and look toward active prevention. The keys are to develop programs that create jobs, reduce poverty, and improve governance, especially in urban areas—before discontented groups take up arms against fellow city-dwellers or join terrorist groups that strike out against the developed countries.

Equally, there are technological means that can help us look through the darkness in ways never thought possible, to find trends and indicators that suggest terrorist activity—especially in remote regions. Specifically, as noted in the *9/11 Commission Report*, the use of remote sensing in rural areas can provide tremendous advantage.[17] (Admittedly, such sensing is less effective inside "feral city" zones.) Douglas S. Way, a professor at Ohio State University and chief scientist at Earth Satellite Corporation, has been particularly effective in arguing how insurgents such as Mao, Castro, and Guevara serve as examples. Their preferred territory, often referred to as "stateless zones," encompass characteristics that hinder government troops and favor illicit groups: rugged terrain, thick vegetation cover, remote from population centers and lines of communication and control, close to foreign borders, and in countries of poor governance.[18] Way and others thus developed global open-source GIS datasets at one-kilometer resolution, as well as detailed maps that show the advantages of environment and geography for terrorist groups. The maps also suggest "priority zones" and identify several locations not previously suspected and worthy of additional monitoring.

Indeed as Andres Oppenheimer noted in the 12 March 2003, *San Diego Union-Tribune*: "In the new U.S. military doctrine, one of the biggest dangers . . . no longer comes from foreign armies or urban guerrillas taking over capital cities and expanding their reach to the interior. Rather, it comes from criminal forces occupying empty spaces in jungles, mountains and other remote areas, and expanding their reach to big cities and centers of power."[19]

The solution to these dilemmas of environment and geography will prove all the more difficult if ignored over time. Admittedly, the intuitive response to situations of such sheer complexity is, classically, to *do nothing at all*— because many of these problems seem just too difficult to address. The more appropriate response is to take an adaptive posture, to avoid the impulse to act purely on instinct, or to recognize what variables and past examples might best inform the basis of future action. It is by no means an exaggeration to argue that new understandings of both geography and geopolitics are needed for addressing the global threat of terrorism.

CHAPTER 18

Dealing with the Roots of Terror[1]

KARIN VON HIPPEL

Al Qaeda's spectacular on September 11, along with the tragically lethal attacks in places such as Nairobi, Bali, and Madrid, attest to its determination, reach, and capabilities. The indoctrination strategy is equally long-term; the extremist madrasas (Islamic boarding schools) epitomize the patient nurturing of potential recruits. Beyond the military, police, legal, and financial activities that have been undertaken to confront this threat, a number of longer-term preventative measures also need to be adopted by governments and international organizations to thwart this movement, network, and organization.[2] At the risk of stating the obvious, the threat posed by transnational terrorism can only be defeated by a coordinated, robust, long-term, transnational response.

Publicly, all states and international organizations have been committed to tackling root causes since September 11, though some were quicker than others in articulating their policies. For example, just after the attacks, the European Union, as did the United Nations and the Organization for Economic Cooperation and Development (OECD),[3] outlined a comprehensive counterterrorist strategy that incorporated a major component aimed at root causes through the use of nonviolent tools. At the same time, the United States government had an additional plan to undermine terrorism, that is, war in Iraq. As was patently obvious in the run-up to the war, it was opposed by a number of European (and other) states, and only served to exacerbate a transatlantic rift that had been evident since the end of the Cold War.

In addition to dealing with the alleged weapons of mass destruction, the United States was positing that a democratic Iraq would pave the way for more democracy in the Middle East and thereby undermine terrorism, while some European states argued that war in Iraq would in fact do more to enhance the appeal and swell the ranks of al Qaeda. For Europe and several of the aforementioned multilateral organizations, the focus was not on regime change, but rather, on a number of socioeconomic reforms in developing states. The U.S. government also officially joined this effort in February 2003, with the publication of the *National Strategy for Combating Terrorism*.[4] This document asserts:

> Ongoing U.S. efforts to resolve regional disputes, foster economic, social, and political development, market-based economies, good governance, and the rule of law, while not necessarily focused on combating terrorism, contribute to the campaign by addressing underlying conditions that terrorists often seek to manipulate for their own advantage.[5]

The strategy paper goes on to describe how the U.S. government cannot do this alone: "The United States has neither the resources nor the expertise to be in every place in the world. . . . Our friends and allies face many of the same threats. It is essential for America to work with its friends and allies in this campaign."[6] While much of the language in the *National Strategy* appears bizarrely out of place, and certainly inconsistent with U.S. behavior since the start of the Bush Administration, at least publicly the U.S. government formally committed to dealing with root causes.

However it transpired that the public strategies of Europe and America converged on the issue of tackling root causes (though not on the regime change component), and however welcome the nonviolent aspects of the U.S. approach may be to European policy makers, the question remains as to how well both power blocks actually understand root causes and what their strategies in fact entail for countering them. Three years since the attacks in America, neither have implemented significant practical measures, in terms of political and socioeconomic reforms, which could fundamentally reduce the appeal and influence of bin Laden and al Qaeda. Three years on, the progress report has been decidedly mediocre.

Beyond the more radical elements of the al Qaeda platform which are considered nonnegotiable, other underlying causes still need to be tackled, while those that are less well understood, or merely assumptions at this stage, need greater clarification. (This discussion takes it as a given that if President Bush would follow through on his promise to push for peace in the Middle East, this would make an enormous contribution to removing a serious obstacle and perceptions of inequity by many Arabs and Muslims.)[7]

Without duplicating much that has been addressed in the previous chapters of this volume, this discussion examines developments in six main areas that have emerged in the public debate as causal and facilitating factors for international terrorism. A closer examination of these factors reveals that while some energy has been dedicated to understanding and tackling them in the three years since the attacks in America, the response has not been adequate. The rhetoric—on both sides of the Atlantic—has not yet been satisfactorily matched by realistic and robust reforms.

Terrorism and Poverty: What Are the Links?

The first area is the complicated link between terrorism and poverty. Since September 11, a number of world leaders, including President Bush, have made a connection between poverty and terrorism. Although conventional wisdom would argue in favor of establishing a direct correlation, the evidence gathered thus far does not fully support this proposition. Indeed, if poverty really were the root cause of terrorism, terrorists would mostly come from the poorest parts of the world, namely sub-Saharan Africa. Thus far, this is not the case.

A Princeton study in 2002 on Israeli and Arab terrorism in the Middle East demonstrated that in this region terrorists not only enjoyed living standards above the poverty line, but also had obtained at the minimum a secondary education.[8] Information gathered thus far regarding the background of al Qaeda members seems to be consistent with these findings, especially regarding the ability of these terrorists to adapt successfully to foreign environments. In alien cities, members of al Qaeda have had no trouble finding employment, renting apartments, attending graduate schools, and enrolling in flying lessons, all of which would have been much more difficult had they been uneducated and indigent. Two additional factors, however, complicate the poverty debate: suicide bombers and education.

Suicide Bombers

A more direct link could be established between "suicide bombers" and poverty in some circumstances, given that the families of "suicide bombers" are generously compensated by a number of charitable organizations. It could thus be argued that the financial reward can become an attractive incentive for a poor family. In the case of the Palestinians, the sponsors of "suicide bombers" included, among others, Saddam Hussein. Yet, in her interviews with potential Palestinian suicide bombers, Nasra Hassan found that most came from middle-class and educated families.[9] In contrast, Jessica Stern's research, which focused on the Kashmir dispute, demonstrated that many volunteers did indeed come from poor families, and often because of the financial reward.[10] Further research is needed to shed light on how relevant financial considerations are with respect to such volunteers in many parts of the world.

Education

Education is an additional factor to consider in the poverty debate. In some Islamic countries, such as Somalia or Pakistan, poor parents send their children to madrasas and Koranic schools because they are heavily subsidized or free of charge. Children also receive food, clothing, and books, at no cost to the family. It has become apparent, however, that children who attend certain radicalized madrasas are taught to despise "corrupting Western influences" from an early age and gain few practical skills to prepare them for working in modern society (for example, some learn no math nor science whatsoever).[11] In the late 1990s, it was estimated that more than 10,000 teachers were instructing three million local students plus an additional 10,000 foreign students in madrasas. Most of these children came from poor families. Combined spending on this type of education was estimated at over $1 billion per year, with three-fourths of the funds coming from abroad, and mostly from Saudi Arabia.

While approximately 30 percent of the Taliban—the hosts for al Qaeda—were educated in such madrasas, many of the known al Qaeda terrorists themselves, such as those who committed the September 11 attacks, were not. Interestingly, many of the hijackers had advanced scientific and technical degrees and were educated in Europe and North America. These discrepancies indicate the need to clarify and categorize educational achievement and standards for different terrorists in order to develop appropriate interventions for these populations.

Support for quality public education could be one way of attacking root causes in some parts of the world. Tentative steps have begun in this direction; for example, the European Union has been exploring innovative approaches to working with the Pakistani madrasa system, in an attempt to engage the "huge untapped source of manpower and funding for educational and development work" in evidence in these communities.[12] The U.S. government has also been applying pressure on Pakistan and other countries to reform the madrasas, with minimal success.[13] Yet the funds dedicated to educational reform thus far, which is sorely needed in all too many parts of the world—such as USAID's commitment in 2002 for $100 million to help reform Pakistan's education system over a five-year period—pale in comparison to the amounts spent on defense. The Pentagon's missile defense system, now being deployed even though evidence does not exist that it actually works, already has cost U.S. taxpayers over $31 billion, and estimates of the total cost are more than $100 billion.[14]

After the war in Afghanistan, Senator Joe Biden proposed a project to build and supply a thousand schools in Afghanistan in order to counter the influence of the madrasas. The idea was soon killed, and not just by the Republican party, but also by his own Democratic colleagues.[15] As George Packer explained, "Spending twenty million dollars on schools in Afghanistan is a harder sell than spending four hundred billion on defense; fear is more compelling than foresight." According to Biden, "This is a place where the President's bragging to me, 'Mr. Chairman, I don't do nuance' . . . where he has an advantage."[16]

It is not only the children of poor countries who are being indoctrinated at extremist schools, but also a large number of educational systems in wealthier Middle East countries. For example, a recent U.S. study highlighted concerns about the textbooks and curricula in Qatar and Saudi Arabia.[17] Thus far Qatar is the only country in the region to completely overhaul its education system, and in this case, reform has been attributed to the modernization package introduced by the ruler, Sheik Hamad Bin Khalifa Thani, rather than as a result of U.S. pressure.

Even if the entire system could be overhauled overnight, there are still millions of children who have already gone through this system, one that began to expand significantly during the 1970s in places such as Pakistan, India and Bangladesh, Indonesia, and parts of Africa as well as the Middle East and North Africa (although not all schools have an extremist agenda and not all students will become terrorists).[18] Policy measures focused on these "graduates" have not even been considered.

Even if many terrorists, and their leaders, are neither poor nor uneducated, they tend to use the plight of the poor as one justification for committing violence and for broadening their appeal. They often claim to speak on behalf of the poor, just as other middle-class, well-educated ideologues have done in the past. Therefore, it could well be argued that a serious effort to fulfill the Millennium Development Goals, as well as being the right thing to do, is essential in order to remove one of the platforms commonly used by terrorists. As Ambassador David Shinn remarked, "What is missing is a major, new, long-term program to reduce poverty and social alienation."[19] Instead of concentrating on the individual terrorist, who is likely to be beyond reach, it may be more important to work on what Louise Richardson of Harvard refers to as "the enabling environment" or "complicit society."

Collapsed and Weak States: Breeding Grounds or Open Markets for Illegal Economic Activity?

When discussing the environment in which terrorism flourishes, a further theory links "failed" states, such as Somalia, to terrorism.[20] The factors that make these places attractive include weak or nonexistent government structures and the inability of the international community to monitor or interfere with trafficking and smuggling pipelines, which are used to move humans, drugs, small arms, natural resources, black money, and potential nuclear materials across porous borders. Terrorists in theory can operate with relative impunity, without fear of a government crackdown on operations, or international intervention.[21]

These attractions may be countered by the difficulties facing terrorists when operating in an insecure and foreign environment, where security is itself highly fragmented and infrastructure unreliable. It should be recalled that when taking refuge in Sudan, bin Laden did not settle in the southern parts of the territory that are considered "lawless," albeit Christian and Animist, but rather in the Muslim north, in Khartoum, an area where the government is and was firmly in control. Similarly, when he established his base in Afghanistan in 1996, the country was no longer a collapsed state, but was instead under the control of the Taliban, except for the northern province of Badakhshan.

While collapsed states may not be the real breeding grounds for terrorists—and there is little hard evidence to support the allegations, particularly in the case of Somalia[22]—they could, in future, become more attractive territories, especially if the international community tightens its grip over terrorist networks in other states. And currently they are at risk for transshipment activity and for providing sanctuary to some terrorists—the recent Report of the Panel of Experts on Somalia to the Security Council described how Somalia not only harbored some of the terrorists who carried out attacks in Mombasa, but also how the territory was used to smuggle weapons into Kenya. These types of interventions can only serve to undermine nascent state authorities and attempts at democratization.

While the al Qaeda network has also penetrated Western societies, at least in Minneapolis, London, Hamburg, or Toronto, they leave behind a paper trail, whereas in weak states it is far more difficult to ascertain their movements and activities. All policy papers recognize the need to strengthen governance and security sectors in these places. For example, the U.S. *National Strategy* likewise declares, "We will ensure that efforts designed to identify and diminish conditions contributing to state weakness and failure are a central U.S. foreign policy goal. The principal objective . . . will be the rebuilding of a state that can look after its own people."[23] Yet here too, unfortunately, little has been done in the past three years to rebuild weak and collapsed states around the world. For example, funds committed to Somalia by OECD states are not only insignificant in scale, but the totals are also no larger today than prior to September 11, and most of it is dedicated to humanitarian efforts, not to nation building, which ideally should be used to support local authorities in Somalia until such time as a national government is reestablished.[24]

Conflicts Hijacked by Religious Extremists

Wars perceived as threatening Islam have been exacerbated due to the participation of "foreign volunteers," many of whom have links to al Qaeda. This occurs in much the same way that past ideological wars, such as the Spanish Civil War, attracted foreign recruits.[25] Bin Laden and other al

Qaeda members—the so-called "Afghan Arabs"—fought against the Soviet occupation of Afghanistan, which is when al Qaeda was founded. While researchers and journalists are now revisiting some of the conflicts penetrated by these "Muslim Mercenaries," not enough is known about their participation in places such as Bosnia, Chechnya, Dagestan, Eritrea, Kashmir, the Philippines, Somalia, Sudan, and Uzbekistan.[26]

Al Qaeda involvement can also transform these territories into breeding grounds for terrorists, as occurred in Afghanistan during the late 1990s. Ayman al-Zawahiri, Osama bin Laden's top lieutenant, wrote that he visited Chechnya with the intention of establishing it as a further training base.[27] These conflicts also provide new recruits and expand the network of affiliates. The presence of these "foreign volunteers" can lead to the improvement of strategies, tactics, and quality of equipment, and to the adoption of more violent methods of confrontation—that is, suicide attacks involving massive civilian casualties as opposed to selective attacks against precise military targets.

Attempts should be made to resolve these conflicts through shrewd use of diplomatic and development tools, before they are corrupted in this manner. For those conflicts that have already been exacerbated, new tools will have to be utilized, but first, a greater understanding of how these conflicts have been manipulated by the al Qaeda movement is necessary. Here, again, too little is being done to resolve these conflicts. The recent Beslan school massacre, in Russia's North Caucasus, provides a horrific example of what can happen if these conflicts are left to fester. It only serves Russian Prime Minister Putin's interests to claim foreign involvement, even though it is still unclear if it was purely a domestic terror attack or if "Muslim Mercenaries" played a role.

Fundamentalist Charities

Financial support that promotes international terrorism comes from a variety of sources, including wealthy individuals, states, diasporas, criminal activities, and charitable organizations. Funding from all sources is dedicated, among other things, to planning and executing attacks, assistance for families of suicide bombers, and long-term indoctrination through extremist madrasas, religious centers, and social support mechanisms. Concerning charitable assistance, a distinction needs to be made between some Islamic charities, such as the Aga Khan Foundation, which provides critical humanitarian and development assistance in neglected rural and urban areas, and others that promote a radical agenda.

Significantly, one of the basic tenets of Islam is charity (*zakat*), and charity given in a way that does not humiliate the receiver. This discreet method of delivery, however, complicates matters and makes it difficult to discern how certain Islamic charities, along with several governments, such as Iran, propagate their extremist ideology and anti-Western sentiment with their aid in many developing countries. Rohan Gunaratna notes, "According to the CIA, one-fifth of all Islamic NGOs worldwide have been unwittingly infiltrated by Al Qaeda and other terrorist support groups."[28] It is important, therefore, to understand how these funding pipelines operate, as well as the extremist advocacy that is channeled through these networks. Incidentally, Western aid agencies may also consider utilizing more discreet delivery mechanisms in Islamic countries as an additional means to avoid humiliation.

While international efforts have uncovered information about the financial activities of some of the Saudi-funded charities, and the Financial Action Task Force (FATF) is trying to implement a more stringent regime to make all charitable organizations more transparent and accountable, greater efforts need to be made to understand and improve our response to radical religious funding and advocacy efforts in many parts of the world. The U.S. government also needs to consider alternative ways of "winning hearts and minds" through their actions, rather than their current policy, which often achieves the opposite effect, for example, by shutting down remittance houses, which are in most cases a lifeline for poor countries.

At the most basic level, it is often simply the dearth of Western international support that makes some developing states vulnerable and susceptible to terrorist ideology. While the religious appeal may not be overwhelming for many families, the lack of alternatives for schooling or health care fuels the growth of the movement. In Somalia, for example, because Western international assistance is not significant in scale, the influence of these Islamic movements has increased. A recent International Crisis Group (ICG) report noted that the fundamentalist movements inside Somalia "owe their rapid growth since 1990 less to genuine popularity than access to substantial external funding."[29] Islamic charitable assistance is rarely noted in UN appeals for Somalia (indeed this is lacking in most UN appeals), and few of these countries or organizations actively participate in the Somalia Aid Coordination Body, established to serve as the permanent coordination body for donors, UN agencies, NGOs, and other international organizations.

Every effort should be made to try to include Islamic NGOs in all international coordinating bodies. Currently the work of these NGOs all too often occurs in parallel to those sponsored by OECD states. At the very least, discussion should be promoted and information exchanged with Islamic NGOs in order to prevent overlap and duplication, improve needs assessments, and importantly, enhance the lives of the poor.

Moreover, it appears that over the last decade, significant amounts of financing for terrorist activities worldwide has come from Saudi Arabian sources. Saudi money has allegedly funded fundamentalist activity in a wide range of places—from Algeria or Chechnya, in support of insurgent groups, to Europe or Central Asia, where the Saudis have provided the funding for mosques and for free scholarships for students of Islamic studies. The influence of these charities has increased on the quiet, though recently in the United States, two publications concerning the Saudi connection have received significant attention.[30]

It must also be pointed out here that it is not just the extreme Islamic groups that utilize this method of influence: Christian fundamentalist organizations in the United States, for example, have been supporting certain sides in conflicts that are perceived as threatening to Christianity, with southern Sudan being the most obvious example. President Bush has been openly supporting the southern Sudanese in this long-standing conflict, primarily due to the influence of the Christian fundamentalist lobby.[31]

Transnational Mobilization and Recruitment

The fifth area concerns a debate as to whether some economic migrants, asylum seekers, and members of certain diaspora communities are joining terrorist groups *after* having spent time in their host country. Mohammed Atta's experience in Hamburg, or Sayyid Qutb's in Colorado, are cited as two examples. It has been suggested that one of the main reasons why immigrants come to support terrorist groups, such as al Qaeda, is the alienation and prejudice they often experience in the West. This marginalization is further reinforced by the fact that many remain outside formal state structures because they are not legal residents. Consequently they seek assistance and support from local mosques and Islamic cultural centers, often the first ports of call for new arrivals, where they can obtain fake passports and identity cards. It appears that some of these individuals are vulnerable to the aggressive recruitment campaigns being carried out by extremist groups operating across Europe and the United States.[32]

Here too, they often access the extreme Islamist literature that advises them on ways to survive in "infidel" countries.[33] Such publications, along with al Qaeda manuals, promote and glorify an isolated existence in Western countries, turning feelings of alienation into a necessary and noble means of survival. Prior to September 11, many were encouraged to attend training camps in Afghanistan from these mosques and centers. In addition, today, as in the past, they are also recruited in prisons throughout the world, in both North and South.[34]

While this may be happening in some cases, it is also true that many were radicalized at home prior to coming to Europe and North America. It was in fact the liberal laws in Europe that prevented most European countries, for example, the United Kingdom and Italy, from returning many wanted radicals to their home countries, for fear they would be tortured or that the government would apply the death penalty. At this stage, too many assumptions are being made on too small a sample size, though it can be said that a fundamental overhaul of Europe's asylum procedures would be a step in the right direction.[35]

The Governance Factor: The Democratic Deficit

Strong, authoritarian states that lack democracy and accountability may be the real breeding grounds for international terrorism.[36] The al Qaeda terrorists who participated in the September 11 attacks, and most of the members of affiliated organizations who have been arrested for other acts of terrorism, come from such states. They oppose what they perceive to be authoritarian, secular rule in their own countries, and view their leaders as corrupted by Western influences. They believe that only through the establishment of Islamic states can these countries be returned to the right path and their former glory.

In these countries, the snowballing anger on the so-called "Arab Street"[37] hones in on the United States and some other Western countries. Ordinary Saudis or Algerians or Egyptians are resentful of their own governments, but are unable to express that anger in any meaningful way that will bring about change. It is far easier to direct that anger at the United States and other developed states, which anyway are supporting their "elitist" and nonrepresentative leaders.

This frustration is so strong in some parts of the world that we often hear two entirely different and competing versions of events. Conspiracy theories abound as to who really committed recent terrorist attacks: Accusations that the CIA and the FBI were behind the Bali bombing, or destroyed the Twin Towers, are perpetuated by extremist imams. These beliefs are being fed to populations in certain parts of the world that are already disillusioned and distrustful of the intentions of the "West," or learned to hate the "West" in school. Moreover, the populations read and hear about generous financial support for the impoverished, but rarely see evidence that the money reaches the poor. This is not necessarily the fault of developed states, which are often forced to work with corrupt governments due to their own conditionality factors to ensure accountability or because they are unable to spend funds that have been committed due to lack of accountable partners on the ground.

Nevertheless, the inability of developed states to realize international development goals contributes to this disillusionment and resentment, and allows more and more ordinary citizens to become susceptible to believing these conspiracy theories. This is the "complicit society" referred to above. Thomas Friedman has argued that every attempt should be made to address the anger on the "Arab Street," as once they move into the "Arab Basement," it is too late to use persuasion and other nonviolent measures.[38]

Conclusions

These six areas—poverty, weak and collapsed states, wars hijacked by Islamic extremists, fundamentalist charities, radicalization in Europe and North America, and the "democracy deficit"—need deeper analysis to understand how they may facilitate terrorist recruitment and support. They also require a response that goes further than that advocated by current policy in both Europe and America: New, more nuanced tools are required. At the very least, both Europe and America should make more of an effort to implement policies committed to since September 11.

As noted at the beginning of this chapter, the threat posed by transnational terrorism can only be defeated through a dedicated and coordinated transnational response, one that not only focuses on the symptoms, but also on the causes, because security and intelligence measures at national, Europe-wide, and even transatlantic levels cannot guarantee that an attack will not take place. All governments have structural weaknesses and vulnerabilities that can be exploited, and no government could be expected to eliminate all vulnerability to terrorist attack. It is simply not possible to prevent attacks in truly globalized, relatively open societies. Thus a complementary campaign that addresses root causes takes on added urgency, and should be spearheaded by the United Nations, as the only neutral and morally legitimate world body, which thus far has been hampered in its own counterterrorism strategy by the transatlantic rift. As former U.S. President Bill Clinton recently remarked, "If you come from a wealthy country with open borders, unless you seriously believe you can kill, imprison, or occupy all your enemies, you have to make a world with more friends and fewer enemies."[39]

Recommended Resources for the Study of Terrorism

Annotated Bibliographies

Annotated Bibliography of Government Documents Related to the Threat of Terrorism and the Attacks of September 11, 2001 (Oklahoma Dept. of Libraries)
http://www.odl.state.ok.us/usinfo/terrorism/911.htm

Bibliography of Future Trends in Terrorism (Library of Congress)
http://www.loc.gov/rr/frd/pdf-files/Future_trends.pdf

CBRN Terrorism: An Annotated Bibliography, by the Center for the Study of Weapons of Mass Destruction
http://www.ndu.edu/WMDCenter/CBRN_Annotated_Bib.pdf

Center for Terrorism Studies (Maxwell AF Base) Reference Bibliography
http://c21.maxwell.af.mil/cts-ref.htm#bibliographies

Chemical, Biological, and Nuclear Terrorism/Warfare: A Bibliography (Naval Postgraduate School)
http://library.nps.navy.mil/home/bibs/chemnuctech.htm

Terrorism and Counterterrorism: An Annotated Bibliography, by James J. F. Forest
http://www.teachingterror.com/bibliography

USAF Counterproliferation Center, *Global War on Terror Bibliography*
http://www.au.af.mil/au/awc/awcgate/cps-terr.htm#agro

University of Texas at Arlington, *Bibliography on Terrorism and Homeland Security Research Resources*
http://libraries.uta.edu/dillard/subfiles/bibterror.htm

Articles and Reports

"A Conceptual Framework for Analyzing Terrorist Groups," by Bonnie Cordes, Brian M. Jenkins et al.
http://www.rand.org/publications/R/R3151

"Al Qaeda, Trends in Terrorism and Future Potentialities: An Assessment," by Bruce Hoffman
http://www.rand.org/publications/P/P8078/index.html

"Al Qaeda's Fantasy Ideology," by Lee Harris
http://www.policyreview.org/AUG02/harris_print.html

"Al-Qaeda's Understudy," by Nasra Hassan
http://www.theatlantic.com/issues/2004/06/hassan.htm

"America's Anti-Terrorist Campaign and Russia's Choice," by Dmitri Trenin
http://www.ceip.org/files/Publications/treninrussiachoice.asp?from=pubdate

"Anthrax Attacks, Biological Terrorism and Preventive Responses," John Parachini, congressional testimony, CT-186, 2001 (Full Document)
http://www.rand.org/publications/CT/CT186/index.html

"Behind the Terror," by Ehud Ya'ari
http://www.theatlantic.com/issues/87jun/yaari.htm

"Combating Terrorism: The 9/11 Commission Recommendations and the National Strategies," by John V. Parachini
http://www.rand.org/publications/CT/CT231-1

"Countering al Qaeda: An Appreciation of the Situation and Suggestions for Strategy," by Brian Jenkins
http://www.rand.org/publications/MR/MR1620/index.html

"Countering the New Terrorism," by Ian Lesser, Bruce Hoffman, John Arquilla, David Ronfeldt, Michele Zanini, and Brian Jenkins
http://www.rand.org/publications/MR/MR989/index.html

"Counterterrorism Intelligence Capabilities and Performance Prior to 9–11"
http://www.fas.org/irp/congress/2002_rpt/hpsci_ths0702.html

"Creating a Trusted Network for Homeland Security," by the Markle Foundation Task Force on National Security in the Information Age (December 2003)
http://www.markletaskforce.org

"Deadly Arsenals: Tracking Weapons of Mass Destruction," by Joseph Cirincione et al.
http://www.ceip.org/files/Publications/DeadlyArsenals.asp?from=pubdate

"Facing Saddam's Child Soldiers," by Peter W. Singer
http://www.brookings.edu/views/op-ed/singer/20030114.htm

"Female Suicide Bombers," by Debra Zedalis
http://www.carlisle.army.mil/ssi/pubs/pubResult.cfm/hurl/PubID=408

"Foreign Policy in the Age of Terrorism," by Henry Kissinger
http://www.cps.org.uk/kissinger.pdf

"Ground Zero, the Day After," by Petra Bartosiewicz
http://www.theatlantic.com/unbound/dispatches/dsp2001-09-19.htm

"Inside al-Qaeda's Hard Drive," by Alan Cullison
http://www.theatlantic.com/doc/200409/cullison

"Inside Jihad U.—The Education of a Holy Warrior," by Jeffrey Goldberg
http://www.indianembassy.org/policy/Terrorism/news_us/education_holy_warri
or_june_25.htm

"Iraq and Weapons of Mass Destruction" (GWU Electronic Briefing Book No. 80)
http://www.gwu.edu/~nsarchiv/NSAEBB/NSAEBB80

"New Terrorists, New Attack Means? Categorizing Terrorist Challenges For the
Early 21st Century," by Rod Propst
http://www.homelandsecurity.org/journal/articles/displayArticle.asp?article=48

"Nuclear and Radiological Terrorism," by Rose Gottemoeller
http://www.ceip.org/files/Publications/Nuclearandradiologicalterrorism.asp

"On Terrorists and Terrorism," by Konrad Kellen
http://www.rand.org/publications/publications/N/N1942

"Political Violence and Stability in the States of the Northern Persian Gulf," Daniel
Byman and Jerrold Green, full report, MR-1021-OSD (1999)
http://www.rand.org/publications/MR/MR1021

"Promoting Democracy and Fighting Terror," by Tom Carothers
http://www.ceip.org/files/Publications/2003-01-carothers-foraffairs.asp?from=
pubdate

"Protecting America's Freedom in the Information Age," by the Markle Foundation Task Force on National Security in the Information Age (October 2002)
http://www.markletaskforce.org

"Regional Demographics and the War on Terrorism," by Brian Nichiporuk
http://www.rand.org/publications/RP/RP1057/index.html

"Should Hezbollah Be Next?" by Daniel L. Byman
http://www.brookings.edu/views/articles/byman/20031101.htm

"Social Science Research Council, September 11th Essays"
http://www.ssrc.org/sept11/essays

"Terror.net: How Modern Terrorism Uses the Internet," by Gabriel Weimann
http://www.usip.org/pubs/specialreports/sr116.html

"Terrorism and Development: Using Social and Economic Development Policies to
Inhibit a Resurgence of Terrorism," by Kim Cragin and Peter Chalk
http://www.rand.org/publications/MR/MR1630/index.html

"Terrorism and U.S. Policy"
http://www.gwu.edu/~nsarchiv/NSAEBB/NSAEBB55/index1.html

"Terrorism in the Horn of Africa" (USIP Special Report 113)
http://www.usip.org/pubs/specialreports/sr113.html

"The Advent of Netwar," by John Arquilla and David Ronfeldt
http://www.rand.org/publications /MR/MR789/index.html

"The Concept and Practice of Jihad in Islam," by Michael Knapp
http://carlisle-www.army.mil/usawc/Parameters/03spring/knapp.htm

"The Culture of Martyrdom," by David Brooks
http://www.theatlantic.com/issues/2002/06/brooks.htm

"The Dynamic Terrorist Threat: An Assessment of Group Motivations and Capabilities in a Changing World," by R. Kim Cragin and Sara A. Daly
http://www.rand.org/publications/MR/MR1782

"The Gospel According to Osama bin Laden," by Reuel Marc Gerecht
http://www.theatlantic.com/issues/2002/01/gerecht.htm

"The Modern Terrorist Mindset: Tactics, Targets and Technologies," by Bruce Hoffman
http://www.ciaonet.org/wps/hob03/

"The Muslim World After 9/11," by Angel M. Rabasa, Cheryl Benard et al.
http://www.rand.org/publications/MG/MG246

"The Logic of Suicide Terrorism," by Bruce Hoffman
http://www.theatlantic.com/issues/2003/06/hoffman.htm

"The Long Hunt for Osama," by Peter Bergen
http://www.theatlantic.com/doc/200410/bergen

"The Real Roots of Terror," by Jack Beatty
http://www.theatlantic.com/unbound/polipro/pp2001-12-05.htm

"The Roots of Terrorism, and a Strategy Against It," by Anatol Lieven
http://www.ceip.org/files/publications/lieventerrorism.asp

"The September 11th Sourcebooks"
http://www.gwu.edu/~nsarchiv/NSAEBB/sept11

"The Transnational Dimension of Cyber Crime and Terrorism," by Abraham Sofaer
http://www-hoover.stanford.edu/publications/books/cybercrime.html

"Trends in Outside Support for Insurgent Movements," by Daniel L. Byman, Peter Chalk, Bruce Hoffman, William Rosenau, David Brannan
http://www.rand.org/publications/MR/MR1405/index.html

"U.S. Proliferation Policy and the Campaign Against Terror," by Lee Feinstein
http://www.ceip.org/files/publications/lieventerrorism.asp

"War Against Terror" (A CNN Special Report)
http://www.cnn.com/SPECIALS/2001/trade.center/index.html

"What Went Wrong?" by Bernard Lewis
http://www.theatlantic.com/issues/2002/01/lewis.htm

"Why Do They Hate Us?" by Peter Ford
http://www.csmonitor.com/2001/0927/p1s1-wogi.html

U.S. Government Reports

2003 Annual U.S. State Department Report, Patterns of Global Terrorism
http://www.state.gov/s/ct/rls/pgtrpt/2003 (April 2004)

2002 Annual U.S. State Department Report, Patterns of Global Terrorism
http://www.state.gov/s/ct/rls/pgtrpt/2002 (April 2003)

Airport Security (U.S. General Accounting Office)
http://www.gao.gov/airptsec.html

Al Qaeda's Training Manual
http://www.usdoj.gov/ag/trainingmanual.htm (on the Dept. of Justice website).

*CONPLAN: United States Government Interagency Domestic Terrorism Concept
of Operations Plan*
http://www.fbi.gov/publications/conplan/conplan.pdf

"Cybersecurity: Getting it Right," by Daniel Wolf
http://www.nsa.gov/ia/Wolf_SFR_22_July_2003.pdf

Government Publications on Terrorism
http://www.lib.umd.edu/GOV/terrorism.html

Homeland Security (U.S. General Accounting Office)
http://www.gao.gov/homelandsecurity.html

*Joint Inquiry into Intelligence Community Activities before and after Terrorist At-
tacks of September 11, 2001*
http://www.gpoaccess.gov/serialset/creports/911.html

Media Interactions with the Public in Emergency Situations: Four Case Studies
http://www.loc.gov/rr/frd/pdf-files/Media_Interaction.pdf

The Network of Terrorism
http://usinfo.state.gov/products/pubs/terrornet

Project Megiddo: An FBI Strategic Assessment of the Potential for Domestic Terrorism
http://permanent.access.gpo.gov/lps3578/www.fbi.gov/library/megiddo/megidd.
pdf

Report of the National Commission on Terrorist Attacks Upon the United States
(the 9-11 Commission Report)
http://www.gpoaccess.gov/911

Sanctions Program and Country Summaries
http://www.ustreas.gov/offices/enforcement/ofac/sanctions/index.html

Specially Designated Nationals (SDN) and Blocked Persons List
http://www.ustreas.gov/offices/enforcement/ofac/sdn/index.html

The Sociology and Psychology of Terrorism: Who Becomes a Terrorist and Why?
http://www.loc.gov/rr/frd/pdf-files/Soc_Psych_of_Terrorism.pdf

Terrorism
http://www.gao.gov/terrorism.html

Terrorism and Organized Crime in the TriBorder Region of Latin America
http://www.loc.gov/rr/frd/pdf-files/TerrOrgCrime_TBA.pdf

Terrorist Financing Rewards Program
http://www.ustreas.gov/rewards/terrorismlist.html

Terrorism: Near Eastern Groups and State Sponsors
http://www.fas.org/irp/crs/RL31119.pdf (Library of Congress).

Terrorism, the Future, and U.S. Foreign Policy
http://www.fas.org/irp/crs/IB95112.pdf (Library of Congress).

Terrorism Information Websites

Al Qaeda's Training Manual
http://www.usdoj.gov/ag/trainingmanual.htm (on the Dept. of Justice website).

America's War Against Terrorism
http://www.lib.umich.edu/govdocs/usterror.html

ANSER Institute For Homeland Security
http://www.homelandsecurity.org

CIA Factbook on Intelligence
http://www.cia.gov/cia/publications/facttell/index.html

CIA World Factbook
http://www.odci.gov/cia/publications/factbook

Center for Arms Control and Non-Proliferation: Terrorism Prevention Handbook
http://www.armscontrolcenter.org/terrorism/handbook

Center for Defense Information: Terrorism Project
http://www.cdi.org/terrorism

Center for Nonproliferation Studies: Terrorism
http://cns.miis.edu/research/terror.htm

Centre for the Study of Terrorism and Political Violence
http://www.st-and.ac.uk/academic/intrel/research/cstpv

Council on Foreign Relations (CFR) Terrorism Website
http://cfrterrorism.org/home

Countering the Changing Threat of International Terrorism
http://www.fas.org/irp/threat/commission.html

CQ Press Information Resources on Terrrorism
http://www.cqpress.com/context

Crissisweb: The International Crisis Group
http://www.intl-crisis-group.org

GlobalSecurity.org
http://www.globalsecurity.org

Henry L Stimson Center: Chemical and Biological Terrorism
http://www.stimson.org/cwc/terror.htm%20

Intelligence and Counterintelligence Links
http://www.kimsoft.com/kim-spy.htm

International Policy Institute for Counter-Terrorism
http://www.ict.org.il

International War on Terrorism—Air War College, U.S. Air University
http://www.au.af.mil/au/awc/awcgate/cps-terr.htm

INTERPOL
http://www.interpol.int

Janes Information Group
http://www.janes.com

Jemaah Islamiyah News Trove
http://jemaahislamiyah.newstrove.com

Library of Congress—Federal Research Division—Terrorism Studies
http://www.loc.gov/rr/frd/terrorism.htm

Library of Congress—"Remembering 9/11" Resources
http://www.loc.gov/loc/lcib/0209/index.html

Marshall Center Information Resource on Terrorism
http://www.marshallcenter.org/site-graphic/lang-en/page-research-bibliographies
   -1/xdocs/library/bibliographies/terrorism%202004.htm

Memorial Institute for the Prevention of Terrorism
http://www.mipt.org (MIPT)

MIPT Knowledge Base on Terrorism
http://www.tkb.org

MI5—The UK Security Service
http://www.mi5.gov.uk

National Commission on Terrorist Attacks Upon the U.S.
http://www.9-11commission.gov

National Security Council
http://www.whitehouse.gov/nsc

South Asia Terrorism Portal
http://satp.org

Strategic Intelligence Resources
http://www.loyola.edu/dept/politics/intel.html

Teaching Terror
  http://www.teachingterror.com

Terrorism Library
  http://www.terrorismlibrary.com

Terrorism Research Center
  http://www.terrorism.com/index.shtml

Terrorism: Attacks and Responses
  http://www.library.vanderbilt.edu/romans/terrorism.html

Terrorist Group Profiles
  http://library.nps.navy.mil/home/tgp/tgpndx.htm

Terrorist Group Profiles #2
  http://www.terrorism/com/terrorism/Groups2.shtml

Terrorism: Questions and Answers
  http://www.terrorismanswers.org/home (Council on Foreign Relations)

Terrorism Info, U.S. State Department
  http://usinfo.state.gov/topical/pol/terror

Uppsala Conflict Database
  http://www.pcr.uu.se/database

U.S. Department of State
  http://www.state.gov

U.S. Dept. of State Counterterrorism Office
  http://www.state.gov/s/ct

U.S. Department of State: Foreign Terrorist Organizations
  http://www.state.gov/s/ct/rls/rpt/fto

U.S. Dept. of State—Winning the War on Terrorism
  http://usinfo.state.gov/is/international_security/terrorism.html

U.S. Dept. of the Treasury
  http://www.ustreas.gov

U.S. General Accounting Office
  http://www.gao.gov

Washington Institute for Near East Policy
  http://www.washingtoninstitute.org

World Intelligence and Security Agencies
  http://www.fas.org/irp/world/index.html

Notes

Preface

1. Roland Paris, *At War's End* (Cambridge: Cambridge University Press, 2004).

2. Professor Klare is the Five-College Professor of Peace and World Security Studies, a joint appointment at Amherst, Hampshire, Mount Holyoke, Smith colleges, and the University of Massachusetts at Amherst.

Chapter 1: Exploring Root Causes of Terrorism

1. See "Kofi Annan Opens Summit on Terrorism's 'Root Causes,'" Agence France-Presse, 22 September 2003, online at http://quickstart.clari.net/qs_se/web news/wed/df/Qun-us-attacks-conference.Rmkg_DSL.html.

2. See "Abstracts of Presentations: International Expert Meeting on Root Causes of Terrorism," organized by the Norwegian Institute of International Affairs Oslo 9–11 June 2003 (hereafter cited as Oslo abstracts), available online at http://www.nupi.no/IPS/IPS?module=Files;action=File.getFile;ID=856/.

3. Ibid.

4. See "Kofi Annan Opens Summit."

5. Oslo abstracts.

6. John E. Mack, "Deeper Causes: Exploring the Role of Consciousness in Terrorism," *Ions Noetic Sciences Review* (June–August 2003): 13.

7. Bernard Lewis, "What Went Wrong?" *Atlantic Monthly*, January 2002, online at http://www.theatlantic.com.

8. Jack Beatty, "The Real Roots of Terror," *Atlantic Monthly*, 5 December 2001, online at http://www.theatlantic.com.

9. Please see Volume 1 for the 1996 and 1998 al Qaeda *fatwas*, as well as discussion on various ideological statement related to political Islam, Wahhabism, and jihad.

10. For a brief history of revolutionary ideologies, please see the chapter by Leonard Weinberg in Volume 1 of this publication.

11. "Chaos in the Roof of the World," *The Economist*, 3 February 2005.

12. Ibid.

13. Ibid.

14. Francis M. Deng, *War of Visions: Conflict of Identities in the Sudan* (Washington, DC: Brookings Institution, 1995), particularly pages 9–97 and 484–515.

15. Ibid., p. 485.

16. Allan C. Brownfeld, "Religious Zionism: A Growing Impediment To Middle East Peace," *Washington Report on Middle East Affairs* 21, no. 9 (December 2002): 71.

17. See the chapter by Allan C. Brownfeld in Volume 1 of this publication.

18. Michael B. Oren, *Six Days of War: June 1967 and the Making of the Modern Middle East* (New York: Oxford University Press, 2002).

19. John E. Mack, "Deeper Causes," p. 14. Mack's observations on religion also paraphrase theologian Paul Tillich.

20. Please see the chapter by J. P. Larsson in Volume I.

21. Jessica Stern, *Terror in the Name of God* (New York: HarperCollins, 2003; Ecco Trade Paperback Edition, 2004), p. 281.

22. Ibid., p. 282.

23. Ibid.

24. Olivier Roy, "America and the New Terrorism: An Exchange," *Survival* 42, no. 2 (Summer 2000): 160.

25. See the chapters by Maha Azzam and Jarret Brachman in Volume I; also see Olivier Roy, "America and the New Terrorism."

26. Please see Volume 1 for the complete text of this *fatwa*.

27. Ibid.

28. Ibid.

29. Marc Sageman, "The Global Salafi Jihad," statement made to the National Commission on Terrorist Attacks upon the United States, 9 July 2003, available online at http://www.9-11commission.gov/hearing/hearing3/witness_sageman.htm.

30. Ibid.

31. See Robert Pape, "The Strategic Logic of Suicide Bombing," in *Terrorism and Homeland Security*, edited by Russell Howard, James Forest, and Joanne Moore (New York: McGraw-Hill, 2005); and Bruce Hoffman, "The Logic of Suicide Bombing," in Howard et al., *Terrorism*.

32. Ibid.

33. David C. Rapoport, "Fear and Trembling: Terrorism in Three Religious Traditions," *American Political Science Review* 78, no. 3 (September 1984): 660–64.

34. Ibid., p. 661 (footnote).

35. Oslo abstracts.

36. *9/11 Commission Report*, as paraphrased in Yonatan Levy, "9/11 Commission Report: The Middle East Dimension," *Policywatch* #890 (Washington, DC: Washington Institute, 6 August 2004), online at http://www.washingtoninstitute.org/distribution/POL890.doc.

Chapter 2: Instability and Opportunity

1. George W. Bush, *The National Security Strategy of the United States* (Washington, DC: The White House, 2002), p. 1.

2. This chapter uses the general definition of terrorism as a tactic, not a phenomenon. Also, by necessity this discussion does not address state agencies that engage in political violence toward their own populations, or state-sponsored terrorism conducted by nonstate actors.

3. Robert I. Rotberg, "Failed States, Collapsed States, Weak States: Causes and Indicators," in *State Failure and State Weakness in a Time of Terror*, edited by Robert I. Rotberg (Washington, DC: Brookings, 2003), pp. 1–25; see also *When States Fail*, edited by Robert I. Rotberg (New York: Routledge, 2004).

4. Robert I. Rotberg (2004), p. 2.

5. Ibid., p. 3.

6. Ibid.

7. Ibid., pp. 3–4.

8. Ibid., p. 4.

9. Ibid., p. 5.

10. Ibid., p. 9.

11. Ibid., p. 10.

12. See the State Failure Task Force for more information on the relationship between political stability and state strength. Available at http://www.cidcm.umd.edu/inscr/stfail (last accessed 6 December 2004).

13. See, for instance, Leonard B. Weinberg and William L. Eubank, "Does Democracy Encourage Terrorism?" *Terrorism and Political Violence* 6, no. 4 (1994): 417–43; see also Leonard B. Weinberg and William L. Eubank, "Terrorism and Democracy: What Recent Events Disclose," *Terrorism and Political Violence* 10, no. 1 (1998): 108–18.

14. These assertions refer to terrorist groups that originate within a state and to terrorist groups that infiltrate a state after developing elsewhere.

15. Bruce Hoffman, *Inside Terrorism* (New York: Columbia University Press, 1998), p. 44.

16. Even decentralized systems such as the United States are susceptible to terrorist development, as we generally see these groups rising out of poor or unmonitored regions in such states as Arkansas, Montana, and Idaho.

17. For example, see Edward D. Mansfield and Jack Snyder, "Democratic Transitions and War," in *Turbulent Peace: The Challenges of Managing International Conflict*, edited by Chester Crocker et al. (Washington, DC: United States Institute of Peace, 2001), pp. 113–26.

18. For example, see Michael Malley, "Indonesia: The Erosion of State Capacity," in *State Failure and Weakness*.

19. Bruce Hoffman, *Inside Terrorism*, p. 26.

20. Rohan Gunaratna, *Inside Al Qaeda: Global Network of Terror* (New York: Berkley, 2002), p. 259.

21. Ibid., p. 266.

22. Ibid.

23. United States State Department, *2003 Global Terrorism Report*, online at http://www.state.gov.

24. Martin Ewans, *Afghanistan: A Short History of its People and Politics* (New York: HarperCollins, 2002), p. 285.

25. Ibid., p. 286.

26. Ibid., p. 256.

27. Ibid.

28. Ibid., p. 282.

29. Kim Cragin and Peter Chalk, *Terrorism and Development: Using Social and Economic Development to Inhibit a Resurgence of Terrorism* (Santa Monica: RAND, 2003), p. 19.

30. Kim Cragin and Peter Chalk, *Terrorism and Development*, pp. 20–21.

31. Ibid., p. 20.

32. Rohan Gunaratna, *Inside Al Qaeda*, p. 247.

33. E. P. Thompson, *Whigs and Hunters: The Origins of the Black Act* (New York: Pantheon, 1975), p. 258.

34. For more on this, please see Edward Mansfield and Jack Snyder, "Democratic Transitions and War."

35. Fareed Zakaria, *The Future of Freedom* (New York: W. W. Norton, 2003).

36. See, for instance, Edward D. Mansfield and Jack Snyder, *Electing to Fight: Why Emerging Democracies Go to War* (Cambridge, MA: MIT Press, 2004).

37. Roland Paris, *At War's End* (New York: Cambridge University Press, 2004).

Chapter 3: Superpower Foreign Policies

1. Samuel P. Huntington, *The Clash of Civilizations and the Remaking of World Order* (New York: Simon and Schuster, 1996).

2. National Commission on Terrorist Attacks Upon the United States, *The 9/11 Commission Report* (Washington: Government Printing Office, 2004), p. 165.

3. Pew Research Center for the People and the Press, *Views of a Changing World*, June 2003, available online at http://people-press.org.

4. Daniel Benjamin and Steven Simon, *The Age of Sacred Terror* (New York: Random House, 2002).

5. Michael Scott Doran, "Somebody Else's Civil War," *Foreign Affairs* 81 (January/February 2002): 22–42.

6. Advisory Group on Public Diplomacy in the Arab and Muslim World, *Changing Minds, Winning Peace: A New Strategic Direction for U.S. Public Diplomacy in the Arab and Muslim World* (Washington, DC: U.S. Department of State, 2003).

Chapter 4: A Failure to Communicate

1. U.S. Congress, Senate, Committee on Foreign Relations, "America's Global Dialog: Sharing American Values and the Way Ahead for Public Diplomacy," Sen-

ate Hearing, 107-692, 107th Congress, 2nd sess., 11 June 2002 (Washington, DC: GPO, 2002), available online at http://purl.access.gpo.gov/GPO/LPS24033.

2. For instance, see "Public Diplomacy by the Numbers," available at http://www.publicdiplomacy.org/14.htm.

3. Reference to Samuel P. Huntington, "The Clash of Civilizations," *Foreign Affairs* (Summer 1993).

4. Reference to Iranian President Mohammad Khatami's proposal calling for a dialogue among civilizations that was later on adopted as theme for the year 2001 by the United Nations; for details see http://www.unesco.org/dialogue2001/en/khatami.htm.

5. Reference to the phrase used by Pakistan's President General Pervez Musharraf; for details see Pervez Musharraf, "A Plea for Enlightened Moderation," *The Washington Post*, 1 June 2004, p. A23.

6. Stephen P. Cohen, *The Idea of Pakistan* (Washington, DC: Brookings Institute Press, 2004), p. 328.

7. "A Year After Iraq War: Mistrust of America in Europe Ever Higher, Muslim Anger Persists," Pew Research Center for the People and the Press, 16 March 2004.

8. Quoted in "Bridging the Great Divide," *The Economist* (1–7 June 2002): 11.

9. Minutes of Cabinet meeting, 9 September 1947, 67/CF/47, National Documentation Center, Cabinet Division, Islamabad.

10. "A Report to the National Security Council by the Executive Secretary on the Position of the U.S. with respect to South Asia" (Declassified), 5 January 1951, NSC 93, NND867400, available at Digital National Security Archive.

11. Quoted in Dennis Kux, *The United States and Pakistan 1947–2000: Disenchanted Allies* (Washington, DC: Woodrow Wilson Center Press, 2001), p. 57.

12. Ibid., p. 130.

13. Ibid., p. 201.

14. Diego Cordovez and Selig Harrison, *Out of Afghanistan* (New York: Oxford University Press, 1995), pp. 33–34.

15. Mary Anne Weaver, *Pakistan: In the Shadows of Jihad and Afghanistan* (New York: Farrar, Straus and Giroux, 2002), p. 8.

16. Quoted in Dennis Kux, *The United States and Pakistan*, p. 287.

17. For a detailed analysis of the plane crash and consequent investigations, see Hassan Abbas, *Pakistan's Drift into Extremism: Allah, the Army and America's War on Terror* (New York: M.E. Sharpe, 2004), pp. 124–32.

18. Zahid Hussain, "Inside Jihad," *Newsline* (February 2001): 22.

19. U.S. Department of State, "Patterns of Global Terrorism 1999" (last accessed 12 April 2003), online at http://www.state.gov/www/global/terrorism/1999report/1999index.html.

20. Text of President Clinton's address to the people of Pakistan on 25 March 2000 (last accessed 1 May 2003), available online at http://www.dawn.com/events/clinton_visit/speech.htm.

21. Ayaz Amir, "The Fourth Junta," *Dawn* (31 March 2000).

22. "Food for thought," *Dawn* (26 March 2000).

23. For full text of the speech see *Dawn* (last accessed October 12, 2003), available online at http://www.dawn.com/2002/01/12/speech020112.html (12 January 2002).

24. Ibid.

25. "Jihad Only Option to Halt U.S.: MMA: Leaders want Bush, Blair to be Tried," *Dawn* (31 March 2003).

26. Khalid Hasan, "CENTCOM Blackout on Pakistan," *Daily Times* (21 May 2003). The report, however, was cached by Google.com, later to be reproduced by South Asia Tribune which is available at http://www.satribune.com/archives/may 18_24_03/Pakistan_Centcom.htm.

27. For Thomas Friedman's views about Iran based on his visit to the country, see http://www.pbs.org/newshour/bb/foreign_correspondence/jan-june02/friedman_6-20.html.

28. Elaine Sciolino, "Iran Chief Rejects Bin Laden Message," *New York Times*, 10 November 2001.

29. "How Iran Entered the Axis," *Frontline*, PBS, also available at http://www.pbs.org/wgbh/pages/frontline/shows/tehran/axis/map.html.

30. For a detailed narrative of the episode, see Stephen Kinzer, *All the Shah's Men: An American Coup and the Roots of Middle East Terror* (Hoboken, NJ: John Wiley and Sons, Inc., 2003).

31. Dr. James Bill, "U.S.-Iran Relations: Forty Years of Observations," Policy Brief, *Middle East Institute* (20 February 2004), also available at http://www.mideasti.org/articles/doc170.html.

32. Laura Secor, "The Democrat: Iran's Leading Reformist Intellectual Tries to Reconcile Religious Duties and Human Rights," *Boston Globe*, 14 March 2004.

33. Mehran Kamrava, "Iranian Shiism under Debate," *Middle East Policy Council Journal* 10, no. 2 (Summer 2003).

34. Afshin Molavi, "Buying Time in Tehran," *Foreign Affairs* (November/December 2004).

35. Jahangir Amuzegar, "Iran's Crumbling Revolution," *Foreign Affairs* (January/February 2003).

36. David L. Phillips, "Pragmatism Needed in U.S.-Iran Relations," *Boston Globe*, 7 March 2004.

37. Graham E. Fuller, "U.S.-Iran Relations: A Road Map For Normalization," *Bulletin* (of The Academic Council of the United States) 9, no. 3 (19 March 1998).

38. For a detailed analysis of some of the ideas discussed in the section, see David Hoffman, "Beyond Public Diplomacy," *Foreign Affairs* (March/April 2002); Richard C. Holbrooke, Charles G. Boyd, and Carla A. Hills, "Improving the U.S. Public Diplomacy Campaign In the War Against Terrorism," Independent Task Force Report, *Council on Foreign Relation*; Christopher Ross, "Pillars of Public Diplomacy: Grappling with International Public Opinion," *Harvard Review* (Summer 2003); Derk Kinnane, "Winning Over the Muslim Mind," *The National Interest*

(Spring 2004); R. S. Zaharna, "American Public Diplomacy in the Arab and Muslim World: A Strategic Communication Analysis," *FPIF Policy Report* (November 2001); Idriss Jazairy, "Public Diplomacy at a Crossroads," *Washington Times*, August 2002; Carl Weiser, "Report Lists 'Public Diplomacy' Failures," *USA Today*, 15 September 2003; and "Talking with the Islamic World: Is the Message Getting Through?" summary of panel discussion, Institute for the Study of Diplomacy, Georgetown University, also available at http://cfdev.georgetown.edu/sfs/programs/isd/pubs/iw_summary_feb19.pdf.

Chapter 5: The Complex Relationship

1. Laila Al Arian, "Perceptions of U.S. in the Arab World," *Washington Report on Middle East Affairs* 23 (September 2004), accessed on 15 December 2004 at http://umi.proquest.com.

2. H. W. Brands, *Into the Labyrinth: The United States and the Middle East 1945–1993* (New York: McGraw-Hill, 1994), p. 19.

3. Dana H. Allin and Steven Simon, "The Moral Psychology of U.S. Support for Israel," *Survival* (September 2003): 124.

4. Douglas Little, "The Making of A Special Relationship: The United States and Israel, 1957–58," *Middle East Studies* 25 (1993): 563–64.

5. Kathleen Christison, "Bound by a Frame of Reference, Part II: U.S. Policy and the Palestinians, 1948–1988," *Journal of Palestine Studies* 27 (Spring 1998): 23.

6. Dana Allin and Steven Simon, "Moral Psychology," p. 126.

7. Ghassan Bishara, "The Political Repercussions of the Israeli Raid on the Iraqi Nuclear Reactor," *Journal of Palestine Studies* 11, no. 3 (Spring 1982): 58.

8. Douglas Little, "Special Relationship," p. 565.

9. Dana Allin and Steven Simon, "Moral Psychology," p. 125.

10. Douglas Little, "Special Relationship," p. 570.

11. Steven Simon, "The New Terrorism," *Brookings Review* (Winter 2003): 19.

12. Maha Azzam, "Al Qaeda: The Misunderstood Wahhabi Connection and the Ideology of Violence," the Royal Institute of International Affairs, Briefing Paper No. 1 (February 2003): 3; also see the chapter by Maha Azzam in Volume I of this publication.

13. Maha Azzam, "Misunderstood Wahhabi," p. 3.

14. "Yemen: President Salih Urges Bush to put More Pressure on Israel," *BBC Monitoring Middle East*, 5 April 2001, http://proquest.umi.com (accessed 27 October 2004).

15. "U.S. Hatred like never before Mubarak Says," *Toronto Star*, 21 April 2004, http://proquest.umi.com (accessed 28 October 2004).

16. Nivien Saleh, "Egypt: Osama's Star Is Rising," *Middle East Policy* 9, no. 3 (September 2002): 43.

17. Ibid., p. 40.

18. Eric Watkins, "The Unfolding U.S. Policy in the Middle East," *International Affairs* 73, no. 1 (January 1997): 6.

19. BBC Monitoring quotes from Middle East Arabic Press, 24 April 2004, http://proquest.umi.com (accessed 29 October 2004).

20. "Iran: Commentary Criticizes U.S. Policy Towards Iraq, Israel," *BBC Monitoring Middle East*, 9 September 2002, http://proquest.umi.com (accessed 29 October 2004).

21. Accessed from http://www.nasrollah.org/english/hassan/speeches/spee2004/khabitat009.htm (24 September 2004).

22. John Miller, Michael Stone, and Chris Mitchell, *The Cell* (New York: Hyperion, 2002), p. 49.

23. Robert Fisk, "Why We Reject the West-By the Saudis' Fiercest Arab Critic," *The Independent*, 10 July 1996, http://proquest.umi.com (accessed 28 October 2004).

24. Accessed from http://www.pbs.org/wgbh/pages/frontline/shows/binladen/who/edicts.html.

25. As quoted in Bernard Lewis, "License to Kill: Usama bin Ladin's Declaration of Jihad," *Foreign Affairs* (November/December 1998): 15.

26. "Purported Bin Laden Tape Urges Holy War" Government CustomWire, 5 January 2004, http://web28.epnet.com (accessed 22 October 2004).

27. Maha Azzam, "Misunderstood Wahhabi," p. 3.

28. Excerpts of auditape remarks attributed to Ayyman al-Zawahiri, Federal News Service, http://lexis-nexis.com (accessed 21 October 2004).

29. "True Muslims Should Act," *USA Today*, 12 February 2003, p. 7A.

30. Robert Fisk, "Why We Reject the West—By the Saudis' Fiercest Arab Critic," *The Independent* (UK), 10 July 1996, p. 21.

31. As quoted in, "Ephraim Karsh, "Intifada II: The Long Trail of Arab Anti-Semitism," *Commentary* (December 2000): 49.

32. Andrew Hammond, "A New Era of Openness," *Middle East* no. 320 (February 2002): 46, http://ehostvgw4.epnet.com (accessed 31 July 2003).

33. Ibid.

34. Steven Simon, p. 20.

35. Richard Murphy, interview with author, New York City, 24 September 2003.

Chapter 6: Political Repression and Violent Rebellion

1. This chapter draws upon some arguments, excerpts, and citations from Mohammed M. Hafez, *Why Muslims Rebel: Repression and Resistance in the Islamic World* (Boulder, CO: Lynne Rienner Publishers, 2003). However, it is not a duplication of a previously published chapter.

2. Martin Kramer, "The Mismeasure of Political Islam," in *The Islamism Debate*, edited by Martin Kramer (Tel Aviv: The Moshe Dayan Center for Middle Eastern and African Studies, 1997); and Daniel Pipes, *In the Path of God: Islam and Political Power* (New Brunswick, NJ: Transaction Publishers, 2002).

3. Nazih Ayubi, *Political Islam: Religion and Politics in the Arab World* (New York: Routledge, 1991); R. Hrair Dekmejian, *Islam in Revolution: Fundamental-*

ism in the Arab World (Syracuse, NY: Syracuse University Press, 1995); and International Crisis Group, "Islamism in North Africa I: The Legacies of History," *Middle East and North Africa Briefing* (20 April 2004).

4. Michael C. Hudson, "Arab Regimes and Democratization: Responses to the Challenge of Political Islam," in *The Islamist Dilemma: The Political Role of Islamist Movements in the Contemporary Arab World*, edited by Laura Guazzone (Reading, NY: Ithaca Press, 1995).

5. International Crisis Group, "Islamism in North Africa II: Egypt's Opportunity," *Middle East and North Africa Briefing* (20 April 2004); and International Crisis Group, "Islamism, Violence and Reform in Algeria: Turning the Page," *Middle East Report* no. 29 (30 July 2004).

6. Aïssa Khelladi, *Les islamistes algériens face au pouvoir* (Algiers: Alfa, 1992), pp. 73–80; and Ahmeda Ayyashi, *al-Haraka al-Islamiyya fi al-Jazair: al-Joudhour, al-Rumouz, al-Masar* (Casablanca: Uyun al-Magalat, 1993), pp. 192–207.

7. Hala Mustapha, *al-Islam al-Siyasi fi Misr: Min Haraket al-Islam ila Jama'at al-'Anf* (Cairo: Markaz al-Dirasat al-Siyasiya wal-Istratijiya, 1992).

8. Hisham Mubarak, *al-Irhabiyun Qadimun: Dirasa Muqarana bayn Mouqif al-Ikhwan al-Muslimin wa Jama'at al-Jihad min Qadhiet al-'Anf, 1928-1994* (Cairo: Markaz al-Mahrousa lil-Nashr al-Khidmat al-Sahafiya, 1995).

9. International Crisis Group, "The Algerian Crisis: Not Over Yet," *Africa Report* no. 24 (20 October 2000). There has been speculation that the GSPC has formed links with al Qaeda, but it is not clear to what extent these links are ideological or operational (see International Crisis Group, "Islamism, Violence and Reform in Algeria: Turning the Page," *Middle East Report* no. 29 [30 July 2004]).

10. Nabil Sharaf al-Din, *Umara wa Muwatinun: Rasd li-Dhahirt al-Islam al-Haraki fi Misr Khilal 'Aqd al-Tisinat* (Cairo: Madbouli, 1998), p. 506.

11. Haider Ibrahim Ali, *al-Tiyarat al-Islamiyya wa Qadhiyat al-Dimuqratiyya* (Beirut: Markaz Dirasat al-Wihda al-Arabiyya, 1996); al-Tahir bin Kharfallah, "Mu'ana al-Sahafa al-Mustaqila fi al-Jazair," *Shuoun al-Awsat* 59 (January–February 1996): 81–95; and Samih Rashid, "Al-Ta'adidiya al-Hizbiyya fi al-Jazair," *Shuoun al-Awsat* 65 (September 1997): 57–77.

12. Ibrahim al-Biyoumi Ghanim, *al-Haraka al-Islamiyya fi al-Jazair wa Azmat al-Dimuqratiyya* (Paris: Umat, 1992), pp. 33–34.

13. M. Al-Ahnaf, B. Botiveau, and F. Frégosi, *L'Algérie par ses islamistes* (Paris: Karthala, 1991), p. 97; and Nazim Abdelwahed al-Jasour, "al-Mawqif al-Faransi min al-Islam Asiyasi fi al-Jazair: Ab'aadih al-Iqlimiyya wal-Dawliyya," *al-Mustaqbal al-Arabi* 202 (December 1995): 46.

14. Ahmeda Ayyashi, *al-Haraka*, p. 248.

15. Hugh Roberts, "From Radical Mission to Equivocal Ambition: The Expansion and Manipulation of Algerian Islamism, 1979–1992," in *Accounting for Fundamentalism: The Dynamic Character of Movements*, edited by Martin E. Marty and R. Scott Appleby (Chicago: University of Chicago Press, 1994), p. 469; and Michael Willis, *The Islamist Challenge in Algeria: A Political History* (Reading: Ithaca Press, 1996), pp. 178–80.

16. Abed Charef, *Algérie: Le Grand Dérapage* (Paris: éditions de l'aube, 1994), pp. 117–18; Camille al-Tawil, *al-Haraka al-Islamiyya al-Musalaha fi al-Jazair: min al-Inqadh ila al-Jama'a* (Beirut: Dar al-Nahar, 1998), pp. 40–41; and Muhammed Qawas, *Ghazwit "al-Inqaz": M'araket al-Islam al-Siyasi fi al-Jazair* (Beirut: Dar al-Jadid, 1998), pp. 107–10.

17. Interview with *al-Wasat*, no. 76, 12 July 1993, part 5.

18. *Middle East Insight*, 13 May 1994.

19. Luis Martinez, *The Algerian Civil War, 1990–1998* (New York: Columbia University Press, 2000).

20. Abdelhamid Mehri, "al-Azma al-Jazairiyya: al-Waq'a wal-Ifaq," *al-Mustaqbal al-Arabi* 226 (December 1997): 5–6. Ben Hajjar, the commander of the *Rabita al-Islamiya lil-Dawa wal Jihad* (The Islamic League for Preaching and Holy Struggle, LIDD), which joined the GIA in 1994, maintained that those who opposed the electoral option were few prior to 1992. But when the FIS was "hit twice" (June 1991 and January 1992), these extremists were the only leaders left to guide the movement (interview in *al-Hayat*, 5 February 2000, p. 8).

21. George al-Rasi, *al-Islam al-Jazairi: min al-Amir 'Abd al-Kader ila Umara al-Jama'at* (Beirut: Dar al-Jadid, 1997), pp. 385–87.

22. The letter was issued on 1 April 1995 and quoted in al-Tawil, *al-Haraka*, pp. 303–4.

23. *al-Hayat*, 26 August 1994.

24. The letter is addressed to the Independent Dialogue Committee and dated 23 November 1993; Abu Abdel Fatah Ali Belhaj, *Ghayat al-Murad fi Qadhaya al-Jihad: Four Letters* (Algeria: al-Jabha al-Islamiya lil-Inqaz, 1994), pp. 135–58.

25. Huda Ragheb Auda and Hasanin Tawfiq Ibrahim, *al-Ikhwan al-Muslimun wal-Siyasa fi Misr: Dirasa fi al-Tahalufat al-Intikhabiya wal-Mumarasat al-Barlamaniya lil-Ikhwan al-Muslimin fi Dhal al-Ta'adudiya al-Siyasiya al-Muqayada, 1984–1990* (Cairo: Markaz al-Mahrous lil-Bihouth wal-Tadrib wal-Nashr, 1995).

26. Muhsin Radhi, *al-Ikhwan al-Muslimun that Qibet al-Barlaman*, Volumes 1 and 2 (Cairo: Dar al-Nashr wal-Tawzia, 1990/1991); and Muhammad al-Tawil, *al-Ikhwan fi al-Barlaman* (Cairo: al-Maktab al-Misri al-Hadith, 1992).

27. Bahgat Korany, "Resticted Democratization from Above: Egypt," in *Political Liberalization and Democratization in the Arab World: Comparative Experiences*, edited by Bhagat Korany, Rex Brynen, and Paul Noble (Boulder, CO: Lynne Rienner, 1998), p. 53.

28. Quoted in Abdel Aati Muhammad Ahmed, *al-Harakat al-Islamiya fi Misr wa Qadhiyet al-Tahawal al-Dimuqrati* (Cairo: Markaz al-Ahram lil-Tarjama wal-Nashr, 1995), p. 109.

29. Hisham Mubarak, *al-Irhabiyun*, pp. 260–62.

30. Ibid., pp. 260–65; and Asef Bayat, "Activism and Social Development in the Middle East," *International Journal of Middle East Studies* 34 (February 2002): 12.

31. Manar al-Shourbaji, "Al-Qadhaya al-Dasturiya wal Qanuniya fi Fatret Ri-

aset Mubarak al-Thaniya," in *al-Tatawur al-Siyasi fi Misr, 1982–1992*, edited by Muhammed Sifa al-Din Kharboush (Cairo: Center for Political Research and Studies, 1994).

32. Amru al-Shawkabi, "Al-M'araka al-Intikhabiya: Dhawahir Jadida," in *al-Intikhabat al-Barlamaniya fi Misr, 1995*, edited by Hala Mustapha (Cairo: Markaz al-Dirasat al-Siyasiya wal-Istratijiya, 1995).

33. Hasanein Tawfiq Ibrahim, *al-Nizam al-Siyasi wal-Ikhwan al-Muslimun fi Misr: Min al-Tasamuh ila al-Muwajiha, 1981–1996* (Cairo: Dar al-Tali'a lil-Tiba'a wal-Nashr, 1998), pp. 139–44.

34. Communiqué in *Al-Hayat*, 8 August 1995.

35. *Al-Hayat*, 30 March 1993.

36. *Al-Hayat*, 28 January 1996.

37. *Human Rights Watch*, "Egypt: Human Rights Abuses Mount in 1993," 22 October 1993; and *Amnesty International*, "Egypt: Indefinite Detention and Systematic Torture: The Forgotten Victims," July 1996.

38. In 1987 the state arrested approximately 4,000 suspected militants. In 1988, the number declined to 1,159, while in 1989 it went back up to 2,114. In 1990, the number declined to 955, but in 1991 it went back up to 1,370; 9,428 were arrested in 1992 and 17,785 in 1993 (Ahmed 1995, pp. 299–300).

39. *Human Rights Watch*, "Egypt: Hostage-Taking and Intimidation by Security Forces," January 1995.

40. Hasan Bakr, *Al-'Anf al-Siyasi fi Misr, 1977–1993* (Cairo: Markez al-Mahrousa lil-Bihouth wal-Tadrib wal-Nashr, 1995), pp. 199–200.

41. Fawaz A. Gerges, *America and Political Islam: Clash of Cultures or Clash of Interests* (New York: Cambridge University Press, 1999).

42. John L. Esposito and John O. Voll, *Islam and Democracy* (New York: Oxford University Press, 1996); and William B. Quandt, *Between Ballots and Bullets: Algeria's Transition from Authoritarianism* (Washington, DC: Brookings Institution Press, 1998).

Chapter 7: Rejection of Political Institutions

1. Oliver Mackson, "Life's Struggles Got Better of Man in Armed Police Showdown," *Times Herald-Record (Middletown, NY)*, 31 December 2004; see also Oliver Mackson, "Russo's Neighbors Lived in Fear of Him," *Times Herald-Record* (Middletown, NY), 26 December 2004; Staff writer, "Man Pleads Guilty, still Suing," *Times Herald-Record* (Middletown, NY), 31 October 1997.

2. Marc Fisher, "War and Peacekeeping: Battle Rages Over the GI Who Said No to U.N. Insignia," *The Washington Post*, 4 March 1996, D01. See also 104th Congress, 2nd sess., House Con Res. 134 (summary Bill Tracking Report, Lexis-Nexis), sponsored by Roscoe Bartlett (R-MD) with a final tally of 43 cosponsors (41 Republicans and 2 Democrats). The Democrats were Ralph M. Hall (D-TX) and James Traficant (D-OH).

3. "The Blue Helmet Blues," *St. Louis Post Dispatch*, 14 September 1996, p. 6B.

A bill to prohibit wear of UN insignia passed 276–130; the bill to retain operational and tactical control of U.S. troops passed 299–109. Democrats supporting both were Ike Skelton and Glenn Poshard (also on Lexis-Nexis, House Resolution 2540).

4. Mark Pitcavage, "Extremism and the Electorate: Campaign '96 and the 'Patriot' Movement," 6 November 1996, online at www.adl.org. Pitcavage tracks 15 races. I conducted an independent Lexus/Nexus search from 1990 to 1998 of "extremis*" or "militia" and "congress" to find articles indicating members of Congress or candidates who spoke to Far Right adherents (such as militias) or were otherwise linked to these organizations. My search turned up eight members and one challenger: Representative Rick Hill (R-MT); Representative Tom Tancredo (R-CO); Representative Joe Scarborough (R-FL); Representative Bob Schaffer (R-CO); Representative Mark Foley (R-FL); Representative Helen Chenoweth (R-ID); Representative Roscoe Bartlett (R-MD); and Representative Steve Stockman (R-TX). In addition, Republican candidate Pat Miller (running for 6th District in Colorado) was reported to have spoken to members of a Boulder militia.

5. Libertarian Party, "The Libertarian Party's Statement of Principles," available at http://www.lp.org/issues/platform/sop.html (accessed 5 November 2002).

6. Libertarian Party news, available at http://www.lp.org/lpnews/0211/denver.html (accessed November 2002).

7. Tom Murse, "Constitution Party: 'We're not a Hate Group.'" *Lancaster New Era* (Lancaster, PA), 26 April 2001, p. B1.

8. Tom Murse, "Constitution Party."

9. U.S. Congress, Senate, Senate Judiciary Committee Subcommittee on Terrorism, Technology, and Government Information, Prepared testimony of John E. Trochmann and Bob Fletcher Militia of Montana 15 June 1995, Federal News Service.

10. Author's interviews with Flathead County, Montana, Sheriff, March 2002, and the Supervisor of a Regional Criminal Intelligence Unit in Washington state, March 2002; Human subjects review board approval on file at Stanford University (March 2002).

11. James E. Duffy and Alan C. Brantley, "Militias: Initiating Contact," July 1997, Federal Bureau of Investigations Bulletin. These militia groups fall into the "Type I and Type II" categories in Duffy and Brantley's typology.

12. Some examples are the 1997 plot by New Hampshire militia at Fort Devens, Massachusetts, the 1997 plot of North American Militia in Michigan to target military bases, and the 1997 attack planned on Fort Hood, Texas, by militia members in Colorado and Kansas. Source: Mark Pitcavage, "Calendar of Conspiracy," 1994–1999 Militia Watchdog, www.militia-watchdog.org.

13. Mark Pitcavage, "Calendar of Conspiracy," 1997–2000, www.militia-watchdog.org.

14. Bernard J. Sussman, "Idiot Legal Arguments," 29 August 1999, available online at www.adl.org.

15. Gerald M. Nagle, "Common Law Courts in the United States," National Center for State Courts, memorandum #IS 96.0472, 30 April 1996.

16. Examples are Georgia inmates filing bogus liens in 1998, a Missouri adherent filing bogus liens in 1997, a Wisconsin man charged with impersonating a U.S. Marshal in 1998, a Florida man charged on multiple counts of driving without a license in 1998, and a 1998 shooting by a Michigan man stopped for driving without a license. See Mark Pitcavage, "Calendar of Conspiracy," Militia Watchdog.

17. Mark Pitcavage, "Special Report #4, Common Law and Uncommon Courts," 25 July 1997.

18. Bernard Sussman, "Idiot Legal Argument."

19. California Franchise Tax Board, 2002. Also IRS Release IR-2002-042, 3 April 2002, "IRS Updates Web Item Debunking Frivolous Tax Arguments."

20. James Aho, *The Politics of Righteousness: Idaho Christian Patriotism* (Seattle: University of Washington Press, 1990). Aho comments in his introduction about the seemingly ordinariness and civility of his Idaho Christian Patriot subjects.

21. State of California Department of Justice, "Organized Crime in California 2000," Annual Report to the California Legislature, 18 September 2001.

22. "9 in Lincoln County are Guilty of Trying to Intimidate Judge," *Saint Louis Post-Dispatch*, 12 June 1999, p. C13.

23. James Aho, *Politics of Righteousness*, 11–12. Aho also writes of being criticized for his characterization of Idaho Christian Patriots as "good people with blind spots."

24. Elinor Burkett, *The Right Women: A Journey Through the Heart of Conservative America* (New York: Touchstone, 1998), p. 86.

25. Biographical sketches of key right wing leaders prepared by Anti-Defamation League, online at www.adl.org.

26. Credited to David Lane, member of The Order.

27. For more on William Pierce and his publications, see www.adl.org/learn/ext_us/Pierce.asp.

28. Mark Pitcavage, "Calendar of Conspiracy," 1999, www.militia-watchdog.org

29. Crimes attributed to those with a right-wing, or antigovernmental ideology (Pitcavage, Calender of Conspiracy, 1994, 1995, 1997, 1998, 1999). This analysis of events is found in Eugenia K. Guilmartin, "An Empirical Analysis of Right Wing Domestic Terrorism in the United States (1995–2001)," Stanford University dissertation (2003), available online at ProQuest http://wwwlib.umi.com/dissertations/fullcit/3085185.

30. Morris Dees and James Corcoran, *Gathering Storm: America's Militia Threat* (New York: HarperCollins, 1996).

31. http://members.aol.com/_ht_a/USSOCM/page3 (accessed May 2002).

32. http://www.hdmsc.org/ (accessed May 2002).

33. Dees, *Gathering Storm*, pp. 169–70.

34. See, for example, Libertarian party policy on extremist groups on the party website (http://www.lp.org).

35. Author's interview, March 2002.

36. Author's interview, Kalispell, Montana, March 2002.

37. Rick Sine, "Right Wing Dropouts" (Santa Clara, CA), *Metro*, 14 March 1996.

38. Staff writer, "House Passes Involuntary Bankruptcy Bill," *Milwaukee Journal Sentinel*, 11 June 2003.

39. Ibid.

40. Author's interview with Ozaukee Corporate Counsel, 2004.

41. Ibid.

Chapter 8: Religious Sources of Violence

1. The introduction page of Sinn Fein's website makes clear that union with Ireland is not the sole goal of the party; see Sinn Fein, "Introduction," www.sinnfein.ie (November 2003). Sinn Fein's President, Gerry Adams, also makes this clear in his book, *Free Ireland: Towards a Lasting Peace* (Niwot, CO: Roberts Rinehart Publishing, 1994).

2. As cited in Mark Juergensmeyer, *Terror in the Mind of God: The Global Rise of Religious Violence* (Berkeley: University of California Press, 2000), p. 145.

3. For a detailed review of Jihad, please see the chapter by Jarret Brachman in Volume 1 of this publication.

4. Michael Sells, *The Bridge Betrayed: Religion and Genocide in Bosnia* (Berkeley: University of California Press, 1998), p. 31.

5. Ibid.

6. Exodus 1:1–14:30 (Authorized King James Version).

7. Romans 8:31 (The Student Bible: New International Version).

8. Juergensmeyer, *Terror in the Mind of God*, p. 146.

9. R. Scott Appleby, *The Ambivalence of the Sacred: Religion, Violence, and Reconciliation* (Lanham, MD: Rowman and Littlefield Publishers, 2000), p. 17.

10. Ibid., p. 17.

11. Ibid.

12. Gary T. Marx, "Religion: Opiate or Inspiration of Civil Rights Militancy Among Negroes?" *American Sociological Review* 32, no. 1 (1967): 64–72; see also Gary T. Marx, *Protest and Prejudice* (London: Harper and Row Publishers, 1967).

13. Ibid., p. 72.

14. Christian Identity is a religious sect that believes that white people of European descent are the descendants of the "Lost Tribes" of ancient Israel and God's Chosen People. Estimates of their current membership are between 25,000 and 50,000.

15. Doug McAdam, *Political Process and the Development of Black Insurgency* (Chicago: University of Chicago Press, 1982).

16. Ibid., p. 128.

17. Ibid., p. 132.

18. Ibid., p. 137.

19. Kevin Neuhouser, "The Radicalization of the Brazilian Catholic Church in Comparative Perspective," *American Sociological Review* 54 (1989): 233–44.

20. Guenter Lewy, *Religion and Revolution* (New York: Oxford University Press, 1974).

21. Ibid., p. 575.

22. "Adherents.com," 16 August 2000, online at http://www.adherents.com.

23. Gilles Kepel, *Jihad: The Trail of Political Islam*, translated by Anthony F. Roberts (Cambridge, MA: The Belknap Press of Harvard University Press, 2002), p. 237.

24. Ibid., p. 247.

25. Cynthia Keppley Mahmood, *Fighting for Faith and Nation: Dialogues with Sikh Militants* (Philadelphia: University of Pennsylvania Press, 1996), p. 151.

26. Bhabani Sen Gupta, "Internationalization of Ethnic Conflict: The Punjab Crisis of the 1980s," in *Internationalization of Ethnic Conflict*, edited by K. M. de Silva and R. J. Mays (London: Pinter Publishers, 1991), p. 52.

27. Ibid., p. 55.

28. Ibid.

29. Scott Thomas, "Religion and International Conflict," in *Religion and International Relations*, edited by K. R. Dark (London: MacMillan Press, 2000), p. 6.

30. Ibid., pp. 6–7.

Chapter 9: Terrorism and Doomsday

1. Herman Kahn, *On Thermonuclear War* (Princeton, NJ: Princeton University Press, 1960), p. 145.

2. Herman Kahn, *On Escalation: Metaphors and Scenarios* (Baltimore, MD: Penguin, 1968), p. 228.

3. Jonathan B. Tucker, ed., *Toxic Terror: Assessing Terrorist Use of Chemical and Biological Weapons* (Cambridge, MA: MIT Press, 2000), p. 10.

4. Jeffrey Kaplan, ed., *Millennial Violence: Past, Present and Future* (Portland, OR: Frank Cass, 2002), p. 48.

5. Ibid., pp. 53–59.

6. Mark Juergensmeyer, *Terror in the Mind of God: The Global Rise of Religious Violence*, 3rd ed. (Berkeley: University of California Press, 2003), p. 149.

7. For a description and analysis of Aum Shinrikyō, please see the chapter by John Parachini in Volume 2 of this publication.

8. Edward Cody, "In Angry Waves, the Devout See an Angry God," *The Washington Post*, 5 January 2005, p. A01.

9. W. Warren Wagar, *Terminal Visions: The Literature of Last Things* (Bloomington: Indiana University Press, 1982), p. 108.

10. Bruce Lincoln, *Holy Terrors: Thinking about Religion after September 11* (Chicago: University of Chicago Press, 2003), pp. 95–96.

11. David C. Rapoport, "Terrorism and Weapons of the Apocalypse," *National Security Studies Quarterly* 5, no. 3 (1999): 50.

12. Jonathan B. Tucker, *Toxic Terror*, p. 11.

13. Mark Juergensmeyer, *Terror in the Mind of God*, p. 126.

14. Ibid., pp. 126–27.

15. Jeffrey Kaplan, *Millennial Violence*, p. 59.

Chapter 10: Fueling the Fires

1. National Commission on Terrorists Attacks upon the United States (the 9/11 Commission), *The 9/11 Commission Report* (New York: W. W. Norton, 2004), p. 50, available online at http://www.gpoaccess.gov/911.

2. Bin Laden used this term in a videotaped message aired on al Jazeera in October 2004, as posted on www.marktaw.com on 1 November 2004.

3. From an audiotape address released on Islamic websites on 16 December 2004, as transcribed by and posted at www.jihadunspun.com on 24 December 2004.

4. From a May 1998 interview with bin Laden recorded by the Public Broadcasting System. Electronic document accessed at www.pbs.org/wgbh/pages/frontline/shows/binladen/who/interview.html on 29 November 2004.

5. Anonymous, *Imperial Hubris* (Washington, DC: Brassey's, 2004), p. 16. Michael Scheuer was identified as the author of this book in Eric Lichtblau, "C.I.A. Officer Denounces Agency and Sept. 11 Report," *New York Times*, 17 August 2004.

6. For discussion, see ibid., pp. 10–19, 129–31.

7. Ibid., pp. 12–13, 129–31, 258.

8. For background and discussion, see John Keay, *Sowing the Wind: The Seeds of Conflict in the Middle East* (New York: W. W. Norton, 2003), pp. 1–119.

9. Describing and defending Britain's interest in Persia, for example, Lord Curzon, then Foreign Secretary, observed in 1919, "We possess in the southwestern corner of Persia great assets in the shape of oil fields, which are worked for the British navy and which give us a commanding interest in that part of the world." Quoted in Stephen Kinzer, *All the Shah's Men* (Hoboken, NJ: John Wiley, 2003), pp. 39–40; see also John Keay, *Sowing the Wind*, pp. 120–40.

10. For background, see Stephen Kinzer, *All the Shah's Men*, pp. 30–82.

11. For background on these developments, see Daniel Yergin, *The Prize* (New York: Simon and Schuster, 1991), pp. 134–61.

12. Ibid., pp. 138, 145.

13. For background, see ibid., pp. 158–61, 269–71.

14. Stephen Kinzer, *All the Shah's Men*, p. 50.

15. Ibid., pp. 30–46, 66–73.

16. For background, see ibid., pp. 158–61, 269–71, 420–22; see also Stephen Kinzer, *All the Shah's Men*, pp. 38–40, 47–52; and Kenneth M. Pollack, *The Persian Puzzle* (New York: Random House, 2004), pp. 27–39.

17. See Stephen Kinzer, *All the Shah's Men*, pp. 52–82; and Kenneth Pollack, *The Persian Puzzle*, pp. 50–57.

18. Daniel Yergin, *The Prize*, p. 452.

19. Ibid., p. 455, see also Stephen Kinzer, *All the Shah's Men*, pp. 73–79.

20. Daniel Yergin, *The Prize*, pp. 456–64.

21. For an account of the coup, see Stephen Kinzer, *All the Shah's Men*, pp. 1–16, 167–92.

22. See Stephen Kinzer, *All the Shah's Men*, pp. 134–215.

23. For discussion, ibid., pp. 75–78.

24. Quoted in ibid., p. 76.

25. For background on this episode, see John Keay, *Sowing the Wind*, pp. 434–42; and Daniel Yergin, *The Prize*, pp. 479–93.

26. For background, see John Keay, *Sowing the Wind*, pp. 120–66.

27. Peter and Marion Farouk Sluglett, "Iraq," in *The Oxford Companion to the Politics of the World*, 2nd ed., edited by Joel Krieger (New York: Oxford University Press, 2001), p. 434.

28. See John Keay, *Sowing the Wind*, pp. 445–50.

29. For background, see Peter and Marion Sluglett, "Iraq," pp. 434–35.

30. For discussion, see John Keay, *Sowing the Wind*, pp. 451–74.

31. For background and discussion, see Michael A. Palmer, *Guardians of the Gulf* (New York: Free Press, 1992), pp. 1–39; Michael B. Stoff, *Oil, War, and American Security* (New Haven, CT: Yale University Press, 1980), pp. 34–150; and Daniel Yergin, *The Prize*, pp. 391–402.

32. For background on these developments, see David S. Painter, *Oil and the American Century* (Baltimore, MD: Johns Hopkins University Press, 1986), pp. 32–51; and Michael Stoff, *Oil, War, and American Security*, pp. 34–61.

33. For discussion of this encounter and its implications, see Michael T. Klare, *Blood and Oil: The Dangers and Consequences of America's Growing Petroleum Dependency* (New York: Metropolitan Books, 2004), pp. 35–37; Aaron Dean Miller, *Search for Security* (Chapel Hill: University of North Carolina Press, 1980), pp. 128–31; and Daniel Yergin, *The Prize*, pp. 403–5.

34. U.S. Senate, Committee on Armed Services, *Crisis in the Persian Gulf Region*, Hearings, 101st Cong., 2nd sess., 1990, p. 10.

35. See Michael Klare, *Blood and Oil*, pp. 37–45; David E. Long, *The United States and Saudi Arabia* (Boulder, CO: Westview Press, 1985), pp. 33–50; David Painter, *Oil and the American Century*, pp. 96–127; and Michael Palmer, *Guardians of the Gulf*, pp. 40–84.

36. For background on labor unrest in al-Hasa, see Alexei Vassiliev, *The History of Saudi Arabia* (New York: New York University Press, 2000), pp. 336–37.

37. See Daniel Yergin, *The Prize*, pp. 446–67, 651–52.

38. For background on these developments, see ibid., pp. 456–71, see also Stephen Kinzer, *All the Shah's Men*, pp. 150–66; and Kenneth Pollack, *The Persian Puzzle*, pp. 57–67.

39. See Stephen Kinzer, *All the Shah's Men*, pp. 1–16, 167–92.

40. For background, see Daniel Yergin, *The Prize*, pp. 470–78.

41. Ibid., p. 477.

42. For background, see Michael T. Klare, *American Arms Supermarket* (Austin: University of Texas Press, 1984), pp. 114–23.

43. See ibid., pp. 121–26; see also Kenneth Pollack, *The Persian Puzzle*, pp. 72–127; and Daniel Yergin, *The Prize*, pp. 637–38, 644–46, 672–82.

44. On Savak, see Kenneth Pollack, *The Persian Puzzle*, pp. 74–75, 114–17.

45. For an account of these developments, see ibid., pp. 117–35.

46. For discussion, see ibid., pp. 124–27, 135–40.

47. For background, see ibid., pp. 117–19, 127–28; see also John Keay, *Sowing the Wind*, pp. 463–65.

48. For background on these events, see Kenneth Pollack, *The Persian Puzzle*, pp. 143–74; and Daniel Yergin, *The Prize*, pp. 681–83, 699–701.

49. For discussion, see John Keay, *Sowing the Wind*, pp. 465–74.

50. Kenneth Pollack, *The Persian Puzzle*, p. 198.

51. Ibid.

52. See Alexei Vassiliev, *The History of Saudi Arabia*, pp. 396–97.

53. Ibid., pp. 395–96.

54. Ibid., p. 396.

55. Ibid., p. 397.

56. From a White House press conference on 1 October 1981 as reported in the *New York Times*, 2 October 1981.

57. Alexei Vassiliev, *The History of Saudi Arabia*, p. 397.

58. For background and discussion, see Steve Coll, *Ghost Wars* (New York: Penguin Press, 2004), pp. 228–31; Anthony H. Cordesman, *Saudi Security and the War on Terrorism* (Washington, DC: Center for Strategic and International Studies, 2002), pp. 1–3, 24–25, 31–32; Gwenn Okruhlik, "Networks of Dissent: Islamism and Reform in Saudi Arabia," *Current History* (January 2002): 22–25; see also Neela Banerjee, "The High, Hidden Cost of Saudi Arabian Oil," *New York Times*, 21 October 2001; and Neil MacFarquhar, "Anti-Western and Extremist Views Pervade Iraqi Schools," *New York Times*, 19 October 2001.

59. See Kenneth Pollack, *The Persian Puzzle*, pp. 198–205.

60. Ibid., pp. 278–86.

61. From a White House press conference on 1 October 1981, as reported in the *New York Times*, 2 October 1981.

62. For discussion, see Anonymous, *Imperial Hubris*, pp. 10–19, 138–40, 148–52.

63. See Jonathan Randal, *Osama: The Making of a Terrorist* (New York: Alfred A. Knopf, 2004), pp. 86–87.

64. Steve Coll, *Ghost Wars*, pp. 85, 112–13.

65. Ibid., pp. 155–58, 162–64; see also Jonathan Randal, *Osama*, pp. 87–93.

66. For an account of this meeting, see Douglas Jehl, "Holy War Lured Saudis As Rulers Looked Away," *New York Times*, 27 December 2001; see also Steve Coll, *Ghost Wars*, pp. 222–23.

67. See Jonathan Randal, *Osama*, pp. 105–8.

68. Ibid., p. 107.

69. Ibid., pp. 107–13.

70. Steve Coll, *Ghost Wars*, p. 229; see also Jonathan Randal, *Osama*, pp. 109–10.

71. From the transcript of an interview with bin Laden conducted by Peter Arnett in March 1997, www.ishipress.com (accessed 29 November 2004).

72. From bin Laden's 1998 *fatwa* calling for jihad against the United States, as published by *Al-Quds Al-Arabic* in London on 23 February 1998, www.emergency.com (accessed 30 May 2002).

73. Quoted in Warren Vieth and Alissa J. Rubin, "Iraq Pipelines East Targets for a Saboteur," *Los Angeles Times*, 26 June 2003.

74. See Daniel Yergin, *The Prize*, pp. 490–92.

75. For background on these events, see Michael Palmer, *Guardians of the Gulf*, pp. 128–49.

76. See Lawrence Freedman and Efraim Karsh, *The Gulf Conflict 1990–1991* (Princeton, NJ: Princeton University Press, 1993), pp. 278, 342–43, 384.

77. Heather Timmons, "Got Oil? Now, Try to Find Tankers to Carry It," *New York Times*, 9 June 2004.

78. Robert F. Worth, "Attack on Iraq Pipeline Cuts Oil Flow to Turkey," *New York Times*, 17 August 2003.

79. See Yochi J. Dreazen and Hassan Hafidh, "Iraq Attacks Staff the Flow of Crude," *Wall Street Journal*, 10 August 2004; Eric Watkins, "Iraqi Oil Exports Hampered by Pipeline Saboteurs," *Oil and Gas Journal* (25 August 2003): 48–49; and Watkins, "Iraq Oil Output to Rise, Despite Sabotage, Minister Says," *Oil and Gas Journal* (24 November 2003): 32–33.

80. Chip Cummings and Hassan Hafidh, "Attack on Iraqi Offshore Terminals Could Choke Off Rebuilding Funds," *Wall Street Journal*, 26 April 2004; and Eric Watkins, "Terrorists Attack Iraq's Persian Gulf Terminals," *Oil and Gas Journal* (3 May 2004): 32–33.

81. For discussion, see John Tierney and Robert F. Worth, "Attacks in Iraq Might Be Signs of New Tactics," *New York Times*, 18 August 2003.

82. Chip Cummings and Hassan Hafidh, "Iraq's Oil Industry Pumps Away," *Wall Street Journal*, 29 November 2004.

83. See David S. Cloud and Greg Jaffe, "U.S. Diplomat Wants More Funds for Iraqi Security," *Wall Street Journal*, 30 August 2004.

84. See Eric Watkins, "U.S. to Deploy Airborne Snipers to Protect Iraqi Pipelines," *Oil and Gas Journal* (13 October 2003): 37.

85. See James Glanz, "Fifteen Miles Offshore, Safeguarding Iraq's Oil Lifeline," *New York Times*, 6 July 2004.

86. Neil MacFarquhar, "After Attack, Company's Staff Plans to Leave Saudi Arabia," *New York Times*, 3 May 2004.

87. Neil MacFarquhar, "Saudi Military Storms Complex to Free Hostages," *New York Times*, 31 May 2004.

88. Quoted in Simon Romero, "Latest Terrorist Attack Increases Doubts About the Ability of Saudi Arabia to Pump More Oil," *New York Times*, 31 May 2004.

89. For discussion, see Simon Romero, "Latest Terrorist Attack Increases Doubts."

90. From a audiotape address released on Islamic websites on 16 December 2004, as transcribed by and posted at www.jihadunspun.com on 24 December 2004.

91. For discussion, see Michael Klare, *Blood and Oil*, pp. 74–84.

92. U.S. Department of Energy, Energy Information Administration (DoE/EIA), *International Energy Outlook 2004* (Washington, DC: DoE/EIA, 2004), Table D1, p. 213.

93. For discussion of this point, see Michael Klare, *Blood and Oil*, pp. 180–202.

Chapter 11: Socioeconomic and Demographic Roots

1. Frederick H. Gareau, *State Terrorism and the United States: From Counterinsurgency to the War on Terrorism* (Atlanta, GA: Clarity Press, 2004).

2. Mark Miller and Jason File, *Terrorism Factbook* (Peoria, IL: Bollix Press, 2001); also see Anthony J. Marsella, "Reflections on International Terrorism: Issues, Concepts, and Directions," in *Understanding Terrorism: Psychoscoial Roots, Consequences, and Interventions*, edited by Fathali M. Moghaddam and Anthony J. Marsella (Washington, DC: American Psychological Association, 2004), pp. 11–47.

3. Karl Philip Gottlieb von Clausewitz, *On War* (Princeton, NJ: Princeton University Press, 1976 [1833]), p. 605.

4. D. Brendan Nagle and Stanley M. Burstein, *The Ancient World: Readings in Social and Cultural History*, 2nd ed. (Upper Saddle River, NJ: Prentice Hall, 2002), p. 40.

5. Audrey Kurth Cronin, "Sources of Contemporary Terrorism," in *Attacking Terrorism: Elements of a Grand Strategy*, edited by James M. Ludes (Washington, DC: Georgetown University Press, 2004), pp. 19–45.

6. For example, see Martha Crenshaw, "Questions to Be Answered, Research to Be Done, Knowledge to Be Applied," in *Origins of Terrorism: Psychologies, Ideologies, Theologies, States of Mind*, edited by Walter Reich (Baltimore: Woodrow Wilson Center Press, 1998), pp. 247–60; Ariel Merari, "The Readiness to Kill and Die: Suicidal Terrorism in the Middle East," in *Origins of Terrorism: Psychologies, Ideologies, Theologies, States of Mind*, edited by W. Reich (Baltimore: Woodrow Wilson Center Press, 1998), pp. 192–207; and Walter Reich, ed., *Origins of Terrorism: Psychologies, Ideologies, Theologies, States of Mind* (Baltimore, MD: Woodrow Wilson Center Press, 1998).

7. Thomas Friedman, "The Core of Muslim Rage," *New York Times*, 6 March 2002.

8. Fathali M. Moghaddam and Anthony J. Marsella, *Understanding Terrorism: Psychosocial Roots, Consequences, and Interventions* (Washington, DC: American Psychological Association, 2004).

9. Paul R. Ehrlich, *Human Natures: Genes, Cultures, and the Human Prospect* (Washington, DC: Island Press, 2000).

10. Matthew Bunn and Anthony Wier, "Preventing a Nuclear 9/11," *The Washington Post*, 12 September 2004, p. B07.

11. Gretchen C. Daily and Paul R. Ehrlich, "Global Change and Human Susceptibility to Disease," *Annual Review of Energy and the Environment* 21 (1996): 125–44; and Steven M. Block, "The Growing Threat of Biological Weapons," *American Scientist* 89 (2001): 2–11.

12. Paul R. Ehrlich et al., *Ecoscience: Population, Resources, Environment* (San Francisco: W. H. Freeman and Co., 1977); Joseph A. Yager and Eleanor B. Steinberg, *Energy and U.S. Foreign Policy* (Cambridge, MA: Ballinger, 1975); and Daniel Yergin, *The Prize: The Epic Quest for Oil, Money, and Power* (New York, NY: Simon and Schuster, 1991).

13. Craig J. Jenkins and Doug Bond, "Conflict-Carrying Capacity, Political Crisis, and Reconstruction," *Journal of Conflict Resolution* 45 (2001): 3–31; see also Audrey Kurth Cronin, "Sources," and Martha Crenshaw, "Questions."

14. Gregory S. Paul, "The Secular Revolution of the West," *Free Inquiry* (Summer 2002): 28–34.

15. Daniel Pipes, "God and Mammon: Does Poverty Cause Militant Islam?" *National Interest* 66 (Winter 2001/2002): 14–21; and Mark Juergensmeyer, *Terror in the Mind of God: The Global Rise of Religious Violence* (Berkeley: University of California Press, 2003).

16. Walter Reich, *Origins of Terrorism*.

17. Daniel Pipes, "God and Mammon."

18. Kim Cragin and Peter Chalk, *Terrorism and Development: Using Social and Economic Development to Inhibit a Resurgence of Terrorism* (Santa Monica, CA: Rand, 2003).

19. Jack A. Goldstone, *Revolution and Rebellion in the Early Modern World* (Berkeley: University of California Press, 1991).

20. Federal Bureau of Investigation, http://www.fbi.gov/mostwant/terrorists/fugitives.htm, 2001.

21. Ariel Merari, "Readiness to Kill."

22. United States Department of Justice (Federal Bureau of Investigation), *Crime in the United States, 1999* (Washington, DC: USGPO, 2001).

23. Trish Saywell, "Crime Unlimited," *Far Eastern Economic Review* (2 November 2000): 72.

24. For example, see Jack Goldstone, *Revolution and Rebellion*.

25. United Nations (Population Division) *World Population Prospects: The 2000 Revision* (New York: United Nations, 2001).

26. Ibid.

27. For example, see Rachid Mimouni, *De la Barbarie en Général et de l'Intégrisme en Particulier* (Paris: Le Préux Clercs, 1992).

28. For example, see Youssef Courbage, "Demographic Change in the Arab World: The Impact of Migration, Education and Taxes in Egypt and Morocco," *Middle East Report* 190, no. 24 (1994): 19–22; and Philippe Fargues, "From Demographic Explosion to Social Rupture," in *Arab Society*, edited by N. S. Hopkins and S. E. Ibrahim (Cairo: American University in Cairo Press, 1997), pp. 75–83.

29. Population Reference Bureau, *2001 World Population Data Sheet* (Washington, DC: Population Reference Bureau, 2001).

30. Philippe Fargues, "Protracted National Conflict and Fertility Change: Palestinians and Israelis in the Twentieth Century," *Population and Development Review* 26 (2000): 441–82.

31. Central Bureau of Statistics of Israel, www.cbs.gov.il/shanton51/sto2-old.pdf (2001).

32. Thomas L. Friedman, "A Foul Wind," *New York Times,* 10 March 2002.

33. Eli Berman, "Sect, Subsidy and Sacrifice: An Economist's View of Ultra-Orthodox Jews," *Quarterly Journal of Economics* 115 (2000): 905–53.

34. Christopher C. Harmon, *Terrorism Today* (London: Frank Cass, 2000).

35. John B. Cobb Jr., "Globalization and Security: The Prospects of the Under-class," in *On the Edge of Scarcity: Environment, Resources, Population, Sustainability, and Conflict,* edited by I. Wallimann (Syracuse, NY: Syracuse University Press, 2002), pp. 4–15.

36. United States Department of Justice (Federal Bureau of Investigation), 2001.

37. Thomas Friedman, "The Core of Muslim Rage," *New York Times,* 6 March 2002.

38. "Warehouses for Refugees," *New York Times,* 28 September 2004, p. A24.

39. Population Reference Bureau, 2001.

40. Benjamin R. Barber, *Jihad vs. McWorld* (New York: Times Books, 1995).

41. Laurence R. Iannaccone, "Why Strict Churches are Strong," *American Journal of Sociology* 99 (1994): 1180–211; Brad S. Gregory, *Salvation at Stake: Christian Martyrdom in Early Modern Europe* (Cambridge, MA: Harvard University Press, 1999); and Sam Harris, *The End of Faith: Religion, Terror, and the Future of Reason* (New York: W. W. Norton, 2004).

42. Christopher C. Harmon, *Terrorism Today,* 2000.

43. Hilary French, "Reshaping Global Governance," in *State of the World 2002,* edited by L. Starke (New York: W. W. Norton, 2002), pp. 175–98.

44. Kim Cragin and Peter Chalk, *Terrorism and Development,* 2003.

45. John P. Holdren, "Population and the Energy Problem," *Population and Environment* 12 (1991): 231–55.

46. Gretchen C. Daily et al., "Optimum Human Population Size," *Population and Environment* 15 (1994): 469–75.

Chapter 12: Intersection of Terrorism and the Drug Trade

1. Few analysts would classify the Kosovo Liberation Army as a terrorist group, for example. Yet it is important to realize that even actors whom the international community may consider legitimate, or at least not fully illegitimate, also profit from the drug trade and that the drug trade is not simply a domain of illegitimate groups. Of course, an obvious interaction with the illicit narcotics trade may undermine the legitimacy of the group over time. The Northern Alliance provides another example. It and the original mujahideen groups from which it emerged were deeply involved in the narcotics trade in Afghanistan since the 1980s. Still, this fact did not stop the United States from supporting them and engaging with them as legitimate allies during the 1980s and after 9/11.

2. The relationship between al Qaeda and drugs is rather murky. Despite the frequent allegation fact that al Qaeda is benefiting from the burgeoning opium econ-

omy in Afghanistan, it is extremely unlikely that al Qaeda is taxing production and processing there. More likely, al Qaeda could be connected to some aspect of the *international* traffic. For circumstantial evidence to this effect, see, for example, Tim McGirk, "Terrorism's Harvest," *Time*, 9 August 2004, p. 41.

3. The exact timing of Sendero Luminoso's control of the Upper Huallaga Valley is placed by different experts between 1986 and 1987. The group actually started organizing in the valley in 1983 and initiated first armed actions there in 1985. However, it was only after 1986 that it managed to consolidate control over the valley and learned to exploit drug production. See Gabriela Tarazona-Sevillano with John B. Reuter, *Sendero Luminoso and the Threat of Narcoterrorism* (Washington, DC: Center for Strategic and International Studies, 1990), p. 110.

4. LaMond Tullis, *Unintended Consequences: Illegal Drugs and Drug Policies in Nine Countries* (Boulder, CO: Lynne Rienner, 1995), p. 96.

5. Enrique Obando, "Subversion and Anti-Subversion in Peru 1980–2," *Low Intensity Conflict and Law Enforcement* 2, no. 2 (Autumn 1993): 323.

6. "Los Intis de la Coca," *Peru Economico*, September 1987.

7. Enrique Obando, "Subversion," p. 323; and Richard Clutterbuck, *Drugs, Crime, and Corruption* (New York: New York University Press, 1995), p. 46. A roughly equal amount went to corrupt officials of the Peruvian police or armed forces who turned a blind eye to coca trafficking. In 1994, there were about 82 such airstrips in the Huallaga Valley, of which 14 were controlled by the army, another 10 known and patrolled by the air force, and about 58 clandestine—a varying number, since on flat ground an airstrip can be made quickly and easily. Richard Clutterbuck, *Drugs*, p. 44.

8. Mark Chernick, "Negotiating Peace Amid Multiple Forms of Violence," in *Comparative Peace Processes in Latin America*, edited by Cynthia J. Arson (Washington, DC: Woodrow Wilson Center Press, 1999), pp. 166–67. Some intelligence sources placed the total income of the guerrilla movement in 1995 as high as $800 million. For example, see International Institute for Strategic Studies, "Colombia's Escalating Violence," *Strategic Comments* 3, no. 4 (May 1997). However, given the size of the Colombian economy and its known difficulties in absorbing illicit monies, this figure is likely inflated.

9. Nazih Richani, *Systems of Violence* (Albany: State University of New York Press, 2002), p. 75.

10. Gonzalo Sánchez, "Introduction: Problems of Violence, Prospects for Peace," in *Violence in Colombia 1990–2000: Waging War and Negotiating Peace*, edited by Charles Bergquist, Ricardo Peñaranda, and Gonzalo Sánchez (Wilmington, DE: A Scholarly Resources Inc. Imprint, 2001), p. 24. The FARC is responsible for a majority of kidnappings committed in Colombia today. Colombia has one of the highest kidnapping rates in the world.

11. Nazih Richani, *Systems of Violence*, p. 75. A study by the Colombian police put FARC's and the AUC's income at a high of $105 million per month (Colombia National Police Internal Document A-4523, Government of Colombia, December 2000); quoted in *War and Lack of Governance in Colombia: Narcos,*

Guerrillas, and U.S. Policy, Edgardo Buscaglia and William Ratliff (Stanford: Hoover Institution on War, Revolution, and Peace, 2001), no. 107, p. 26.

12. According to police estimates, as cited by Richani, *Systems of Violence*, p. 109. In a Colombian TV interview, Carlos Castaña asserted that 70 percent of the AUC's income came from drugs.

13. Edgardo Buscaglia and William Ratliff, *War*, p. 5.

14. U.S. Department of State, Bureau for International Narcotics and Law Enforcement Affairs, *International Narcotics Control Strategy Report* (Washington, DC: U.S. Department of State, 2000).

15. The leftist guerrillas are believed to control around 70 percent of the opium poppy-producing municipalities; the right-wing paramilitaries aligned with the narcotraffickers are estimated to control about 26 percent of the municipalities. Camilo Echandia, "La Amapola en el Marco de las Economicas del ciclo Corto," *Analisis Politico*, no. 27 (January–April 1996). Colombia is now the Western Hemisphere's largest producer of heroin. Afghanistan is the world's largest producer of heroin.

16. U.S. Congress, House of Representatives, Committee on International Relations, "United States Policy Towards Narco-Terrorism in Afghanistan," Statement of Karen B. Tandy, Administrator, Drug Enforcement Agency, 12 February 2004.

17. Cynthia McClintock, *Revolutionary Movements in Latin America: El Salvador's FMLN & Peru's Shining Path* (Washington, DC: United States Institute of Peace Press, 1998), p. 73.

18. The common salary range—$20–$500 per month—was about three to eight times the salaries of most of Peru's teachers (Cynthia McClintock, *Revolutionary Movements*, p. 292). For comparison, the salary of top military generals in Peru was less than $200 per month, and about $10 for enlisted personnel (David Scott Palmer, "Peru, the Drug Business and Shining Path: Between Scylla and Charybdis?" *Journal of Interamerican Studies and World Affairs* 34, no. 3 [Special Issue: Drug Trafficking Research Update, Autumn 1992], p. 70). Sendero Luminoso also rewarded its other members and sympathizers by providing them with food, housing, livestock, etc.

19. Nazih Richani, *Systems of Violence*, pp. 124, 148.

20. Raul Gonzales, "Coca y subversion en el Huallaga," *QueHacer*, no. 48 (September–October 1987), p. 67.

21. Commented a coca-plantation employee to a Lima journalist: "From [the day the SL came] our salaries went up, and there aren't so many abuses. The Senderistas come every week and ask the townspeople how they are being treated by the growers, if there have been abuses, what problems we have" (interview reproduced by Gabriela Tarazona-Sevillano, *Threat*, p. 124).

22. Nazih Richani, *Systems of Violence*, pp. 99, 110.

23. Quoted in Barnett R. Rubin, *The Fragmentation of Afghanistan* (New Haven, CT: Yale University Press, 1995), p. 245.

24. LaMond Tullis, *Unintended Consequences*, p. 22; and Cyrus Ernesto Zirakzadeh, *Social Movements in Politics: A Comparative Study* (New York: Longman,

1997), p. 213. Sendero Luminoso also provided a system of law and order, even if a brutal one, that was previously missing.

25. Nazih Richani, *Systems of Violence*, p. 89. The FARC also supplied the provision of social services by blackmailing major international companies and forcing them to invest in local schools, vocational training, etc. According to a survey by Edgardo Buscaglia of 1,500 individuals concerning informal institutions in Colombia's war zones, 68 percent of the sample population used health services established by the FARC and many also used mediation services provided by the FARC. At the same time, 91 percent of the population perceived municipal authorities as corrupt and 67 percent viewed local officials as incompetent in the provision of public services (Buscaglia & Ratliff, *War and Lack of Governance*, pp. 8–9). The FARC has also taken over other roles of the state by dispensing justice and stipulating laws regarding the carrying of arms, fishing, hunting, working hours, liquor consumption, prostitution, drug abuse, and cutting of trees; see also James Dao, "The War on Terrorism Takes Aim at Crime," *New York Times*, 7 April 2002.

26. Ricardo Vargas Meza, ed., *Drogas, Poder y Region en Colombia*, Volumes 1 and 2 (Bogota: CINEP, 1994).

27. Please see the chapter on Hamas by Matthew Levitt in Volume 1 of this publication.

28. Clutterbuck, *Drugs, Crime*, p. 24. The remoteness and inaccessibility of the territory where cover could be found in Vietnam-like savannahs was apparently one of the major reasons why the SL attempted to build a support base there.

29. Sendero Luminoso justified its participation in the drug trade, despite its anti-Marxist character, by explaining that the narcotics are destined for the United States, and hence contribute to the corrosion and demoralization of "Yankee imperialists" (Gabriela Terrazona-Sevillano, *Threat*, p. 118).

30. The MRTA was created in late 1983 as an armed Marxist alternative to the Shining Path. A follower of Che Guevara's "foco-strategy," the MRTA often operated through "Robin Hood" tactics, such as stealing food trucks and distributing the food to the poor, and attacking symbols of capitalism.

31. James Anderson, *Sendero Luminoso: A New Revolutionary Model?* (London: Institute for the Study of Terrorism, 1987), p. 1.

32. Sendero Luminoso apparently persuaded some farmers that the MRTA had betrayed them by pacting with the *narcos* on the prices (Cynthia McClintock, *Revolutionary Movements*, p. 138). The drug traffickers, at least for a time, helped Sendero Luminoso against the MRTA by providing it with men and arms. The drug dealers apparently resented the fact that the MRTA tried to not only tax the peasants but also control the processing stage of the coca industry, and thus threatened the interests of the *narcos* (Raul Gonzales, "Coca y Subversion," p. 69). Ironically, once the MRTA was out of the picture and the group did not face a competitor, it apparently also tried to get involved with the cocaine-processing part of the cycle, thus threatening the turf of the *narcos*.

33. Presentation by Jose Olarte (mayor of Calamar, Guaviare) at Georgetown University and National Endowment for Democracy Conference on "Local Gov-

ernment Amidst the Armed Conflict: The Experience of Colombian Mayors," Georgetown University, Washington, DC, 27 September 2000 (quoted in Angel Rabasa and Peter Chalk, *Colombian Labyrinth: The Synergy of Drugs and Insurgency and its Implications for Regional Stability* [Santa Monica: RAND, 2001], p. 26).

34. The policy of protecting coca production, taxing the *narcos*, and recruiting people in the lower end of the drug business was laid out formally in the unpublished "Conclusions" of the FARC's Seventh Conference (quoted in Angel Rabasa and Peter Chalk, *Colombian Labyrinth*, p. 26).

35. Mark Chernick, "Negotiating Peace," p. 166. The FARC's overall taxation system is progressive, and the poor peasants are exempted from at least some taxation (see also Nazih Richani, *Systems of Violence*, p. 70).

36. It is important to note that the Colombian drug dealers have an intimate relationship not only with the insurgents, but also with many Colombian politicians and members of the armed forces and corruption of the political system and the military is very high in Colombia.

37. Nazih Richani, *Systems of Violence*, p. 112.

38. Jenny Pearce, *Colombia: Inside the Labyrinth* (London: Latin American Bureau, 1990), p. 247.

39. Barnett Rubin, "The Political Economy of War and Peace in Afghanistan," http://institute-for-afghan-studies.org/ECONOMY/political_economy_of_war_peace.htm.

40. Barnett Rubin, *Fragmentation of Afghanistan*, p. 263.

41. Phil Stewart, "Colombia Trumpets UN Study Showing Record Drop in Coca," *Boston Globe*, 18 March 2003; United States, Office of National Drug Control Policy, "Pulse Check: Trends in Drug Abuse, January 2004" (Washington: ONDCP), http://www.whitehousedrugpolicy.gov/publications/drugfact/pulsechk/january04/index.html.

42. Interview with U.S. government officials, September 2004.

43. Scott B. MacDonald, "Afghanistan," in *International Handbook on Drug Control*, edited by Scott B. MacDonald and Bruce Zagaris (Westport: Greenwood Press, 1992), p. 317.

44. Interview with U.S. government officials, August 2004 and October 2004; see also Howard W. French, "A Corner of China in the Grip of a Lucrative Heroin Habit," *New York Times*, 23 December 2004.

45. The military was dispatched to the area after 1982, when the state of emergency was declared.

46. It is important to recognize that although the drug economy does provide peasants with means of subsistence, its illicitness also results in serious negative consequences for the overall economy of the country due to its effects on inflation and exchange rates among others. For a detailed analysis, see Mauricio Reina, "Drug Trafficking and the National Economy," in *Violence in Colombia 1990–2000: Waging War and Negotiating Peace*, edited by Charles Bergquist, Ricardo Peñaranda, and Gonzalo Sánchez (Wilmington: A Scholarly Resources Inc. Imprint, 2001), pp. 75–94.

47. Jose E. Gonzales, "Guerrillas and Coca in the Upper Huallaga Valley," in *Shining Path of Peru*, edited by David Scott Palmer (New York: St. Martin's Press, 1994), p. 125. The *narcos* also took advantage of the government's acquiescence and started a campaign of terror that terrified the local populace. They also started paying the *cocalero* farmers smaller prices. Both lower prices and the increased terror alienated the populace from Sendero Luminoso and the *narcos* and motivated it to support the military and provide it with intelligence. Thus, even though Carbajal's policy ultimately resulted in some negative externalities for the local populace, it was effective against the guerrillas. Sendero Luminoso operated in the UHV since 1983, undertaking some military activity in 1984. Carbajal managed to push the guerrillas out of the Upper Huallaga Valley, but SL returned in 1985 when a strong anti-narcotics policy was undertaken, and consolidated its control over the Valley by 1986.

48. Jose Gonzales, "Guerrillas and Coca," pp. 126–28.

49. Gabriela Tarazona-Sevillano further maintains that the hostility of the peasants was so large that the police soon found themselves outgunned and outmanned by the insurgency (*Threat*, Tarazona-Sevillano, p. 129). The *dirty war* was the government's counterinsurgency policy that indiscriminately killed civilians suspecting of sympathizing with the insurgents.

50. Raul Gonzales, "Las armas de un general," *QueHacer* 62 (December 1989–January 1990), pp. 38–43. Even under Arciniega's rule, however, there were allegations that the army still carried out human rights abuses and harassed the peasants, and that the number of disappearances increased.

51. Jose Gonzales, "Guerrillas and Coca," pp. 135–36; see also Melvyn Levitsky, Testimony of the Director of the Bureau of International Narcotics Matters, U.S. Department of State. Hearings of U.S. Senate, Committee on Governmental Affairs, Permanent Subcommittee on Investigation, 26–29 September. 101st Congress, 1st session (Washington, DC: U.S. Government Printing Office, 1989). The extent of his corruption is questionable. It is true that Belaunde's and Garcia's governments, as well as the military, were extraordinarily corrupt. Some authors, such as David Scott Palmer, for example, have suggested that given the economic crisis, General Arciniega was forced to rely, to a significant extent, on the drug money to finance his military opposition (David Scott Palmer, "Peru, the Drug Business," p. 71). It is also true, however, that it was the standard practice in Peru to accuse one's political enemies of drug corruption, and the police regularly used this method in its turf wars with the military.

52. In a revealing statement, a coca grower from UHV declared: "We are very disappointed, because we thought we had governmental and military support, but now we are thinking it was only Arniciega who understood us and had the courage to live among us." Jose Gonzales, "Guerrillas and Coca," p. 136.

53. The capture of Guzman shattered his image as invincible god, reduced the decision making capacity of the remaining Sendero Luminoso members (since the group was strictly hierarchically organized around Guzman), and secured further important intelligence on the remaining top echelons of the group. See for example, Cynthia McClintock, *Revolutionary Movements*, pp. 90–91.

Chapter 13: Terrorism and Export Economies

1. Lisa Anderson, "Shock and Awe: Interpretations and Events of September 11," *World Politics* 56 (January 2004): 304.

2. Ivo H. Daalder and James M. Lindsay, "Nasty, Brutish, and Long: America's War on Terrorism," *Current History* (December 2001): 403–8; and James D. Wolfensohn, "Making the World a Better and Safer Place: The Time for Action Is Now," *Politics* 22, no. 2 (2002): 118–23.

3. Samuel P. Huntington, "The Age of Muslim Wars," *Newsweek*, 17 December 2001, pp. 42–48.

4. Norman Angell, *The Great Illusion: A Study of the Relation of Military Power in Nations to Their Economic and Social Advantage*, 3rd ed. (New York: Putnam, 1911).

5. Richard Rosecrance, *The Rise of the Trading State: Commerce and Conquest in the Modern World* (New York: Basic Books, 1986).

6. Kenneth N. Waltz, *Theory of International Politics* (New York: McGraw-Hill, 1979).

7. Hans Morgenthau, *Politics Among Nations: The Struggle for Power and Peace*, 6th ed. (New York: Knopf, 1985 [1948]).

8. Kenneth N. Waltz, *Theory of International Politics*, 1979; Geoffrey Blainey, *The Causes of War* (New York: The Free Press, 1988).

9. Katherine Barbieri, "Economic Interdependence: A Path to Peace or a Source of Conflict?" *Journal of Peace Research* 33, no. 1 (1996): 29–49.

10. Bruce Russett and John R. Oneal, *Triangulating Peace: Democracy, Interdependence, and International Organizations* (New York: W. W. Norton, 2001); Kristian Skrede Gleditsch, "Expanded Trade and GDP Data," *Journal of Conflict Resolution* 46, no. 5 (2002): 712–25; and Michael Mousseau, Håvard Hegre, and John R. Oneal, "How the Wealth of Nations Conditions the Liberal Peace," *European Journal of International Relations* 9, no. 2 (2003): 277–314.

11. Jack S. Levy and Katherine Barbieri, "Sleeping with the Enemy: The Impact of War on Trade," *Journal of Peace Research* 36, no. 4 (1999): 463–79.

12. Alan S. Milward, *War, Economy and Society: 1939–1945* (Berkeley, CA: University of California Press, 1977); Jeffrey L. Hughes, "The Origins of World War II in Europe: British Deterrence Failure and German Expansionism," in *The Origin and Prevention of Major Wars*, edited by Robert I. Rotberg and Theodore K. Rabb (Cambridge: Cambridge University Press, 1989), pp. 281–321.

13. Marshall D. Sahlins, *Stone Age Economics* (Hawthorne: Aldine de Gruyter, 1972); and Colin A. M. Duncan and David W. Tandy, eds., *From Political Economy to Anthropology: Duncan Situating Economic Life in Past Societies* (London: Black Rose, 1994).

14. Emile Durkheim, *The Division of Labor in Society*, translated by George Simpson (Glencoe, IL: Free Press, 1933[1893]); Karl Polanyi, *The Great Transformation: The Political and Economic Origins of Our Time* (Boston: Beacon, 1957 [1944]); Joseph Schumpeter, *Imperialism/Social Classes: Two Essay by Joseph*

Shcumpeter, translated by Heinz Norden (Cleveland: World, 1968 [1919]); and Max Weber, *Economy and Society: An Outline of Interpretive Sociology*, edited by Guenther Roth and Claus Wittich, translated by Ephraim Fischoff (Berkeley, CA: University of California Press, 1978).

15. Marshall D. Sahlins, *Stone Age Economics*, 1972.

16. Herbert Simon, "A Behavioral Model of Rational Choice," *The Quarterly Journal of Economics* 69, no. 1 (1955): 99–118.

17. Michael Mousseau, "Market Prosperity, Democratic Consolidation, and Democratic Peace," *Journal of Conflict Resolution* 44, no. 4 (2000): 478–80; and Michael Mousseau, "Globalization, Markets, and Democracy: An Anthropological Linkage," in *Globalization and Civilizations*, edited by Mehdi Mozaffari (London: Routledge, 2002), pp. 97–124.

18. Michael Mousseau, "Market Prosperity," 2000; Michael Mousseau, "Comparing New Theory with Prior Beliefs: Market Civilization and the Democratic Peace," in *Conflict Management and Peace Science* (forthcoming, 2005); and Michael Mousseau, Håvard Hegre, and John R. Oneal, "How the Wealth of Nations Conditions the Liberal Peace."

19. Karl Polanyi, *The Great Transformation*; Fernand Braudel, *Afterthoughts on Material Civilization and Capitalism*, translated Patricia Ranum (Baltimore: Johns Hopkins University Press, 1979); Janet L. Abu-Lughod, *Before European Hegemony: The World System, A.D. 1250–1350* (New York: Oxford University Press, 1989).

20. Maxine L. Margolis, "Introduction to the Updated Edition," in *The Rise of Anthropological Theory: A History of Theories of Culture*, edited by Marvin Harris, updated ed. (Walnut Creek, CA: AltaMira Press, 2001), pp. vii–xii.

21. Geert Hofstede, *Culture's Consequences: Comparing Values, Behaviors, Institutions, and Organizations across Nations*, 2nd ed. (Thousand Oaks, CA: Sage, 2001 [1980]); and Ronald Inglehart and Wayne E. Baker, "Modernization, Cultural Change, and the Persistence of Traditional Values," *American Sociological Review* 65, no. 1 (2000): 19–52.

22. Ross E. Burkhart and Michael S. Lewis-Beck, "Comparative Democracy: The Economic Development Thesis," *American Political Science Review* 88, no. 4 (1994): 111–31; and Carles Boix and Susan C. Stokes, "Endogenous Democratization," *World Politics* 55, no. 4 (2003): 517–50.

23. Gabriel A. Almond and Sidney Verba, *The Civic Culture: Political Attitudes and Democracy in Five Nations* (Princeton, NJ: Princeton University Press, 1963); and Seymour Martin Lipset, "Some Social Requisites of Democracy: Economic Development and Political Legitimacy," *American Political Science Review* 53, no. 1 (1959): 69–105.

24. Rondo Cameron, *A Concise Economic History of the World: From Paleolithic Times to the Present*, 3rd ed. (New York: Oxford University Press, 1977).

25. Janet L. Abu-Lughod, *Before European Hegemony: The World System, A.D. 1250–1350* (New York: Oxford University Press, 1989), pp. 212–47.

26. Ibid., pp. 115–20.

27. Ibid., p. 115.

28. Lauro Martines, *Power and Imagination: City-States In Renaissance Italy* (New York: Vintage Books, 1979).

29. Fernand Braudel, *Afterthoughts on Material Civilization and Capitalism*, pp. 26–81.

30. Gordon S. Wood, *The Creation of the American Republic, 1776–1787* (Chapel Hill: University of North Carolina Press, 1998).

31. Lisa Anderson, "Shock and Awe," p. 305.

32. Michael Mousseau, "The Sources of Terrorism," *International Security* 28, no. 2 (2003): 196–98.

33. Steeped in the English school, Western analysts claim, after the fact, that al Qaeda targeting of the World Bank and the International Monetary Fund shows that al Qaeda seeks to disrupt the U.S. economy (see, for example, Don Van Natta Jr. and Leslie Wayne, "Threats and Responses," *New York Times*, 2 August 2004). However, this view assumes that the leaders of al Qaeda think in terms of liberal rationality like Western analysts do. In fact, deeply embedded in the norms of reciprocity, the leaders of al Qaeda probably have very little understanding of liberal economics. Given that Western analysts themselves are not sure of how the targeting of buildings that house financial markets will impact the economy, it is most likely that the leaders of al Qaeda have given little or no thought of the economic impacts of their targets.

34. Ted Robert Gurr, Keith Jaggers, and Will H. Moore, "The Transformation of the Western State: The Growth of Democracy, Autocracy, and State Power Since 1800," *Studies in Comparative International Development* 25 (1990): 73–108.

35. Lisa Anderson, "Shock and Awe," p. 305.

Chapter 14: Terrorism, Interdependence, and Democracy

1. For a detailed analysis of Islamic traditions and concepts related to jihad, please see the chapter by Jarret Brachman in Volume I of this publication.

2. Benjamin R. Barber, *Jihad vs. McWorld* (New York: Times Books, 1995).

3. Benjamin R. Barber, *Fear's Empire: War, Terrorism and Democracy* (New York: W. W. Norton, 2004).

4. See Benjamin R. Barber, *Jihad vs. McWorld*.

5. For example, see the chapter by Matthew Levitt on Hamas and social underpinnings of terrorism, in Volume I of this publication.

6. Please see the chapter by Mohammed Hafez on repressive governments in the Muslim World, in this volume.

7. Please see the chapter by Susanna Pearce in this volume, and the chapters by Maha Azzam, James Aho, and Allan Brownfeld in Volume I of this publication.

8. See http://www.e-alliance.ch/wsf.jsp.

9. See http://www.jubilee2000uk.org and http://www.un.org/millenniumgoals.

10. See www.civworld.org for details.

Chapter 15: Human Security and Good Governance

1. This quote is believed to be attributed to Chief Seattle, but there is some disagreement about its exact origin.

2. Stephen M. Walt, "International Relations: One World, Many Theories," *Foreign Policy* (Spring 1998): 1, http://proquest.umi.com (accessed on 21 July 2003) as first cited in Cindy R. Jebb, *Bridging the Gap: Ethnicity, Legitimacy and State Alignment in the International System* (Lanham: Lexington Books, 2004), p. 242.

3. United Nations Development Program (UNDP) Report, 1994, 3, 22–23 as quoted by Peter H. Liotta, *The Uncertain Future* (Lanham: Lexington Books, 2003), pp. 4–5.

4. "A Human Security Doctrine for Europe," The Barcelona Report of the Study Group on Europe's Security Capabilities, 15 September 2004, p. 9.

5. Fritjof Capra, *The Web of Life: A New Scientific Understanding of Living Systems* (New York: Anchor Books Doubleday, 1996), pp. 104, 158, 160, 209. Capra refines his universal living-systems theory as he integrates the social and human domains of a living system inherit to a human system. He adds the criterion of meaning.

6. Fritjof Capra, *The Hidden Connections: Integrating the Biological, Cognitive, and Social Dimensions of Life into a Science of Sustainability* (New York: Doubleday, 2002), p. 81.

7. Ibid., p. 35.

8. Fritjof Capra, *The Web of Life*, p. 158; and Fritjof Capra, *The Hidden Connections*, pp. 70–71.

9. Fritjof Capra, *The Hidden Connections*, pp. 70–71; and Fritjof Capra, *The Web of Life*, p. 162.

10. Fritjof Capra, *The Web of Life*, p. 168.

11. Fritjof Capra, *The Hidden Connections*, p. 219.

12. Fritjof Capra, *The Hidden Connections*, pp. 71–72; and Fritjof Capra, *The Web of Life*, pp. 158, 168–72.

13. Fritjof Capra, *The Hidden Connections*, pp. 13, 71–72; and Fritjof Capra, *The Web of Life*, p. 169.

14. Fritjof Capra, *The Web of Life*, pp. 172, 192–93.

15. Humberto R. Maturana and Francisco J. Varela, *The Tree of Knowledge: The Biological Roots of Human Understanding* (Boston: Shambhala, 1998) pp. 75, 99; and Fritjof Capra, *The Hidden Connections*, p. 36.

16. Fritjof Capra, *The Hidden Connections*, pp. 10, 35, 100; Fritjof Capra, *The Web of Life*, pp. 219–20; and Humberto Maturana and Francisco Varela, *The Tree of Knowledge*, p. 57.

17. Humberto Maturana and Francisco Varela, *The Tree of Knowledge*, p. 57; Fritjof Capra, *The Hidden Connections*, pp. 10, 35, 100; and Fritjof Capra, *The Web of Life*, pp. 219–20. See also Peter Senge, *The Fifth Discipline* (New York: Currency Doubleday, 1990).

18. Fritjof Capra, *The Hidden Connections*, pp. 10, 35, 100; Fritjof Capra, *The*

Web of Life, pp. 219–20; and Humberto Maturana and Francisco Varela, *The Tree of Knowledge*, p. 57.

19. Fritjof Capra, *The Web of Life*, pp. 172–74.

20. Humberto Maturana and Francisco Varela, *The Tree of Knowledge*, p. 172; and Fritjof Capra, *The Web of Life*, pp. 267–68.

21. Fritjof Capra, *The Web of Life*, p. 267.

22. Fritjof Capra, *The Web of Life*, pp. 267–68.

23. Fritjof Capra, *The Hidden Connections*, pp. 116–19; and Fritjof Capra, *The Web of Life*, p. 228.

24. Fritjof Capra, *The Hidden Connections*, pp. 35–37; and Fritjof Capra, *The Web of Life*, p. 295.

25. Fritjof Capra, *The Hidden Connections*, p. 73.

26. Fritjof Capra, *The Hidden Connections*, p. 73.

27. Portions of the discussion concerning globalization are taken from Cindy Jebb, *Bridging the Gap*, pp. 242–46.

28. Please see the chapter in this volume by Benjamin Barber, as well as his 1992 article, "Jihad vs. McWorld," *Atlantic Monthly* (March 1992).

29. Hans-Henrik Holm and Georg Sorensen, *Whose World Order? Uneven Globalization and the End of the Cold War* (Boulder, CO: Westview Press, 1995), pp. 6–7.

30. Ibid., p. 5.

31. Jessica T. Mathews, "Power Shift," in *Strategy and Force Planning*, 3rd ed, edited by the Naval War College Strategy and Force Planning Faculty (Newport, RI: Naval War College Press, 2000), pp. 94–95.

32. Jessica Stern, "Will Terrorists Turn to Poison," *Orbis* 37, no. 3 (Summer 1993): 5, http://ehostvgw6.epnet.com (accessed 23 November 2001). In this article Stern primarily addresses biological and chemical weapons.

33. Bruce Hoffman, "Low-Intensity Conflict: Terrorism and Guerilla Warfare in the Coming Decades," in *Terrorism: Roots, Impacts, Responses*, edited by Lance Howard (New York: Praeger, 1992), p. 139.

34. U.S., The White House, *A National Security Strategy for a New Century* (December 1999): 2.

35. Mahmud Faksh explains that the 1990–1991 Gulf crisis exposed the illegitimacy and ineffectiveness of past ideologies based on Marxism, liberalism, and secular nationalism. The resultant ineffective policies "turned Muslims inward in search of indigenous ways of life and governance. This, of course, in the context of these societies could only mean Islamization." These points are discussed in Mahmud Faksh, *The Future of Islam in the Middle East: Fundamentalism in Egypt, Algeria, and Saudi Arabia* (Westport, CT: Praeger, 1997), p. 24.

36. The failure of secular nationalism's institutions and legitimacy, and the following quote is taken from Mark Jurgensmeyer, *Terror in the Mind of God: the Global Rise of Religious Violence* (Berkeley: University of California Press, 2000), p. 24.

37. This idea of terrorism becoming a political movement comes from Bruce Hoffman, "Lecture to the Terrorism Seminar," at West Point, April 2002.

38. Ebere Onwudiwe, "Africa's Other Story," *Current History* 101, no. 655 (May 2002): 225–29.

39. "Special Report: Terrorism in the Horn of Africa," United States Institute of Peace (January 2004): 2.

40. There is much written about the debate of what constitutes terrorism. For our purposes here, terrorist activities "have a political purpose, and they are conducted outside normal political bounds, involving symbolic violence usually perpetrated against innocent victims in order to weaken the bonds between the legitimate government and society" see Cindy Jebb, *Bridging the Gap*, pp. 129–30, for further explanation.

41. Louise Richardson, "Global Rebels: Terrorist Organizations as Trans-National Actors," in *Terrorism and Counterterrorism: Understanding the New Security Environment*, edited by Russell Howard and Reid Sawyer (Guilford, CT: McGraw-Hill, 2002), pp. 69–71.

42. For more on the relationship between failed states and terrorism, please see the chapter in this volume by Erica Chenoweth.

43. Jessica Stern, "The Protean Enemy," *Foreign Affairs* 82(4) (July/August 2003): 28.

44. Ibid., pp. 29 and 32.

45. Foreign Military Studies Office, *Islam and Africa*, Draft of this work forthcoming on the FMSO website: http://fmso.leavenworth.army.mil, pp. 4–62.

46. "Special Report," USIP, p. 2.

47. Ibid., pp. 2–3.

48. Foreign Military Studies Office, *Islam and Africa*, Draft of this work forthcoming on the FMSO website: http://fmso.leavenworth.army.mil, p. 1.

49. Ibid., p. 1.

50. Ibid., pp. 1–2.

51. The efforts of the Combined Joint Task Force in the Horn of Africa illustrate a living-systems approach to combating terrorism with nonlethal means. The task force directly confronts the human insecurities that are facing the nations within the Horn of Africa, and in doing so indirectly combats terrorism, while facilitating good governance. See the longer version of Cindy R. Jebb and Madelfia A. Abb, "Human Security and Good Governance: A Living Systems Approach to Combating Terrorism," Paper presented at International Studies Association National conference, March 2005, Honolulu, Hawaii.

Chapter 16: Terrorism and the State

1. Daniel Chirot and Clark McCauley, *Why not Kill Them All? The Logic of Mass Political Murder and Finding Ways of Avoiding it* (Princeton: Princeton University Press, forthcoming).

2. Carl von Clausewitz, *On War*, edited and translated by Michael Howard & Peter Paret (Princeton: Princeton University Press, 1989), p. 99.

3. Alan Forrest, "*La Patrie en Danger*: The French Revolution and the First *Levee en Masse*," in *The People in Arms: Military Myth and National Mobiliza-*

tion since the French Revolution, edited by Daniel Moran and Arthur Waldron (New York: Cambridge University Press, 2003), pp. 8–32.

4. Benedict R. O'G. Anderson, *Imagined Communities: Reflections on the Origins and Spread of Nationalism* (London and New York: Verso, 1991).

5. John Horne, "Defining the Enemy: War, Law and the *Levee en Masse* from 1870 to 1945," in *The People in Arms*, pp. 100–123.

6. Ibid., p. 113.

7. Robert A. Pape, *Bombing to Win* (Ithaca, NY: Cornell University Press, 1996).

8. John R. C. Arter, *Airpower and the Cult of the Offensive* (Maxwell Air Force Base: Air University Press, 1998), http://64.233.161.104/search?q=cache:tt3l8n NVNKAJ:www.maxwell.af.mil/au/aul/aupress/CADRE_Papers/PDF_Bin/carter.pdf +air+power+Ethiopia+1936&hl=en (accessed 27 December 2004).

9. United States Strategic Bombing Survey, *Summary Report (European War)* (Washington, DC: U.S. Government Printing Office, 1945), http://www.anesi.com/ ussbs02.htm#tbba (accessed 27 December 2004).

10. United States Strategic Bombing Survey, *Summary Report (Pacific War)* (Washington, DC: U.S. Government Printing Office, 1946), http://www.anesi.com/ ussbs01.htm (accessed 27 December 2004).

11. Clemens Brechtelsbauer, "Fur Kaiser und Reich: His Imperial German Majesty's U-boats in WWI" (6. Finale), http://uboat.net/history/wwi/part6.htm (accessed 27 December 2004).

12. U.S. Merchant Marines, "U.S. Merchant Marines in WWII," http://www. usmm.org/ww2.html (accessed 27 December 2004).

13. Terry Hughes and John Costello, *The Battle of the Atlantic* (New York: Dial Press, 1977).

14. Clay Blair, *Silent Victory: The U.S. Submarine War Against Japan* (Philadelphia: J. B. Lippincott, 1975).

15. William McGee, "British Merchant Navy at War: 1939–1945," http://www. british-merchant-navy.co.uk/ (accessed 27 December 2004).

16. Robert A. Pape, *Bombing to Win.*

17. *Physicians for Human Rights*, "Panama: 'Operation Just Cause'—The Human Cost of the U.S. Invasion," 16 December 1990, http://www.phrusa.org/re search/health_effects/humojc.html (accessed 27 December 2004).

18. Robert A. Pape, *Bombing to Win.*

19. *Human Rights Watch*, "Civilian Deaths in the NATO Air Campaign" (February 2000), http://www.hrw.org/reports/2000/nato/Natbm200.htm#P37_987 (accessed 27 December 2004).

20. John Donnelly and Anthony Shadid, "Civilian Toll in U.S. Raids Put at 1,000. Bombing Flaws, Manhunt Cited," *Boston Globe*, 17 February 2002, sec. A1.

21. Brad Knickerbocker, "Who Counts the Civilian Casualties?" *Christian Science Monitor*, 31 March 2004, http://csmonitor.com/2004/0331/p15s01-wogi.html (accessed 27 December 2004).

22. UNICEF, "Iraq Surveys Show 'Humanitarian Emergency,'" *Information Newsline*, 12 August 1999, http://www.unicef.org/newsline/99pr29.htm (accessed 27 December 2004).

23. Rudolph J. Rummel, *Death by Government* (New Brunswick, NJ: Transaction, 1996).

24. Daniel Chirot and Clark McCauley, *Why not Kill Them All?*

25. Martin van Crevald, *The Transformation of War* (New York: Free Press, 1991).

26. Thomas X. Hammes, *The Sling and the Stone: On War in the 21st Century* (St. Paul: Zenith Press, 2004).

27. Ibid.

28. Arthur Waldron, "From Jaures to Mao: The *Levee en Masse* in China," in *The People in Arms* pp. 189–207.

29. League of Researchers of South African Historical Battlefields, "The Centenary of the Anglo-Boer War, 1899–1902" (Pretoria: League of Researches of South African Historical Battlefields, 1996), http://www.icon.co.za/~dup42/abw.htm (accessed 27 December 2004).

30. Martha Crenshaw, "How Terrorism Declines," in *Terrorism Research and Public Policy*, edited by Clark McCauley (London: Frank Cass, 1991), pp. 69–87.

31. Clark McCauley, "Terrorism Research and Public Policy: An Overview," in *Terrorism Research and Public Policy*, edited by Clark McCauley (London: Frank Cass, 1991), pp. 126–44.

32. For more on the relationship between state repression and violence, please see the chapters in this volume by Audrey Cronin and Mohammed Hafez.

33. Robert A. Altemeyer, *Right-Wing Authoritarianism* (Winnipeg: University of Manitoba Press, 1981).

34. Clark McCauley, "Psychological Issues in Understanding Terrorism and the Response to Terrorism," in *Psychology of Terrorism*, Volume III, *Theoretical Understandings and Perspectives*, edited by Christopher Stout (Westport: Praeger, 2002), pp. 3–30.

35. Thomas X. Hammes, *The Sling and the Stone*, p. 47.

36. Ibid., pp. 84–85.

37. *Al Jazeera*, full transcript of Bin Laden's speech, 1 November 2004, http://english.aljazeera.net/NR/exeres/79C6AF22-98FB-4A1C-B21F-2BC36E87F61F.htm (accessed 27 December 2004).

Chapter 17: Digging Deep

1. Marc Sageman, *Understanding Terror Networks*, Foreign Policy Research Institute (1 November 2004). Sageman based his conclusions on a review of biographical information available on 400 terrorists.

2. For a visual representation of this, please see the "Earthlights" image developed by NASA, available online at http://antwrp.gsfc.nasa.gov/apod/ap001127.html.

3. For an in-depth examination of the Soviet biological weapons program, one of the best available sources is Ken Alibek's *Biohazard* (New York: Random House, 1999).

4. Based on lecture notes and drawn from discussions with Professor Arthur

Waldron, the University of Pennsylvania. The "engineering" approach bears remarkable similarity with the thought process and implementation of the Bottom-Up Review as well as the 1997 and 2001 Quadrennial Defense Reviews.

5. Roger Trinquier, *Modern Warfare: A French View of Counterinsurgency* (Fort Leavenworth, KS: Combat Studies Institute), available online at http://www-cgsc.army.mil/carl/resources/csi/trinquier/trinquier.asp.

6. Quoted by Joe Klein in "Closework," *New Yorker*, 1 October 2001, p. 45.

7. See for example, "Water Scarcity In The Middle East: Regional Cooperation as a Mechanism Toward Peace." Hearing before the House Of Representatives Committee on International Relations, 5 May 2004 (93–528PDF, Serial No. 108–118), online at http://www.house.gov/international—relations; and the World Bank's Middle East and North Africa Water Initiative, online at http://lnweb18.worldbank.org/mna/mena.nsf/Attachments/RWISpring02/$File/RWINewsletterSpring02.pdf.

8. National Intelligence Council, *Global Trends 2015: A Dialogue about the Future with Non-Governmental Experts* (Washington, DC: Central Intelligence Agency, 2000). Online at http://www.cia.gov/cia/reports/globaltrends2015/.

9. Erla Swingle, "Megacities," *National Geographic Magazine* (November 2002).

10. United Nations Population Division, *World Urbanization Prospects: The 2001 Revision* (New York: United Nations). Online at http://www.un.org/esa/population/publications/wup2001/WUP2001report.htm.

11. These figures are compiled from National Intelligence Council, *Global Trends 2015* (2000); Erla Swingle, "Megacities," 2002; and United Nations Population Division, *World Urbanization Prospects* (2001).

12. These figures are compiled from National Intelligence Council, *Global Trends 2015* (2000); Erla Swingle, "Megacities," 2002; and United Nations Population Division, *World Urbanization Prospects* (2001).

13. Richard J. Norton, "Feral Cities," *Naval War College Review* vol. 56 (August 2003): 132–50.

14. Robert Kaplan, "The Coming Anarchy," *Atlantic Monthly* vol. 273 (February 1994): 44–75.

15. For example, see "Terrorist and Organized Crime Groups in the Tri-Border Area (TBA) of South America," a July 2003 report prepared by the Federal Research Division, Library of Congress under an Interagency Agreement with the Director of Central Intelligence Crime and Narcotics Center, online at http://www.loc.gov/rr/frd/pdf-files/TerrOrgCrime_TBA.pdf; also see Jihad Watch, "Terror's South American Front," www.jihadwatch.org/archives/001217.php.

16. Jonathan Lash, "The Johannesburg Summit," *Ideas Into Action* (September 2002). Online at http://ideas.wri.org/success_stories.cfm?ContentID=371.

17. National Commission on Terrorists Attacks Upon the United States (the 9/11 Commission), *The 9/11 Commission Report* (New York: W. W. Norton, 2004).

18. Douglas S. Way, "Targeting Terrorists: Can GIS Lead the Attack?" Online at http://www.geoplace.com/gw/2003/0310_gw/0310cvr.asp.

19. Andres Oppenheimer, 12 March 2003, *San Diego Union-Tribune*, as cited in Douglas S. Way, "Targeting Terrorists."

Chapter 18: Dealing with the Roots of Terror

1. Portions of this chapter will also appear in the conclusion to Karin von Hippel, ed., *Europe Confronts Terrorism* (New York: Palgrave Macmillan, 2005).

2. Al Qaeda has increasingly been defined in these terms. For example, see Marc Sageman, *Understanding Terror Networks* (University of Pennsylvania Press, 2004). Also, see the March 31, 2003 testimony of Magnus Ranstorp to the National Commission or Terrorist Attacks upon the U.S. (9/11 Commission).

3. See http://www.europa.eu.int for more information. The OECD-DAC Secretariat has also been at the forefront for exploring potential root causes and their implications for development cooperation; see the OECD's most recent report, "A Development Co-operation Lens on Terrorism Prevention: Key Entry Points for Action," 11 April 2003, DCD/DAC(2003)11/REV1; and see also the UN publication, "Annex, Report of the Policy Working Group on the United Nations and Terrorism," A/57/273, S/2002/875.

4. U.S., The White House, *National Strategy for Combating Terrorism*, February 2003; online at http://www.whitehouse.gov/news/releases/2003/02/counter_terrorism/counter_terrorism_strategy.pdf.

5. Ibid., p. 23.

6. Ibid.

7. For more on this topic, please see the chapter by Ruth M. Beitler in this volume.

8. Alan B. Krueger and Jitka Maleckova, "Education, Poverty, Political Violence and Terrorism: Is There a Causal Connection?" Working Papers, Research Program in Development Studies, Woodrow Wilson School, Princeton University (May 2002).

9. Nasra Hassan, "An Arsenal of Believers," *New Yorker*, 19 November 2001, pp. 36–41.

10. Jessica Stern, "Pakistan's Jihad Culture," *Foreign Affairs* (November/December 2000).

11. See Jessica Stern, "Meeting with the Muj," *Bulletin of the Atomic Scientists* 57, no. 1 (January/February 2001): 42–51.

12. As noted in Brigid Smith, "Review of Primary Education in Pakistan During Last 10 Years; Madrassah Schooling: Potential for Growth," Consultancy to European Commission: Pakistan, ARCADIS BMB and EUROCONSULT, Pakistan, April 2002, p. 8, paragraph VI; see also "Pakistan: Madrasas, Extremism and the Military," *ICG Asia Report 36*, International Crisis Group, Brussels, 29 July 2002.

13. See Febe Armanios, "Islamic Religious Schools, Madrasas: Background," Report for Congress (Washington: Congressional Research Service, October 2003), p. 6.

14. See Bradley Graham, "The Bush Record: Missile Defense Interceptor System

Set, But Doubts Remain Network Hasn't Undergone Realistic Testing," *The Washington Post*, 29 September 2004, p. A01.

15. See George Packer, "A Democratic World," *New Yorker*, 16 and 23 February 2004, pp. 100–108.

16. Ibid., pp. 107–8.

17. Armanios, p. 4.

18. Ibid.; see also Uzma Anzar, "Islamic Education: A Brief History of Madrassas with Comments on Curricula and Current Pedagogical Practices," Washington: World Bank (March 2003).

19. David Shinn, "Fighting Terrorism in East Africa and the Horn," *Foreign Service Journal* (September 2004), p. 42.

20. See, for example, "Banks-to-Terror Conglomerate Faces U.S. Wrath," *The Daily Telegraph* (London), 28 September 2001. This article claimed that "between 3,000 and 5,000 members of the al Qa'eda and al-Itihad partnership are operating [in Somalia], with 50,000 to 60,000 supporters and reservists."

21. For more on the relationship between failed states and global terrorism, please see the chapter by Erica Chenoweth in this volume.

22. For more information, see Ken Menkhaus, "Somalia: Next Up in the War on Terrorism?" *CSIS Africa Notes*, 6 (January 2002); Andre Le Sage, "Prospects for Al Itihad and Islamist Radicalism in Somalia," *Review of African Political Economy* 27, no. 89 (September 2001); "Somalia and the 'War' on Terrorism," *Strategic Comments* 8, no. 1 (January 2002); and Karin von Hippel, "Terrorist Space," *World Today* (February 2002).

23. *National Strategy for Combating Terrorism*, p. 23.

24. For financial contributions to Somalia, see http://www.sacb.info.

25. For more on the role of ideology and terrorist recruitment, please see the chapters by Maha Azzam, Jarret Brachman, and Leonard Weinberg in Volume I, and the chapter by Susanna Pearce in this volume.

26. For a detailed analysis of the Bosnian mujahideen, please see the chapter by Evan Kohlmann in Volume 2 of this publication.

27. As cited in Lawrence Wright, "The Man Behind Bin Laden: How an Egyptian Doctor Became a Master of Terror," *New Yorker*, 16 September 2002, pp. 80–81.

28. Rohan Gunaratna, *Inside Al Qaeda: Global Network of Terror* (New York: Columbia University Press, 2002), p. 6.

29. "Somalia: Countering Terrorism in a Failed State," *ICG Africa Report 45* (23 May 2002), p. 13.

30. See, for example, "Terrorist Financing: Report of an Independent Task Force," sponsored by the Council on Foreign Relations, Maurice R. Greenberg, Chair, William F. Wechsler and Lee S. Wolosky, Project Co-Directors, 2002.

31. From author interviews in Geneva, New York, and East Africa.

32. For more on the innovative recruitment tactics used by extremists and terrorist organizations in Europe and the United States, please see the chapter by Madeleine Gruen in Volume I of this publication.

33. For examples of this literature, please see the chapters by Martha Brill Olcott and by James Forest in Volume 2 of this publication.

34. For an analysis of terrorist recruitment in prisons throughout the United States, please see the chapter by Michael Waller in Volume 1 of this publication.

35. Alison Pargeter, a research fellow at the Centre for Defense Studies, King's College London, is undertaking a research program on this topic.

36. Please see the chapter in this volume by Mohammed Hafez regarding the relationship between political repression and terrorism.

37. Although the term is inappropriate because the anger is also felt by many non-Arabs in other parts of the world.

38. Thomas Friedman, *New York Times*, 23 October 2002.

39. Quoted in James McElvoy, "Light and Verity," *Yale Alumni Magazine* (January/February 2004): 13.

Select Bibliography and Resources for Further Reading

Abbas, Hassan. *Pakistan's Drift into Extremism: Allah, the Army and America's War on Terror*. New York: M. E. Sharpe, 2004.

Abou El-Fadl, Khaled. *Islam and the Challenge of Democracy*. Princeton, NJ: Princeton University Press, 2004.

Advisory Group on Public Diplomacy in the Arab and Muslim World. *Changing Minds, Winning Peace: A New Strategic Direction for U.S. Public Diplomacy in the Arab and Muslim World*. Washington, DC: U.S. Department of State, 2003.

Aho, James. *The Politics of Righteousness: Idaho Christian Patriotism*. Seattle: University of Washington Press, 1990.

Amuzegar, Jahangir. "Iran's Crumbling Revolution." *Foreign Affairs* (January/February 2003).

Anderson, Benedict R. O'G. *Imagined Communities: Reflections on the Origins and Spread of Nationalism*. London and New York: Verso, 1991.

Anderson, James. *Sendero Luminoso: A New Revolutionary Model?* London: Institute for the Study of Terrorism, 1987.

Anderson, Lisa. "Shock and Awe: Interpretations and Events of September 11." *World Politics* 56 (January 2004): 304.

Anonymous. *Imperial Hubris*. Washington, DC: Brassey's, 2004.

Anzar, Uzma. "Islamic Education: A Brief History of Madrasas with Comments on Curricula and Current Pedagogical Practices." Washington: World Bank, 2003.

Appleby, R. Scott. *The Ambivalence of the Sacred: Religion, Violence, and Reconciliation*. Lanham, MD: Rowman and Littlefield Publishers, 2000.

Armanios, Febe. "Islamic Religious Schools, Madrasas: Background." Report for Congress. Washington: Congressional Research Service, 2003.

Armstrong, Karen. *The Battle for God*. New York: Alfred A. Knopf, 2000.

Ayoub, Mahmoud M. "Martyrdom in Christianity and Islam." In *Religious Resurgence: Contemporary Cases in Islam, Christianity, and Judaism*. Edited by Richard T. Antoun and Mary Elaine Hegland. Syracuse, NY: Syracuse University Press, 1987.

Ayubi, Nazih. *Political Islam: Religion and Politics in the Arab World*. New York: Routledge, 1991.

Bar, Shmuel. "The Religious Sources of Islamic Terrorism." *Policy Review* 125 (June/July 2004): 27–37.

Barber, Benjamin R. *Fear's Empire: War, Terrorism and Democracy*. New York: W. W. Norton, 2004.

Barber, Benjamin. "Jihad vs. McWorld." *Atlantic Monthly* (March 1992).

Barber, Benjamin R. *Jihad vs. McWorld*. New York: Times Books, 1995.

Barber, Benjamin R. *A Place For Us: How To Make Society Civil And Democracy Strong*. New York: Hill and Wang/Farrar and Strauss, 1998.

Barber, Benjamin R. *Strong Democracy: Participatory Politics For A New Age*. Berkeley: University of California Press, 1984.

Barber, Benjamin R. "The War of All Against All: Terror and the Politics of Fear." In *War After September 11*. Edited by Verna V. Gehring. Lanham, MD: Rowman and Littlefield Publishers, Inc., 2002.

Beatty, Jack. "The Real Roots of Terror." *Atlantic Monthly* (December 2001).

Benjamin, Daniel, and Steven Simon. *The Age of Sacred Terror*. New York: Random House, 2002.

Bergquist, Charles, Ricardo Peñaranda, and Gonzalo Sánchez, ed. *Violence in Colombia 1990–2000: Waging War and Negotiating Peace*. Wilmington, DE: A Scholarly Resources Inc. Imprint, 2001.

Berlet, Chip, and Matthew N. Lyons. *Right Wing Populism in America*. New York: Guilford, 2000.

Blank, Jonah. "Kashmir: Fundamentalism Takes Root." *Foreign Affairs* 78, no. 2 (November–December 1999).

Brands, H. W. *Into the Labyrinth: The United States and the Middle East 1945–1993*. New York: McGraw-Hill, 1994.

Brownfeld, Allan C. "Religious Zionism: A Growing Impediment To Middle East Peace." *Washington Report on Middle East Affairs* 21, no. 9 (December 2002).

Buscaglia, Edgardo, and William Ratliff. *War and Lack of Governance in Colombia: Narcos, Guerrillas, and U.S. Policy*. Stanford: Hoover Institution on War, Revolution, and Peace, 2001.

Bush, George W. *The National Security Strategy of the United States*. Washington, DC: The White House, 2002.

Capra, Fritjof. *The Hidden Connections: Integrating the Biological, Cognitive, and Social Dimensions of Life into a Science of Sustainability*. New York: Doubleday, 2002.

Capra, Fritjof. *The Web of Life: A New Scientific Understanding of Living Systems*. New York: Anchor Books Doubleday, 1996.

Chernick, Mark. "Negotiating Peace Amid Multiple Forms of Violence." In *Comparative Peace Processes in Latin America*. Edited by Cynthia J. Arson. Washington, DC: Woodrow Wilson Center Press, 1999.

Christison, Kathleen. "Bound by a Frame of Reference, Part II: U.S. Policy and the Palestinians, 1948–1988." *Journal of Palestine Studies* 27 (Spring 1998): 20–34.

Clawson, Patrick L, and Rensselear W. Lee III. *The Andean Cocaine Industry*. New York: St. Martin's Press, 1996.

Clutterbuck, Richard. *Drugs, Crime, and Corruption*. New York: New York University Press, 1995.

Cobb Jr., John B. "Globalization and Security: The Prospects of the Underclass." In *On the Edge of Scarcity: Environment, Resources, Population, Sustainability, and Conflict*. Edited by Michael N. Dobkowski and Isidor Wallimann, pp. 4–15. Syracuse, NY: Syracuse University Press, 2002.

Cody, Edward. "In Angry Waves, the Devout See an Angry God." *Washington Post*. 5 January 2005, p. A1.

Cohen, Stephen P. *The Idea of Pakistan*. Washington, DC: Brookings Institute Press, 2004.

Cordesman, Anthony H. *Saudi Security and the War on Terrorism*. Washington, DC: Center for Strategic and International Studies, 2002.

Cordovez, Diego, and Selig Harrison. *Out of Afghanistan*. New York: Oxford University Press, 1995.

Courbage, Youssef. "Demographic Change in the Arab World: The Impact of Migration, Education and Taxes in Egypt and Morocco." *Middle East Report* 190, no. 24 (1994): 19–22.

Cragin, Kim, and Peter Chalk. *Terrorism and Development: Using Social and Economic Development to Inhibit a Resurgence of Terrorism*. Santa Monica: RAND, 2003.

Crenshaw, Martha. "Questions to be Answered, Research to be Done, Knowledge to be Applied." In *Origins of Terrorism: Psychologies, Ideologies, Theologies, States of Mind*. Edited by Walter Reich, pp. 247–60. Baltimore: Woodrow Wilson Center Press, 1998.

Cronin, Audrey Kurth. "Sources of Contemporary Terrorism." In *Attacking Terrorism: Elements of a Grand Strategy*. Edited by James M. Ludes, pp. 19–45. Washington, DC: Georgetown University Press, 2004.

Daily, Gretchen C., and Paul R. Ehrlich. "Global Change and Human Susceptibility to Disease." *Annual Review of Energy and the Environment* 21 (1996): 125–44.

Daily, Gretchen C., Anne H. Ehrlich, and Paul R. Ehrlich. "Optimum Human Population Size." *Population and Environment* 15 (1994): 469–75.

Dees, Morris. *Gathering Storm: America's Military Threats*. New York: HarperCollins, 1997.

Dekmejian, R. Hrair. *Islam in Revolution: Fundamentalism in the Arab World*. 2nd ed. Syracuse, NY: Syracuse University Press, 1995.

Deng, Francis M. *War of Visions: Conflict of Identities in the Sudan*. Washington, DC: Brookings Institution, 1995.

Diamond, Larry Jay, Marc F. Plattner, and Daniel Brumberg. *Islam and Democracy in the Middle East*. Baltimore, MD: Johns Hopkins University Press, 2003.

Dobratz, Betty A., and Stephanie L. Shanks-Meile. *The White Separatist Movement in the United States: White Power White Pride*. Baltimore: Johns Hopkins University Press, 2000.

Doran, Michael Scott. "Somebody Else's Civil War." *Foreign Affairs* 81 (January/February 2002): 22–42.

Ehrlich, Paul R. *Human Natures: Genes, Cultures, and the Human Prospect*. Washington, DC: Island Press, 2000.

Ehrlich, Paul R., and Jianguo Liu. "Some Roots of Terrorism." *Population and Environment* 23 (2002): 183–92.

Ehrlich, Paul R., Anne H. Ehrlich, and John P. Holdren. *Ecoscience: Population, Resources, Environment*. San Francisco: W. H. Freeman and Co., 1977.

Entelis, John P. *Islam, Democracy and the State in North Africa*. Bloomington: Indiana University Press, 1997.

Esposito, John. *The Islamic Threat: Myth or Reality?* 3rd ed. New York: Oxford University Press, 1999.

Esposito, John L. *Unholy War: Terror in the Name of Islam*. New York: Oxford University Press, 2002.

Esposito, John L., and John O. Voll. *Islam and Democracy*. New York: Oxford University Press, 1996.

Everingham, Susan S., and C. Peter Rydell. *Modeling the Demand for Cocaine*. Santa Monica: RAND, 1994.

Ewans, Martin. *Afghanistan: A Short History of its People and Politics*. New York: HarperCollins, 2002.

Fargues, Philippe. "From Demographic Explosion to Social Rupture." In *Arab Society*. Edited by Nicholas S. Hopkin and Saad E. Ibrahim, 3rd ed., pp. 75–83. Cairo: American University in Cairo Press, 1997.

Freedman, Lawrence, and Efraim Karsh. *The Gulf Conflict 1990–1991*. Princeton, NJ: Princeton University Press, 1993.

French, Hilary. "Reshaping Global Governance." In *State of the World 2002*. Edited by Linda Starke, pp. 175–98. New York: W. W. Norton, 2002.

Gareau, Frederick H. *State Terrorism and the United States: From Counterinsurgency to the War on Terrorism*. Atlanta, GA: Clarity Press, 2004.

Gerges, Fawaz A. *America and Political Islam: Clash of Cultures or Clash of Interests*. New York: Cambridge University Press, 1999.

Goldstone, Jack A. *Revolution and Rebellion in the Early Modern World*. Berkeley: University of California Press, 1991.

Gonzales, Jose E. "Guerrillas and Coca in the Upper Huallaga Valley." In *Shining Path of Peru*. Edited by David Scott Palmer, pp. 123–44. New York: St. Martin's Press, 1994.

Gregory, Brad S. *Salvation at Stake: Christian Martyrdom in Early Modern Europe*. Cambridge, MA: Harvard University Press, 1999.

Gunaratna, Rohan. *Inside Al Qaeda: Global Network of Terror*. New York: Columbia University Press, 2002.

Hafez, Mohammed M. *Why Muslims Rebel: Repression and Resistance in the Islamic World*. Boulder, CO: Lynne Rienner, 2003.

Hammes, Thomas X. *The Sling and the Stone: On War in the 21st Century*. St. Paul: Zenith Press, 2004.

Harmon, Christopher C. *Terrorism Today*. London: Frank Cass, 2000.

Harris, Sam. *The End of Faith: Religion, Terror, and the Future of Reason*. New York: W. W. Norton, 2004.

Hefner, Robert W. *Civil Islam: Muslims and Democratization in Indonesia*. Princeton, NJ: Princeton University Press, 2000.

Hoffman, Bruce. *Inside Terrorism*. New York: Columbia University Press, 1998.

Hoffman, David. "Beyond Public Diplomacy." *Foreign Affairs* (March/April 2002).

Hofstede, Geert. *Culture's Consequences: Comparing Values, Behaviors, Institutions, and Organizations Across Nations*. 2nd ed. Thousand Oaks, CA: Sage, 2001[1980].

Holdren, J. P. "Population and the Energy Problem." *Population and Environment* 12 (1991): 231–55.

Holm, Hans-Henrik, and Georg Sorensen. *Whose World Order? Uneven Globalization and the End of the Cold War*. Boulder, CO: Westview Press, 1995.

Howard, Russell, James Forest, and Joanne Moore, ed. *Terrorism and Homeland Security*. New York: McGraw-Hill, 2005.

Huntington, Samuel P. *The Clash of Civilizations and the Remaking of World Order*. New York: Simon and Schuster, 1996.

Iannaccone, L. R. "Why Strict Churches Are Strong," *American Journal of Sociology* 99 (1994): 1180–211.

Jenkins, J. Craig, and Doug Bond. "Conflict-Carrying Capacity, Political Crisis, and Reconstruction." *Journal of Conflict Resolution* 45 (2001): 3–31.

Juergensmeyer, Mark. *Terror in the Mind of God: The Global Rise of Religious Violence*. Berkeley: University of California Press, 2000.

Junger, Sebastian. "Terrorism's New Geography." *Vanity Fair* (December 2002): p. 194–206.

Kahn, Herman. *On Escalation: Metaphors and Scenarios*. Baltimore: Penguin, 1968.

Kahn, Herman. *On Thermonuclear War*. Princeton, NJ: Princeton University Press, 1960.

Kamrava, Mehran. "Iranian Shiism under Debate." *Middle East Policy Council Journal* 10, no. 2 (Summer 2003).

Kaplan, Jeffrey, ed. *Millennial Violence: Past, Present and Future*. Portland, OR: Frank Cass, 2002.

Kaplan, Jeffrey, and Leonard Weinberg. *The Emergence of a Euro-American Radical Right*. NJ: Rutgers University Press, 1998.

Karsh, Ephraim. "Intifada II: The Long Trail of Arab Anti-Semitism." *Commentary* (December 2000): 49–53.

Keay, John. *Sowing the Wind: The Seeds of Conflict in the Middle East*. New York: W. W. Norton, 2003.

Kepel, Gilles. *Jihad: The Trail of Political Islam*. Translated by Anthony F. Roberts. Cambridge, MA: Harvard University Press, 2002.

Kepel, Gilles. *The War for Muslim Minds: Islam and the West*. Translated by Pascale Ghazaleh. Cambridge, MA: Harvard University Press, 2004.

Kinzer, Stephen. *All the Shah's Men: An American Coup and the Roots of Middle East Terror*. Hoboken, NJ: John Wiley and Sons, Inc., 2003.

Klare, Michael T. *American Arms Supermarket*. Austin: University of Texas Press, 1984.

Klare, Michael T. *Blood and Oil: The Dangers and Consequences of America's Growing Petroleum Dependency*. New York: Metropolitan Books, 2004.

Klein, Joe. "Closework." *New Yorker*. 1 October 2001.

Kramer, Jane. *Lone Patriot: The Short Career of an American Militiaman*. New York: Pantheon, 2002.

Kramer, Martin, ed. *The Islamism Debate*. Tel Aviv: The Moshe Dayan Center for Middle Eastern and African Studies, 1997.

Kux, Dennis. *The United States and Pakistan 1947–2000: Disenchanted Allies*. Washington, DC: Woodrow Wilson Center Press, 2001.

Laqueur, Walter. "Postmodern Terrorism." *Foreign Affairs* 75, no. 5 (1996): 24–36.

Laqueur, Walter. "The Terrorism to Come." *Policy Review* 126 (August/September 2004): 49–64.

Lewis, Bernard. "License to Kill: Usama bin Ladin's Declaration of Jihad." *Foreign Affairs* (November/December 1998): 14–19.

Lewis, Bernard. "What Went Wrong?" *Atlantic Monthly* (January 2002).

Lewy, Guenter. *Religion and Revolution*. New York: Oxford University Press, 1974.

Lincoln, Bruce. *Holy Terrors: Thinking about Religion after September 11*. Chicago: University of Chicago Press, 2003.

Liotta, Peter H. *The Uncertain Certainty: Human Security, Environmental Change, and the Future Euro-Mediterranean*. Lanham, MD: Lexington Books, 2003.

Liotta, Peter H., and Allan Shearer. *Gaia's Revenge: Climate Change and its Impact on Security*. Westport, CT: Praeger Publishers, forthcoming.

Liotta, Peter H., and James F. Miskel. *The Fevered Crescent: Security and Insecurity in the Greater Near East*. Gainesville: University of Florida Press, forthcoming.

Long, David E. *The United States and Saudi Arabia, Ambivalent Allies*. Boulder, CO: Westview Press, 1985.

MacDonald, Scott B. "Afghanistan." In *International Handbook on Drug Control*. Edited by Scott B. MacDonald and Bruce Zagaris. Westport, CT: Greenwood Press, 1992.

Mack, John E. "Deeper Causes: Exploring the Role of Consciousness in Terrorism" *Ions Noetic Sciences Review* (June–August 2003).

Mahmood, Cynthia Keppley. *Fighting for Faith and Nation: Dialogues with Sikh Militants*. Philadelphia: University of Pennsylvania Press, 1996.

Mansfield, Edward D., and Jack Snyder. "Democratic Transitions and War." In

Turbulent Peace: The Challenges of Managing International Conflict. Edited by Chester Crocker et al., pp. 113–26. Washington, DC: United States Institute of Peace, 2001.

Mansfield, Edward D., and Jack Snyder. *Electing to Fight: Why Emerging Democracies Go to War.* Cambridge, MA: MIT Press, 2004.

Marsella, Anthony J. "Reflections on International Terrorism: Issues, Concepts, and Directions." In *Understanding Terrorism: Psychosocial Roots, Consequences, and Interventions.* Edited by Fathali M. Moghaddam and Anthony J. Marsella, pp. 11–47. Washington, DC: American Psychological Association, 2004.

Marx, Gary T. "Religion: Opiate or Inspiration of Civil Rights Militancy Among Negroes?" *American Sociological Review* 32, no. 1 (1967): 64–72.

Maturana, Humberto R., and Francisco J. Varela. *The Tree of Knowledge: The Biological Roots of Human Understanding.* Boston: Shambhala, 1998.

McCauley, Clark. "Psychological Issues in Understanding Terrorism and the Response to Terrorism." In *Psychology of Terrorism.* Volume 3: *Theoretical Understandings and Perspectives.* Edited by Christopher Stout, pp. 3–30. Westport, CT: Praeger, 2002.

McCauley, Clark, ed. *Terrorism Research and Public Policy.* London: Frank Cass, 1991.

McClintock, Cynthia. *Revolutionary Movements in Latin America: El Salvador's FMLN & Peru's Shining Path.* Washington, DC: United States Institute of Peace Press, 1998.

Merari, Ariel. "The Readiness to Kill and Die: Suicidal Terrorism in the Middle East." In *Origins of Terrorism: Psychologies, Ideologies, Theologies, States of Mind.* Edited by Walter Reich, pp. 192–207. Baltimore, MD: Woodrow Wilson Center Press, 1998.

Michel, Lou, and Dan Herbeck. *American Terrorist: Timothy McVeigh and the Oklahoma City Bombing.* New York: HarperCollins, 2001.

Miller, Aaron Dean. *Search for Security.* Chapel Hill: University of North Carolina Press, 1980.

Miller, John, Michael Stone, and Chris Mitchell. *The Cell.* New York: Hyperion, 2002.

Miller, Mark, and Jason File. *Terrorism Factbook.* Peoria, IL: Bollix Press, 2001.

Mimouni, Rachid. *De La Barbarie En Général Et De L'intégrisme En Particulier.* Paris: Le Pré aux Clercs, 1992.

Mitchell, Richard G. *Dancing at Armageddon: Survivalism and Chaos in Modern Times.* Chicago: University of Chicago Press, 2002.

Moghaddam, Fathali M., and Anthony J. Marsella. *Understanding Terrorism: Psychosocial Roots, Consequences, and Interventions.* Washington, DC: American Psychological Association, 2004.

Molavi, Afshin. "Buying Time in Tehran." *Foreign Affairs* (November/December 2004).

Moran, Daniel, and Arthur Waldron, eds. *The People in Arms: Military Myth and*

National Mobilization since the French Revolution. New York: Cambridge University Press, 2003.

Mousseau, Michael. "Comparing New Theory with Prior Beliefs: Market Civilization and the Democratic Peace." In *Conflict Management and Peace Science,* forthcoming, 2005.

Mousseau, Michael. "Globalization, Markets, and Democracy: An Anthropological Linkage." In *Globalization and Civilizations.* Edited by Mehdi Mozaffari, pp. 97–124. New York: Routledge, 2002.

Mousseau, Michael. "Market Prosperity, Democratic Consolidation, and Democratic Peace." *Journal of Conflict Resolution* 44, no. 4 (2000): 478–80.

Mousseau, Michael. "The Sources of Terrorism." *International Security* 28, no. 2 (2003): 196–98.

Nagle, D. Brendan, and Stanley M. Burstein. *The Ancient World: Readings in Social and Cultural History.* 2nd ed. Upper Saddle River, NJ: Prentice-Hall, 2002.

National Commission on Terrorist Attacks Upon the United States. *The 9/11 Commission Report.* Washington, DC: Government Printing Office, 2004.

Neiwert, David A. *In God's Country: The Patriot Movement and the Pacific Northwest.* Pullman: Washington University Press, 1999.

Obando, Enrique. "Subversion and Anti-Subversion in Peru 1980–2." *Low Intensity Conflict and Law Enforcement* 2, no. 2 (Autumn 1993).

Painter, David S. *Oil and the American Century.* Baltimore, MD: Johns Hopkins University Press, 1986.

Palmer, David Scott. "Peru, the Drug Business and Shining Path: Between Scylla and Charybdis?" *Journal of Interamerican Studies and World Affairs* 34, no. 3 (Special Issue: Drug Trafficking Research Update, Autumn 1992).

Palmer, David Scott. "The Revolutionary Terrorism of Peru's Shining Path." In *Terrorism in Context.* Edited by Martha Crenshaw, pp. 249–308. University Park: The Pennsylvania State University Press, 1995.

Palmer, Michael A. *Guardians of the Gulf.* New York: Free Press, 1992.

Pape, Robert A. *Bombing to Win.* Ithaca, NY: Cornell University Press, 1996.

Pape, Robert A. "The Strategic Logic of Suicide Terrorism." *American Political Science Review* 97, no. 3 (2003): 343–61.

Paris, Roland. *At War's End.* Cambridge: Cambridge University Press, 2004.

Pearce, Jenny. *Colombia: Inside the Labyrinth.* London: Latin American Bureau, 1990.

Peterson, Peter G. "Diplomacy and the War on Terrorism." *Foreign Affairs* 81, no. 5 (2002): 74–96.

Pew Research Center for the People and the Press. *Views of a Changing World.* June 2003. Available online at: http://people-press.org.

Pillar, Paul R. *Terrorism and U.S. Foreign Policy.* 2nd edition. Washington: Brookings Institution Press, 2003.

Pipes, Daniel. "God and Mammon: Does Poverty Cause Militant Islam?" *National Interest* 66 (Winter 2001/2002): 14–21.

Pipes, Daniel. *In the Path of God: Islam and Political Power.* New Brunswick, NJ: Transaction Publishers, 2002.

Pollack, Kenneth M. *The Persian Puzzle.* New York: Random House, 2004.

Rabasa, Angel, and Peter Chalk. *Colombian Labyrinth: The Synergy of Drugs and Insurgency and Its Implications for Regional Stability.* Santa Monica, CA: RAND, 2001.

Randal, Jonathan. *Osama: The Making of a Terrorist.* New York: Alfred A. Knopf, 2004.

Rapoport, David C. "Fear and Trembling: Terrorism in Three Religious Traditions." *American Political Science Review* 78, no. 3 (September 1984): 658–77.

Rapoport, David C. "Terrorism and Weapons of the Apocalypse." *National Security Studies Quarterly* 5, no. 3 (1999): 49-67.

Reich, Walter, ed. *Origins of Terrorism: Psychologies, Ideologies, Theologies, States of Mind.* New York: Cambridge University Press, 1990.

Reina, Mauricio. "Drug Trafficking and the National Economy." In *Violence in Colombia 1990–2000: Waging War and Negotiating Peace.* Edited by Charles Bergquist, Ricardo Peñaranda, and Gonzalo Sánchez. Wilmington, DE: A Scholarly Resources Inc. Imprint, 2001.

Richani, Nazih. *Systems of Violence.* Albany: State University of New York Press, 2002.

Richardson, Louise. "Global Rebels: Terrorist Organizations as Trans-National Actors." In *Terrorism and Counterterrorism: Understanding the New Security Environment.* Edited by Russell Howard and Reid Sawyer. Guilford, CT: McGraw-Hill, 2003.

Roberts, Hugh. "From Radical Mission to Equivocal Ambition: The Expansion and Manipulation of Algerian Islamism, 1979–1992." In *Accounting for Fundamentalism: The Dynamic Character of Movements.* Edited by Martin E. Marty and R. Scott Appleby. Chicago: University of Chicago Press, 1994.

Rosecrance, Richard. *The Rise of the Trading State: Commerce and Conquest in the Modern World.* New York: Basic Books, 1986.

Rotberg, Robert I. "Failed States, Collapsed States, Weak States: Causes and Indicators." In *State Failure and State Weakness in a Time of Terror.* Edited by Robert I. Rotberg, pp. 1–25. Washington, DC: The Brookings Institute, 2003.

Rotberg, Robert I., ed. *When States Fail.* Princeton, NJ: Princeton University Press, 2004.

Roy, Olivier. "America and the New Terrorism: An Exchange." *Survival* 42, no. 2 (Summer 2000).

Rubin, Barnett R. *The Fragmentation of Afghanistan.* New Haven, CT: Yale University Press, 1995.

Rummel, Rudolph J. *Death by Government.* New Brunswick, NJ: Transaction, 1994.

Russett, Bruce, and John R. Oneal. *Triangulating Peace: Democracy, Interdependence, and International Organizations.* New York: W. W. Norton, 2001.

Rydell, C. Peter, and Susan S. Everingham. *Controlling Cocaine: Supply Versus Demand Programs*. Santa Monica, CA: RAND, 1994.

Sageman, Marc. *Understanding Terror Networks*. Philadelphia: University of Pennsylvania Press, 2004.

Saleh, Nivien. "Egypt: Osama's Star Is Rising." *Middle East Policy* 9 (September 2002): 40–44.

Sells, Michael. *The Bridge Betrayed: Religion and Genocide in Bosnia*. Berkeley: University of California Press, 1998.

Sick, Gary. *All Fall Down: America's Tragic Encounter with Iran*. 1st ed. New York: Random House, 1985.

Simon, Steve. "The New Terrorism." *Brookings Review* (Winter 2003): 18–24.

Smith, Brent. *Terrorism in America: Pipe Bombs and Pipe Dreams*. Albany: SUNY Press, 1994.

Stern, Jessica. *Terror in the Name of God: Why Religious Militants Kill*. New York: HarperCollins, 2003.

Stoff, Michael B. *Oil, War, and American Security*. New Haven, CT: Yale University Press, 1980.

Tarazona-Sevillano, Gabriela, with John B. Reuter. *Sendero Luminoso and the Threat of Narcoterrorism*. Washington, DC: Center for Strategic and International Studies, 1990.

Thomas, Scott. "Religion and International Conflict." In *Religion and International Relations*. Edited by K. R. Dark. New York: St. Martin's Press, 2000.

Timmerman, Kenneth R. *Preachers of Hate: Islam and the War on America*. New York: Crown Forum, 2003.

Tucker, Jonathan B., ed. *Toxic Terror: Assessing Terrorist Use of Chemical and Biological Weapons*. Cambridge, MA: MIT Press, 2000.

Tullis, LaMond. *Unintended Consequences: Illegal Drugs and Drug Policies in Nine Countries*. Boulder, CO: Lynne Rienner, 1995.

U.S. Department of State. *2003 Global Terrorism Report*. http://www.state.gov.

U.S. Department of State, Bureau for International Narcotics and Law Enforcement Affairs. *International Narcotics Control Strategy Report*. Washington, DC: U.S. Department of State, 2000.

United Nations (Population Division). *World Population Prospects: The 2000 Revision*. New York: United Nations, 2001.

Van Natta, Don Jr., and Leslie Wayne. "Threats And Responses: Financial Impact; Al Qaeda Seeks to Disrupt U.S. Economy, Experts Warn." *New York Times*. 2 August 2004.

Vargas Meza, Ricardo, ed. *Drogas, Poder y Region en Colombia*. Bogota: CINEP, 1994.

Varshney, Ashutosh. *Ethnic Conflict and Civic Life: Hindus and Muslims in India*. New Haven, CT: Yale University Press, 2002.

Vassiliev, Alexei. *The History of Saudi Arabia*. New York: New York University Press, 2000.

von Clausewitz, Karl Philip Gottlieb. *On War*. Princeton, NJ: Princeton University Press, 1976 (1833).

von Hippel, Karin, ed. *Europe Confronts Terrorism*. New York: Palgrave Macmillan, 2005.

von Hippel, Karin. "The Roots of Terrorism: Probing the Myths." *Political Quarterly* 73, special supplement no. 1 (September 2002): 25–39.

von Hippel, Karin. "Terrorism as a Problem of International Cooperation." In *Terrorism and the UN: Before and After September 11*. Edited by Thomas Weiss and Jane Boulden. Bloomington: Indiana University Press, 2004.

Wagar, W. Warren. *Terminal Visions: The Literature of Last Things*. Bloomington: Indiana University Press, 1982.

Walt, Stephen M. "International Relations: One World, Many Theories." *Foreign Policy* (Spring 1998).

Way, Douglas S. "Targeting Terrorists: Can GIS Lead the Attack?" Online at the Geoplace.com website: http://www.geoplace.com/gw/2003/0310/0310cvr.asp.

Weinberg, Leonard B., and William L. Eubank. "Does Democracy Encourage Terrorism?" *Terrorism and Political Violence* 6, no. 4 (1994): 417–43.

Weinberg, Leonard B., and William L. Eubank. "Terrorism and Democracy: What Recent Events Disclose." *Terrorism and Political Violence* 10, no. 1 (1998): 108–18.

Wickham, Carrie Rosefsky. *Mobilizing Islam: Religion, Activism, and Political Change in Egypt*. New York: Columbia University Press, 2002.

Wiktorowicz, Quintan. *Islamic Activism: A Social Movement Theory Approach*. Bloomington: Indiana University Press, 2004.

Willis, Michael. *The Islamist Challenge in Algeria: A Political History*. Reading, UK: Ithaca Press, 1996.

Wolfensohn, James D. "Making the World a Better and Safer Place: The Time for Action Is Now." *Politics* 22, no. 2 (2002): 118–23.

Yager, Joseph A., and Eleanor B. Steinberg. *Energy and U.S. Foreign Policy*. Cambridge, MA: Ballinger, 1975.

Yergin, Daniel. *The Prize: The Epic Quest for Oil, Money, and Power*. New York: Simon and Schuster, 1991.

Zaharna, R. S. "American Public Diplomacy in the Arab and Muslim World: A Strategic Communication Analysis." *FPIF Policy Report* (November 2001).

Zakaria, Fareed. *The Future of Freedom*. New York: W. W. Norton, 2003.

Index

About the Editor and Contributors

JAMES J. F. FOREST, Ph.D., is Director of Terrorism Studies and Assistant Professor of Political Science at the U.S. Military Academy, where he teaches undergraduate courses in a range of subjects and directs research initiatives for the Combating Terrorism Center. Recent publications include *Homeland Security and Terrorism* (with Russell Howard and Joanne Moore, 2005), *Teaching Terror: Knowledge Transfer in the Terrorist World* (2005), a 200-page *Annotated Bibliography of Terrorism and Counterterrorism* (2004), available online at the Center's website (http://ctc.usma. edu), and *Terrorism and Oil in the New Gulf* (with Matt Sousa, forthcoming). His research has also appeared in the *Cambridge Review of International Affairs*, the *Journal of Political Science Education*, and the *Encyclopedia of Intelligence and Counterintelligence* (2005). Dr. Forest received his graduate degrees from Stanford University and Boston College and undergraduate degrees from Georgetown University and De Anza College.

MADELFIA A. ABB is a Lieutenant Colonel in the U.S. Army and Professor of Military Science at Seton Hall University. Her research explores theories in complexity, chaos, management, and living systems in search for contemporary understanding and application in the realm of organizational learning, leadership, military effectiveness, and operational-strategic planning.

HASSAN ABBAS, a former government official from Pakistan, is a Ph.D. candidate at the Fletcher School of Law and Diplomacy, Tufts University.

He has also remained associated with Harvard Law School, first as a Research Fellow (2002–3) and later as a visiting scholar (2004). His publications include *Pakistan's Drift into Extremism: Allah, the Army and America's War on Terror* (2004).

BENJAMIN R. BARBER, Ph.D., is the Gershon and Carol Kekst Professor of Civil Society and Distinguished University Professor at the University of Maryland. An internationally renowned political theorist, he has published seventeen books, including *Fear's Empire: War, Terrorism and Democracy* (2004); *A Place For Us: How To Make Society Civil And Democracy Strong* (1998); *Jihad vs. McWorld* (1995); and *Strong Democracy: Participatory Politics For A New Age* (1984). He was also a founding editor and for ten years editor-in-chief of the distinguished international quarterly *Political Theory*.

MICHAEL BARKUN, Ph.D., is Professor of Political Science in the Maxwell School at Syracuse University. His ten books include *A Culture of Conspiracy: Apocalyptic Visions in Contemporary America* (2003), *Religion and the Racist Right: The Origins of the Christian Identity Movement*, Revised edition (1997), and *Disaster and the Millennium* (1974). His numerous articles and book chapters deal with terrorism, millennialism, and international law, and he has served as a consultant to the Federal Bureau of Investigation.

RUTH MARGOLIES BEITLER, Ph.D., is an Associate Professor of International Relations and Comparative Politics in the Department of Social Sciences. She is author of *The Path to Mass Rebellion: An Analysis of Two Intifadas* (2004) and numerous articles and chapters on the Middle East, including "Egypt as a Failing State: Implications for U.S. National Security" (with Cindy Jebb, 2003) and "Tactical Deception and Strategic Surprise in Al Qaeda Operations" (with Richard Schultz, *Middle East Review of International Affairs*, 2004).

ERICA CHENOWETH is currently completing her Ph.D. in international relations and public policy at the University of Colorado at Boulder. She has researched and written extensively on topics such as terrorism, state capacity, and international security, and her work has appeared in book chapters and academic conference presentations.

PAUL R. EHRLICH, Ph.D., is Bing Professor of Population Studies at Stanford University. His research deals with a wide variety of topics including the ecology and evolution of natural populations, environmental science, and human ecology, evolution, and behavior. He has published more than 900 scientific papers and popular articles and more than forty books. Ehrlich is a member of the U.S. National Academy of Sciences and has received the Crafoord Prize of the Royal Swedish Academy of Sciences (an explicit substitute for the Nobel Prize in areas in which the latter is not given), a MacArthur Prize Fellowship, and dozens of other prizes and honors.

VANDA FELBAB-BROWN is a Ph.D. candidate in the Security Studies Program of the Political Science Department at MIT, writing her dissertation on the relationship between the production and trafficking of illicit commodities and military conflict. She has authored several book chapters, articles, and conference papers on issue of drugs and conflict. She is the Research Associate for Seminar XXI, Washington, DC.

EUGENIA K. GUILMARTIN, Ph.D., is an Assistant Professor at the United States Military Academy and a Major in the U.S. Army. She has conducted extensive research on American right-wing domestic terrorism, including her doctoral thesis (at Stanford University). She is the author of *Political Bullies* (publication forthcoming).

MOHAMMED M. HAFEZ, Ph.D., is a Visiting Professor in the Department of Political Science at the University of Missouri—Kansas City, where he teaches courses on Terrorism and Political Violence, Religion and Politics, Politics of the Middle East, and Arab-Israeli Conflict. His publications include *Why Muslims Rebel: Repression and Resistance in the Islamic World* (2003), and he has been a Harry Frank Guggenheim Foundation fellow and a United States Information Agency fellow.

CINDY R. JEBB, Ph.D., is a Colonel in the U.S. Army, currently serving as Professor and Director of Comparative Politics and Security Studies in the Department of Social Sciences at the U.S. Military Academy. Colonel Jebb has served in numerous command and staff positions in the United States and overseas, to include a tour as the Deputy Commander of the 704th Military Intelligence Brigade, which supported the National Security Agency. Her published works include *Bridging the Gap: Ethnicity, Legitimacy, and State Alignment in the International System* (2004) and *Mapping Macedonia: Idea and Identity* (with P. H. Liotta).

MICHAEL T. KLARE, Ph.D., is the Five College Professor of Peace and World Security Studies (a joint appointment at Amherst, Hampshire, Mount Holyoke, and Smith Colleges and the University of Massachusetts at Amherst), a position he has occupied since 1985. Klare has written widely on various aspects of U.S. military policy, the international arms trade, human rights, and the relationship between resource competition and international security. His most recent books are *Resource Wars: The New*

Landscape of Global Conflict (2001) and *Blood and Oil: The Dangers and Consequences of America's Growing Petroleum Dependence* (2004).

P. H. LIOTTA, Ph.D., is Tenured Professor of Humanities at Salve Regina University and Executive Director of the Pell Center for International Relations and Public Policy. He has served as a faculty member at the Naval War College, the American College of Athens, and the United States Air Force Academy. His publications include *The Fevered Crescent: Security and Insecurity in the Greater Near East* (with James F. Miskel, forthcoming); *Mapping Macedonia: Idea and Identity* (with Cindy R. Jebb, Praeger, 2004) and *The Uncertain Certainty: Human Security, Environmental Change, and the Future Euro-Mediterranean* (2003).

JIANGUO (JACK) LIU, Ph.D., is Rachel Carson Chair in Ecological Sustainability and Director of the Center for Systems Integration and Sustainability at Michigan State University. He is interested in integrating ecology with other disciplines (e.g., socioeconomics and demography) to address complex issues in coupled human and natural systems. In recognition of his efforts and achievements in research, teaching, and service, Liu has been given a number of awards and honors, including a Career Award from the National Science Foundation and an Aldo Leopold Leadership Fellowship from the Ecological Society of America.

CLARK R. McCAULEY, Ph.D., is Professor of Psychology at Bryn Mawr College and Director of the Solomon Asch Center for Study of Ethnopolitical Conflict at the University of Pennsylvania. He is also a consultant and reviewer for the Harry Frank Guggenheim Foundation for research on dominance, aggression and violence. His published works include *The Psychology of Ethnic and Cultural Conflict* (with colleagues, Praeger, 2004), and *Why not Kill Them All? The Origins of Genocide* (under review, with Dan Chirot).

JAMES F. MISKEL, Ph.D., is Vice President for Policy Studies at Alidade, Inc. in Newport, Rhode Island. He is a former Professor and Associate Dean of Academics at the Naval War College and is widely published on national security issues. He also teaches in the Norwich University master's degree program in Diplomacy and International Relations. His publications include *The Fevered Crescent: Security and Insecurity in the Greater Near East* (with P. Liotta, forthcoming).

MICHAEL MOUSSEAU, Ph.D., is Associate Professor of International Relations at Koç University in Istanbul, Turkey. His research is on the political economy of values and institutions and the implications for conflict within and among nations and has appeared in *Conflict Management and*

Peace Science (2004), *European Journal of International Relations* (2003), *Journal of Peace Research* (1997 and 1999), *Journal of Conflict Resolution* (1998 and 2000), *International Interactions* (2002), *International Security* (2003), and *International Studies Quarterly* (2003). He received his Ph.D. in Political Science from the State University of New York at Binghamton.

SUSANNA PEARCE is currently completing her Ph.D. in Political Science at Trinity College, Dublin. Her research has focused on the nature and impact of religion on political conflicts, and her work has appeared in several publications and conference presentations.

PAUL R. PILLAR is a Visiting Professor in the Security Studies Program at Georgetown University. He has had a twenty-eight-year career in the U.S. Intelligence Community during which he has been deputy chief of the Counterterrorist Center at CIA and, most recently, National Intelligence Officer for the Near East and South Asia. He is the author of *Negotiating Peace* (1983) and *Terrorism and U.S. Foreign Policy* (2003).

KARIN VON HIPPEL, Ph.D., is the Co-Director of the Post-Conflict Reconstruction Program at the Center for Strategic and International Studies. She previously worked as part of a small independent research team investigating the UN Integrated Missions and was a member of Project Unicorn, a counterterrorism police advisory panel in London. She has researched and published widely on topics such as root causes of terrorism; diasporas, remittances and development; UN reform; and military intervention and nation-building. Recent publications include *Europe Confronts Terrorism* (forthcoming) and *Democracy by Force* (2000).